S0-BYG-489

LAS VEGAS

RICK GARMAN

DISCOVER LAS VEGAS

When Las Vegas was first stumbled upon, it must have seemed like a mirage shimmering in the distance. Miles of unrelenting, unforgiving terrain through rocky sun-scorched deserts and mountains finally gave way to a valley verdant with trees and plants fed from natural springs. It was a refuge from the harsh world beyond its borders offering rest, comfort, and possibility.

This oasis later became a rest stop of sorts along the Old Spanish Trail, a place for travelers to pause during their long journey across the untamed West of the early 1800s. Native Americans who inhabited the area had a name for the place, the Spanish term for "The Meadows." They called it Las Vegas.

Hundreds of years later, Las Vegas remains a literal oasis. It is considered to be the most geographically isolated major city in the United States, surrounded by mountains with miles of nothing but scrub brush and dirt in every direction beyond its glittery borders. The nearest metropolis of major significance is more than 200

the dancers of *Jubilee!* at Bally's

miles away, so the city still acts for some as a place to stop on their way elsewhere.

But for millions of people, Las Vegas has become more than a pit stop; it has become the destination, a figurative oasis where one can shrug off the harsh realities of the world beyond its borders.

The city still surprises upon first viewing. Drive in from Los Angeles along I-15 through the desolate and barren stretches of desert and it's easy to imagine heading toward the edge of the world. (Okay, the billboards every mile or so advertising $5.95 prime rib specials and the traffic jams of SUVs might make it difficult to truly cast yourself as the lone survivor of some global apocalypse, but you're headed toward a land of fantasy, so just go with it.)

Passing through the middle of nowhere, I-15 suddenly takes a turn to the left, circles around a stony outcropping, and there it is: the gleaming gold tower of Mandalay Bay, the hulking black pyramid of Luxor, the big green monster that is the MGM Grand, the giant

Las Vegas skyline

space needle jutting into the sky at Stratosphere, and, of course, there's the white and gold edifice of the Mirage.

Las Vegas and surrounding Clark County are a region of mind-boggling proportion when you look at the numbers and the consistent litany of "most," "biggest," and "more than any other" ascriptions. It is home to more than 1.8 million residents, with more than 5,000 new transplants arriving every month, making it one of the fastest growing metropolitan areas in America for the last decade or more. It draws about 40 million people annually to its shiny palaces of excess, making it the number-one tourist destination in the country.

The city hosts eight of the ten biggest hotels in the world: the Stratosphere has the tallest observation tower west of the Mississippi; the Luxor has the biggest indoor atrium; and the most expensive privately financed construction project in the nation's history, the CityCenter, costing over $7 billion will be ready for its first occupants in 2009.

Need rest? You can usually find a place to do it here with about 135,000 hotel rooms in the area and thousands more on the way,

Wynn Las Vegas Golf Club

more than in any other city in the world. On the other hand, the nationwide hotel occupancy rate hovers around 65 percent, while the occupancy rate in Vegas is over 90 percent, meaning you may have trouble finding a room that someone isn't already sleeping in.

Looking for comfort? You've got that here, too, with world-class dining, spas, and other comforting distractions available at every turn.

And what about possibility? Yes, they've got that covered here as well in the form of games of chance. There is no other spot on earth where you'll find more slot machines concentrated in a smaller geographical area. There is more square footage of casino space in Las Vegas than in any other city. And all that square footage adds up to big gaming revenue, more than $10 billion annually and growing every year.

But those 40 million folks aren't just dropping their money in video poker machines. It is estimated that tourism brings in more than $39 billion a year from accommodations, dining, entertainment, and, of course, shopping. Las Vegas is now considered to be the number-one

New York-New York

shopping destination in the country and proudly displays, as evidence, The Forum Shops at Caesars Palace, an ornate mall that generates one of the highest incomes per square foot of any mall in the world.

Set the numbers aside, though, and the city still looms large, both legendary and mythic at the same time. This is where Elvis married Priscilla and made his big comeback; where Frank, Dean, and Sammy turned the moniker "The Rat Pack" from an insult into an institution; where Liberace mastered the complexities of camp and made "wink-wink, nudge-nudge" humor safe for America. Vegas hosted Howard Hughes and the mafia, perfected topless reviews and all-you-can-eat buffets, encompassed both high class and the lowest common denominator, blending all of the larger-than-life ingredients to create the place we love to call Sin City.

As Vegas glitters in the distance from I-15, motorists generally react with something like "It shouldn't be there. It doesn't look real. What kind of demented imagination would place this jaw-dropping, visual overload of a city smack-dab in the middle of a desert?"

Well, I suppose that's why they call it an oasis.

Circus Circus

MGM Grand's *Crazy Horse Paris*

Caesars Palace

The Steak House at Circus Circus

Contents

The Neighborhoods

The bulk of the must-see attractions are concentrated in and around The Strip, a four-mile section of Las Vegas Boulevard South. This area has some of the priciest real estate in the world and, oddly enough, is not actually in the city of Las Vegas; it's just outside the border in Paradise Township, an unincorporated section of Clark County. Because Las Vegas has so much crammed into The Strip, this book splits up the area into three sections for easier digestion, with separate sections for other areas around town.

SOUTH STRIP

Whether you drive into town from Los Angeles or fly into McCarran Airport, this section of The Strip is the first one you'll see upon your arrival. In fact, there are McCarran taxiways less than a block from some of the major hotels in the area. There are no signs declaring this the "South Strip," but it is generally regarded to be the section of Las Vegas Boulevard South from Russell Road northward to Harmon Avenue and includes major casino-hotels like **MGM Grand, New York-New York, Monte Carlo, Mandalay Bay, Luxor Las Vegas,** and **Excalibur.** It's here, also, that you'll find the massive **CityCenter** development of hotels, casinos, condos, and more due to open in 2009. The major cross street through the neighborhood is Tropicana Avenue, accessible from I-15.

CENTER STRIP

The central part of The Strip, from Harmon Avenue north to Spring Mountain/Sands Avenue, is home to the heaviest concentration of casinos, hotels, attractions, and restaurants. If walking is your only option, you may want to consider this area first. It includes such high-profile buildings as the **Bellagio, Caesars Palace, The Mirage, Treasure Island, The Venetian, Paris Las Vegas,** and **Flamingo Las Vegas,** among others. The major cross street in this area is Flamingo Road, accessible from the freeway. If you're coming from the airport, travel north on Paradise Road to Flamingo and head west about a mile.

NORTH STRIP

After years of a development boom on the South and Center Strip, the North Strip has begun to blossom again with the addition of **Wynn Las Vegas** and plans afoot for as many as a half dozen major hotel, casino, and condominium projects. The boundaries of the North Strip are considered Spring Mountain/Sands on the south up to St. Louis Avenue on the north. In addition to Wynn, other famous places in this section of The Strip include the **Stratosphere, Sahara, Riviera,** and **Circus Circus.** The major cross street here is Sahara Avenue, accessible from I-15.

JUST OFF THE STRIP

This neighborhood is a little more nebulous in definition, although it generally includes locations within a mile or two of the South, Center, and North Strip. It includes places on the major (and minor) Strip cross streets, like Tropicana, Harmon, Flamingo, Spring Mountain/Sands, Convention Center, and Sahara, and on the streets paralleling The Strip, such as Koval, Audrie, and Paradise on the east, and Frank Sinatra, Dean Martin, and Industrial on the west. Major casino-hotels in these areas include the **Las Vegas Hilton, Hard Rock Hotel, Rio All Suite Hotel & Casino, The Palms,** and **Orleans.**

DOWNTOWN

This is the place where it all started. The Downtown Las Vegas boundaries are vaguely defined, but in general, this area comprises everything adjacent to Las Vegas Boulevard from St. Louis Avenue north to Washington Avenue and from I-15 on the west to Maryland Parkway on the east. This includes the **Fremont Street Experience,** the main attraction for Downtown and home to such Glitter Gulch favorites as **The Golden Nugget, Four Queens, Main Street Station,** and **Fitzgerald's.** It's worth noting that more than any other place in town, it's best to stay on the main touristy thoroughfares of Las Vegas Boulevard and Fremont Street, especially at night. While these sections are safe, anything too far off the beaten track starts to become very rough, filled with gang, drug, and prostitution activity.

EAST AND SOUTH OF LAS VEGAS

The hotels and casinos in **Henderson** and the locals' hangouts on **Boulder Highway** are the main attractions that may lure you to this area. **Green Valley Ranch** is a stunning resort that can compete with the major hotels and casinos on The Strip. And **Sam's Town** and **Sunset Station** offer high quality accommodations for surprisingly low prices. A variety of shopping opportunities can also be found in this region, with major malls, discount warehouses, and high-end boutiques all competing for your attention. There are also plenty of dining options, from fast food to chain restaurants to gourmet bistros.

NORTH AND WEST OF LAS VEGAS

The areas in the north and west part of Las Vegas are **Summerlin** and the **city of North Las Vegas.** In these suburbs surrounding The Strip you'll find the kind of shopping and dining options that you'll recognize from your hometown, plus several notable "locals'" casinos. Noteworthy hotels/casinos here include **Red Rock Resort** and **Santa Fe Station,** and there are abundant dining, recreation, and entertainment options in this region as well.

Planning Your Trip

Planning a trip to Las Vegas requires some time and energy for all the details, but let's start with the basics. To get the full Las Vegas experience I recommend staying a minimum of three full days. By seven days, the roster of new activities begins to dwindle considerably and the wallet begins to thin, especially if some of those activities have included trips to the casinos.

Obviously, the bulk of the action takes place on The Strip. This is where you'll find the major hotels, shows, attractions, restaurants, and shopping highlights that most people want to experience. If you've never been to Las Vegas, you can focus on the big stuff and get it all done in two very full days or three slightly more relaxed ones. Add in a day for each of the other areas of town you may want to visit, including the Downtown area with its "Old Vegas" style, the Lake Las Vegas vicinity with its relaxed beauty, Lake Mead or Red Rock Canyon for recreation and scenic opportunities, and some hidden gems interspersed around town, like the Liberace Museum or Ethel M. Chocolate Factory, for a bit of local flavor.

If you have been to Vegas before, give yourself a day or two to see the attractions on and around The Strip that aren't as obvious, such as the Mirage Dolphin Habitat, The Atomic Testing Museum, or the Springs Preserve. Then add more time to really explore the outlying areas or take some interesting side trips to Hoover Dam or even the Grand Canyon. A day should cover each of the areas you want to visit unless you're a big fan of a specific activity; if you're an avid golfer, for instance, schedule in some additional time to get around town and hit the best courses.

WHEN TO GO

The best time for you to go to Vegas may not necessarily be the best time for other people, since everyone has different priorities and ideas about what makes a vacation truly special. Do you want to go when the crowds are thin and rates are cheap or do you want to go when the weather is good and there are lots of special things to do? In Vegas, those factors are usually mutually exclusive.

What it all ultimately comes down to is flexibility. Although not everyone has the luxury of being able to choose when they can take their next vacation, even the option of two different time periods in the same month can save a lot of money. A room that costs $300 a night one week could cost half that the next.

Off Season

If getting the cheapest room rates is of paramount importance, then you'll have to make sacrifices in a few other key areas, namely weather and entertainment options. The cheapest times of the year in Las Vegas are the last couple of weeks in December leading up to Christmas, parts of January and February, and late July through August. In December, January, and February, you'll have to deal with cool weather (when most of the hotels close their outdoor pools). In July and August, the pools are open, but it's often so hot it's next to impossible to spend more than a few minutes outside enjoying them.

The weather plays a factor in keeping the crowds lighter, hence the lower room rates (in Vegas, demand equals higher prices). At the same time, the decrease in visitors leads to a decrease in the amount and quality of entertainment in the city. During late December, for instance, you'll find very few

Mirage Dolphin Habitat

big-name headliner shows and many of the permanent production shows go on hiatus. So that means your amusement may be limited to how much fun you can wring out of a slot machine.

High Season

The best weather can be found late March through May and late September through October. With generally sunny skies and warm (but not insanely warm) temperatures, these are the times of year when Vegas has the most climatic appeal.

Not surprisingly, these seasons are also when the big crowds show up, driving up room rates. Leisure travelers and the convention crowd descend on the city in droves, making the lines long and the prices high. The good news is that there is no lack of things to do; all the production shows and showrooms are open for business and waiting to take your money.

WHAT TO TAKE

Generally speaking, Las Vegas is a very casual town, so unless you're planning on going to a lot of very expensive restaurants and upscale clubs, you can leave the fancy duds at home. While some of the nicer dining establishments may frown upon jeans and a T-shirt, only a handful of them will actually turn away guests in such attire. Nightclubs are a bit more restrictive, with many asking for "casual elegance" or "dress to impress."

Take a glance at the forecast before packing, just to make sure the weather generalities for your specific travel period are going to hold true. Just because it's July and it's usually hot with no rain doesn't mean it actually will be that way when you get there. Lightweight pants, dresses, and shorts for the summer, and heavier pants and sweaters with a jacket for the winter are the general rules of thumb. And since you'll be doing a lot of walking, a comfortable pair of shoes is a must.

For security purposes, a wallet with a chain, a purse with a strap long enough to wear diagonally (as opposed to casually slung over the shoulder), or even a fanny pack worn tightly around the waist are a good idea. The latter, worn in front, may not be the most fashion-forward statement, but it'll help reduce the risk of theft.

Explore Las Vegas

THE BEST OF VEGAS

For anyone who's never been to Vegas before, the place to spend the most time is The Strip. This four-mile stretch of Las Vegas Boulevard South has most of the big hotels and casinos, some of the best (and usually most expensive) restaurants, all of the high-profile shows and attractions, and perhaps, if you're lucky, a showgirl or an Elvis impersonator.

DAY 1
Morning

Before you begin your day of adventure, power up with a solid breakfast at one of the buffets in the South Strip area, such as the **Mandalay Bay Bayside Buffet.**

Start on the South Strip and glory in the faux–Big Apple madness at **New York-New York** and gawk at the sheer enormity of the biggest casino in Las Vegas and second biggest hotel in the world at **MGM Grand.**

Once you've seen the big things on the South Strip, catch the **Las Vegas Monorail** at the MGM Grand and ride it up to the Paris/Bally's station.

Depending on how much time you spent on the South Strip, you may be ready for lunch before you start seriously exploring. Your options here include the charming street-side dining of **Mon Ami Gabi** at Paris, the theme madness of **Margaritaville** at Flamingo Las Vegas, the celebrity chef masterpieces of **Bobby Flay's Mesa Grill** at Caesars Palace, or the terrific **buffets** at Bellagio or The Mirage.

Afternoon

After fueling up, head over to the 50-story Eiffel Tower replica at **Paris Las Vegas** where you can travel to the top for a bird's-eye view of The Strip. Be sure to check out all that **Bellagio** has to offer, including the stunning **Bellagio Fountains** water show out front and the beautiful garden conservatory inside.

From there, walk over the pedestrian bridge to **Caesars Palace** and have your photo taken with one of the toga-clad models who walk through the place for just such an occasion. Hide your credit cards from yourself and walk out through **The Forum Shops,** a wildly themed Roman shopping experience.

The Mirage, Treasure Island, The Venetian, and its new sister hotel, **Palazzo,** are all also in this area and are all worthy of your time.

By now, it should be time for you to start thinking about dinner. If you want to stay in the vicinity, **Fix** at Bellagio, **Delmonico Steakhouse** at The Venetian, and **Le Village Buffet** at Paris Las Vegas are all terrific options.

Evening

Now that you're refueled, you can head back out for a little Las Vegas nightlife. First, take in a show, perhaps. **Mystère, KÀ,** and **O** by Cirque du Soleil; the **Blue Man Group; Rita Rudner;** and **Penn & Teller** are popular, but there is a little something for everyone in this town, from magicians to dancers, simplicity to spectacle, high art to lowbrow, and just about everything in between.

Afterward, check out the booming club scene. Almost every hotel has a high-energy dance club and at least one or two super-swank ultra-lounges. The hottest "in" spot seems to change on a weekly basis, but the gigantic **Pure** at Caesars Palace; **Rain, Moon,** and ghostbar at The Palms; and **Tao** at The Venetian seem to be permanently hardwired into the city's hip and trendy network.

And, of course, you'll want to try your hand at the games of chance, which seem to be a lot more raucously fun in the wee hours. You've seen just about every major casino on the South and Center Strip area, so you can pick the one you liked the best, but if it were up to me, I'd head to **The Mirage** for its fun but classy atmosphere or the **Bellagio** if you're feeling like you need the high-roller treatment.

DAY 2

Morning

Did you get any sleep? Come on, admit it. You stayed up until five in the morning gambling, didn't you? Take the morning to relax by grabbing a quick (and inexpensive) nosh at one of the food courts at **Luxor, Monte Carlo,** or **New York-New York;** getting a spa treatment at one of the world-class facilities such as **Qua Baths & Spa at Caesars Palace** or **The Canyon Ranch Spa Club;** or even lounging by the pool if the weather is cooperating.

Afternoon

Head up to the North Strip area to check out the sights and play some more. **Wynn Las Vegas,** a $2.7-billion palace of excess, is one of the new kids on the block here and is definitely worth a look; you could stop for lunch at the fantastic **Wynn Buffet.** Across the street, you'll find the enormous **The Fashion Show mall,** with more than two million square feet of retail heaven. Further up the street, you should at least snap a photo of **The Riviera** since it is rumored to be heading toward a date with a wrecking ball.

Also in the vicinity is **Circus Circus,** which is really only noteworthy if you've got children in tow. Everyone else can skip this one.

Paris Las Vegas

COURTESY HARRAH'S ENTERTAINMENT

Finish your afternoon at the **Stratosphere** with a ride to the top of the tallest observation tower west of the Mississippi and, if you dare, a spin on one of the extreme thrill rides at the top.

Evening

In the evening, a visit to **Downtown Las Vegas** is in order. Catch the terrific light and sound show at the **Fremont Street Experience** and wander through historic casinos for a little low-limit gambling at places like **The Golden Nugget, Binion's,** and **Four Queens.** The **Triple George Grill** or the **Main Street Station Garden Court Buffet** are two terrific options for dinner.

Cap off your two-day tour with a stroll down Fremont Street through the burgeoning nightlife district with fun and funky bars like **The Griffin** and **Beauty Bar.**

LUCK BE A LADY

The research says that most people who come to Las Vegas do not list gambling as the primary reason for their visit. These mysterious people claim they travel all this way to the hot Nevada desert for the shopping, the shows, the restaurants, the spas, or the comfy hotel room beds and robes.

While it is true that Las Vegas has a lot to offer besides slot machines, let's get serious for a minute. Gambling is an inherent part of the very fabric of this city and many people find it a key part of the allure. If you're one of them, here's the perfect travel strategy for you.

Where to Gamble

As a basic rule, my definition of a good casino is one in which I win. But in order to win, you have to play, and some casinos do a better job than others at creating an environment that makes you want to play in the first place. An open and easily navigable floor plan, plenty of room for personal space, good (but not harsh) lighting, lots of gaming options, and overall visual appeal are the ingredients that make a winning experience even more so and may soften the blow of a losing one.

the casino at Red Rock Resort

On The Strip, the casinos that seem to do the best job of attaining these goals are **Mandalay Bay,** huge but not overwhelming, with a delightfully understated South Seas theme; **Wynn Las Vegas,** which does a better job than Bellagio of looking upscale without feeling intimidating; **Bally's,** smaller than most Strip casinos but also easier to navigate and friendlier; and **New York-New York** and **Paris Las Vegas,** each of which do their respective themes with a great deal of visual panache.

Venture off The Strip and you'll find several other casinos that fit the bill quite nicely, including **Main Street Station** and **The Golden Nugget** in Downtown Las Vegas, both with a much more congenial atmosphere than what you're probably used to; and **Red Rock Resort** and **Green Valley Ranch,** featuring stunning designs and a terrific entertainment quotient that make them worth the drive to the edges of town.

Where to Stay

Since most gamblers will spend more time in the casino than they do in the hotel room, they really only need to find a nice hotel in a convenient location that will leave enough money in their wallet for them to waste in the casino.

On The Strip you'll want to focus on the mid-range hotels, which are becoming more of a rarity, but are there if you look closely. **Bally's** is one of the best choices, located at the center of the Center Strip, walking distance to a dozen other casinos, relatively inexpensive, and still nicely appointed. Other choices include **The Flamingo, Luxor, New York-New York,** and **Monte Carlo,** all of which offer solidly comfortable accommodations in great locations at prices that usually won't bust your budget before you get anywhere near a slot machine.

Another option is the Downtown Las Vegas area, offering lower-limit gambling and friendlier casinos. Although most of the hotels in this area don't have much ambience—things just aren't as spiffy and shiny as they are on The Strip—you can still find fine rooms at very decent prices and still be close to many casino options. Leading the herd in this area would be **The Golden Nugget** and **Main Street Station.**

Gambling on a Budget

Even as recently as a few years ago, penny slot machines were mostly relegated to a few seedy Downtown Las Vegas gaming parlors. These days, every major casino has them, including posh joints like **Bellagio** and **Wynn Las Vegas.** Put in a penny and win thousands. But, of course, nothing is as easy as that. Most modern penny slots will allow you to bet one penny, but the most you can usually win on that bet is a few more pennies. In order to hit the big prizes, you have to play multiple coins on multiple lines, usually driving the maximum bet well into the $3–$4-per-pull range.

If your budget won't allow you to play more than a few coins or you're looking for a blackjack table with something less than a $10-per-hand limit, you can still find them if you try.

Generally speaking, you're going to want to get off The Strip and either go to Downtown Las Vegas or to the local neighborhoods where limits are often lower (and payouts often greater). Most of the Downtown casinos like

the **Four Queens** and **Fremont** have a wide variety of machines and tables that will require smaller upfront investments. Likewise, the neighborhood casinos like **Boulder Station** and **The Cannery** allow you to spend more time playing with less money.

How to Maximize Your Play

The Strip has the lowest reported payouts on slot machines, with Downtown Las Vegas doing a little better and the neighborhood casinos doing better still. Combine the lower limits you'll find at these so-called locals' casinos and it's plain to see why the smart gambler gets as far away from Las Vegas Boulevard as they possibly can. The **Red Rock Resort** and **Green Valley Ranch** are my personal favorites, allowing you to stretch your dollar without sacrificing comfort, but **Santa Fe Station, Sunset Station,** and the **Orleans** are terrific alternatives.

Stretching your gambling dollar goes beyond what you put in and take out, though. Your very first stop when you walk into any casino should be at the players' club desk, where you can sign up for a rewards card. These cards, when used religiously, will earn you points that can be traded in for everything from free meals to hotel rooms to cash. Every casino has one and many are good at multiple locations, so you can wander the city and find the place that suits you best. The rewards of these particular rewards clubs vary wildly, but generally speaking, the less fancy and less conveniently located casinos offer the best deals. Pay special attention to **Station Casinos Boarding Pass** and **Club Coast,** which offer a generous return on your gambling investment.

RAT PACK RETRO

Las Vegas is a town that loves to reinvent itself. Buildings that would otherwise be considered "classic" in some other city are considered out of date here and are imploded with impunity to make way for something bigger, better, and grander. Because of that, the history of Las Vegas that we all know and love—The Rat Pack, Elvis, Bugsy Siegel—is fading fast. The places where those famous faces used to play are mostly gone: The Dunes, The Sands, The Desert Inn, The Aladdin, and The Frontier. Those that remain have either been completely redone (Caesars Palace, the Flamingo, The Sahara) or are shadows of their former selves destined for a date with a wrecking ball (The Tropicana, The Riviera). But if you're looking for a vintage Vegas experience, there are still some places to go to find it, and this travel strategy is designed with that in mind.

Historical Sites

On the southwest corner of Las Vegas Boulevard and Sahara Avenue sits a desolate and dusty lot that is one of the most important sites in the city's history. It is here in 1941 that a place called **El Rancho** opened. With only 80 rooms, a couple of restaurants, a showroom, a small casino, and a pool, El Rancho was not important because of what was on the property but because of where that property was located: on the north end of what would eventually become The Strip. As the first resort hotel in the area, it paved the way for places like The Flamingo, The Dunes, the Stardust, and pretty much everything else that followed it. At some point in the next few years there will be a massive development of hotels, casinos, and entertainment on this plot of land, but it will always be an important piece of history.

Another key place to visit for your historical tour of the city is the **Fremont Street Experience,** the street where Las Vegas *really* started in Downtown. It is lined with classic

the lobby of Caesars Palace

gambling halls like **El Cortez** (1941), **The Golden Nugget** (1946), **Binion's** (1951), the **Four Queens** (1955), and the granddaddy of them all, **The Golden Gate,** originally opened as The Hotel Nevada way back in 1906.

But if you want to go back—way back—you can go just north of Downtown to the **Old Las Vegas Mormon Fort,** one of the first structures in the entire area, built in 1855 by Mormon settlers from Utah.

Classic Hotels

On The Strip, the oldest continually operating hotel was **The Frontier,** which opened in 1942, but that hotel closed in 2007, just shy of its 65th birthday. The **Flamingo** opened in 1946, but none of its original buildings are standing today. **The Sahara,** despite its 1952 origins, is more of a product of the 1970s and 1980s today.

So that means the oldest rooms on The Strip that you can actually still stay in are located at **The Riviera,** a nine-story hotel tower built in 1955. The Downtown area has **El Cortez,** with rooms dating back to 1941, and **The Golden Gate,** with rooms that have been in use since 1906.

For the most part, you don't actually want to stay in most of these hotel rooms because no matter how many coats of paint or layers of wallpaper, they are more "old" than "classic." So if you're looking for a true old-time Vegas experience but don't want to give up the creature comforts, go for a room at **Caesars Palace.** It opened in 1966 and the original rooms are still in operation, but you won't give up quality just to get a taste of history.

Frank, Sammy, Dean, and Elvis

The stages on which the legendary performers of Vegas entertained the masses have mostly been removed, even in hotels that still exist. The Congo Room at The Sahara and the Circus

Maximus showroom at Caesars Palace are gone, but there are a few that still exist and are worth a pilgrimage.

At **Harrah's,** you can not only have a seat in the former Sammy Davis, Jr. showroom, but you can see a great show to boot, with comedian **Rita Rudner.** The showroom at the **Flamingo** never had a famous name, but it has hosted more than a few famous faces, including Wayne Newton, The Supremes, and Ella Fitzgerald.

And, of course, what Las Vegas visit would be complete without a trip to the **Las Vegas Hilton** to see **Barry Manilow**? Not because he "wrote the songs," but because the theater in which he performs is the same one that saw Elvis make his 1968 "comeback" when the hotel was known as The International.

Vegas On Screen

Las Vegas has been a favorite for moviemakers all the way back to 1946 when The Frontier (closed in 2007) made an appearance in the Roy Rogers (and Trigger!) movie *Helldorado.* Since then, the city has played background and foreground to dozens, if not hundreds, of films both big and small.

It should come as no surprise that the bulk of the places that showed up in old movies either don't exist anymore or are completely unrecognizable. In the original *Ocean's 11* with Frank Sinatra and Dean Martin, the group conspired to rob five casinos, including the long-gone Desert Inn and Sands, plus the still-in-existence but totally remodeled **Sahara, Flamingo,** and **Riviera.** The 2001 *Ocean's 11* remake was filmed all over Las Vegas, with the bulk of the action happening at **Bellagio.** Likewise, the 2007 sequel *Ocean's 13* is worth a viewing for some more current Vegas exteriors and interiors.

Portions of Elvis Presley's classic *Viva Las Vegas* were filmed at the Desert Inn (now the site of **Wynn Las Vegas**) and the **Flamingo.**

24-HOUR PARTY SCENE

Some of the best nightlife hot spots in the nation are located in Sin City; clubs so epic on almost every measurable (and nonmeasurable) scale that they have become the nexus of Vegas after dark. But partying in Vegas needn't be restricted to the hours when the nightclubs are open. These days, Vegas is not just a 24-hour town, it's a 24-hour *party* town, and here is the strategy for getting the most out of it.

Hotels

Choosing the right hotel for your party vacation is key for a lot of reasons. You want to make sure it is centrally located so you can get to the hot spots easily without worrying about driving, but beyond that is the cache involved with the right address. Do you really want to meet the girl or guy of your dreams at a chic nightclub and then have to tell them you're staying at Circus Circus?

Instead, you want to focus your energy on the places where the party extends beyond the nightclubs into the entire property itself at a place like **The Palms.** Home to four unbelievably popular clubs, one of the premier concert venues in town, a pool area that stays hot even after the sun goes down, a recording studio that draws famous faces, a tattoo parlor, and more, this is Party Central and should be at the top of your list. **Hard Rock** is only a point or two below The Palms on the "cool" scale, but its location means you'll have to cab it to get to most of the nightlife spots you'll want to go to. Then there's **Planet Hollywood,** which caters to the same trendy clientele, but has yet to prove itself worthy among the glitterati.

TAO LAS VEGAS/WARREN JAGGER

Tao nightclub at The Venetian

the terrace nightclub at Pure, Caesars Palace

COURTESY HARRAH'S ENTERTAINMENT

Nightlife

Almost every hotel worth its salt has a nightclub or ultra-lounge, and most have more than one. It's not easy to say with any authority which of the clubs will be the current spot for the "in crowd," since it seems to change on a weekly basis depending on which booze-addled "celebutante" (I'm not naming names) shows up where. But there are a few places that will always be at the top of the list for the party-faithful.

As of this writing, **Tao** at The Venetian is ruling the roost of the nightclub scene in Las Vegas. With its post-apocalyptic Chinese decor, slamming dance floor, and parade of celebrities in the VIP booths, this is the first choice for many and has lines to get in that prove it. The clubs at The Palms are always packed with beautiful faces who want to see and be seen, so be sure to put **ghostbar, Rain, Moon,** and **The Playboy Club** on your list. Then there's always **Pure** at Caesars Palace, four clubs in one

(including the **Pussycat Dolls Lounge**) that make up the biggest party space in the city.

Strip Clubs

If you're looking to put a little sin in your Sin City vacation, you're not the only one. Vegas is the place where fantasies come true, illicit behavior is not only tolerated but encouraged, and sex, booze, and gambling are the staple crops.

At least, that's what the television commercials would have you believe. In fact, while the hedonistic image of Las Vegas has become a part of our pop culture lexicon ("What happens in Vegas…"), the reality is it's all just a tantalizing ruse, a tease, a facade. Sure, the sin may look real, but so does that Eiffel Tower in front of Paris Las Vegas.

Straight men have seemingly limitless opportunities to see scantily clad females. Strip clubs or gentlemen's clubs abound and cater to just about every taste. You've got the posh **Treasures,** with enough marble and gilt edges

COURTESY MGM MIRAGE

Bare Pool Club at The Mirage

to make you think you're in one of the expensive hotel lobbies. Then there's the earthier attitude at places like the **Girls of Glitter Gulch** along Fremont Street. They've even got what claims to be the largest strip club in the world: **Sapphire,** a 71,000-square-foot behemoth with multiple stages, bars, and shimmying things to look at.

But keep in mind before you enter one of these establishments that the women (and, in some cases, the men) are strictly for watching. Touching is forbidden and will get you more acquainted with the big, burly bouncer than with any of the dancers.

The options are much more limited for women, since most of the strip clubs are geared toward straight men, and the few that do have male dancers are not really worth your time or energy. Instead, head to The Strip for the raucous **Chippendales** and **Thunder From Down Under** revues.

Poolside Parties

It used to be that the pool at most Las Vegas hotels was a place to relax, catch some sun, and maybe go for a swim. Now, many of the pool areas have been transformed into daytime (and a few nighttime) versions of nightclubs with live DJs, lounge-style seating arrangements, bars, and restaurants. Several hotels even allow topless sunbathing.

Just like its nightclub counterpart, The Venetian's **Tao Beach Club** seems to be the most popular right now. It has gloriously over-the-top cabanas and day beds (they come with their own mini-fridges and televisions), plus a pool that turns into a floating dance floor at night. Similar and equally decadent facilities can be found at Mandalay Bay's **Moorea Beach Club** and The Mirage's **Bare Pool Club.**

And the good news is you don't have to be staying at the hotel to enjoy these places.

HIGH ROLLERS

Las Vegas is a city that revels in the concept of indulgence—a place where if money is no object, you can buy just about anything, anytime. If what you want isn't sitting on a store shelf, the concierge will find it for you and make sure the wait to get it is filled with all manner of pampering. In this city there are unlimited ways to separate you from your money, and the more you have of it, the better. Here are just a few suggestions for those with the bank accounts to support such decadent displays of wealth.

Hotels

The standard rooms at **Wynn Las Vegas, Red Rock Resort, The Ritz-Carlton Lake Las Vegas, The Four Seasons, The Venetian,** and **Bellagio** are more luxurious than most people's homes and will cost for a weekend what a lot of people pay in rent for entire month. If your bill is less than $300 on a Saturday night at one of these places, something is seriously wrong.

But you're not interested in anything that could be termed "standard," are you? You're interested in the suites, which range from extravagant to downright silly, both in terms of size and cost. Those high-roller suites you've heard so much about on endless Travel Channel specials are usually only available to people who do crazy things like bet $1,000 on a hand of blackjack with regularity, but if you've got the bucks, you can rent them.

The most extravagant can be found at **The Palms,** where they have a variety of fantasy suites. One comes with its own indoor basketball court, another features a private bowling alley, and one has a full nightclub with DJ setup. If you're feeling especially naughty, you can get the room with a stripper pole in the middle of a *Showgirls*-worthy stage.

the lobby of the Bellagio

Restaurants

For dining, your choices are virtually limitless, but if you're feeling like going for broke (either figuratively or literally), you should go for the most special of the special-occasion restaurants. Legendary French chef **Joël Robuchon** came out of retirement to open a namesake restaurant at MGM Grand that charges more than $360 per person for dinner, while **Restaurant Guy Savoy** at Caesars Palace matches or beats that, depending on what you order. Both have collected epicurean awards by the truckload and true "foodies" insist it is worth every penny. Other establishments in or approaching this rarified strata include **Bouchon** at The Venetian, **Charlie Palmer Steak** at the Four Seasons, and **Alex** at Wynn Las Vegas; they all serve award-winning cuisine from award-winning chefs at eye-popping prices.

The Forum Shops at Caesars Palace

Entertainment

If you're going all out, you might as well go for the good seats at the city's top shows. *O* by Cirque du Soleil at Bellagio and *Love,* also by Cirque du Soleil, at The Mirage are just two examples of productions where the top tickets will run you at least $150 per person. You could also check out whatever headliner is playing in the big showrooms or arenas, where tickets can set you back as much as $500 per person. Granted, that figure is usually reserved for the Barbra Streisands of the world, but even Madonna is going to run you $250 a pop.

Nightlife

Las Vegas has become one of the premier destinations for nightclub action in the world, eclipsing famed party spots like Miami and Ibiza with an over-the-top menu of all-night diversions. But many of these clubs are not cheap, so here's where that big bank account of yours could come in handy.

The hottest of the hot spots in town are clubs that offer a wide variety of environments at one location with slamming nightclubs, cool ultra-lounges, and outdoor areas. Some examples of those types of venues include **Tao** at The Venetian, **Pure** at Caesars Palace, **Body English** at The Hard Rock, and all of the clubs at The Palms. These places regularly charge at least $20 per person just to get in the door, with VIP and front-of-line passes easily going for twice that. If you want to sit down, you'll usually have to buy bottle service at a VIP table, which usually starts at around $300, depending on what kind of bottle you're getting. Throw in drinks that range from $8 for fancy water to more than $1,000 for a shot of extraordinarily rare tequila and it's a good thing you have all those unlimited funds.

Shopping

Via Bellagio, The Forum Shops at Caesars Palace, **The Esplanade** at Wynn Las Vegas, **The Miracle Mile Shops** at Planet Hollywood,

COURTESY HARRAH'S ENTERTAINMENT

the Arctic Ice Room in the Qua Baths & Spa at Caesars Palace

Wynn Las Vegas is only available to guests of the hotel and they will have to pay $500 for the privilege of playing 18 holes.

But that kind of exclusivity is for the more active-minded, so perhaps you'd prefer to lounge poolside at **The Four Seasons** where attendants hand out cool towels and spray guests with Evian water. Or you could rent a cabana for a couple hundred dollars a day that will include everything from plasma screen televisions to wireless Internet service.

If the hot desert sun is just too much for your sensitive skin, perhaps you'd prefer to do your relaxing indoors at one of the world-class spas in town. **Spa Bellagio** and the **Qua Baths & Spa** at Caesars Palace have treatments, massages, and other bits of personalized pampering that will easily set you back as much as what those other folks are paying for the round of golf at the Wynn.

and Venetian's **Grand Canal Shoppes** have stores with names that make people on Rodeo Drive and 5th Avenue swoon: Armani, Baccarat, Dolce and Gabbana, Gucci, Harry Winston, Prada, Tiffany, and Versace are just a few of the high-end shops you'll find.

Recreation and Relaxation

Go outside for some recreation and you can turn things like a simple round of golf into exercise for your wallet as well. The golf club at

Gaming

To cap off your money-is-no-object tour of Vegas, you're going to have to go wild in the casinos: $500-a-pull slot machines, $300-a-hand blackjack, and no-limit Texas Hold 'Em are just a few examples of games you can play. You can find these games just about anywhere, but if you're looking for the well-heeled crowd, head to **Wynn Las Vegas** or **Bellagio.** With their fine appointments and exclusive airs, you'll feel like the true high-roller you are.

BEYOND THE GLITZ

Most people come to Vegas and do the same things everyone else does. They gamble, eat at a buffet or a celebrity chef restaurant, see the big-name shows, go to the trendy nightclubs, and never, ever venture more than a block or two off The Strip. For them, Vegas has become a destination where the rules of engagement may be extravagant, but they rarely stray from the expected.

But maybe you're the type of person that eschews convention and enjoys blazing new trails, or at least trails less trodden. Perhaps you like to gamble but not necessarily in a casino, don't like eating in chain restaurants, prefer alternative music, and hate the thought of spending $8 for a bottle of beer (after paying $20 to get into the bar in the first place). If you describe yourself as alternative, nontraditional, an adventurer, or just your own person who wants unique experiences, here's the itinerary for you.

Non-Gaming Hotels

I've heard there are people who want to come to Vegas, but don't want to gamble. I've never actually met a person like this, but just in case you fall into this category, it is possible to experience this city without ever going near a slot machine—well, once you leave the airport, that is.

There are literally hundreds of non-gaming hotels in this city, some just as nice as, if not nicer than, the casino-hotels. And you can even find a few of them on The Strip! THEhotel, despite its silly name, is attached to Mandalay Bay but is worlds apart in many ways. You can enter and leave without ever seeing the casino, and the all-suite accommodations are among the best on The Strip. **The Four Seasons,** a luxurious destination of its own also at Mandalay Bay, and **The Signature,** high-end hotel-condominium units at MGM Grand, are also good options.

Get off The Strip and you have a whole host of affordable non-gaming hotel choices from Marriott to Motel 6. But the best non-gaming hotels are located at **Lake Las Vegas,** where you'll find unparalleled rooms, service, and amenities at **The Ritz-Carlton Lake Las Vegas** and **Loews Lake Las Vegas.** Both are world-class resorts that could compete with high-end hotels in any city.

Dining Diversions

If you eat at a restaurant or buffet on The Strip, you'll probably have to pass through a casino to get there and will usually pay more to do so. While it is true that the places that have turned this city into a dining Mecca are mostly found at major Strip hotels, there are places worthy of your attention elsewhere, ranging from cheap and affordable eats to gastronomic delights.

Scattered around the Downtown Las Vegas area are a number of fun, fine, and funky eateries including the terrific **Triple George Grill,** an American diner with an affordably upscale twist; **Andre's,** a classic French restaurant; and **El Sombrero Café,** a decidedly downscale Mexican joint in business since 1950.

Elsewhere in the Las Vegas metropolitan area you can find some fantastic food of all types if you're willing to drive to find it. My personal favorites include the farm-food gone mad at **Hash House a Go Go; Lotus of Siam,** which was called the best Thai restaurant on the continent by *Gourmet* magazine; the simply amazing Italian subs at **Capriotti's;** the deep South influences on the nouvelle cuisine at **Rosemary's;** and **The Cupcakery,** which should need very little explanation.

Shopping Options

Some of the biggest and most successful malls in America are located here in Vegas, but generally speaking, what you'll find there is what you'll find at the mall in your town, only more expensive. The area of town you'll most want to focus your attention on is known as the **Las Vegas Arts District.** Located between the North Strip casinos like the Stratosphere and Downtown Las Vegas, this area is home to a variety of art galleries, independent furniture and accessories boutiques, and some especially noteworthy vintage clothing stores. **The Attic** is famous nationally from an American Express commercial, but it is more famous locally as the place for fun and affordable fashions. Similar in tone, but more exclusive in execution, is **D'Loe House of Style Then and Now,** which focuses on fabulous getups from the 1930s through the 1970s, and has gained the attention of both *Italian Vogue* and *Elle* magazines. For the musically inclined, head directly to **Zia Records.** It's technically a chain, but it's a small chain located mainly in the Southwest, and nobody does alternative music better.

© RICK GARMAN/VERN GARMAN

Krave nightclub at Planet Hollywood

Alternative Entertainment

Zia Records has weekly in-store concerts from local rock and indie bands, and you can find touring acts of this stripe at clubs and venues scattered all over town. Your best bet is to pick up a copy of *Las Vegas Weekly,* the local alternative newspaper that does a good job of keeping up on whatever you call the opposite of trendy.

If what you're more interested in is the nontraditional bar and club scene, it's not easy to find in this town without venturing into neighborhoods that are best left unexplored. Bridging the gap between places Paris Hilton would enjoy and places she wouldn't be caught anywhere near are a host of bars that some alternative types might sneer at, but are good enough for most of the rest

of us. You can start at **Beauty Bar** in Downtown Las Vegas for its fun, non-threateningly intelligent vibe, then venture over to **The Sand Dollar Blues Lounge** for some authentic live blues music and cheap drinks. Later in the evening, move on to a more hard-core venue like **The Double Down Saloon,** where the motto is "You Puke, You Clean."

For the gay and lesbian crowd, the nightlife scene is not as well-organized geographically as it is in other major cities, but the coolest clubs these days are **Krave,** the only major "alternative lifestyle" club near The Strip, and the Paradise Avenue bars including **Gypsy,** a longtime favorite dance club, and **Piranha,** a dance/lounge combo that has been drawing big crowds.

SIGHTS

In other cities, a hotel is just a place for sleeping in. Somewhere to hang your hat while you run out to see all the cool tourist attractions and major sights that particular city has to offer. In Las Vegas, the bulk of the cool tourist attractions and major sights *are* the hotels, or at least they're inside them. Those dancing fountains shooting geysers of water high in the air? In front of the Bellagio hotel. The faux volcano spewing water and flame? In front of The Mirage.

All the images seen on television or on film or read about or heard about are affiliated in one way or another with a hotel or casino. The vast majority of the well-known sights in the Las Vegas area—the Bellagio fountains, the Mirage Volcano, the Paris Las Vegas Eiffel Tower Experience—were created as ways to lure people near a slot machine or gaming table in the hope that they'll pull out their wallets and start losing. Some may view this with cynicism, suggesting that the artificial wonders of Las Vegas are the equivalent of carnival barkers, promising a lot of flash and delivering very little substance.

In some cases, those folks would be right, but those sights aren't listed here. The sights in this book are the best of the bunch—the things that are worthy of existing on their own merits, regardless of whether there happen to be slot machines lurking behind them. These are the sights that make jaws drop with "how did they do that?" wonder, arouse giggles at the sheer audacity of the thing, or cause the audience to stop for a moment and appreciate what's in front of them.

COURTESY HARRAH'S ENTERTAINMENT

HIGHLIGHTS

LOOK FOR (TO FIND
RECOMMENDED SIGHTS.

(Best Peek into the Future: At a cost of more than $7 billion, **CityCenter** is just a construction project now, but it will revolutionize the Vegas skyline by 2009 (page 30).

(Best "Ancient" Wonder: A giant pyramid. A sphinx. An obelisk. This is true Las Vegas, where ancient Egypt gets a makeover at **Luxor Las Vegas** (page 31).

(Best Modern Wonder: Take a bite of the Big Apple with a delirious Sin City update at **New York-New York** (page 35).

(Best Things in Life Are Free: The fact that it's free to see the beautiful **Bellagio Fountain Shows** is merely icing on the cake (page 38).

(Best Blast from the Past: Caesars **Palace** has gotten a light and bright makeover, but of all the older hotels, it has remained the most true to its historic essence (page 40).

(Most Influential Sight: When Steve Wynn built **The Mirage,** it changed everything we knew or thought about a Las Vegas hotel (page 41).

(Best Photo Opportunity: At 50 stories high, the **Paris Las Vegas Eiffel Tower Experience** offers some of the best views for picture-snapping (page 43).

(Best Architecture: If it weren't for the ring-a-ding of the slot machines, you'd almost swear you were actually in Venice at **The Venetian** (page 44).

(Best Views: The **Stratosphere Tower Observation Decks** are too high up for most cameras to get good pictures, but the views from about 1,000 feet in the air are fantastic anyway (page 48).

(Best Brain Food: Most of Las Vegas is built around the concept of getting you to *not* think, but the amazing cultural, historical, and natural facilities at the **Springs Preserve** will balance out the brainlessness of your visit (page 50).

(Best History Lesson: The original Glitter Gulch has gotten an upgrade with the light and sound show of the **Fremont Street Experience,** but it doesn't change the historic, old-Vegas vibe of the place (page 52).

South Strip   Map 1

(CITYCENTER

3780 Las Vegas Blvd. S., 866/722-7171,
www.citycenter.com

HOURS: Open 24 hours

Regardless of the fact that you won't be able to enter CityCenter until late 2009, this spot is a sight unlike any that Vegas has ever seen. What it is now is a lot of construction—$7.4 billion of it as of this writing (probably more by the time you read this). It's considered to be the most expensive privately financed construction project in American history. And for a city that has gotten used to massive buildings (many of the world's largest hotels are here), this place will be almost beyond comprehension.

When it is complete, it will be a city within a city, spreading across 76 acres between Bellagio and Monte Carlo, encompassing more than 18 million square feet of floor space. The centerpiece will be a 61-story hotel with more than 4,000 rooms and suites, a massive casino, restaurants, entertainment facilities (including a custom showroom for an Elvis-themed Cirque du Soleil production), shopping, convention space, and more.

Most places would've stopped there, but no, there's more—much more. Three more boutique hotels are going into the space, including the 50-story Vdara with more than 1,500 condominium hotel units (privately owned residences that can be rented); The Mandarin Oriental, the first Las Vegas entry of the famed Asian hotelier, with a 400-room hotel and more than 200 condominiums; and The Harmon Hotel and Residences, with 400 rooms and even more condos. With these and other residential components, there will be more than 7,000 units, most of which will be available for you to stay in.

But we're not done yet. There will be more than a half-million square feet of additional shopping, dining, and entertainment; park-like grounds and common areas; more than 18,000 parking spaces; and its own futuristic people mover. It'll take more than 12,000 employees just to make it all run.

So take a moment as you walk by to have a look at the construction and realize that you are seeing the future of Las Vegas.

EXCALIBUR

3850 Las Vegas Blvd. S., 800/937-7777,
www.excalibur.com
HOURS: Open 24 hours (casino)
When Excalibur opened in 1990, it was the opening shot in a theme war that was about to engulf The Strip. True, The Mirage opened a year before, but its theme was slightly more subtle—if a Polynesian rainforest can be subtle, that is.

Nothing about Excalibur is subtle. It looms, as all great castles should, over the intersection of Las Vegas Boulevard and Tropicana Avenue with great cartoonish delight. It's the place Mickey Mouse and his pals would probably hang out if they ever made it to Vegas. With candy-colored turrets, a valet parking area that looks like a drawbridge, and a moat with a wizard and a dragon, the Excalibur once was the height of delirious Vegas wackiness.

Since then, more delirious and more wacky hotels have come along to overshadow it and Excalibur has somehow managed to fade in the Vegas zeitgeist, especially for repeat visitors. It's hard to believe that a castle-themed, 4,000-room hotel can become background noise, but there you have it. Whether it's because they eventually got rid of the wizard and dragon or

just that a castle can't compete with the skyline of New York City right across the street, the end result is the same: Excalibur is not the must-see it used to be.

And that's too bad, really, because it still qualifies as a sight in its own right. You may not spend as much time here as you will at some of the other more entertaining visual wonders in the neighborhood, but you really should stop to see it, both outside and in. Forget the competition for a minute and The Knights of the Round Table regalia throughout is just as much of a hoot as it was when it first opened.

🄲 LUXOR LAS VEGAS
3900 Las Vegas Blvd. S., 800/288-1000, www.luxor.com
HOURS: Open 24 hours (casino)
Once a masterpiece of thematic kitsch, the Luxor is now slightly less giggle-inducing since the corporate owners have undertaken a project to de-Egypt the building. What was once a riot of hieroglyphics and "Walk Like an Egyptian" fun is now much more upscale, hip, and serious.

The exterior is still quite a sight, from the tip of the pyramid, shining a light heavenward that's said to be visible from space, to the base of the world's largest indoor atrium. Even those who park out back should walk out to the front of the building and enter from the sidewalk in order to pass the Obelisk and Sphinx.

The main floor is home to the casino and the art deco lobby under the soaring, and somewhat dizzying, interior of the pyramid.

The main attractions however are up a set of escalators (to the left of the front doors or directly inside from the parking garage and pool area). The IMAX movie theater, arcade, and other fun stuff are found on this level of the hotel, although at press time many of the current attractions were under consideration for being replaced with nightclubs, restaurants, and other adult diversions.

This is not the hotel's first redesign. The original version opened in 1993 and featured a lazy Nile River ride around the casino area, complete with boats and narration. This was back in the days when they were trying to convince everyone that Vegas was a family-friendly destination.

SOUTH STRIP WALKING TOUR

Starting and ending point: MGM Grand
Approximate distance: 2-3 miles
Approximate time: 3-4 hours
Best time: Morning

1. Start at the **MGM Grand** lobby near the back of the hotel. This is convenient whether you're driving and entering from the parking garage or taking the monorail, both of which will deposit you near the check-in desk. Walk west toward The Strip through the casino to get a full sense of just how big the thing is. You can catch the **MGM Grand Lion Habitat** just before you exit the building – use the doors on the south side directly adjacent to the habitat.

2. As you come out, you'll be looking across Tropicana Avenue at the **Tropicana.** Take the pedestrian bridge across the street and at least wave to the old gal. By the time you read this, the hotel should be in the middle of a major transition as they tear down the majority of the hotel and rebuild it bigger and, in theory, better. Whether or not you stop in is up to you and should depend on how much construction madness you have to navigate to get inside.

3. Use the pedestrian bridge heading west across The Strip toward The **Excalibur.** You can't miss it – it's that big Disney-esque castle

COURTESY MGM MIRAGE

New York-New York

on the corner. But don't go inside (don't worry, I'll get you back there). Instead, hop on the free monorail shuttle out front.

4. The monorail will ferry you to **Mandalay Bay,** a South Seas beauty that may not be as heavily themed as its neighbors, but is still pretty to look at. Follow the signs for the arena

---

Although the Luxor is not as over the top and wacky as it used to be, it is still quite a sight to behold.

MANDALAY BAY

3950 Las Vegas Blvd. S., 877/632-7000,
www.mandalaybay.com
HOURS: Open 24 hours (casino)

Whereas Excalibur helped to define the wacky theme era of Las Vegas and Luxor refined it to an art form, sister hotel Mandalay Bay took the concept of theming and went in a totally different direction: upscale. While most places were seeking inspiration from well-known locales,

Mandalay Bay took its name from an obscure reference in a Rudyard Kipling novel. Who knew that Vegas could be esoteric?

But the fact that it isn't as giggle-inducing as some of its competition doesn't change the fact that this is still a remarkable achievement, both from a visual and ambience perspective. The South Seas detail is there, but it is more subtle and, because of that, more evocative in more meaningful ways.

Start on the corner in front of the hotel and note the graceful winged creatures guarding a temple-like gate while the gleaming gold towers soar behind it. That's a photo opportunity.

and convention center and you'll pass through the restaurant row, where you can get a picture of yourself next to the headless Lenin statue outside of the Red Square eatery. Further down that hall (much further) is the **Mandalay Bay Shark Reef** aquarium, which is not one of my personal favorites, but fans of our fishy friends should probably put it on their "must see" list.

5. Follow the signs in the casino toward the House of Blues and you'll find the **Mandalay Place** mall right next to it. This small shopping gallery is built on a bridge between Mandalay Bay and your next stop, but on your way you should stop and get a sugar boost with some of the sweet temptations at **The Chocolate Swan.**

6. Follow that mall to **Luxor Las Vegas.** The mall-level entrance deposits you on the second-floor attractions level, good for a dizzying photo of the interior of the pyramid.

7. Then follow the signs for the Luxor's shopping area, and you'll find an adjacent indoor walkway that will lead you to Excalibur. See, I told you I'd get you back here. The walkway deposits you on the second-floor entertainment and restaurant level, but a quick escalator ride will bring you down into the casino. Gambling history buffs may want to scour the casino for the Megabucks machine that paid off the single

largest jackpot in history, more than $37 million. Next, head toward the front door and you'll be back on the corner of Tropicana and The Strip.

8. Take the pedestrian bridge across Tropicana to **New York-New York.** You'll enter on the second floor overlooking the Central Park-themed casino, which is a great spot for a picture of one of the most visually entertaining casinos in town. Head down the escalators and bear to your right to wander through the Greenwich Village homage packed with eateries that may be tempting (**Jody Maroni's** sausages are fantastic). Keep going past this and you'll find your way outside to the Brooklyn Bridge exit.

9. If you use this exit along the bridge replica, you're heading north toward your next destination, **Monte Carlo,** a white and gold facsimile of French Riviera gaming that you should at least snap a picture of, just so you can say you got all the big ones. Keep heading north on the sidewalk.

10. Just past Monte Carlo is where construction is underway on the massive $7 billion **CityCenter,** a complex of hotels, gaming, entertainment, and shopping that will transform the skyline of The Strip in 2009.

11. Use the crosswalk by Monte Carlo to make your way across The Strip back to the MGM Grand.

Inside, the lush foliage and warm lighting spotlight the tropical touches throughout, from lazy palm-frond ceiling fans to rare parrots in the lobby. It's the kind of place that if it were reduced to about a tenth of its size wouldn't be at all out of place on some island resort, seeming to calmly tell you to relax and enjoy your vacation instead of trying to get you all amped up and excited like many other hotels. Think of it as the difference between a blended drink with lots of fruit sticking out of it and a vodka with Red Bull.

Head through "restaurant row" at the back of the property and you'll find a windowed hallway that gives pretty good views of the center-

piece of the hotel: the beach area. It's only open to guests, so unless you're staying there, you'll have to make do with a picture from afar—but it'll be worth it. A lazy river ride, multiple pools, dense landscaping, and an actual beach alongside a giant wave pool make this one of the most photo-worthy relaxation spots in town.

MANDALAY BAY SHARK REEF
3950 Las Vegas Blvd. S., 877/632-7000,
www.mandalaybay.com
HOURS: Daily 10 A.M.-11 P.M.
COST: $15.95 adult, $10.95 child (under 13)
More than 1,200 species of marine life, including

COURTESY MGM MIRAGE

Mandalay Bay

15 varieties of the namesake predators, call the Shark Reef home. A giant two-million-gallon aquarium is the centerpiece of the facility, but it's more than just fish in a bowl, with other wildlife (crocodiles, etc.), flora, and tons of educational information.

The experience starts with a descending, winding walk through a humid rainforest area filled with plants and animals of the non-swimming variety. Informational placards give the lowdown on the species at every stop, but don't expect a dissertation.

Past the piranha pit (luckily, they don't make you swim through) is the main attraction, an underwater room done like the wreck of a sunken ship, with glass walls facing the massive aquarium. This is where visitors can get up close and personal with the sharks, always with a nice thick pane of glass keeping the sharks on their own side. A warning: People with water phobias may not want to spend a lot of time in this area. With water all around and above, it can be a little disconcerting.

I mention this from experience, having been ruined from enjoying water activities by a trip to see *Jaws* when I was in third grade. I've never

gotten over it. But that's probably a discussion for another time.

People with mobility issues should note that the Shark Reef is located at the far south end of the property, through the casino, past the restaurant row and concert venues, and down a very, very long hallway. It's quite a hike even for people who don't have walking difficulties.

MGM GRAND

3799 Las Vegas Blvd. S., 800/929-7111,
www.mgmgrand.com
HOURS: Open 24 hours (casino)

Grand is the operative word here with the largest casino in Las Vegas (at more than 171,000 square feet) and one of the largest hotels in the entire world (more than 5,000 rooms).

When the place first opened in 1993, the size was a major component of the marketing campaign, as was the family-friendly *Wizard of Oz* theme. Bigger! Better! Fun for the kids, too! That experiment failed and subsequent redesigns reconfigured the casino to offer more intimate gaming spaces and relegated the Dorothy and Tin Man statues to the basement.

The look of the place now is not quite as

chuckle-inducing as it used to be, and that's both a good and a bad thing, depending on how you look at it. Fans of kitsch won't find it here anymore, but the ritzy design, which enhances the "we swear it's not that big" feeling, is still worth a photo or three for its opulent, Hollywood-glamour aesthetic.

Of course, no matter how much they try to disguise it, the sheer scope of the MGM Grand is daunting on just about every level, with massive bronze lions outside and real ones inside. For those who are determined (and if crowds are light), the trip from the parking garage to The Strip entrance can be done in less than 15 minutes, but it will probably be a sweaty trip. Just don't try to do it on a Friday or Saturday night. Tons of very popular restaurants and several incredibly trendy nightclubs draw hordes of people here on the weekends.

Dorothy may not be in Vegas anymore, but the Emerald City is still just as enticing.

MGM GRAND LION HABITAT

3799 Las Vegas Blvd. S., 800/929-7111,
www.mgmgrand.com
HOURS: Daily 11 A.M.–10 P.M.

Just inside the main entrance from The Strip is a delightful change of pace from the frenetic madness of everything that surrounds it at this soaring glass habitat for the namesake corporate mascots. You may not hear them roar like they do at the end of MGM movies, but the lions that live here are no less majestic.

Actually, to be clear, they don't really live here. More than two dozen lions are a part of this collection, and every day a select few are brought in from their own ranch for a six-hour stint of allowing tourists to take pictures of them. I can think of worse jobs.

The habitat at the MGM Grand seems relatively small, but that's only because it's a small part of one of the world's biggest hotels. It's a perspective thing. Go during the week if you can. Weekends bring out the crowds, and since there is limited space to press your nose against the glass, you may have to elbow your way past people to get a good view.

But just because it's not as "grand" as some

other parts of the building, it's still pretty cool with trees, rocks, water, and various other lounge furniture for the lions to lie around on, which is what they usually do. This isn't exactly the sort of place where the lions play with giant balls of yarn or chase down elk.

A glass-walled tunnel leads guests through the habitat to the requisite lion-themed gift shop. The good news is a portion of the profits here go to conservancy efforts, and they even have photo opportunities on occasion with lion cubs.

This is a must for animal lovers, but even those who don't know what channel *Animal Planet* airs on should enjoy this. Take a cue from the lazy lions and relax for a few minutes.

◀ NEW YORK-NEW YORK

3790 Las Vegas Blvd. S., 800/693-6763,
www.nynyhotelcasino.com
HOURS: Open 24 hours (casino)

A year after this hotel opened in 1997, Bellagio came along and Las Vegas started getting all serious and stuff. Perhaps it was because everyone realized there was no way they could top the audacious, delirious, hyperkinetic amalgam of everything Gotham here at New York-New York.

Stand outside and stare for a while. You'll probably have no other choice. There's a Statue of Liberty in front of the hotel, complete with a tugboat at its base. The entrance along The Strip looks just like the Brooklyn Bridge. Look up for a view of the skyline, featuring scaled-down versions of the Chrysler and Empire State Buildings (yes, the hotel rooms are in those towers). Oh, and just in case that's not stimulating enough, they threw in a roller coaster winding through the whole thing just to kick it up a notch.

Inside, the amusing details continue. The casino is done as Central Park, complete with lots of trees and twinkling lights (but alas, no lawns for picnicking). Core facilities and bathrooms are disguised behind New York Stock Exchange and Public Library facades. There's even a Greenwich Village area that doubles as a shopping arcade and food court, complete with graffiti-covered mailboxes and manhole covers in the "streets."

The one thing not present is any overt visual representation of a pre-September 11th New York City. The giant mural over the art deco–inspired check-in desk was redone to remove the Twin Towers from the landscape and there are no photos in the rooms anymore featuring those reminders of that terrible day.

It's just as well. This is fantasy New York, where the streets are clean, the smells are good, and the bandits taking your money are of the one-armed variety and they never do it at gunpoint.

NEW YORK-NEW YORK TRIBUTE TO HEROES

3790 Las Vegas Blvd. S., 800/693-6763,
www.nynyhotelcasino.com
HOURS: Open 24 hours (casino)

It's rare to find anything "real" in Las Vegas. They build fake versions of everything from New York to Rome. They pump in scented air to make the experiences more enjoyable. They even hide the clocks and rarely let guests see if it's day or night outside. Las Vegas is all about getting as far away from reality as you can get.

That this touching memorial exists at all is impressive. The fact that it's in front of a giant hotel-casino, along one of the busiest intersections in the world, is almost miraculous.

In the days and weeks following the September 11th terrorist attacks, a makeshift tribute popped up on the fence in front of New York-New York Hotel and Casino as people left cards, photos, signed T-shirts, and stuffed animals out of sympathy, honor, and grief. Facing a marketing nightmare anyway (representations of the Twin Towers were throughout the building in artwork and photography), officials of the hotel began removing the objects from the fence, but as soon as they were taken down, more would pop up in their place.

They do deserve credit for what they did next. Even though the rest of the hotel was scrubbed of any visual reminder of 9/11 (artwork and photos were changed or removed), hotel personnel collected and catalogued everything that was left on the fence and then built a permanent display for rotating sets of select items along the sidewalk in the shadow of the Statue of Liberty.

It's totally out of place here, yet it would be completely wrong if it didn't exist. We always say trite things like "We'll never forget," but why don't you take a minute away from the slot machines and showgirls on your next Vegas vacation and prove it. It doesn't get more real than this.

Center Strip   Map 2

BELLAGIO

3600 Las Vegas Blvd. S., 888/987-7111,
www.bellagio.com
HOURS: Open 24 hours (casino)

Just as sister hotel The Mirage set the tone for Las Vegas hotels for the decade that followed its opening, so too did Bellagio, moving everything in the city up a rung (or 12) on the luxury ladder and proving that good taste had a place on The Strip.

Taken as a whole, Bellagio still stuns from its own fountain-filled lake in front to the Italian renaissance pool out back. Take some time as you start the long walk from the sidewalk to the building and notice the details: lush

landscaping blooming with colors; ornate balustrades and graceful lanterns lining the cobblestone drive; a sun-dappled color scheme that perfectly evokes the Mediterranean seaside village it pretends to be.

Inside, things are no less impressive. Come in through the heavy glass and iron revolving door and the lobby embraces immediately, bursting with vivid hues in the floral arrangements, floor treatments, and the giant glass sculpture overhead. The latter consists of more than 2,000 hand-blown glass flowers created by renowned artist Dale Chihuly. In addition to being simply beautiful, it instantly sets the tone for the entire hotel: elegant and sophisticated, but not stuffy.

COURTESY MGM MIRAGE

Bellagio

The casino is a visual feast as well with thick carpeting, luxurious wall treatments, and colorful canopies over the gaming tables. They even managed to turn the ultimate pedestrian Las Vegas symbol, the slot machine, into something less "common" by encasing them in rich woods and grouping them in well-ordered arrangements that foster a sense of a much more intimate space.

Bellagio undeniably ushered in a new era of opulence for the city. The downside, of course, is that it also ushered in an era of sky-high prices that many people can't afford. The good news is they don't charge you anything to walk through the front door and appreciate the results of what they accomplished.

BELLAGIO CONSERVATORY AND BOTANICAL GARDENS

3600 Las Vegas Blvd. S., 888/987-7111, www.bellagio.com

HOURS: Open 24 hours

COST: Free

If there were fewer people, this would be a great place to pause and unwind, but even though the hordes descend on this grand, indoor garden doesn't mean it isn't worth seeing. Thousands of colorful plants and flowers are on display under a large glass atrium allowing natural light to spill inside, a rarity in Vegas.

Each display is themed, changing every few months in keeping with a season or holiday. Springtime usually brings a riot of colors, arching up the trellises and often shaped into birds or bees; autumn brings out the horns o' plenty and perhaps a turkey or three worthy of a Rose Parade float; Chinese New Year is a big draw for Vegas and the conservatory, with Asian-inspired flowers and decor; and December offers a majesty of holiday ornaments, trees, and blooms in a winter setting right out of a movie.

These seasonal masterpieces (and others) are designed and cared for by more than 100 horticulturalists, who grow the plants in an off-site greenhouse, then bring them into the

CENTER STRIP WALKING TOUR

Starting and ending point: Bellagio
Approximate distance: 2 miles
Approximate time: 3-4 hours
Best time: Evening

1. Enter **Bellagio** and head straight to the **Bellagio Conservatory and Botanical Gardens,** just off the lobby and adjacent to the doors that come in from the parking garage. Spend a few minutes appreciating the artistry that goes into creating these floral masterpieces. Go out the back of the gardens and walk down the hall to find the giant chocolate fountain at the **Jean-Phillippe Patisserie** (3600 Las Vegas Blvd. S., 702/693-7111, www .bellagio.com, Sun.-Thurs. 7 A.M.-11 P.M., Fri.-Sat. 7 A.M.-midnight). If you love chocolate, this is like a holy shrine. If you don't like chocolate, I have nothing else to say to you.

2. Next head outside to catch one of the **Bellagio Fountain Shows,** the epic water, light, and sound show that is entertaining no matter how many times you've seen it. The fountain show is best viewed after the sun goes down to get the full effect of the colorful lights that accompany it.

3. Walk north along The Strip to the pedestrian bridge that crosses Flamingo Road and you'll arrive at **Caesars Palace,** a Roman-themed wonderland located here since 1966. The pedestrian bridge deposits you in an outdoor plaza that leads to the casino. Traverse it

carefully – it's easy to get lost, but if you get turned around, just keep following the signs for the Forum Shops and that's the direction you want to go.

4. Wander through **The Forum Shops at Caesars Palace** to take a gander at the silliness of a Gap in ancient Rome, plus you may catch the fountain shows inside the mall if your timing is right. They're a good amusement, but not worth going out of your way to see, so if it's a choice of waiting 30 minutes to see the next one or moving on with your life, I suggest the latter.

5. Keep going through the mall and eventually you'll be deposited back on The Strip. Turn to your left and you'll see a moving sidewalk that will take you into **The Mirage.** Angle to your right through the casino and you'll stumble onto the tropical rainforest and the aquarium behind the check-in desk. Exit the front door to the valet parking area for a view of the Mirage volcano show.

6. Alongside the valet parking area is a stop for a tram that will take you to neighboring **Treasure Island.** It deposits you on the second floor at the back of the property near the parking garage, and as you exit, turn right to take an escalator down to the main casino floor. Feel free to explore, but if you want to skip this one, walk straight ahead to the exit through Buccaneer Bay, where they have the

hotel to set up the displays. Each involves thousands of flowers and plants at an annual cost that hotel officials will only divulge as being "in the millions."

It's quite an achievement, this oasis of sight and smell—take a minute to inhale deeply. The delicious aromas are intoxicating and a welcome relief from the smoke-filled casinos nearby.

The gardens are located adjacent to the main lobby, on the way to the Spa Tower built in 2004. That hallway leading to the new wing is where the big staircase that Julia Roberts walked down in *Ocean's 11* used to be.

◖ BELLAGIO FOUNTAIN SHOWS
3600 Las Vegas Blvd. S., 888/987-7111,
www.bellagio.com
HOURS: Shows every 30 minutes Mon.-Fri. 3 -8 P.M., Sat.-Sun. noon-8 P.M.; every 15 minutes nightly 8 P.M.-midnight
COST: Free

To call it a fountain is a gross understatement. Located in the 22-million-gallon lake in front of Bellagio, it's more of an epic water ballet as streams and geysers seem to twirl, dance, and explode in careful choreography to the music.

There are more than 1,200 water-shooting devices in the lake. The Oarsmen are the smallest,

awful pirate show you shouldn't bother seeing unless you're desperate for entertainment or a glutton for punishment.

7. Instead, turn right and you'll find a pedestrian bridge that will lead you across The Strip to **The Venetian.** It delivers you to the second-floor walkway overlooking the outdoor St. Mark's Square replica (and **Gondola Rides**) with an entrance to the **Grand Canal Shoppes** mall. With its replica of the Grand Canal, this is where you'll find the indoor gondola rides. You can wander through the mall or take the escalators down to the main casino floor. Be sure to look up as you go for some really stunning artwork on the walls and ceilings. Turn right as you get off the escalators and follow the signs for the front desk. It's worth the extra few steps to see the Grand Hall and lobby area, highly impressive marble affairs with enough filigree to fill the Louvre. Exit the main doors to the valet parking area.

8. As you come out of The Venetian, head to The Strip and turn left on the sidewalk. This will lead you past **Harrah's** and **Imperial Palace** to the **Flamingo Las Vegas,** one of the oldest continually operating resorts on The Strip, opened in 1946. Whether you choose to stop in any of these places is totally up to you. I personally wouldn't put them high on my "sightseeing" tour since about the only good photo opportunities are

of more slot machines, but if you feel like losing a few bucks, these aren't bad places in which to do it.

9. Keep going past The Flamingo and you'll come to a pedestrian bridge that crosses over Flamingo Road to **Bally's.** Take the elevated moving sidewalk inside this hotel and pause for a minute to remember that this was the scene of one of the most devastating hotel fires in U.S. history: 87 people died here in 1980 when the hotel was known as the MGM Grand. Pass through the casino, and on your right, just past the main casino cage, is a walkway lined with shops and restaurants. Take it.

10. That walkway will lead you to the back of **Paris Las Vegas.** Turn right and you'll follow a cobblestone Parisian street scene to the main casino, where you'll find the ticket counter for the **Paris Las Vegas Eiffel Tower Experience.** After you've finished, go out any of the main doors of the hotel to The Strip.

11. Turn left as you exit and you'll see the hotel that was once known as The Aladdin, but has now made the successful transition to its current state as **Planet Hollywood.** The swank casino and equally swank **Miracle Mile Shops** that surround the building are both worth a look.

12. Return to Bellagio via the crosswalk near Planet Hollywood or via the pedestrian bridge near Bally's.

emitting the targeted streams of water that go back and forth, left and right, adding to the dancing illusion. Mini-, Super-, and Extreme-Shooters use between 120 and 500 pounds-per-square-inch of compressed air to blast water straight up—more than 500 feet up in some cases. That's about as tall as the building behind them.

The sound system pumps out more than 56,000 watts of music through speakers located all around the lake. A lighting system is comprised of more than 5,000 575-watt bulbs, giving the fountains a white or colored glow at night (which, by the way, is the best time to view them).

It takes a team of roughly three dozen engineers to maintain and run the fountains. The shows are controlled by a computer that allows designers to select a piece of music, upload it to the system, and then click and point on the various water-shooting devices to create a ballet. Once done, the new show is saved to the computer and the operator simply presses "play" and watches the magic begin.

And magic is a good word for it. It's easy to get cynical about stuff like this, especially after seeing it a time or four. But get up close and really pay attention. There's nothing else like this anywhere in the world.

The shows are free of charge, but <u>the best viewing areas are from the restaurants or bars lining the lake on the hotel side,</u> so it may cost the price of a meal or a drink. Barring that, pretty much anywhere along The Strip sidewalk still offers a terrific view.

CAESARS PALACE

3570 Las Vegas Blvd. S., 800/634-6661,
www.caesarspalace.com

HOURS: Open 24 hours (casino)

Opened in 1966, Caesars Palace was once considered the most decadent of Las Vegas hotels. Back then, people couldn't believe anyone would spend that much money to build a hotel and casino. Of course, the $10 million spent to build the entire thing back then would barely cover the cost of a half-dozen hotel rooms these days.

Caesars was not the first themed hotel on The Strip. The Frontier had a western flair, and the Dunes, Sands, and Sahara all had desert or Arabian elements. But Caesars Palace took the concept of hotel theming to a whole new level with an ornate Roman temple design, statuary, fountains, and toga-clad employees taking drink orders and posing for pictures with the guests.

These days, a modern makeover has removed some of the Bacchanalian glamour, but there's still enough left of the old gal to get an appreciation for the way things used to be done in Las Vegas. For instance, the fountains leading up to the main entrance and the lighted porte cochere are all new, but they have the same basic layout and essentially the same design as the originals.

Inside, virtually all trace of the old has been scrubbed away, which tugs at the historic heartstrings a little, but truth be told, the place had started to get a little dingy before they began throwing money at it again. While it's easy to miss the smoky chandeliers and dark, clubby atmosphere in theory, the elegantly redesigned interiors are a much more user-friendly reality.

The casino wanders and rambles through the building, so take the time to stroll and appreciate the details both small (the paintings and architectural design elements are indi-

vidual masterpieces) and large (yes, that's supposed to be a replica of the Roman Colosseum housing a 4,000-seat showroom).

The adjacent Forum Shops mall continues the theme with a Roman street scene, moving statuary, and an indoor "sky" that changes from night to day. (For more details, see the *Shopping* chapter.)

Oh, and they still have people wandering around wearing togas and sandals to take pictures with. The Caesars of yore is long gone, but the Caesars of today still puts on a good show.

FLAMINGO LAS VEGAS

3555 Las Vegas Blvd. S., 800/732-2111,
www.flamingolv.com

HOURS: Open 24 hours (casino)

Most people think the Flamingo was the first hotel-casino on The Strip. Heck, some people even think this was the first hotel-casino in Las Vegas. Not true on either account.

Downtown Las Vegas and the casinos along Glitter Gulch had been booming for more than three decades when the Flamingo opened in 1946 (except for that unpleasant period when they outlawed gambling, but we won't speak of that). Once business moved south to what would eventually become The Strip, there were already two major resorts (El Rancho and The Frontier) up and running years before The Flamingo was even a twinkle in Bugsy Siegel's eye.

Mobster Benjamin Siegel muscled his way into controlling an already under-construction casino, turning it into something bigger and grander than originally envisioned or ever considered for Las Vegas (hence the "Bugsy's Folly" nickname). After using up a lot of the mafia's money and suffering through a less than spectacular opening in late 1946, Siegel was killed in Los Angeles in a hail of gunfire, never getting a chance to see his vision turn into the lasting success it has become.

If he were still around, he wouldn't recognize the place. In fact, there isn't a single wall still standing from that original structure; the last remains of it were torn down in 1999. Today, the hotel doesn't compare in grandeur to its newer, more expensive neighbors, but there are still enough photo-worthy opportunities around to use up a bit of film. Be sure to wander out near the pool, a tropical paradise complete with live animals that rivals or beats any other on The Strip.

Some say the ghost of Benjamin Siegel still wanders through the rose garden near the pool. If it's good enough for Bugsy to haunt, it's good enough for you.

It's worth noting that the current corporate owners, Harrah's Entertainment, were considering some major changes to their properties at press time. This could mean some revamping of The Flamingo and several of its neighbors, so don't be surprised if you see scaffolding when you visit.

◖ THE MIRAGE

3400 Las Vegas Blvd. S., 800/627-6667,
www.mirage.com
HOURS: Open 24 hours (casino)

When The Mirage opened in 1989, it set a new standard for Las Vegas hotel-casinos. Built at the then-staggering cost of $750 million (a drop in the bucket compared to the multibillions spent today), The Mirage changed the long-accepted formula of lavishing on the casino while skimping on the rest of the building. In years past, restaurants and shows were almost an afterthought, public areas were little more than hallways to a slot machine, attractions were virtually unheard of, and standard rooms were little more than motel-level accommodations.

But casino impresario Steve Wynn had a different vision. His dream was to create a full package where guests would be pampered in luxury from the moment they stepped out of the cab. To say it changed everything is an understatement. The award-winning restaurants and celebrity chefs at hotels up and down The Strip today wouldn't be here if it weren't for the high-class dining The Mirage introduced when it opened. Without the multimillion-dollar showroom and spectacle of the long-running Siegfried and Roy extravaganza, we wouldn't have Cirque du Soleil or The Blue Man Group. Even the gleaming white and gold

tri-wing hotel tower design was copied at Bellagio, Treasure Island, Monte Carlo, and Mandalay Bay, to name a few.

Today, there are bigger, grander, and more expensive hotels in the area, but The Mirage still impresses. Once guests walk in the front doors, they can walk through an indoor tropical rainforest—an actual living ecosystem under a giant dome with fragrant flowers and plants. Behind the check-in desk is a large aquarium packed with dozens of species of colorful fish.

And out front? Well, yes, of course there's a volcano. With hundreds of trees atop a waterfall, the faux-cano belches fire, geysers, and rumbling sound effects every 15 minutes from dusk to midnight. When it first opened, it literally stopped traffic on The Strip. Today, it's become just another bit of background noise, but remember, without it, the things that eclipse its attention-getting status wouldn't exist.

All of The Mirage's aforementioned attractions are free of charge.

MIRAGE SECRET GARDEN & DOLPHIN HABITAT

3400 Las Vegas Blvd. S., 800/627-6667,
www.mirage.com
HOURS: Mon.-Fri. 11 A.M.-5:30 P.M.; Sat., Sun., and major holidays 10 A.M.-5:30 P.M., hours vary by season
COST: $15 adult, $10 child (4-12), free for children under 4

Undoubtedly the most un-Vegas thing to see in Vegas, this sanctuary is home to a veritable *Wild Kingdom*'s worth of animals and includes one of the most highly regarded dolphin habitats in the world.

The Secret Garden portion of the program is a small zoo-like facility housing many of the lions, tigers, elephants, and other animals that were used in Siegfried and Roy's former show. I give this part of the facility short shrift only because the animals, while beautiful, are much less interactive. If you've seen one tiger behind a fence, you've seen them all, but you can never get enough of playing with dolphins, and that's where you should really spend the bulk of your time.

COURTESY MGM MIRAGE

Mirage Secret Garden & Dolphin Habitat

Three pools are home to more than a dozen Atlantic bottle-nosed dolphins, most born and raised here over the last 15 years or so, making it one of the most successful breeding programs anywhere. While it is undeniably true that these animals would probably be better off in their native ocean environments, the reputation of this facility and the obvious care they give the animals makes all but the most rabid of animal activists a little more at ease.

An observation platform overlooking the main pool is the first stop as the animal handlers give guests an overview of the facility and a bit of education on the dolphins themselves. This is not SeaWorld, so there is no "show" to speak of. People don't water-ski on the backs of dolphins or do lots of crazy aerial stunts. If the dolphins are feeling frisky, though, which they usually are, they will do some jumping, diving, and fish-grabbing to keep guests amused.

From there, the tour goes indoors to a room overlooking another of the pools, the location of many a dolphin birth as captured on the videos playing nonstop. A winding passage leads

visitors down one level so they can get an underwater view of this pool and the dolphins swimming merrily along.

Visitors wind up back at the main pool where, if they're lucky, they may actually get a chance to play "catch" with the dolphins as they bat a big ball out into the crowd and wait patiently until someone throws it back in. It's a hoot on just about every level.

PARIS LAS VEGAS

3665 Las Vegas Blvd. S., 888/266-5687, www.parislv.com

HOURS: Open 24 hours (casino)

It seems silly to call a giant Las Vegas hotel-casino romantic, but if any of them come close to justifying the use of that word, it's this one. Done with an early 1900s "City of Lights" theme, the cobblestone streets, Parisian-style buildings, and outdoor park-like setting will make you want to stroll hand-in-hand with a loved one. Or eat a chocolate pastry. Your call.

The details here are astounding. The intricate and ornate exterior of the building, done

Paris Las Vegas

in a faithful French rococo style, wouldn't look out of place on just about any street in Paris if it weren't for the massive size issues. There's a full-scale replica of the Arc de Triomphe in the valet parking area and, of course, that half-scale replica of the Eiffel Tower soaring overhead.

But it's inside where the designers' visions really grab hold. The casino area is filled with trees and twinkling lights under exhibition-style metal garden trellises. Overhead, a blue sky illuminates the room with white, fluffy clouds floating here and there—at least, that's how it seems until you notice it's just a very well done painting. Around the edges of the casino are building facades straight out of 1905 Paris. It's all charming and fun, and if it weren't for all of those slot machines and blackjack tables, you might be able to fool yourself into believing you were actually there.

Okay, maybe that's pushing things a little. But for those whose powers of fantasy aren't that well developed, there are always the French pastries baked fresh every day. That should bring on a Parisian mood really fast.

◖ PARIS LAS VEGAS EIFFEL TOWER EXPERIENCE

3665 Las Vegas Blvd. S., 888/266-5687, www.parislv.com

HOURS: Daily 9:30 A.M.–12:30 A.M. weather permitting; hours may vary seasonally

COST: Mon.-Thurs. $9 adult, $7 child (6-12) and senior, Fri.-Sat. $12 adult, $10 child (6-12) and senior, free for children under 6

Soaring some 50 stories over The Strip, this version of the Eiffel Tower at Paris Las Vegas is only half the size of the original, but it dominates the landscape on this section of Las Vegas Boulevard since most of the neighboring buildings top out around 35–40 stories. The only reason people don't stop and stare more often, marveling at how gloriously out of place it is in the middle of the desert, is because this is

Las Vegas and, by the time it was built in 1999, people had come to expect such silliness.

The elevators up to the observation deck are located inside the casino, naturally. But before you go, take a moment to note the feet of the tower intruding through the faux-sky ceiling. Construction crews built the Eiffel Tower replica first and then put up the casino around it.

While I probably don't need to mention it to people with height issues since they're probably smart enough not to go anywhere near this thing, here's a note of caution: For the record, there's a dizzying glass-elevator ride to the top. Since the three-sided lift has windows on all sides, the only escape for those who can't stomach it is to stare at the floor.

The observation deck at the top is small—there's only room for a few dozen people at a time—but if you can muscle your way to the sides, the views are terrific. At half the height of the Stratosphere Tower and more centrally located, the Eiffel Tower provides one of the best bird's-eye views in town. It's an especially terrific place to view the Bellagio fountain show directly across the street.

By the way, for the romantically inclined, this is a great and memorable place to pop the question. In fact, the ceremony itself can be held here. Paris Las Vegas offers full Eiffel Tower wedding packages.

(THE VENETIAN

3355 Las Vegas Blvd. S., 888/283-6423,
www.venetian.com
HOURS: Open 24 hours (casino)

With faithful re-creations of St. Mark's Square, the Grand Canal (complete with gondolas), and other Venice landmarks, The Venetian is a veritable masterpiece of its own. The architecture and artwork throughout are museum-quality—the kind of building that usually takes 100 years to reach landmark status, but instead achieved it the day it opened in 1999.

It's interesting to note that when the hotel opened, it was considered a beautiful failure. So many things went wrong in the first year of operation that many, including myself, figured this billion-dollar palace of excess was an

exercise in what not to do. But they made it through their growing pains, learned their lessons quickly, and have turned what could've been a disaster into one of the most talked about, most successful hotels on The Strip.

Management issues aside, The Venetian mastered the locale-theme madness that gripped The Strip at places like Paris and Luxor by bringing Venice landmarks to Las Vegas and adding enough art and design to turn it into a full-fledged experience. The Strip–facing portion of the hotel is the first of two replicas of St. Mark's Square, with a gondola canal, the Bridge of Sighs, and the famous clock tower completing the effect.

Past the doors that lead to the check-in desk are the Louvre-worthy paintings and sculpture in the lobby along with the Grand Hall, a towering three-story colonnade to the casino with enough marble to pave a road to Los Angeles.

Navigating through the mostly forgettable casino, visitors arrive at the Grand Canal Shoppes, well worth the journey. (This highly themed mall is covered in detail in the *Shopping* chapter.)

If you can wrangle access to the newer Venezia tower (reserved for guests, but you can usually get there via the elevators just off the main lobby), you should. The artwork and architectural detail here are even more jaw-dropping in their complexity and quality than in the original building.

By the way, that big building next door is Palazzo, a sister property to The Venetian. It was not open at press time, but will be by the time this book hits the stands. You can expect more Italian-inspired art and elegance plus a new casino, more shopping, and 3,000 more rooms.

VENETIAN GONDOLA RIDES

3355 Las Vegas Blvd. S., 888/283-6423,
www.venetian.com
HOURS: Sun.-Thurs. 10 A.M.-11 P.M., Fri.-Sat. A.M.-midnight
COST: Indoor rides $15 adult, $7.50 child (12 and under); outdoor rides $12.50 adult, $5 child (12 and under)

People who have taken gondola rides in the real Venice tell me the Vegas version is actually a more satisfying experience on many levels. It's cleaner, it smells better, and it's actually substantially cheaper than the real thing. Of course, here guests are guided by a singing gondolier through a shopping mall or in front of a casino, but if you want to get picky about the whole thing, then buy a plane ticket to Italy.

If you don't do the private gondola ($60 inside, $50 outside), you have to be a bit of an exhibitionist to fully enjoy the ride. Since the indoor canal runs down the center of the Grand Canal Shoppes and the outdoor one is visible from a huge chunk of The Strip, there are lots and lots of people standing and staring, taking pictures to show the neighbors when they get home. If you don't want to be a part of Bill and Edna's slideshow, don't get on the boat.

But if you do, it's one of those classic "only in Vegas" experiences, despite the fact that it's a carbon copy of what they do in Italy.

North Strip   Map 3

CIRCUS CIRCUS BIG TOP & MIDWAY
2880 Las Vegas Blvd. S., 800/444-2472,
www.circuscircus.com

HOURS: Open 24 hours (casino), circus acts every 30 minutes from 11 A.M.-midnight

Although the experience includes a lot of noisy kids, it's kind of a hoot to see traditional circus acts (none of that fancy Cirque du Soleil stuff here) performing high above a bank of slot machines.

Billed as the world's largest permanent circus, it includes the kind of Barnum & Bailey aerialist feats of derring-do we've grown to know and love. Trapeze artists, tightrope walking, and all other manner of spinning and flying will definitely keep the kids entertained and might even amuse the parents long enough to look up from the blackjack table.

Surrounding the circus "stage" is a midway with carnival-style games for the young and young at heart. This is the kind of thing where visitors can pay a few bucks to toss a

Circus Circus

NORTH STRIP WALKING AND RIDING TOUR

Starting and ending point: Wynn Las Vegas
Approximate distance: 2 miles
Approximate time: 3-4 hours
Best time: Morning

1. Start at **Wynn Las Vegas,** which, at an estimated $2.7 billion, is the most expensive hotel ever built in this country. There's a lot to look at here, including the beautiful gardens near the lobby, the lovely casino, and a Ferrari dealership, if you are so inclined. Exit the building through the shopping gallery and that will lead you to the northeast corner of The Strip and Sands Avenue.

2. Take the pedestrian bridge across the street to the west toward **The Fashion Show** mall. This three-million-square-foot temple to commerce is the largest in Las Vegas and one of the largest in the United States. It has everything from the usual mall suspects to things you probably won't find in the one down the road from you. Have someone hide your credit cards.

3. Exit the mall and turn left to head north on The Strip. The next thing you'll pass will most likely be a big hole in the ground or a construction site. This is the place where The Frontier Hotel and Casino, one of the original resorts on The Strip since 1941, used to stand until it was purchased in 2007 and torn down

(or at least that was the plan as of this writing). What will go in its place is a Las Vegas version of the famed New York Plaza Hotel, except subtracting Eloise and adding a casino.

4. Behind the future Plaza you'll notice a tall gold building under construction as of this writing. That's the new Trump International (yes, that Trump), a condo-hotel tower due to open in 2008. There will be no casino, so even if you happen to be reading this after the place is open, there's not going to be a lot for you to see or do there.

5. Keep heading north along The Strip and you'll pass another big construction zone on your side of the street. That's where the Stardust used to be located and where they are building a $4-billion complex of hotels and casinos called **Echelon Place.** It's due to open in 2010.

6. Across the street you'll notice **The Riviera,** one of the last remaining casinos from one of Vegas's many boom periods. Opened in 1955 with Liberace as the main entertainment, the hotel has gone downhill in recent years and it really isn't worth the energy to cross the street to see it, unless you just want to say you did.

7. Instead, walk a little further north and you'll find **Circus Circus** on your side of the

ring, shoot a water pistol, or sink a basket for a small chance at winning a stuffed animal that probably cost about $0.30 to manufacture. Oh well, apparently it's never too early to learn the basic concept of gambling.

The circus acts are free of charge to view. The midway is free of charge to enter; prices vary per game.

ECHELON PLACE

3000 Las Vegas Blvd. S., www.echelonplace.com
HOURS: Open 24 hours

Yes, I'm sending you to another construction site. Why? Because although this one may not be as expansive or expensive as CityCenter down the road, it will be no less important

to the history of the Las Vegas Strip when it opens in 2010.

Located on a plot of more than 66 acres between the former Frontier (future site of The Plaza) and Circus Circus, this is the place where not one but two legendary casinos once held sway over the city. The Royal Nevada opened here in 1955, but suffered financially and was eventually absorbed into its bigger, better, and more famous neighbor, The Stardust, which opened in 1958. At the time this was the hot area of The Strip, with hotels like The Sahara, The Riviera, The Frontier, The Thunderbird, and The Desert Inn all acting as a focal point for the building boom of the era.

But as development moved south, this

street. This one is worth wandering through, if for no other reason than they have live, free circus acts inside above the casino and, for thrill-ride aficionados, an indoor amusement park called **Adventuredome at Circus Circus** out back. When you come out of the hotel, turn left and continue heading north.

8. The big empty lot you see at the corner of Sahara and The Strip is noteworthy. That is the location of the very first hotel-casino to be built on what would eventually become The Strip. It was called El Rancho and opened in 1941, years before the Flamingo did. It burned to the ground in 1960 and the plot of land has been vacant ever since. At some point in the not-too-distant future, there will be a major development of hotels and condos there done by the same company (MGM Mirage) that already owns most of The Strip. Across the street you'll see The Sahara, but don't go there yet. We'll get that one on the way back.

9. Continue north and you'll pass **Bonanza Gift Shop**, billed as the world's largest souvenir shop. I don't know who verifies claims like this, but I'm willing to let it pass because if you're looking for that truly tacky Vegas souvenir (and I mean that in a good way), this is the place to go. From Elvis to aliens, they've got it here.

10. Continue north for another couple of blocks and you'll reach the pinnacle of your walking tour in more ways that one with the **Stratosphere.** You can't miss it; it's that 1,000-foot tower looming over everything. Go inside and take a ride up to the top to see just how far you've walked, and if you're feeling brave, take a trip on one of the extreme thrill rides.

11. When you come back down, head back the way you came, going a couple of blocks south back to **The Sahara.** This is another hotel that isn't much to look at as of this writing, but the place has new owners as of 2007 that are promising major changes to glam up the place. Regardless of its state, you'll need to walk through it to get to the Las Vegas Monorail station out back. I recommend this rather than walking all the way back just because it's easier.

12. You could stop at the **Las Vegas Hilton** on your way, but that's not officially part of the North Strip, so I'm not going to include it here. Instead, get off at the Las Vegas Convention Center stop (the next one past the Las Vegas Hilton) and go across the street to the southwest corner of Desert Inn and Paradise Road. You'll see a red awning over a bus stop. This is where buses will come pick you up to take you back to Wynn Las Vegas.

neighborhood suffered a steady decline. Not that it ever became dangerous or even seedy, but by comparison to the fantastic palaces that sprung up down the street, the North Strip area looked, well, worn. Old. Tired.

Echelon Place will be a lynchpin in changing all of that. When it is complete, it will feature more than 5,000 rooms in multiple hotels on the property, including the 3,300-room Echelon Resort and casino; a 1,000-room version of the chic Los Angeles hot spot The Mondrian; 600 more rooms in the South Beach transplant Delano; and a 400-room Shangri-La from one of the leading hotel companies in Asia.

Of course, there will also be the requisite casino, which, at more than 140,000 square

feet, will be the second largest on The Strip; entertainment in multiple theaters, including a 4,000-seat amphitheater; restaurants; 350,000 square feet of shopping; a million square feet of convention space; and multiple pools, spas, and recreation facilities to support it all.

The total price tag on the development is expected to exceed $4 billion, but it's not the cost of the thing that makes it important. Instead, it's what it means to this formerly old, tired area. Before they even imploded the hotel that preceded it, multiple plans for major developments in the area were announced, turning this portion of The Strip into the neighborhood to watch for the next decade.

EL RANCHO HISTORIC SITE

Corner of Las Vegas Blvd. S. and Sahara Ave.

HOURS: Open 24 hours

It looks like just a big, empty, dusty lot and, well, it is. But this particular empty lot at the corner of Sahara Avenue and The Strip has tremendous historic importance. It was here, on a hot day in 1938, that hotel magnate Thomas Hull's car broke down just outside of the Las Vegas city limits. Remember, at that time, what would eventually become The Strip was nothing more than a mostly deserted highway and a bunch of scrub brush leading to the Glitter Gulch excitement of Downtown Vegas.

As Hull sat there baking in the merciless desert sun, he envisioned a cool pool on that dusty stretch of desert—a respite from the heat. He returned to his Los Angeles–based business and announced to his associates that he was going to buy the land and build an oasis amid the desert sand.

The El Rancho Vegas resort opened in 1941, a $425,000 hotel and casino with a western theme, 80 rooms, restaurants, a showroom, and, of course, a big sparkling pool visible from the highway. It was the first hotel to be built on The Strip; the first hotel to have an integrated air-conditioning system (air blown over ice); and is the first known location of an all-you-can-eat buffet, which cost $1.

The success of the property brought speculators south, and classic hotels like The Frontier, the Flamingo, The Dunes, The Sands, and The Stardust quickly followed, each outdoing the last in terms of size and status. By the time 1960 rolled around, El Rancho was considered past its prime and probably wouldn't have lasted a lot longer even if fate hadn't intervened in the form of a fire that burned the place to the ground.

The desert reclaimed the land and this has been an empty field ever since. There are no plaques, no memorials, and no evidence that anything ever existed here, but this, in fact, is where it all began.

And perhaps it is fitting that this is also the site of the future of the Las Vegas Strip. In 2007, the MGM Mirage Corporation bought the property and much of the land that abuts their Circus Circus hotel and casino, totaling approximately 100 acres. They plan to build an enormous collection of hotels, casinos, entertainment, shopping, and convention facilities with construction due to start toward the end of the decade, and an opening date sometime in the next decade.

◖ STRATOSPHERE TOWER OBSERVATION DECKS

2000 Las Vegas Blvd. S., 800/998-6937, www.stratospherehotel.com

HOURS: Sun.-Thurs. 10 A.M.-1 A.M., Fri.-Sat. 10 A.M.-2 A.M.
COST: $9.95

Not for the weak of constitution, these indoor and outdoor observation decks are located more than 100 stories above the earth, offering unparalleled views of the entire Las Vegas Valley. They don't call it the Stratosphere for nothing.

High-speed elevators shuttle visitors quickly to the top—a bit of a stomach-churning experience for those sensitive to such things. Once there, visitors have the choice of the indoor area, with slanted glass walls allowing the brave to look straight down about 1,000 feet and telescopes to aid in picking out the details in the distance, or the outdoor deck with fences supplying the barrier between sightseers and an unpleasant end.

Speaking of which, in case you're wondering, the answer is yes. Since the tower opened in 1996, several people managed to get past the elaborate safety and security systems in order to make the ultimate exit. Miraculously, no one else was injured when their journeys came to an end on the concrete below.

But let's not think of such troublesome thoughts. Instead, take a minute or 10 or 30 to simply gaze at the vistas from what seems to be cloud level. Hyperbole? On more than one occasion, I've been in the tower and seen helicopters flying *below* me.

Note: The outdoor observation deck is subject to closure during inclement weather or high winds.

COURTESY WYNN LAS VEGAS/ROBERT MILLER

Wynn Las Vegas

WYNN LAS VEGAS

3131 Las Vegas Blvd. S., 888/320-9966,
www.wynnlasvegas.com

HOURS: Open 24 hours (casino)

At a cost of $2.7 billion, this is not only the most expensive hotel-casino ever built (so far), it is one of the most expensive buildings, period. Steve Wynn, the mastermind behind The Mirage, Bellagio, and Treasure Island, took what he learned from those experiences and threw a lot more money at it. What he wound up with is a luxurious resort that may not have any showstopping single elements, but certainly has enough opulent details to add up to an overall successful package.

Out front rises a 10-story manufactured mountain, with hundreds of trees and plants (many rescued from the old Desert Inn golf course out back), and surrounding waterfalls that cascade into reflecting pools. The other side of the mountain, facing the hotel, has more waterfalls and pools, with a light and sound show playing nightly. There are no public viewing areas for the show—you have to be in a restaurant or a bar to see it and pay the requisite tabs for eating or drinking while doing so. I personally don't find it worth the money or effort, but some people think it's kind of cool, so if you have some extra cash burning a hole in your pocket and nothing else to do with your time, go for it.

Inside the hotel, the design is certainly impressive, with colorful mosaic tiles forming intricate patterns in the public areas; a big conservatory garden under a skylight with seasonal flowers and plants; lots of rich fabrics and woods everywhere; and a bold color scheme of reds and chocolate browns lending a dramatic flair. There is no theme to speak of—nary a pirate in sight—unless luxury can be counted as a theme of its own.

Next door is the sister hotel **Encore,** another couple of billion dollars' worth of Vegas excess due to open in 2008.

Just Off The Strip   Map 4

HARD ROCK HOTEL
4455 Paradise Rd., 800/473-7625,
www.hardrockhotel.com
HOURS: Open 24 hours (casino)

The casino and public areas of the Hard Rock are cramped, loud, and overwhelming. This is rock and roll, baby!

The natural extension of the rock-themed restaurant chain has become one of the most successfully hip hotels in Las Vegas. The crowds here are relentlessly young, pretty, and willing to throw around ridiculous amounts of cash, so those who don't fit into that category may not want to spend a lot of time here.

But music fans should at least stop by to see the bits of history contained within the Hard Rock's walls. Scattered throughout are memorabilia displays of music stars new and old, including costumes, guitars, gold records, and ephemera from some of the biggest names in the business. Exhibits change often but, in the past, I've seen everything from a Jimi Hendrix guitar to one of Courtney Love's baby-doll dresses. Fans looking for nice mementos from Pat Boone or Pasty Cline won't be happy here.

Past the pulsing crowds, the gaming tables and slot machines are worth a look. The craps tables are shaped like grand pianos and many of the slots have guitar stalks for handles. It's a cute touch.

As mentioned, this is a haven for the see-and-be-seen set and a refuge for the famous, nearly famous, and formerly famous. And if you're lucky, you might bump into one of those big names whose memorabilia is housed in display cases nearby (well, probably not Hendrix). I met Hootie here. You know, of Blowfish fame. Just thought you'd want to know.

There is no charge to view the displays.

Potential visitors should note that the current owners, Morgan's Hotel Group, plan a multibillion-dollar renovation and expansion that will be well underway by the time you pick up this book. A new hotel tower, an expanded casino, new concert venues, and much more are in the works.

RIO'S *MASQUERADE VILLAGE SHOW IN THE SKY*
3700 W. Flamingo Rd., 888/752-9746,
www.playrio.com
HOURS: Shows daily 3, 4, 5, 6:30, 7:30, 8:30, and 9:30 P.M.
COST: Free

Mardi Gras takes flight with colorful parade-style floats appearing to, well, float above the casino floor. Meanwhile, singers, dancers, musicians, and other entertainers shake their bon bons on the floats and a big center stage. While this isn't exactly Broadway-caliber entertainment, it's pretty good for a free Vegas show.

The specifics of the show change from time to time, so I won't expend a lot of energy describing it here, but it usually involves a lot of amped-up party music ("Conga" is a perennial favorite) pounding on the sound system while the dancers strut their stuff on the stage and throughout the audience. It's fun and yet instantly forgettable all at the same time, the entertainment equivalent of junk food.

Above the audience, floats filled with musicians and singers move about on tracks in the ceiling. There's a paddle wheel–style boat, a big swan, and something that looks vaguely like a multilevel gazebo. Since this is a Carnivale in Rio–style affair, there's lots of bead-throwing to keep things interesting. And you don't even have to flash anyone to get some.

The glory of all of this is that it's totally free. Very little is in Vegas anymore, so appreciate this one while it's still around.

◖ SPRINGS PRESERVE
333 S. Valley View Blvd., 702/822-7700,
www.springspreserve.org
HOURS: Opens daily at 10 A.M., closing time varies by season
COST: $18.95 adult, $10.95 child (5-17), $13.45 senior (65 and up)

The chunk of land that eventually became Las Vegas was attractive to the people who wandered

WELCOME TO FABULOUS LAS VEGAS

A little more than a mile south of Russell Road on the 5200 block of Las Vegas Boulevard South, located in the middle of the highway with very little fanfare, is one of the most iconic symbols of the city: the Welcome to Fabulous Las Vegas sign.

The Chamber of Commerce commissioned the sign in the late 1950s, at the peak of the early Strip boom. Up the street were such classic hotels as the Tropicana, The Desert Inn, The Riviera, The Sands, The Dunes, and the Sahara, some of which have managed to survive to this day. Closest to the location of the sign was The Hacienda, a Spanish-style resort on the land that is now home to Mandalay Bay.

The sign was designed by local artist Betty Willis and built by the Young Electric Sign Company, the manufacturers of just about every neon sign in Vegas for decades. It went up in 1959 and the people who were responsible must still be kicking themselves for not copyrighting the design. That's why it turns up on books, websites, brochures, and more – no one has to pay for its usage.

But perhaps in the long run it was better

LAS VEGAS NEWS BUREAU/LVCVA

that people could use it wherever they wanted. In doing so, the sign has become the ultimate shorthand for the city's zeitgeist, an instantly recognizable shape that heralds the beginning of another wild Vegas adventure.

through all those years ago because of the natural Artesian springs that fed the area. Although those springs dried up in the 1960s, the land surrounding them, just north and west of The Strip, remained a protected environment. Now the area has been turned into the Springs Preserve, a 180-acre cultural, recreational, and environmental education facility that should absolutely be on your list of things to visit while in Las Vegas.

Start your journey in the Origen Experience, an interpretive center with displays, interactive exhibits, live animals, a theater, and more that explores the cultural and ecological development of the region. Far from a dry museum experience, this hands-on facility has fun features like a dizzying multimedia walk across the Hoover Dam as it was being built and a

flash-flood display with thousands of gallons of water.

Beyond that is the Desert Living Center, a series of LEED Platinum Certified buildings that dig deeper into environmental concerns, including alternative energies and building materials, recycling, conservation, and more. Educational without being preachy about the whole thing, this is a must for adults and especially parents who are concerned about the earth.

The rest of the facility features nature trails, archaeological sites, historic structures, an eight-acre botanical garden with cooking demonstrations, an 1,800-seat amphitheater for concerts (Jewel opened the place), a children's playground, a Wolfgang Puck restaurant, gift shops, and the future home of the Nevada State Historical Museum.

Downtown   Map 5

◖ FREMONT STREET EXPERIENCE

Fremont St. btwn. Main and 4th Sts.,
www.vegasexperience.com
HOURS: Open 24 hours (street), top of every hour
dusk-midnight (shows)
COST: Free

Fremont Street was the main drag of Las Vegas
when it was founded more than 100 years ago.
Heck, it was just about the only drag to speak
of. As the early gambling halls sprang up and
the city grew, the main action was still centered on Fremont and it was here that such
legendary hotel-casinos as the Golden Nugget,
Binion's, The Four Queens, The Mint, and
The Golden Gate laid claim to their fame.

As the buildings grew taller and the neon
signs announcing them grew larger, the area
took on the nickname of Glitter Gulch, the
towering lights creating a canyon of sorts that
made you want to put on some Dean Martin
tunes and cruise in a convertible.

But as the main action moved south to The
Strip, Downtown began to decline, and so the
city took a drastic step in the early 1990s by
closing the street to auto traffic, putting in a
pedestrian mall with an overhead canopy, and
presenting a light and sound show they called
The Fremont Street Experience.

Purists howled, but the result is a stunning
multimedia display with more than 12 million
LED lights and a massive sound system. Every
hour on the hour after dusk, the neon lights of
Glitter Gulch go dark and the giant canopy
lights up with a dazzling spectacle.

The video-quality display features a variety of
rotating shows set to classic and contemporary
music. For instance, as 1940s-era big band music
plays, the display shows horns, music notes, and
zoot-suited hoofers all blending in a kaleidoscope
of color. A British rock show features music from
The Who, The Stones, and The Beatles while
guitars and double-decker buses flash by above.
There are holiday-themed shows, an alien invasion, an underwater adventure, a patriotic rouser,
NASCAR racers, and many others.

This is absolutely one of the best free shows
in town and absolutely worth a trip to Downtown. Yes, purists may miss that cruise in a
convertible down Glitter Gulch, but the Fremont Street Experience is a great example of
why progress is not always a bad thing.

THE GOLDEN GATE

One Fremont St., 702/385-1906,
www.goldengatecasino.net
HOURS: Open 24 hours (casino)

This hotel is not only the oldest in Las Vegas,
it's the oldest in the entire state of Nevada and
one of the oldest buildings still standing in the
state today. Originally opened in 1906 as the
Hotel Nevada, it was one of the earliest significant structures in the town, which wouldn't
become officially incorporated for another five
years. Located directly across the street from the
train depot, where The Plaza hotel now stands,
the hotel charged the royal sum of $1 for a 10-
by 10-foot room and was one of very few "respectable" businesses to offer a casino, albeit a
small one.

The gambling equipment was put away
when the practice was outlawed in 1909, but
it came back out in 1931 after the law was re-
pealed, and there have been people winning
and losing here ever since.

The hotel has undergone a series of name
changes, remodeling, and expansions, but the
basic core of the building is exactly like it was
more than 100 years ago.

It's also worth noting that this is the location of the San Francisco Shrimp Bar and
Deli, home to the famous shrimp cocktail that
you've seen in all of those Travel Channel specials. They started serving it in 1959 and it still
costs only $0.99.

THE GOLDEN NUGGET

129 E. Fremont St., 702/385-7111,
www.goldennugget.com
HOURS: Open 24 hours (casino)

Even though this Downtown Las Vegas main-

LAS VEGAS NEWS BUREAU/LVCVA

The Fremont Street Exprerience is an exciting pedestrian promenade that is home to more than 12 million lights, making it one of the largest LED screens in the world.

stay has been open since 1946, it didn't actually become a hotel until 1977 under the tutelage of future Strip mastermind Steve Wynn. Until then it was "just" a casino—but what a casino it was. Anchoring the heart of Glitter Gulch, it has been a comforting, constant presence and has outlived hotels and casinos that came before and after it.

As is the case with many older hotels, especially ones in this neighborhood, it went through a series of declines, ownership changes, and reversals of fortune, but in 2006 the property was bought by the Landry Restaurant chain and they have managed to breathe life back into the property. The Grand Dame of Downtown Las Vegas been reborn.

The casino was completely remodeled, turning what had been a crowded, smoky, and chaotic space into a warm blaze of earth tones—elegant and upscale yet still Downtown-friendly. They also added terrific new restaurants; redid the showroom, the spa, and the lobby; and built a fantastic multilevel pool

deck, complete with a water slide that passes through a shark-filled aquarium.

With all the changes, they did manage to keep some elements of what made the hotel great in the first place, including personal service and a more convivial atmosphere. Oh, and they also kept the hotel's namesake, The Hand of Faith, billed as the largest gold nugget on public display in the world. Weighing in at more than 61 pounds, you can find it behind glass in the restaurant and shopping hall just off the main lobby.

The end result of all the effort Landry's put into this hotel is one that could compete on almost any level with the big resorts on The Strip and has returned a Vegas "classic" back to sight status.

THE NEON MUSEUM

Fremont St. btwn. Main St. and Las Vegas Blvd.,
www.neonmuseum.org
HOURS: Open 24 hours

While Downtown for the Fremont Street Experience, it's worth the time to wander around the pedestrian mall from Main Street to Las Vegas Boulevard to get a good look at some authentic bits of Vegas history. Scattered along Fremont and the adjacent side streets are a dozen or so classic neon signs, rescued and restored by The Neon Museum, a nonprofit organization devoted to preserving this unique art form.

The organization is in the process of raising money to build a permanent home for its massive collection, but for now, you'll have to make do with the horse and rider from The Hacienda and one of the original Aladdin's lamps, among other gems scattered throughout the area. Each has an informational sign with additional information to distinguish it from the other neon flashing all around.

But that "other" neon is worth noting even if it isn't an official part of the museum. Vegas Vic is the iconic cowboy host of Glitter Gulch, erected in 1951 as the mascot for the now-defunct Pioneer Club casino. Perfectly rendered in blue, yellow, and red neon, he is a snapshot of a bygone era from the tip of his spurs to the tip of the cigarette dangling from his lips (hey, it was 1951—cowboys smoked). Across the street you'll see his gal pal, Vegas Vicky, erected in 1980 and originally named Sassy Sally for the small casino this cowgirl sat on. Her name was changed in the 1990s when the Fremont Street Experience was erected and, owing to typically wacky Vegas tradi-

LAS VEGAS NEWS BUREAU/LVCVA

Vegas Vicky watches over the Fremont Street Experience

tion, they even had a wedding ceremony for Vic and Vicky.

Both the official and unofficial exhibits are free of charge.

GAMING

You came to Las Vegas for the restaurants, spas, shows, golfing, shopping, and nightclubs, right? But did you know you can also gamble in Las Vegas?

According to studies from the Las Vegas Convention and Visitors Authority, the majority of people who come to Las Vegas do not list gambling as their primary reason for the visit. Even more stunning is the fact that the restaurants, spas, shows, shopping, nightclubs, and hotel room rates generate more income than gaming does.

These new studies reflect a 180-degree shift from the way things used to be in Sin City. All those other temptations used to only exist as a way to get people into the casino and most were priced well below cost as loss leaders. But a few years back, the smart people who run these billion-dollar places started charging more and more for all the sideline attractions, upping the quality and quantity as they went, and the crowds came in droves.

Virtually every state in America now has some form of legalized gambling, with many Native American reservations offering full Las Vegas–style action. Why fly all the way to Vegas to play a slot machine when there's one just down the road on a riverboat? Vegas had to up the ante to keep the people coming and now gaming is not the primary focus.

Of course, that doesn't change the fact that a lot of attention is paid to the games of chance and a lot of income is generated from them. In March 2005, people wagered more than $13 billion at Nevada casinos and, for the first time in history, the casinos kept more

COURTESY STATION CASINOS

HIGHLIGHTS

LOOK FOR ◖◗ TO FIND
RECOMMENDED GAMING.

◖◗ **Best Table Games:** There are plenty of open seats at relatively affordable tables at the **Luxor Las Vegas** (page 63).

◖◗ **Best Slot Selection:** You'll certainly have plenty of slot machines to choose from at **MGM Grand,** the largest casino in Vegas (page 63).

◖◗ **Best Energy:** With its riot of Big Apple kitsch, the casino at **New York-New York** is almost as energetic as the games inside (page 65).

◖◗ **Most Customer-Friendly Casino:** The dealers and fellow gamblers at **Bally's** seem to be much more willing to smile, chat, and assist in gaming adventures (page 66).

◖◗ **Best for High-Rollers:** Those with the bank accounts to back up a serious poker face should make the high-stakes games at **Bellagio** their destination (page 68).

◖◗ **Most Entertaining Casino:** Gambling should be fun, and with the "Dealertainers" (dealers dressed up like famous people) at **Imperial Palace,** it's definitely good for a smile (page 69).

◖◗ **Best Decor Overhaul:** Many of the major casinos have gotten interior overhauls lately, but none can top the stunning and modern decor at **Planet Hollywood** (page 71).

◖◗ **Best Trendy Casino:** The kind of action

craps in Times Square, New York-New York

found at the **Hard Rock** has little to do with gaming and more to do with the hip, happening, and trendy crowd that plays here (page 74).

◖◗ **Best Old-School Gambling:** The former home of the World Series of Poker has been around for decades, and while it's not quite as dark and smoky as it used to be, **Binion's** is still the best casino for the Old Vegas vibe (page 76).

◖◗ **Best Budget Casino:** The newly renovated casino at **El Cortez** is not only a fun and friendly place to gamble, it's a bargain, to boot (page 77).

◖◗ **Best Fresh-Air Casino:** It's virtually impossible to get away from the cigarette smoke in a Vegas casino, but the one at **Main Street Station** seems to do the best job of moving the fresh air around (page 78).

than $1 billion of that money, a figure that has either remained constant or has grown every year since. That's a big chunk of change, so it's no surprise that visitors can gamble just about anywhere, anytime, on just about anything.

But with so many options, how do you decide what's going to be the best place for you to gamble? This chapter leads off with some basic instruction and practical advice on how to play the most popular casino games in Las Vegas. It is in no way meant to be an encyclopedic gambler's bible, but should be enough to get you started if you're a beginner.

You'll also find details on what each of the major (and some minor) casinos have to offer. I don't spend a lot of time talking about specific machines or table games (blackjack, craps, roulette, Let It Ride, Caribbean Stud, 3-Card poker) within those casinos, since things change too often to give an accurate reporting of them, and just about everyone offers the same thing anyway. Instead, the following casino profiles cover the look, feel, and ambience of the casino, including any special features worth noting, like low-limits, high-limits, or no-limits gaming.

Gaming Tips

SLOT STRATEGIES

If I need to explain to you what a slot machine is, then you probably shouldn't be going anywhere near a casino. But just in case: A slot machine is a device with a handle, push-button, or both, and spinning reels (either mechanical or video) that have a variety of symbols on them. A player puts in money, pulls the handle or pushes the button, and watches as the reels spin. If the symbols match up in a predetermined way, then the player wins money. If they don't, the player loses. It's that simple and much more complicated all at once.

Slot machines these days are nothing more than a computer chip, which decides through a random sequence whether a player has won or lost as soon as they push the button. This computer chip is called a Random Number Generator (RNG) and it sits there constantly spitting out strings of digits that equate to a loss or a win on the slot machine. The RNG has the capability to generate thousands of numbers a second and each one means something different in terms of payout.

When the "Spin Reels" button is pressed (or "Bet Credit" button before the handle is pulled), the RNG stops on whatever number it had generated at that exact second. That number determines whether a player has lost or won, and if it's the latter, how much. Everything else—the handle, the reels, the bright lights, the sound—is just for show.

That's the easy part. The complicated part is the variation on the theme. Slots accept everything from pennies to $100,000 tokens, although the most common are quarter, dollar, and nickel machines. All machines accept as few as one coin and may take hundreds at a time (in the case of modern penny slots), but a limit of two or three is common.

By the way, when I speak of types of coins, I'm speaking in terms of a monetary unit and not actual coins. Most modern slot machines do not accept or pay out in real coins anymore. They have mostly been replaced with a system that accepts bills of various denominations and pays out with a paper ticket that can be put in another machine or redeemed at the cashier window or change booth. Casual gamblers miss the rain of coins into the metal bin, but most people have embraced the new system as easier, cleaner, and more convenient.

There are two basic types of machines: flat-top and progressive. A flat-top machine has a fixed amount that can be won if a player is lucky enough to get the right combination on the reels. Amounts vary from 2,500 coins to 25,000 and beyond.

A progressive machine works sort of like the lottery. As people pump more money into it, the top jackpot grows until somebody gets the correct combination. Most are linked to a group of machines in the casino or even around the city or state, and the jackpots can be huge: The largest single jackpot ever won was more than $39 million on a Megabucks slot machine at Excalibur.

Individual progressive machines, where each unit has its own progressive jackpot not linked to any other machine, are very common.

Beyond this, the variations are endless. As gaming has developed, so have the slot machines that offer a variety of side games or bonuses that try to lure gamblers. There are "Wheel of Fortune," "Jeopardy," "Deal or No Deal," and "The Price is Right" games that have similar gimmicks to the popular TV game shows they are modeled after. There are "Monopoly" and "Yahtzee" games that allow gamblers to play the famous board games while they gamble. Movie, TV, and music themes, from Elvis to Frank Sinatra, are everywhere. Some have pinball games attached, while others offer a variety of arcade-style video games as bonuses.

Before sitting down at any slot machine, it's important to read the front of it carefully. It will explain exactly how to play that particular machine.

Don't let anybody try to tell you that there is some technique to winning at the slots. It's

GAMING

all random luck. But here are a few "rules" I try to live by when playing that don't always work, but do often enough to make me remember them.

First, try to find a group of machines where lots of people are playing and winning. The casinos can increase the payouts on certain groups of machines at certain times, so, generally speaking, if there's an area of the casino where no one is gambling or winning, there's probably a reason. Find an empty machine next to someone with a lot of credits on their meter and sit down—you may be just as lucky.

Second, it is an old wives' tale that machines on aisles or near the doors pay better than those buried in the casino. And yet, I've won more often on machines in those locations than I have elsewhere (and trust me, I pay attention to stuff like this). The theory behind it is just basic PR: The casinos try to get the people walking by to see players winning in the hopes it will lure them to play as well. Whether or not you believe it's true will most likely depend on your future experience.

You can also try visiting the slots near a showroom just after a show or near the restaurants or buffets near mealtimes. This is the same concept as above, where the casinos hope to lure people coming out of the shows or restaurants into the casino.

Finally, and most importantly, don't keep dumping money into a machine that isn't paying back something. Despite that sure feeling you've got that it's about to hit big, it probably won't.

BLACKJACK

This is the most popular card game in the casinos by far, primarily because it is relatively easy to learn.

The object of blackjack, put simply, is for the player to get a higher point total on the cards he is dealt than the dealer's cards, without going over 21. Number cards (2–10) are worth a like number of points, face cards (jack, queen, king) are worth 10 points, and the ace is worth either 1 or 11 points, player's choice.

Before sitting down at a table, it's impor-

tant to check the table limit—the cheapest tables are usually $1 per hand, but those games are few and far between. These days, $5 is the most common rock-bottom limit and $10- or $15-per-hand tables are much more common. From there, they can go upwards of $1,000 per hand.

Players place their money on the table and the dealer changes it into chips. Then it's time to place a bet, at least the minimum or more, and the game is on.

Although there are still blackjack tables that use a single or double deck of cards, most blackjack games these days use six or seven decks of cards delivered from a device called a shoe. There are two major differences between the two. The first (and significantly less important) is that in single- or double-deck games, players receive their cards face down and hold them like they would in any other card game (but only using one hand!), whereas in multiple-deck games, the cards are dealt face up and players are not allowed to touch them.

The other major difference has to do with the payouts for getting a blackjack, but I'll cover that a little further on.

Players are dealt two cards to start and have an opportunity to draw as many more as they want. It doesn't matter whether other people are sitting at the table—the game is between the player and the dealer. The trick is that players only get to see one of the dealer's cards while the other is hidden, keeping the dealer's total a mystery (hence the whole gambling concept).

To indicate the desire for more cards, a player simply brushes the tabletop toward himself with his hand as if to say "I want more." If he doesn't want additional cards, he waves his hand over the top of his cards as if to say "no more." With a single deck, the player brushes the table with his cards for more, or, conversely, slides them under his chips, indicating that the player is done.

If a player winds up with a higher point total than the dealer, he doubles his money (a $5 bet brings in an additional $5). If a player has a lower point total than the dealer, he loses his bet. If a player ties the dealer, it's called a "push" and nothing is won or lost.

If it's a multi-deck game and a player is lucky enough to get 21 on the first two cards (a face card or a 10 and an ace), he has blackjack and is paid 3:2 on his wager (a $5 bet brings in an additional $7.50), provided the dealer doesn't have or get 21 as well. Drawing to 21 (two cards plus any additional) wins the standard (doubling the bet placed), as long as the dealer doesn't do the same thing.

If it's a single- or double-deck game, most casinos these days only pay 6:5 for a blackjack. That means instead of winning $7.50 on a $5 bet, the player only wins $6. They say it's to take back the edge from people who can count cards, but that's just a bunch of hooey. Avoid these tables whenever possible. The payouts should be clearly printed on the tabletop or on a sign nearby.

Players have three major options in the game of blackjack. They can "Double Down," whereby they double their bet on certain hands; they can "Split," which is when a player has two cards of the same value (two eights for instance) and splits them into two separate hands; or they can take "Insurance," giving them the option to take a smaller loss when the dealer is showing an ace (and therefore might have blackjack).

Unlike slots or video poker, there is a measure of skill involved in playing blackjack. Here are some basic hints that may improve your game.

Most casinos require their dealers to draw a card if they have less than 17 and stop drawing once they reach 17. This will be important to remember in the next couple of hints.

As a general rule, always draw an additional card or more if your initial two cards total 11 or less. There's no way you're going to go over 21, so go for it.

You usually don't want to draw an additional card if your initial hand totals 17 or more. Since the dealer is playing to 17, you stand a better chance of winning with your original hand than you do getting a small enough card to keep from busting.

If your point total on the first two cards is between 12 and 16, it depends on what the dealer is showing as to whether or not you want

to draw. The most common strategy is to assume that the dealer has a 10 or face card hidden, so if they are showing an eight, consider it 18 and draw accordingly. If they are showing a three, consider it 13 and remember that they will have to draw an additional card—since the casino requires them to draw on anything less than 17—and will hopefully bust.

Many dealers will help you with counting your card totals and will even encourage a smart move or discourage a dumb one. Watch for a few minutes before sitting down at a table and find a dealer who helps the players if you feel like you need it.

You should also watch the table for a few minutes to gauge the "fun level" of the players. As a beginner, it's good to find a lively table with people who are laughing and jovial—you'll have a better time and will probably find others to help you in those sticky situations where you're unsure what to do. Don't go for a table full of stone-faced hard-core gamblers unless you think the peace and quiet might help you concentrate.

POKER GAMES

The explosion in popularity of poker, mostly driven by the tournaments broadcast endlessly on the Travel Channel, ESPN, and GSN, has caused a similar explosion of poker and poker-based games in the casinos. Some of these games have been around forever and a few are recent additions, quickly growing in popularity.

Caribbean Stud Poker

This variation on regular five-card stud poker requires players to have a basic knowledge of winning poker hands, like pairs, three-of-a-kind, flushes, and so on. If you have that, you can play Caribbean Stud easily. Players place a bet in the Ante box on the table and another, if they wish, in the Progressive box. The players are dealt five cards each and the dealer gets five with one turned up and the rest face down. There is no draw, so the five cards that the players start with are the ones they are stuck with. If a player thinks he might have

GAMING

a winning hand, he places another bet in the "Bet" box (must be twice the original bet). The dealer reveals his cards and whoever has the better hand wins. The cool thing about this is that the payouts get bigger the better a player's winning hand. For example, if a player has two pair, he wins 2:1 on his "Bet." This goes up to a Royal Flush paying 100:1 on a "Bet." The Progressive works just like a slot progressive and grows between wins. It is paid when a player has placed a Progressive bet and gets at least a flush.

Let It Ride

This is another variation on five-card stud poker and requires knowledge of winning poker hands. There are three betting spots in front of the players labeled 1, 2, and $. A player places an equal bet on each of the spots and is then dealt three cards while the dealer gets two, face down. The player's job is to decide if her cards can create a winning five-card hand when combined with the dealer's two mystery cards (minimum win is a pair of 10s). If so, the player puts her cards under the 1-spot wager and waits until the end, or, if not, the player can signal that she wants the 1-spot wager returned to her. The dealer reveals one of his cards and the player can reconsider whether or not she has a winning hand in progress. If so, the cards go under the 2-spot or, as above, the player signals to have that bet returned. At this point, there's only the $-spot wager left and one card remaining to be turned over. The player can either fold and lose her bet or risk it by placing the cards under the $-spot bet. The fifth card is revealed and payouts are awarded on a sliding scale, with a pair usually paying 1:1 on remaining bets all the way up to a royal flush paying 100:1.

Pai Gow Poker

Yet another poker-variation game, this one is actually a bit too complex to explain in such limited space, but once you get your head around it, you'll wonder what all the fuss was about. Once wagers have been placed, the dealer rolls a pair of dice to determine who will receive the first cards from the deck. Players and the dealer are dealt seven cards and must make two poker hands from them—one of five cards and one of two cards. The five-card hand must be higher in value than the two-card hand (for instance, if a player has a bunch of nothing in his five-card hand and a pair of aces in his two-card hand, he automatically loses). Both of the player's hands must be higher than the dealer's two hands to win. If the player only beats one of the dealer's hands, it is a "push" and the player neither wins nor loses. If the dealer beats the player on both, the player loses his bet. The complicated part comes in with the concept of a "banker," the role of which can be requested by any player before any hand is dealt—read up online or in a book for more details on how this aspect works.

Texas Hold 'Em

Players are dealt two cards and must determine from them whether they want to stay in the game or fold based upon their potential. If they think they have a shot at creating something good with subsequent cards dealt, they go ahead and make a wager. Players are wagering against each other and not the dealer, who does not participate. The dealer then puts out three community cards (known as The Flop). All players use these community cards with their two cards to try to create a good poker hand. Additional bets and folds happen here. Another community card is dealt (known as The Turn or Fourth Street) and the final round of betting occurs. Then the final community card (known as The River or Fifth Street) is revealed and whoever has the best five-card hand out of the seven cards in play (their two and the five community ones) wins the pot. There is actually a bit more complexity to this game surrounding the wagering, so be sure to study up or get a lesson before you sit down at a table.

3-Card Poker

This is probably my favorite table game for its fast pace and chance to win big on small wagers. Each player places a bet on either the "Ante" spot, the "Pair Plus" spot, or both. Three cards are dealt and the player has to make the best three-card poker hand out of them (high card, pair, three of a kind, flush, three-card straight, or three-card straight flush) with no additional draw. If the player made an "Ante" bet and thinks she has a hand that may beat the dealer's, she places another wager in the "Bet" spot that matches her "Ante." The cards are revealed, and if the player has a better hand than the dealer, the player wins even money on her "Ante" and "Bet." If the dealer has at least a queen and the player has a flush or better, the player wins a bonus payout on her "Bet." That "Pair Plus" wager is just between the cards and the player herself—it doesn't matter what the dealer has or if the player wins or loses on the Ante/Bet wager. If the player has at least a pair, she wins 1:1 on that bet. A flush pays 3 or 4:1 depending on the casino, a straight pays 6:1, three-of-a-kind pays 30:1, and a straight flush pays 40:1. Get a straight flush (which I have several times—it's easier with only three cards) and you have turned a $5 bet into $200. How cool is that?

OTHER TABLE GAMES

While blackjack is the most popular table game, there are literally dozens of other options—some omnipresent and some quite scarce. What follows is a brief rundown of the most common table games found in a casino. Anyone interested in learning more about these games should check with the casinos; almost all of them offer free instruction sessions. How-to guides are also available, both on the Web and at bookstores.

Craps

Trying to explain craps in a paragraph is like trying to explain nuclear physics with a crayon and a napkin. There are just too many possible ways to bet to go through here, but a simple game can be done with minimal study. Players place bets on the Pass or Don't Pass line. If the shooter (the person rolling the dice) gets a 7 or an 11, Pass bets win and Don't Pass bets lose. If the shooter rolls a 2, 3, or 12, the op-

posite is true. If any other number is rolled, it is called "the point" and that's where all the other additional wagers start coming into play. The shooter keeps going until he either rolls that number again (Pass bets win, Don't Pass bets lose) or rolls a 7 (the opposite). Then there are Come line bets, point bets, odds bets, hard-way rolls…beginners should take a lesson or pick up a book if they want to go any further.

Roulette

A ball. A spinning wheel. Where is it going to land? That's what players bet on in roulette. The wheel has 38 slots on it with numbers between 1 and 36 (in red or black), plus 0 and 00 (in green). A few wheels have only the 0, but they are rare. "Outside" bets are the simplest and include red or black, even or odd, first 12 (numbers 1–12), second 12 (13–24), and third 12 (25–36). "Inside" bets go on the grid of numbers between 1 and 36 and can be

Nevada law permits a wide variety of gaming, ranging from traditional card-and-dice games to those available on high-tech electronic gaming devices.

GAMING

single-number bets (just 17, for instance), double-number bets (the line between 16 and 17 covers both), and so on. The wheel spins, the ball drops, and if a player put a chip on a space that matches where the ball dropped (be it red or black, even or odd, or the specific number), he wins! If it doesn't match, he loses.

Baccarat

Despite the intimidating surroundings (tables are often located in lavish lounges), this is actually an easy game to master. The player places a bet on whether she thinks the "banker" (or dealer) will win or whether the player will win. The banker deals two cards to each player and to himself. Play is between the dealer and the player, so it's not important what the other

people at the table have. Aces count as one point, number cards count as their face value, and face cards and tens count as zero. The player combines the point values of her two cards, and if it's over 9, she removes the first number (so a 4 and a 7 totals 11 and is reduced to 1). Whoever is closer to 9 wins, so if the player has bet on the banker and the banker gets a higher point total, the player still wins. If the player bet on herself, her point total needs to be higher to win.

Mini-Baccarat

This is exactly the same as Baccarat, except that in the regular version, the role of the banker passes around the table (that's right, you may have to deal the cards). In mini-baccarat, the cards stay with a house dealer.

South Strip   Map 1

So let's get real for a second. You don't care about what a casino looks like, how well it's lit, or how much space there is between machines. All you care about is whether or not you're going to win there, right?

The number one question I get asked is some form of "What's the best casino to gamble at to make sure I win?" Folks, if I knew that, I wouldn't be writing this book. I'd be living on an island somewhere with all of my gaming riches.

All I can share is where I've had the best, most consistent luck in the hope that maybe, just maybe, that luck might rub off on you on your next visit. If it does, I expect a reward.

This, of course, is absolutely no guarantee that you will win anything in the casinos where I have won in the past, and doesn't mean that places I've done lousy in won't bring you a windfall. This is strictly for fun, as all good gaming should be.

Of the South Strip casinos, I have had the most consistent luck at Luxor. Two of the four largest slot machine jackpots I've ever won were at this casino on the *exact same machine* (double-triple-diamond dollar machine near

the main casino cage, if it's still there) about a year apart, believe it or not.

I do okay at New York-New York, Tropicana, and Mandalay Bay, although I usually walk away from these places with about the same amount I walked in with. That's not a bad thing, believe me.

MGM Grand, Excalibur, and Monte Carlo have been less than kind to me in the past, although on a recent trip to MGM Grand I did make a couple hundred dollars before I left. Unfortunately, that relatively minor win (at least for my wallet) didn't come close to what I've lost there over the years.

EXCALIBUR
3850 Las Vegas Blvd. S., 800/937-7777, www.excalibur.com
HOURS: Open 24 hours
This is not the most enjoyable place to gamble in Las Vegas for a couple of reasons. First, the castle-themed joint is still a major draw for families, so a lot of kids occupy the public spaces that lead to that favorite slot or table game. Second, the whole room is modeled as the inside of a castle, not exactly the most

warm or inviting place in the world. With dark colors, low ceilings, and too much crammed into too little space, this is not the first place I think of when I want to blow some dough.

Still, the 100,000 square feet of gaming at Excalibur does offer everything a person could want and need from a casino and the kooky-castle theme is just kooky enough to provide some smiles. And, just in case you believe in lightning striking twice, the Excalibur has the claim to fame of being the location where the largest single slot machine jackpot in history was won: more than $39 million on a Megabucks machine in March 2003.

LUXOR LAS VEGAS

3900 Las Vegas Blvd. S., 800/288-1000, www.luxor.com

HOURS: Open 24 hours

At more than 120,000 square feet, this is one of the biggest casinos in town. Terrific spacing between machines and tables plus high-enough ceilings and a warm glow of light make the experience of gambling here a pleasurable one.

All the usual suspects are here—slot machines of all denominations with the latest ticket-in-ticket-out technology, a high-limit gaming area, more video poker than in most Strip casinos, the most popular table games, a sports book, a keno lounge, a poker room, and more. Much of the kitschy Egypt design that once ruled this particular roost is no longer here. A sleeker, much more modern design has taken its place. It's not quite as much fun as it once was, but it's still a pleasant place to gamble.

This is one of the few casinos that still has what I lovingly refer to as "Big Giant Slots," those enormous eight-foot-tall monsters that are terrific fun for group gambling. Get yourself a roll of coins (most still accept and dispense them instead of the tickets) and watch the crowds form as you pull the big lever.

MANDALAY BAY

3950 Las Vegas Blvd. S., 877/632-7000, www.mandalaybay.com

HOURS: Open 24 hours

With 135,000 square feet of gaming space,

the Mandalay Bay casino is remarkably free of the kind of overwhelming flashing and noise that doom many casinos to unpleasantness. Instead, the banks of slot machines and table games are more subtly arranged and displayed, upping the class factor and reducing the stress factor by considerable degrees.

The whole thing is done in varying shades of white and gold with a South Seas theme that is thankfully just as muted as the rest of the casino. This place isn't about flash, it's about going uptown and getting down to business.

As with most casinos on The Strip, there isn't a lot of video poker here, but they have the real kind in a very nice poker room plus a sports book, a keno lounge, and all of the popular table games.

MGM GRAND

3799 Las Vegas Blvd. S., 800/929-1111, www.mgmgrand.com

HOURS: Open 24 hours

With more than 171,000 square feet of space, the

the casino at New York-New York

COURTESY MGM MIRAGE

GAMING

PLAYERS' CLUBS

Every casino in town has some version of a players' club. They require some personal information, like your address and possibly your email or phone number, but putting up with the occasional bit of junk mail can reap some serious rewards.

Members are given a card with a magnetic stripe on the back – the same size and look as a credit or ATM card. On the front of slot and video poker machines, there are readers where these cards can be inserted. This tracks play and members accumulate points.

Cards can also be used at table games by simply showing them to the dealer or pit boss. They swipe or otherwise record the cards and then watch members as they gamble to determine how much credit they should be getting. Higher wagers and longer stays at a table generate higher point totals.

Those points build up and can then be used later for different types of awards. What they offer depends on the casino, how generous the reward system is, and, of course, how many points a member has accumulated. The mini-mum is usually a couple bucks off the buffet while the maximum can be free rooms, shows, meals, cash back, or more.

Keep in mind that no matter how much free stuff members get, they will have spent significantly more in the casino than they would have if they had just paid for those buffets themselves. Formulas vary from place to place, but even the most generous casinos require that a member lose $100 or more before they get even a buck's worth of comps. The moral of the story is don't gamble to get free stuff, but if you are going to gamble anyway, take advantage of the system.

What follows is a rundown of the major players' clubs, the casinos they are valid in, and my impressions of each. This is not a comprehensive list by any means – there is only room to cover the big ones that encompass several casinos under one card. Just be sure to check individual casinos to see what they have to offer.

MGM Mirage: This club allows members to earn points and redeem them at any of the hotels under their corporate umbrella, including

casino at the MGM Grand is officially the most "grand" in Las Vegas—larger than any other and big enough to house three football fields and a few concession stands to go with them.

The good news is that a series of redesigns over the years have broken up the space effectively, creating several smaller gaming areas that reduce the former effect of playing a slot machine in the middle of an airplane hangar. It's all wrapped up in a Hollywood glamour package—vaguely art deco, kind of dark and glam in areas, with lots of glitz and shiny packaging.

With that much space, it's no surprise that pretty much every game imaginable can be found here, and probably multiple instances of it. Don't like the blackjack table you're playing at? Walk a few hundred feet and you'll find another six to choose from.

MONTE CARLO

3770 Las Vegas Blvd. S., 800/311-8999, www.montecarlo.com

HOURS: Open 24 hours

The casino at Monte Carlo tends to get overlooked a lot. With flashier and bigger places like New York-New York just steps away, it's easy to understand why. But that's too bad because the Monte has a lot to offer in a package that's a lot more easily digestible than most.

It has a simple, open layout—one oversized football field of a room (90,000 square feet) with table games in the center and slots and video poker around the edges. The French Riviera theme is underplayed here, which is good because themes that aren't executed properly can get annoying really fast. But the lack of a strong theme also leaves some people asking, "What did that place look like?"

Bellagio, Circus Circus, Excalibur, Luxor, Mandalay Bay, MGM Grand, The Mirage, Monte Carlo, New York-New York, and Treasure Island. Their formula is that every point is worth a penny, and those pennies can be used at restaurants, hotels, and the casinos for Free Play, a system that, in effect, turns those pennies into cash.

My experience with this particular club has not been particularly rewarding. I am only a moderate gambler and the most I've ever managed to get out of being a member, besides the Free Play points, are discounted room offers from member hotels, but that's better than nothing.

Harrah's Total Rewards: This players' club covers Bally's, Caesars Palace, The Flamingo, Harrah's, Paris Las Vegas, and the Rio and extends the brand to everything from vacation getaways to credit cards. Total Rewards points can be used for the typical buffet or room comps, but also toward shopping sprees, sweepstakes entries, and more, making this one of the most comprehensive and imaginative clubs around. The fact that you have drop a lot of coin to get the good stuff should not be surprising to you.

Station Casinos Boarding Pass: Good at Boulder Station, Green Valley Ranch, Palace Station, Red Rock Resort, Santa Fe Station, Sunset Station and Texas Station, the Boarding Pass is a really generous club in more ways than one. Moderate gamblers receive plenty of discounted and free room offers at their neighborhood hotel-casinos, plus anytime a member has their card in a machine, they are automatically eligible to win the Jumbo Jackpot. This is a progressive cash award that starts at $100,000 and is guaranteed to hit before it reaches $150,000. It can be won by any player at any casino at any time just by spinning the reels or dealing a hand of video poker – even if a player loses the spin or hand on the machine, they can still win the big jackpot. Plus, all members actively playing a machine when the award hits win $50 in free slot play. Note: The details of the Jumbo Jackpot promotion change from time to time, so be sure to check with the casino before you start trying to win it.

The casino has more than 2,200 slots and video poker machines, all the major table games, a keno lounge, a poker room, and a sports book.

NEW YORK-NEW YORK
3790 Las Vegas Blvd. S. 800/693-6763,
www.nynyhotelcasino.com
HOURS: Open 24 HOURS

New York-New York is the only casino in town where the room commands as much attention as the games within it.

First, there's the overall Central-Park-gone-mad theme, complete with trees, plants, and arboretum-style trellises festooned with twinkling lights. Then, there are the faux Big Apple landmarks, like the Stock Exchange, Greenwich Village, Times Square, and even a big red apple spinning like a disco ball over one of the bars. Beautifully painted murals capture landmarks of the city throughout the ages, all rendered in a jazzy art deco style, which carries over to the signage and even the change booths.

Fun touches abound, like the fake manhole covers in the fake streets and the roller coaster roaring above the ceiling evokes the rumble of a subway train. It's all big giddy fun and it's almost impossible to tear your eyes away long enough to actually look at the cards being dealt.

Oh yeah, there is gambling: more than 2,000 slots, all the major table games, and a race and sports book. It gets very crowded here, but maybe that's just another nod to NYC.

TROPICANA
3801 Las Vegas Blvd. S., 888/826-8767,
www.tropicanalv.com
HOURS: Open 24 hours

At press time, the owners of the Tropicana had

announced plans to tear down the bulk (but not all) of the hotel and rebuild it bigger and better to the tune of a couple of billion dollars. This will be done in phases and the casino will remain open while it is happening, so what you find when you walk in the door will depend on when you walk in the door.

Currently, the inside of the place is like a time capsule, with dark smoky mirrors, heavy wood trim, big crystal chandeliers, low ceilings, and cramped walkways. It practically cries out for an Extreme Makeover, hence the new construction.

If you manage to make it there while the old casino is still intact, you should stroll inside to get a glimpse at history before it's gone. While the slot machines may not all be the latest and greatest, there is certainly enough here in the 61,000-square-foot space to keep gamblers interested, and the table games, all arranged under a stunning stained glass atrium, are often available for lower limits than can be found at neighboring casinos.

On the other hand, if the room has been redone by the time you visit, then you can be one of the first on your block to say you've seen the new Tropicana.

Center Strip   Map 2

I've won big at The Venetian on more than one occasion, including the largest single video poker win in my illustrious gambling career, netting me more than $4,100 for being smart enough to keep that ace of diamonds to match the king, queen, jack, and 10 that were lurking underneath. Although my overall track record at this casino is spotty, the last few times I've visited, I've left with more money than I came in with, so that's pretty cool.

Bally's is my second favorite of the bunch in terms of adding to my bottom line. I seem to do really well on the table games and quarter video poker here, but then I often go and ruin it by trying to play the $5 slots. Just say no!

Paris, The Mirage, and Harrah's have been pretty good to me in the past, with Harrah's being one of my most consistently dependable spots for slots. No major wins at any of them, but enough to make me happy.

Bellagio and Treasure Island have all been break-even–type places for me, while Caesars and Imperial Palace have almost always left me with a thinner wallet. I haven't wasted, er, I mean wagered enough money at Planet Hollywood or Bill's yet to give an informed opinion about them. If you go, let me know how you do!

BALLY'S

3645 Las Vegas Blvd. S. 800/634-3434, www.ballyslv.com

HOURS: Open 24 hours

When it opened in 1973 as the MGM Grand, this was the biggest hotel and biggest casino in the world. Nowadays, its 67,000-square-foot space, set up in a relatively simple rectangular design, seems almost quaint. But that's part of its appeal. You know where you are, you know where you're going, and with more than 1,500 slots and dozens of table games, there's more than enough to keep you away from the all-you-can-eat buffet.

There is more video poker here than at many Strip casinos, plus keno, a poker "room" (more of a corner, really), a high-level gaming area, and one of the city's most well regarded race and sports books.

All of this is great, but it's the people here who make this a worthwhile gambling destination. As a general rule, the dealers seem friendlier, offering smiles, encouragement, and even subtle advice at times on whether to hit or stand. This seems to attract a more genial gambler to the tables as well, so instead of the stone-faced everyman-for-himself types, these folks are willing to cheer wins and commiserate in losses. It makes losing money a little more enjoyable.

LAS VEGAS CASINO TIPS

- Most Las Vegas casinos are open 24 hours a day, 365 days a year.

- Visitors must be 21 to even enter the gaming area, much less play the games. Young-looking guests should be sure to carry some form of identification, such as a driver's license or passport, because casino personnel may ask for proof of age.

- There are cameras, security, and undercover operatives that watch every square inch of the casino at all times. Don't even think about trying to cheat – you'll get caught and you will go to jail.

- Be sure to pay attention to limits on table games, slots, and video poker. If a gambler messes up and winds up betting more or less than they could or should have, the casino isn't going to listen to any excuses.

- Most casinos offer free or heavily discounted drinks to people playing the games, including slot machines. Cocktail servers abound in most casinos, but remember, they live off the tips, so be generous, especially if the drink is free.

- Most casinos offer free gaming lessons on the various card and table games. Check with the main casino cage or the guest services counter of any hotel-casino for schedules. These gaming lessons can be valuable in more ways than one. In addition to the knowledge they impart, many casinos offer discount coupon books to people who take the time to learn how to play the games.

- Most casinos make it really easy to get money. Almost all offer ATMs, check cashing, and systems to take cash advances from credit cards. I highly recommend leaving those bank cards, credit cards, and checkbooks at home. Only bring as much money as you're willing to lose – most of the time, you will.

- Most casinos these days have gone coinless. The slot and video poker machines feature a ticket system, which allows players to insert bills of any denomination at the start and then pull out paper tickets at payout. These tickets can either be inserted in other machines or cashed in. The casino cages and change booths redeem them and, depending on the casino, the slot attendants may pay guests out as well. Most casinos also have automated teller-style machines that take the tickets and redeem them for cash.

- Almost every casino in town has attendants walking around so gamblers can get bills changed for the slots (break a $100 bill down to $20 bills, for instance), or there are change booths and/or automated teller machines sprinkled throughout. Gaming chips can be purchased at any table or the main cashier cage (ask an attendant where it is) and are usually redeemable at the cashier cage only.

- Always remember that gambling should not be looked at as a way to make money! Most of the time, it isn't. Viewed as a form of entertainment, the slots and table games can provide a much better time (and perhaps lose you less money).

- Most casinos have gaming (slot/player) clubs where members earn points toward meals, shows, or rooms by gambling in their casino. Signing up requires giving away some personal information (like your address and perhaps email), but that junk mail they send often includes some deep discounts on future visits.

- Most casinos offer perks to gamblers who drop a lot of money at their tables or slots. Make sure somebody sees you spending money and then casually ask if their show is any good or which restaurant is best. It's not a guarantee, but often they'll give you discount coupons or freebies just to keep you happy and gambling.

COURTESY HARRAH'S ENTERTAINMENT

the casino at Bally's

It is worth noting that the owners of this casino, Harrah's Entertainment, are planning a major revision of their properties in the area that could result in this casino closing or being substantially redone by the time you read this.

BILL'S GAMBLIN' HALL & SALOON
3595 Las Vegas Blvd. S., 702/737-2100,
www.billslasvegas.com
HOURS: Open 24 hours

If the big casinos on The Strip seem too intimidating, Bill's offers a really fine alternative. At 30,000 square feet, this place could fit inside the MGM Grand about 7.5 times, and while some people may find the limited options too limited, others really enjoy the more intimate feel.

Although crowded to the brim with slots, video poker, and gaming tables, the room is still a charmer with a turn-of-the-(last)-century San Francisco design evoking a classic gambling parlor. There are rich, heavy woods, beautiful chandeliers and glasswork, and some wonderful art throughout the space. All are worthy of taking a gander at, providing relaxing relief to the blinking lights.

There is a small sports book and a keno lounge to add to the fun.

For those of you looking at the address, yes, this used to be The Barbary Coast, but was purchased by Harrah's Entertainment in 2007 and converted to the Bill's brand name. The company has made little secret of their intention to tear the place down at some undefined point in the future, so if you see a big hole in the ground when you walk by, you can at least tell your friends what used to be there.

◖ BELLAGIO
3600 Las Vegas Blvd. S., 888/987-6667,
www.bellagio.com
HOURS: Open 24 hours

In terms of games, there's really nothing at Bellagio that can't be found elsewhere, often with lower limits. But what sets this place apart is the presentation of those games: Bellagio takes the concept of an elegant salon and stretches it to more than 116,000 square feet.

The slots don't sit there all naked and open like at those other "lesser" places. Here, the banks of machines are encased in wood, lending an air of class to the proceedings. The gaming tables are under colorful awnings and luxurious light fixtures. The thick carpeting, the wall treatments, and even the seats are all of a higher quality and design than those found elsewhere.

This big-money vibe continues to the games themselves. While there are some nickel or penny slots, the majority require higher denominations of play. There's never a $1 blackjack table here and I don't remember the last time I even saw a $5 table. Most start at $10 or $15 and go up from there. This is serious gambling and the place attracts serious gamblers.

The casino includes a beautiful poker room and a similarly appointed high-limit gaming room, plus keno and a giant, high-tech sports book with more than 200 seats.

CAESARS PALACE

3570 Las Vegas Blvd. S., 800/634-6661,
www.caesarspalace.com

HOURS: Open 24 hours

When it opened in 1966, this casino was as opulent as they came. The decadent Roman Empire theme extended in every direction, with towering columns, gracefully carved statuary, fountains, and more marble than you could shake a chariot at.

Today, the theme thing has been done, redone, done better, and done to death, so the fact that Caesars Palace seems more sedate is only because there are other wilder, more over-the-top places to compare it to.

The whole place has gotten a new millennium makeover. Instead of the classic dark, smoky gambling hall it used to be, everything is light and bright, done in varying tones of white, cream, and gold. The space is a rambling affair—it's easier to get turned around here than in any other casino in the city, in my opinion—but with several different gaming areas, it provides guests with plenty of options for places to sit down and play. In addition to the thousands of slot and video poker machines, there is an enormous sports book (completely open to the rest of the

casino and near a nightclub, so a little less appealing than some), a poker room, keno, and more.

HARRAH'S

3475 Las Vegas Blvd. S., 800/392-9002,
www.harrahs.com

HOURS: Open 24 hours

Three decades' worth of expansions have turned what was once a small riverboat-themed casino into an 86,000-square-foot monster that seems to meander in every direction with almost no rhyme or reason. But it could be worth the navigational frustration.

The slots are notorious for being some of the best-paying in town. That's not scientifically proven or consistent, but I've won more often than I've lost. There's one area, on the lower level about halfway through the casino near the buffet, that usually has rows of Blazing 7 machines that people seem to win on all the time. You may not, but it may be worth a $20 bill to find out.

The dealers are almost infallibly friendly, a welcome relief from the cool demeanor at most Strip casinos. A small sports book, a poker room, and a keno parlor complete the offerings.

Plans are afoot from the corporate owners of this place to make some major changes in the years ahead. The details of those plans are super-secret as of this writing, but don't be surprised if you walk in and it looks different than how I've described it here.

◖ IMPERIAL PALACE

3535 Las Vegas Blvd. S., 800/634-6441,
www.imperialpalace.com

HOURS: Open 24 hours

The overall experience of gambling at the Imperial Palace is sort of like playing cards in your weird uncle's basement. It's dark, it's smoky, and a little dingy, but it's also often a blast since your uncle likes to dress up as Elvis and sing in between hands.

Okay, maybe it was just my family.

The hotel hosts the celebrity impersonation extravaganza *Legends in Concert* and they've brought the star look-alikes out of the showroom and into the casino. The Dealertainer

Pit is a ring of gaming tables featuring dealers dressed up like Elvis, Barbra Streisand, Marilyn Monroe, and other celebrities. It's great silly fun to have Babs or Elton singing and chatting during a game of what would otherwise be the same old blackjack.

The rest of the 75,000-square-foot casino is mostly forgettable, but they do have a lot of slot machines and video poker, a small sports book, keno, and a newer poker room on the third floor.

This is another one of those casinos owned by Harrah's Entertainment that may fall to a wrecking ball in the next couple of years or get some sort of major makeover by the time you read this. You have been warned.

THE MIRAGE

3400 Las Vegas Blvd. S., 800/627-6667,
www.mirage.com

HOURS: Open 24 hours

A major makeover in 2006 changed the subtle Polynesian theme into a darker, sleeker, more chic gambling den of iniquity—a nightclub that has spilled off the dance floor and into the ca-

sino. The black sculptured ceilings and glam new wall treatments and fixtures lend the place a definite air of class, but some of the casual fun of the earlier decor was lost in the process.

No worries, this is still a remarkable place to enjoy yourself while emptying your wallet. With more than 100,000 square feet of space, there are plenty of ways to do just that, including all of the latest slots and table games (with an emphasis on Asian favorites like Pai Gow poker), a sports book, a poker room, and more. Most of the slots and table game limits are high, but there are enough low-ish limits to keep budget gamblers going for a while.

In the evenings, the machines and tables near the lounges and clubs are perfect for listening to live music from some really terrific bands.

PARIS LAS VEGAS

3665 Las Vegas Blvd. S., 888/266-5687,
www.parislv.com

HOURS: Open 24 hours

This is another one of those casinos that is done with such highly themed flair that the decor of the room attracts almost as much at-

the casino at Paris Las Vegas

tention as the games inside it. Presented in a stunning early 20th-century Paris style, the park-like setting of the main casino comes complete with trees, gas lamps, cobblestone walkways, and a blue sky overhead. The legs of the Eiffel Tower come down out of the sky and anchor themselves into the casino floor, making it seem like the machines should take francs (okay, euros) instead of dollars.

There are more than 2,000 slot and video poker machines with a really good mix of denominations, but the table games don't enjoy the same wide range of affordability. It's rare to find anything less than a $10 blackjack table here.

A race and sports book, a poker room, and a keno lounge complete the package.

☾ PLANET HOLLYWOOD

3667 Las Vegas Blvd. S., 877/333-9474, www.aladdincasino.com

HOURS: Open 24 hours

The twice-bankrupt Planet Hollywood restaurant chain bought the bankrupt Aladdin in 2004 and made a lot of big pronouncements on how they were going to turn the *Arabian*

Nights–themed white elephant into a swanky and sophisticated place. Snickering ensued, mostly from me. But while I love to be right, I also proudly admit when I'm wrong—and in this case, I was really, really wrong.

The new-as-of-2007 casino is a gorgeous masterpiece—Hollywood glamour done as both a flash-forward and a throwback with both modern and retro touches everywhere you look. The dark woods are offset by giant columns of light and vibrant splashes of color, turning what had been a confusing and haphazard themed casino into an upscale gambling salon.

They have plenty of slots and all the usual table games on their 100,000-square-foot floor, plus a poker room, race and sports book (catered by the famous Pink's Hot Dogs), and a high limit area on the mezzanine floor.

I never really liked The Aladdin, but Planet Hollywood is a place I want to go back to again and again.

TREASURE ISLAND

3300 Las Vegas Blvd. S., 800/944-7444, www.treasureisland.com

HOURS: Open 24 hours

When Treasure Island opened, it was a riot of pirate kitsch, with gold doubloon–filled chests, skulls and crossbones, and eye-patched scurvy mates everywhere. But seeking to revamp their image from a family-friendly destination, the owners recently gave it a face-lift, dumping the pirate paraphernalia and adopting a new moniker, "T.I." Most of the attention was paid to the nightclubs, leaving the casino without a theme—it's just blandly upscale now.

Which isn't to say that, with 95,000 square feet offering more than 2,000 slot and video poker machines, table games, a sports book, and more, it's not worth a visit. Be warned: On weekends, the new sexed-up attitude draws young, pretty people on the prowl. Head to the far side of the casino away from the nightclubs and you'll be happier...unless you are also a young, pretty person on the prowl, in which case you don't need my help anyway.

the grand hall at The Venetian

THE VENETIAN

3355 Las Vegas Blvd. S., 888/283-6423,
www.venetian.com

HOURS: Open 24 hours

For such a beautifully detailed hotel, the casino at The Venetian is remarkably bland. Beige walls, boring floor coverings, and almost none of the exciting artistry present elsewhere in the building conspire to make this 120,000-square-foot gargantuan forgettable on just about every level.

So why include it? Simply put, it's because I've won a lot of money here. I know that isn't terribly objective, but I have to say that walking away with so much dough that you can't actually close your wallet really perks up your image of a place.

There's no promise you'll do as well, but there are plenty of ways to try with more than 2,500 slot machines of all denominations, a surprising amount of video poker, table games of all stripes and colors (most with $15-per-hand minimums on busy weekends), a sports book, a poker room, keno, and more.

North Strip   Map 3

The clear winner for me in the North Strip area is the Stratosphere. Over the years, I have hit many of the biggest slot machine jackpots I've ever been lucky enough to win here, including a $3,700 bonanza on a $5 double-triple-diamond machine. Even when I don't do *really* well, I seem to do pretty well, so I'm a big fan.

While I'm not a fan of the ambience, I've also made a profit at Circus Circus in the past, and although I've won some sizeable coin at Wynn Las Vegas, it's very hit-and-miss, so it isn't my first choice for a gambling destination.

I've never won a dime at the Sahara, but I have to admit that I haven't spent a lot of time trying.

CIRCUS CIRCUS

2880 Las Vegas Blvd. S., 800/444-2472,
www.circuscircus.com

HOURS: Open 24 hours

I never think of Circus Circus as a place to gamble. Despite their massive 107,000-square-foot casino with a couple thousand slots, all the standard table games, a sports book, a poker room, and more, the frenetic pace makes it less than appealing, in my opinion.

Part of that mood-killer is the Big Top theme, with garish colors, in-your-face signage, narrow walkways, and a general lack of elbow room. The other part of it is the demographic appeal. As the only major hotel-casino on The Strip with amenities that appeal to children, it's got lots of them around. Even though they aren't allowed in the casino per se, the walkways around and through the space are packed with families on the way to the circus acts or indoor theme park.

Having said all that, Circus Circus is the only reasonable gambling alternative for parents who have brought their children to town.

SAHARA

2535 Las Vegas Blvd. S., 888/696-2121,
www.saharacasino.com

HOURS: Open 24 hours

Just before this book went to press, the Sahara was purchased by a Los Angeles–based hotel and nightclub magnate who promised major changes for the entire building. That's good news, because it needs it.

Over the more than 50 years since the Sahara opened, the casino has gone through a series of expansions and thematic changes that have left it a bit schizophrenic in execution. The main area is all *Arabian Nights* detail, with colorful tile work, jewel-encrusted lamps, and Persian carpet madness. A separate area is race car–themed, with corrugated aluminum wall covering, chain-link fencing, and concrete as the main design elements. Bridging the two areas is a low-ceilinged no-man's-land of slot machines, a place that looks like it hasn't been redecorated since 1972.

The full package is a bit disconcerting for anyone paying attention to design elements, but, to be honest, no one comes here for that. They come here for the friendly dealers and very low limits. The Sahara is the only major hotel-casino on The Strip that regularly features $1 blackjack tables. In a day and age when it's next to impossible to find anything less than $10 tables, this is a welcome holdover from eras past.

The casino has more than 85,000 square feet of space, with slots, video poker, all major table games and a few rare ones (like Spanish 21), a small sports book, and a keno lounge.

As mentioned, the new owner will probably make some big moves that will include both visual and content changes in the casino, so don't be surprised if you go looking for those $1 blackjack tables and find they don't have them anymore.

STRATOSPHERE

2000 Las Vegas Blvd. S., 800/997-6737,
www.stratospherehotel.com
HOURS: Open 24 hours

The Stratosphere is a good alternative to the busier, more expensive casinos down the street.

With 86,000 square feet of space, the gaming area here is bigger than it initially seems. The main casino has all of the table games (many with lower limits than nearby casinos) and tons of slots and plenty of video poker, but off to the side is another space with more slots and video poker, and beyond that is yet another room, and beyond that still another. It's nice to have different areas to move to if you feel like you aren't doing well in a certain spot.

Keno, a poker room, and a sports and race book round out the amenities.

WYNN LAS VEGAS

3131 Las Vegas Blvd. S., 888/320-9966,
www.wynnlasvegas.com
HOURS: Open 24 hours

Steve Wynn spent $2.7 billion to build this place (opened in spring 2005) and it's obvious that a big chunk of that change went into the casino. Thick carpeting and intricate tile mosaics line the floors, luxurious drapes and rich fabrics line the walls, and finely carved woods, elegant lighting fixtures, and above-average furnishings abound. The effect is a bit busy at times, but the deep red and chocolate brown color scheme helps mute what could've been "too much."

Slots come in all varieties, from pennies to $500 a pull and beyond. Table games are pricey—$15 a hand for blackjack is the lowest I've seen. Separate baccarat and poker rooms are nearby.

Just Off The Strip   Map 4

Of the casinos listed in this section, I've had the best luck at the Rio and the Las Vegas Hilton. Regarding the latter, I remember very clearly a few years ago, before they put in the coinless slots, trying to navigate my way to the change booth with six or seven buckets of dollar coins stacked up my body. Although the coins are gone, the winnings have remained relatively consistent here.

The Rio, on the other hand, is less consistent, but usually when I hit, I hit big. I've gotten more video poker royal flushes here than in any other single casino in the city.

The Orleans and Gold Coast have been break-even affairs for me, while I did great at The Palms the first time I visited and have done lousy every time since.

The Hard Rock has brought out the worst luck for me of the bunch. I almost always leave poorer (and feeling really old and fat, to boot).

GOLD COAST

4000 W. Flamingo Rd., 800/331-5334,
www.goldcoastcasino.com
HOURS: Open 24 hours

Even though it's less than a mile from The Strip, the Gold Coast offers a gaming experience more akin to the neighborhood casinos significantly further away. With lower limits on everything and traditionally higher payouts, the casino here is a terrific alternative to the pricey, stingy Strip casinos nearby.

When they remodeled, expanded, and upgraded the joint a few years ago, it changed what used to be a run-down, dark affair into a pleasant space, scrubbed clean and bright with natural light pouring in through many windows. High ceilings add to the appeal, giving this place a feeling of spaciousness beyond its 120,000-square-foot size.

They've got plenty of slots and tons of video poker. A poker room, a race and sports book, and a sizeable keno lounge are typical amenities, but the Gold Coast is also one of the few casinos in the area to offer a bingo parlor.

☾ HARD ROCK HOTEL

4455 Las Vegas Blvd. S., 800/473-7625,
www.hardrockhotel.com
HOURS: Open 24 hours

Visiting the casino at the Hard Rock is like going to a really expensive, really loud rock concert. With only 30,000 square feet of space, there is rarely a free square inch of area to call your own, especially on busy weekend nights. Throw in a holiday and it's pretty much impossible to get anywhere near the gaming tables, which dominate the circular casino, forcing the relatively few slot machines and fewer video poker machines to the edges like groupies held at bay by burly bouncers.

The good news is an expansion is in the works and could even be complete by the time you read this, so perhaps things won't be as crowded as it is now.

Owing to its namesake, loud rock music is pumped into the casino, adding to the general din. A relaxing game of blackjack or a mindless hour on the slots is not on the agenda here.

Still, the music memorabilia scattered throughout and the fun touches like guitar-necked slot machine handles and piano-shaped craps tables may make it all worthwhile for serious music fans.

LAS VEGAS HILTON

3000 Paradise Rd., 800/732-7117, www.lvhilton.com
HOURS: Open 24 hours

Schizophrenic—that's the best word to describe this place.

The main casino is buttoned-down, with a traditional layout under sparkly chandeliers and a quiet gold color scheme. It's lovely and inviting and makes you want to sit down at a blackjack table with a glass of wine and a fine cigar.

Then there's the Spacequest Casino, a highly themed area designed to look like a 24th-century space station. It's wacky and geeky and makes you want to sit down at a slot machine with a Zima and a pack of clove cigarettes.

Taken in their individual contexts, the casinos at the Hilton satisfy their completely opposite missions—one for serious gambling, the other for fun gambling. But crossing from one to the other can be disconcerting.

The 100,000 square feet of gaming offers a wide variety of slots and table games of all denominations and limits, a high-limit area, and an enormous 400-seat race and sports book that is widely regarded as being one of the finest in town.

ORLEANS

4500 W. Tropicana Ave., 800/675-3267, www.orleanscasino.com

HOURS: Open 24 hours

At more than 135,000 square feet, this casino is one of the biggest in Vegas and it feels like it. With few dividing walls, the gaming space seems too big and impersonal. The Big Easy–style decor doesn't help, since it's more along the lines of what might be found at a theme park instead of the faithful designs found at other theme casinos.

That's the bad news, but setting aside the

barn-like ambience, there are tons of gaming options at almost all price points. Penny, nickel, quarter, and dollar slots are evenly balanced with video poker machines of all varieties. About the only people who will be disappointed are those looking for a big selection of higher-limit slots—there are a few, but only a few.

They have all the standard table games, a finely equipped race and sports book, a poker room, and a keno lounge.

THE PALMS

4321 W. Flamingo Rd., 866/942-7777, www.palms.com

HOURS: Open 24 hours

The crowd here practically defines dichotomy. You have the young, trendy folks lured by the ultra-swank clubs and celebrity sightings. Then you have the older folks lured by low limits, high payouts, and a cheap food court. It makes for some unusual bedfellows, a bling-bling "gansta," for example, sitting next to a little old lady in a sweater with a poodle on it. They seem to get along just fine, though.

The design elements are a genuine delight,

GAMING

COURTESY HARRAH'S ENTERTAINMENT

Rio All Suite Hotel & Casino

with nary a hard edge in sight, as the space ebbs and flows throughout the 95,000-square-foot area. There is a sports book, two high-limit gaming areas, a poker room, a keno lounge, and more.

Experts and novices alike say the slots pay off better here than anywhere else in town. I've done okay, but not with any level of consistency to be able to join in with the trumpeting crowd.

RIO ALL SUITE HOTEL & CASINO

3700 W. Flamingo Rd., 888/752-9746,
www.playrio.com
HOURS: Open 24 hours

I like about half the casino here and I dislike the other half. The Masquerade Village section is good, with high ceilings and roomy spacing between the machines. If you can put up with the occasional singing, dancing, and bead-throwing from the free show several times a day, it's a comfortable place to gamble.

The older section of the building, on the other hand, has low ceilings, tightly packed machines and tables, and an oppressive Carnivale in Rio theme—way too claustrophobic for my taste. And there's no escaping the singing

and dancing—even over here. Cocktail servers randomly jump up on small stages to croon a tune or shake a tail feather. They call them "Bev-ertainers." Make your own jokes.

The casino encompasses more than 120,000 square feet, with more than 1,600 slot machines (including lots of video poker), all the normal table games, and a 170-seat race and sports book.

TERRIBLE'S

4100 Paradise Rd., 800/640-9777,
www.terribleherbst.com
HOURS: Open 24 hours

Although it is tiny in comparison to the big Strip palaces nearby, the gaming space at Terrible's is noteworthy primarily for its very low limits on everything from slots to video poker to table games. If budget gambling is on the agenda, it can be done here, without having to travel miles to the cheap casinos in Henderson or on Boulder Highway.

With fewer than 800 machines (many Strip casinos have three times that amount) and only a handful of table games, there isn't a lot to choose from here, but they cover the basics like blackjack, roulette, and craps. They've also got a bingo parlor that seats around 200 people.

Downtown   Map 5

Even though Downtown Las Vegas offers historically higher payouts than The Strip, I've never done very well at any of the Downtown casinos. Of them, I've hit the occasional small jackpot at the Golden Nugget, done pretty well at 3-Card poker at Main Street Station, and that 17 on roulette at Four Queens will forever remain in my heart.

Binion's, The Cal, and Fitzgerald's have all resulted in a break-even or loss report by the time I walked out.

BINION'S

128 E. Fremont St., 800/622-6468, www.binions.com
HOURS: Open 24 hours

Opened in 1951, Binion's Horseshoe became

an almost instant classic—an Old Vegas staple that stayed old-school while everyone else went and got all fancy. This was one of those dimly lit, smoked-filled rooms—a favorite of serious gamblers and young hipsters who were looking for that *Swingers* vibe.

But times changed and a series of less-than-fine management decisions led to the casino's closure in 2004.

Enter Harrah's, the mega-billion-dollar gaming empire, who swept in and bought the place in a co-venture with a smaller gaming company. Together they reopened the casino, spiffed it up a bit, and started rebuilding the business. Harrah's part of the deal was up in 2005 and they walked away with the World

Series of Poker and the rights to the Horseshoe part of the name, so now it's just Binion's.

But despite some new carpet and slots, this is still a terrific place to try to recapture the Old Vegas mystique. The 50,000-square-foot space has about 1,000 slots and video poker machines, all of the requisite table games, and even without the World Series, a legendary poker room.

THE CALIFORNIA

12 Ogden Ave., 800/634-6255, www.thecal.com

HOURS: Open 24 hours

Popular with Hawaiian and Asian tourists, The Cal, as it is affectionately known, has an understated Polynesian theme in the casino. Well, except for the carpet. That riot of colors underfoot is about as far from understated as it could be. But never mind that. Instead, focus on the fact that this is one of the cleanest, most comfortable casinos in the Downtown area, where dark, dingy, and tightly packed seem to rule the roost in most cases.

More than 60,000 square feet of gaming space take up two floors with lots of low-limit slots (pennies, nickels, and quarters vastly outnumber the dollars here), plenty of video poker for fans of the game, all of the traditional table games, a keno lounge, and a small sports book.

◖ EL CORTEZ

600 Fremont St., 800/634-6703, www.elcortezhotelcasino.com

HOURS: Open 24 hours

The El, as it is known locally, dates back to the 1940s, but at first glance you'd never guess it these days. A 2007 remodeling turned what had been a crowded, smoky, and worn-around-the-edges also-ran back into the sparkling landmark it deserves to be.

Key to the redesign were changes to the casino where they took out more than half of the machines in order to give the customers more room to breathe, reorganized the layout of the tables and slots to provide a more open feeling, and totally redid all the woodwork, walls, carpeting, furnishings, and lights in the bargain. The overall effect is simply beautiful, with dark cherry

stained frames around coppery wall panels, giving an ambience of inviting warmth.

Even though they took out a bunch of the one-armed bandits, there is still a lot to do here, with more than 1,000 slots and video poker, plenty of table games of most varieties, a race and sports book, a keno lounge, and more—all with lower limits than you'll find on The Strip.

Most of the staff has been here for years and considers this place home, a feeling they will extend to you, should you choose to visit. And you should.

FITZGERALD'S

301 Fremont St., 800/274-5825, www.fitzgeralds.com

HOURS: Open 24 hours

A few years ago, this place was packed with blarney. And by that, I mean blarney stone and all other manner of Irish kitsch imaginable: four-leaf clovers, rainbows, pots o' gold, and even a giant leprechaun (Mr. O'Lucky, to his friends) on the outside of the building.

Happily, a new owner came on board (the first African-American casino owner in Las Vegas) and slowly started stripping away the most egregious bits of the decor (bye, Mr. O'Lucky). The casino remains a little too densely packed for my tastes, but it's still one of the top choices for Downtown Vegas gambling.

Two levels of 42,000 square feet feature more than 1,000 slots and video poker, table games, a keno lounge, and a small race and sports book.

By the way, Mr. O'Lucky met a tragic end. He was saved by the good folks at The Neon Museum, who hoped to restore him and put him on display somewhere. But then, in 2004, a fire broke out in the Neon Boneyard and our favorite giant leprechaun was no more. Rest in peace, Mr. O'Lucky.

FOUR QUEENS

202 Fremont St., 800/634-6045, www.fourqueens.com

HOURS: Open 24 hours

The main draw of the Four Queens for me has always been the table games. In fact, this was the first place I ever played roulette, betting $2 on my lucky number 17. Since then, I keep coming back because they have some of the friendliest dealers in town. These are the kinds of dealers who will help you count when you've drawn four cards and can't add that fast, will discreetly (or sometimes flat out) tell you whether or not to hit again, and seem genuinely disappointed when you don't win. It makes gaming more enjoyable when you aren't sitting across the table from a stone-faced dealer who you think may be chuckling inside every time they draw a 21 to your two-face card stand.

Arranged under a bright (but not too bright), garden-like canopy of lights and mirrors, the table games are the best bet here, but they do have plenty of slot and video poker machines and a small keno area to fill out their 32,000 square feet of gaming space.

Oh, I almost forgot. I have a witness who will attest to the fact that when I put my very first $2 on that roulette table all those years ago, the wheel was spun and the ball landed on 17.

THE GOLDEN NUGGET
129 E. Fremont St., 800/634-3454,
www.goldennugget.com
HOURS: Open 24 hours

One of the classic Vegas stories goes like this: The famed high-roller hits the skids and loses everything, only to get one last chance at redemption through a winner-takes-all roll of the dice—and it comes up 7. The story is mostly apocryphal, but it is the embodiment of the Vegas allure and the recent history of The Golden Nugget.

After years as the Grand Dame of Downtown, the hotel suffered a string of owners who let it slide, certainly not into disrepair, but it had become a shadow of its former glory. Now new owners have come in and rolled the dice on a major makeover and they definitely hit a 7 all the way around.

The casino has been completely revamped with new gold, cream, and brown earth tones set off by blazing oranges and reds that turn

the space into a warmly inviting gambling parlor. New machines, new gaming tables, and a new attitude came with it that make this a casino that could compete with the upscale ones on The Strip.

They have everything you need here, including slots and video poker, all major table games, a race and sports book, a poker room, and a high-limit area, plus a typically Downtown friendly staff and modest limits. The Grand Dame is back!

◖ MAIN STREET STATION
200 N. Main St., 800/465-0711,
www.mainstreetcasino.com
HOURS: Open 24 hours

Located two short blocks away from the bright lights of Fremont Street, Main Street Station is one of those hidden gem–type places. Done with a turn-of-the-last-century San Francisco motif, the casino features elegantly carved wood paneling and trim, beautiful stamped-tin ceilings, charming gas lamps, stained glass windows, and lazy fans. It's one of the most lovely and understated rooms in town.

It's also one of the freshest. A combination of a very high ceiling and a high-tech air-purification system makes this casino noticeably less smoky than the others in the Downtown area and even better for deep breaths than some of the big casinos on The Strip. People with cigarette smoke allergies or strong aversions shouldn't go anywhere near a casino, but if you absolutely must, this one should be high on your list.

At only 28,000 square feet, the casino here is microscopic when compared to the big Strip palaces. Four of these could easily fit inside The Venetian casino. But they do a lot with the space they have, offering nearly 1,000 slots and video poker machines, a couple dozen table games, and keno without resorting to the overcrowding found elsewhere in the neighborhood.

RESTAURANTS

For most of its storied existence, Las Vegas was considered a must-visit destination in just about every category—except for restaurants. Rife with cheap steakhouses and half-hearted attempts at gourmet cuisine, the city was a veritable wasteland when it came to dining.

Today, even the snobbiest of foodies recognizes that Las Vegas is one of, if not *the,* premier restaurant destinations in the world. Name a celebrity or award-winning chef and you'll probably find one of his or her eateries here—Emeril Lagasse, Wolfgang Puck, Sue Milliken, Susan Feniger, Bobby Flay, Alessandro Stratta, Daniel Boulud, Thomas Keller, Julian Serrano, Alain Ducasse—the list goes on and on. These culinary artists didn't get rich and famous by accident and now, instead of traipsing all over the world to sample their cooking, you can do it in one four-mile stretch of road. Highlighted here are the best of the best from these epicurean masters, so you can skip the nearly great and go directly to the truly great.

The downside to having food heaven here in Las Vegas is that the classic bastions of $1.99 prime rib dinners are gone, or at the very least banished to the hinterlands. Checks of more than $100 per couple are common at the finer dining establishments and even a simple burger is going to run $10 at most Strip restaurants. It's a wonder anyone has anything left over to gamble with.

But sprinkled liberally throughout this chapter are plenty of suggestions for fantastic meals at everyday prices and even a few

HIGHLIGHTS

LOOK FOR (TO FIND
RECOMMENDED RESTAURANTS.

(**Best Desserts:** The Chocolate Swan is a heavenly dessert emporium featuring handmade chocolates, delicate Italian gelato, and pastries so rich and flavorful, you'll want to crawl into the case and live there (page 84).

(**Best Three-Figure Splurge:** Got an extra $200? That's probably the least it's going to cost you to eat at **L'Atelier de Joël Robuchon,** but almost everyone agrees it's absolutely worth every dime (page 84).

(**Best Ethnic Fare:** Does it get any better than grilled meat on skewers? I don't think so, and you'll find plenty of fantastic proof at **Pampas Brazilian Grille** (page 89).

(**Best High-End Buffet:** The Buffet at **Wynn Las Vegas** costs more than what most people pay for a traditional restaurant meal, but the food more than makes up for the bill (page 95).

(**Best Sandwiches:** The spicy Italian delights at **Capriotti's** will make you forget about chain sub shops forever (page 98).

(**Best Southern Food:** Okay, so fried chicken smothered in gravy may not be the healthiest thing in the world, but you'll die happy with the southern cooking delights at **M&M Soul Food** (page 99).

(**Best French Fare:** Longtime Vegas favorite André Rochet upped the ante with **Alizé,** his gorgeous French wonder located high atop The Palms (page 101).

(**Best Atmosphere:** Liberace used to own **Carluccio's Tivoli Gardens** and he decorated the place, which hasn't changed in decades (page 102).

(**Best Comfort Food:** Bacon-wrapped meatloaf is just one of the comfort-food specialties at the classic American grill **Triple George Grill** (page 104).

(**Best Budget Buffet:** Just because a buffet is cheap doesn't mean it's not good, and just because it's good doesn't mean it has to be expensive, as evidenced by the fantastic **Main Street Station Garden Court Buffet** (page 104).

COURTESY OF MAIN STREET STATION

Main Street Station Garden Court Buffet

PRICE-RATING SYMBOLS

The following listings indicate the general price range of entrées with $ symbols next to the name of the restaurant. Here's what they mean:

$ **Entrées mostly less than $15**
$$ **Entrées mostly between $15 and $30**
$$$ **Entrées mostly more than $30**

Keep in mind that these price denotations are strictly for the cost of the entrée and whatever may come with it. It does not include side dishes, additional courses, desserts, beverages, tax, or tip, except in the case of buffets, which include all that stuff at no additional cost. So just because a restaurant receives a single $ price denotation doesn't necessarily mean that the bill will end up being less than $15.

Also note that the $$$ price category is open-ended and could include entrées that cost $31 or $131; however, if a place is really expensive, that will be noted in the review.

suggestions of where the near mythic 99-cent shrimp cocktail or jumbo hot dog may still be found.

And don't forget the buffets. Las Vegas may not have invented the concept of an all-you-can-eat smorgasbord, but it certainly perfected it, and no visit to the city would be complete without sampling at least one. Following are a wide variety of these, from the relatively inexpensive—offering good food for great prices—all the way up to the places that charge sit-down restaurant prices but serve sit-down-restaurant–worthy food (or better).

In between the high and the low, the quick bites and the heavy buffets, I've included a bunch of moderately priced "hidden gems." These are the types of places that don't get big awards or fancy write-ups in the food critic category, but offer really good to really great meals for reasonable prices.

RESTAURANTS

South Strip   Map 1

AMERICAN
ESPN ZONE $

3790 Las Vegas Blvd. S. (inside New York-New York), 702/933-3776, www.espnzone.com/lasvegas
HOURS: Sun.-Thurs. 11:00 A.M.-11:00 P.M., Fri.-Sat. 11:00 A.M.-midnight

Sports fans should absolutely put this on their must-see list, but even non-sports fans will enjoy this place. The multilevel facility features several dining rooms, a bar, an expansive video game arcade, big screens showing any sporting event they can find, and lots of memorabilia. A warning: It's always crowded and always loud. A wide-ranging menu offersAmerican grill dishes (sandwiches, burgers, salads, pasta, steak, ribs, etc.), and while it's not exactly cheap, the portions are huge and it's all

good. Don't miss the decadent desserts—they're worth saving room for!

HARLEY DAVIDSON CAFÉ $

3725 Las Vegas Blvd. S., 702/740-4555, www.harley-davidsoncafe.com
HOURS: Sun.-Thurs. 11 A.M.-11 P.M., Fri.-Sat. 11 A.M.-midnight

Hearty, stick-to-your-ribs food and motorcycles. What more could you want? Most of the menu items are high-calorie traditional, with a down-home "do you want gravy with that?" flair (southern fried steak, fried chicken, baby back ribs, barbecue, meatloaf, etc.), but there are a few lighter and fancier items that almost feel out of place (salmon teriyaki?). Portions are huge and prices moderate. The Harley memorabilia, including photos of almost every celebrity

EATING CHEAP ON THE STRIP

The days of really satisfying, really cheap meals are over, especially on The Strip. But for those who don't feel like paying an arm and a leg for a meal or just want something quick to eat so they can get back to the casino, there are a few options. Highlighted below are a few less expensive places that may not win any awards, but will keep you going until you get to the better restaurants for dinner.

Jody Maroni's Sausage Kingdom at New York-New York (3790 Las Vegas Blvd. S., 702/740-6969, Sun.-Thurs. 8 A.M.-8 P.M., Fri.-Sat. 8 A.M.-10 P.M.) is a great place for a quick, inexpensive (most under $5) hot dog that kicks the butt of much more expensive franks. A few bucks more will buy some of the more exciting sausages (tequila chicken and traditional Italian are faves).

There are three branches of three famous delicatessens around the Center Strip, and although the sandwiches are not necessarily cheap, they are cheaper than the food at most other traditional restaurants in the area. **The Stage Deli** at The Forum Shops at Caesars Palace (3570 Las Vegas Blvd. S., 702/893-4045, Sun.-Thurs. 8 A.M.-10:30 P.M., Fri.-Sat. 8 A.M.-11:30 A.M., takeout open later) is a New York institution and has one of those deli menus that take 30 minutes just to get through. Most sandwiches are less than $10.

Speaking of New York institutions, the **Carnegie Deli** (3400 Las Vegas Blvd. S., 702/791-7111, daily 7 A.M.-2 A.M.) has taken up residence at The Mirage. A huge menu offers a mind-boggling array of choices, and most sandwiches are around the $10 price point.

The West Coast deli contingent can cheer with the arrival of Los Angeles's landmark **Canter's Deli** (3300 Las Vegas Blvd. S., 702/894-7111, daily 11 A.M.-midnight). Like their New York counterparts, the selections are vast and they have plenty of under-$10 choices.

Over at Imperial Palace (3535 Las Vegas Blvd. S., 702/731-3311), there are three terrific cheap-eats restaurants, including **Burger Palace** (daily 7 A.M.-11 P.M.), **Pizza Palace** (daily 11 A.M.-11 P.M.), and **Betty's Diner** (not a palace, but open daily 6 A.M.-midnight). They serve what their name implies (burgers, pizza, and diner food, respectively) and the food is not only good, but it's remarkably cheap. Full meals are possible for less than $10 and a quick bite, in many cases, for half that.

Over at **Bally's** (3645 Las Vegas Blvd. S., 702/739-4111), there's a fantastic little coffee and pastry stand adjacent to the front desk. They offer some really great baked goods (including yummy, huge chocolate chip cookies), all for less than $5.

Finally, if all you care about is fuel or you just need a taste of something you recognize, there are food courts at Luxor (3900 Las Vegas Blvd. S., 702/262-400), Monte Carlo (3770 Las Vegas Blvd. S., 702/730-7777), Excalibur (3850 Las Vegas Blvd. S., 702/597-7777), The Fashion Show mall (3200 Las Vegas Blvd. S., 702/369-1613), and The Riviera (2901 Las Vegas Blvd. S., 702/734-5110), featuring names like McDonald's, Nathan's Hot Dogs, Pizza Hut Express, Krispy Kreme, Wendy's, Subway, Burger King, Quiznos, and more. Hours vary by store and by location, but most are open from early morning through late night. Keep in mind that a Quarter Pounder (for instance) here costs more than the one at home. Yes, even the golden arches are not immune to the higher prices in Vegas.

who has ever ridden one with their bikes, is also worth a look. A fully stocked logo store is also on the premises.

HOUSE OF BLUES LAS VEGAS $$

3950 Las Vegas Blvd. S. (inside Mandalay Bay), 702/632-7600, www.hob.com
HOURS: Mon.-Sat. 10 A.M.-9 P.M., Sun. 8 A.M.-8 P.M.

A modern take on a southern honky-tonk roadhouse is the theme of both the restaurant and what they serve. Jambalaya, gumbo, and pulled-pork sandwiches are just a few examples on the really unique menu, better than a boring burger any day. Of special note is the Sunday Gospel Brunch, a wide-ranging Creole/Cajun/barbecue buffet served while a gospel choir entertains. Not only is the food good, but it'll make you feel better about going to that strip club the night before.

MONTE CARLO PUB & BREWERY $

3770 Las Vegas Blvd. S. (inside Monte Carlo), 702/730-7777, www.montecarlo.com
HOURS: Daily 11 A.M.-2 A.M.

Terrific, classic American pub fare is served in a warm (if somewhat clichéd) atmosphere, providing a solid alternative to similarly priced buffets that may provide bigger quantities but rarely provide this kind of quality. Sandwiches, burgers, salads, and pastas are the main attractions, but be sure to check out the brick-oven pizzas—traditional to trendy, but better than the home-delivery kind any day. Everything goes great with their specialty ales, all microbrewed on-site (High-Roller Red amber ale is a favorite, while Silver State Stout will appeal to Guinness fans everywhere).

RAINFOREST CAFÉ $

3799 Las Vegas Blvd. S. (inside MGM Grand), 702/891-8580, www.rainforestcafe.com
HOURS: Daily 8 A.M.-midnight

The experience of dining in a rainforest surrounded by jungle sights and sounds is the primary draw here, especially for families. There are enough fun things to look at (hey, it's an elephant!) to keep the kids entertained and a broad-ranging selection on the menu to satisfy even the pickiest of eaters. While dishes are billed as "inspired" by food from Mexico, the Caribbean, and Asia, what is served is mostly traditional American food (sandwiches, burgers, pizza, pastas, etc.) with a little pizzazz. It's satisfying and generously proportioned, but don't come just for the food—come for the eco-friendly environment.

WOLFGANG PUCK BAR AND GRILL $$

3799 Las Vegas Blvd. S. (inside MGM Grand), 877/793-7111, www.wolfgangpuck.com
HOURS: Sun.-Thurs. 11:30 A.M.-10:30 P.M., Fri.-Sat. 11:30 A.M.-11:30 P.M.

Mr. Puck didn't get his face on all of those frozen entrees in your grocery store for nothing, and this casual restaurant goes a long way toward explaining the whole phenomenon. Expensive for what it is, yet cheaper than any of his other restaurants in town, the Bar and Grill is a good entry point to Wolfgang's food, which in this case includes signature dishes like duck sausage with spicy mustard, foccacia with veal meatballs, and, of course, plenty of the upscale pizzas that helped make him famous. A full menu of sandwiches to steaks accompanies, and it's all good, although perhaps not enough so to justify the prices at times. If you have to eat at a Wolfgang Puck restaurant and don't want to spend a fortune doing so, this is where you should go.

BUFFETS

MANDALAY BAY BAYSIDE BUFFET $$

3950 Las Vegas Blvd. S. (inside Mandalay Bay), 702/632-7402, www.mandalaybay.com
HOURS: Daily 7 A.M.-10 P.M.

For some, this buffet is forgettable, but others swear by the quantity and quality of the food, especially the all-you-can-eat crab legs, a perennial favorite. I'm somewhere in between on the issue, feeling that what they do right, they do *really* right (carving station, desserts, aforementioned crab legs), and the rest is merely okay. The dining room is certainly worth noting. It's beautiful, with big windows overlooking the Mandalay Bay beach area.

COURTESY MGM MIRAGE

The Chocolate Swan

DESSERTS

◖ THE CHOCOLATE SWAN ⑤

3930 Las Vegas Blvd. S. (in the Mandalay
Place Shopping Mall), 702/632-9366,
www.chocolateswan.com

HOURS: Daily 8 A.M.–10 P.M.

You'll thank me later. Seriously. Fans of dessert (especially those involving chocolate) should make a beeline for this small slice of heaven on earth where everything is made on-site with a level of care and attention to detail that borders on ludicrous. Perfectly sculpted caramels, peanut brittle, pastries, pies, insanely rich Italian ice cream, and chocolate-covered anything-you-can-think-of are the staple crops here, accompanied by a very satisfying coffee and cordial menu. Go eat at one of the fancy restaurants, but skip dessert and come here instead for an after-dinner delight.

FRENCH

FLEUR DE LYS ⑤⑤⑤

3950 Las Vegas Blvd. S. (in Mandalay Bay),
877/632-1766, www.mandalaybay.com

HOURS: Daily 5:30–10:30 P.M.

Chef Hubert Keller imported his highly regarded French cooking skills from San Francisco to the Las Vegas desert and the result has become one of the must-visit destinations for the epicurean set. But even the epi-curious will enjoy the meal as an experience that you definitely won't find at your local Applebee's. Three-, four-, or five-course prix fixe meals (with menus that change often) take their sweet time in presentation and delivery, allowing you to linger and luxuriate—no wolfing down the appetizers here! The cuisine is definitely French-inspired (words like brioche and confit are thrown about with aplomb), but the basics behind it (lobster, steaks, game hens, lamb, etc.) will reassure the less adventurous in your group.

◖ L'ATELIER DE JOËL ROBUCHON ⑤⑤⑤

3799 Las Vegas Blvd. S. (in MGM Grand),
702/891-7925, www.mgmgrand.com

HOURS: Sun.-Thur. 5:30-10 P.M., Fri.-Sat. 5:30-10:30 P.M.

I'm directing you to the "cheaper" L'Atelier instead of its parent restaurant next door simply because the bill you get at this place will cause heart palpitations, but may not actually kill you as the other one might. Robuchon, named the Chef of the Century in France, was lured out of retirement to open these Las Vegas venues and has created what has been billed as the most expensive, most extravagant, and yes, the best dining experience in the country. The menu changes regularly, so naming dishes here is pointless, but rest assured that the French delicacies at both restaurants are gastronomic adventures; complex in taste, texture, and structure in ways that are probably lost on average folks like myself. People who appreciate the finest of fine food and don't mind paying outrageous sums of money for it need to call way ahead to get reservations here.

GOURMET

AUREOLE ⑤⑤⑤

3950 Las Vegas Blvd. S. (in Mandalay Bay),
877/632-1766, www.aureolelv.com

HOURS: Daily 6-10 P.M.

Chef Charlie Palmer brought his famed New York eatery here years ago and has been wowing the local foodies ever since. His delightful nouvelle cuisine creations are relentlessly chic and a bit intimidating for those not used to the finer foods in life (lamb, venison, and other non-cow meats make regular appearances), but even casual gourmands will have an experience worth remembering. The meals are prix fixe between $69 and $95 and include three courses of culinary masterworks. Don't miss the four-story wine tower with aerialists fetching your desired bottle of grape.

IRISH
NINE FINE IRISHMEN ⑤
3790 Las Vegas Blvd. S. (in New York-New York), 702/740-6463, www.ninefineirishmen.com
HOURS: Daily 11 A.M.-11 P.M. (bar open later)
Ireland has never been a celebrated food country, but if more Irish restaurants were like this one, things could change. Serving up traditional fare in a countryside manor setting (complete with cozy dining areas and an enormous, intricately carved bar direct from the home country), this casual dining experience provides an affordable alternative to the high-priced theme restaurants and interchangeable cafés that line The Strip. Standouts include the caramelized apricot and pork sausage served on a bed of potatoes and veggies or the traditional fish and chips. And save room for dessert. Irish cream. That's all I'm saying.

MEXICAN
BORDER GRILL ⑤⑤
3950 Las Vegas Blvd. S. (in Mandalay Bay), 702/632-7403, www.bordergrill.com
HOURS: Sun.-Thurs. 11:30 A.M.-10:30 P.M., Fri.-Sat. 11:30 A.M.-11 P.M.
Chefs Sue Milliken and Susan Feniger of *Two Hot Tamales* fame are south-of-the-border cuisine experts, having been schooled by authentic Mexican chefs. So it's no surprise that their restaurant has been such a success. The empanadas, the Gaucho Steak (with roasted garlic and Serrano chiles), and the quesadillas with delicate cheeses are true standouts on a menu full of standouts. Even the guacamole, served spicy with hints of red onion and jalapeño, is done with real originality. The boldly colorful fiesta of a dining room is yet another special treat.

RUSSIAN
RED SQUARE ⑤⑤
3950 Las Vegas Blvd. S. (in Mandalay Bay), 702/632-7407, www.mandalaybay.com
HOURS: Sun.-Thu. 5 P.M.-11 P.M., Fri.-Sat. 5 P.M.-midnight
Say what you want about the Bolsheviks, they knew how to eat. The coy Russian Revolution decor is really just a way of saying they are in on the joke—do you think those are real pigeon droppings on the giant headless statue out front? But get past the nudges and winks and you find some stunning cuisine—caviars, Roquefort-crusted filet mignon and other fine chops, lots of fresh seafood, and sauces...oh, the sauces. They could teach the French a thing or two. The bar serves every vodka known to man and becomes a very popular night spot later in the evening.

SEAFOOD
EMERIL'S NEW ORLEANS FISH HOUSE ⑤⑤
3799 Las Vegas Blvd. S. (in MGM Grand), 702/891-7374, www.emerils.com
HOURS: Daily 11:30 A.M.-2:30 P.M. and 5:30-10:30 P.M.
There's a reason Mr. Lagasse is the most famous chef in the universe, and evidence can be found here on a daily basis. His Creole twists on everything fish are delights from top to bottom. While it's tough to get good seafood way out here in the desert (and veterans of the New Orleans version of this restaurant will most likely be disappointed in the Vegas version), the selections flown in daily for Emeril's place are among the best in town. Non-seafood lovers even have some beef- and poultry-based options to choose from, all with that kick-it-up-a-notch flair.

STEAKHOUSE
CHARLIE PALMER STEAK ⑤⑤⑤
3960 Las Vegas Blvd. S. (in the Four Seasons), 702/632-5120, www.charliepalmersteaklv.com
HOURS: Daily 5-10:30 P.M.
The guy who hit a home run with Aureole did it again with his version of a classic American steakhouse. Chops are huge, using ounce

measurements for the sake of propriety, but pounds would be more accurate. The menu changes often, but whatever version of a rib eye is being offered will undoubtedly satisfy. Poultry and seafood dishes are fine, but this is all about the cow. It's expensive to eat here and there are other steakhouses that I like

better for less money, but for the best steak on this part of The Strip, this is it. Don't worry if you have to wait for a table. The lounge in front features comfy couches and chairs to relax in with a pre-dinner cocktail (and even includes free, live entertainment on Fridays and Saturdays).

Center Strip   Map 2

AMERICAN
FIX ⑤⑤⑤
3600 Las Vegas Blvd. S. (in Bellagio), 702/693-8400, www.fixlasvegas.com
HOURS: Sun.-Thurs. 5 P.M.-midnight, Fri.-Sat. 5 P.M.-2 A.M.
Trendy eateries usually turn me off, but this place, while fitting in the trendy category, does things with such style and serves such terrific food that I'm willing to get over it. Exciting twists on classic American diner food

COURTESY MGM MIRAGE

Fix at the Bellagio

include plenty of pastas, enticingly fresh seafood (the scallops are a dream come true), and grill selections that are out of this world. The last involves cooking over cherry wood, lending the tender steaks a slightly fruity flavor that will make you want all your meat prepared this way. Desserts are not to be missed and service is impeccable.

GRAND LUX CAFÉ ⑤
3355 Las Vegas Blvd. S. (in The Venetian), 702/414-3888, www.grandluxcafe.com
HOURS: Daily 24 hours
From the same folks who do The Cheesecake Factory, this slightly swankier place serves almost insane portions for moderate prices. There are no surprises on the menu—it's the kind of sandwiches, burgers, pastas, and American main courses that you'll find at your local TGIFriday's—but it's all prepared with a higher level of care and presentation. If the fancy menus and prices at most Vegas restaurants are a turnoff, this is a safe and satisfying place to turn. And yes, they do have their sister restaurants' desserts.

MARGARITAVILLE ⑤
3555 Las Vegas Blvd. S. (in the Flamingo Las Vegas), 702/733-3302, www.margaritavillelasvegas.com
HOURS: Daily 11 A.M.-2 A.M.
I have to admit I don't get the whole parrot head thing, but you don't have to be a Jimmy Buffet fan to enjoy the silly spectacle here, if for no other reason than they have the food to back it up. Many of the dishes have a Caribbean zing to them (jerk spices abound), but it

COURTESY HARRAH'S ENTERTAINMENT

wasting away at Margaritaville

shouldn't scare you away from the hearty sandwiches, burgers, salads, wraps, and especially the fajitas they serve up here. The margarita-spewing volcano is just a bonus. Outdoor dining on two Strip-facing balconies is a real treat if the weather is nice.

PINK'S SPORTS LOUNGE $

3667 Las Vegas Blvd. S. (in Planet Hollywood), 702/785-5555, www.aladdincasino.com
HOURS: Daily 10 A.M.-2 A.M.

Anyone who has ever been to Los Angeles should know about Pink's, the legendary hot dog stand that regularly has lines down the street full of people eager to get a taste of what have been called the best dogs in the country. Now that they have taken over the food concessions at the Planet Hollywood race and sports book, you can find out for yourself why they are so popular. They serve them with a range of toppings, from their most famous chili dog to the same with bacon on top, one with red spicy onions, another with pastrami and Swiss cheese, and so on, plus

burgers and other fast fare. Purists complain that they couldn't possibly be as good here as in their original location, but with very reasonable prices, you can go and judge for yourself and not be out a lot of money or time for your effort.

STACK $$

3400 Las Vegas Blvd. S. (in The Mirage), 702/791-7111, www.stacklasvegas.com
HOURS: Sun.-Thurs. 5 P.M.-11 P.M., Fri.-Sat. 5 P.M.-midnight

Done by the same people who do Fix at Bellagio, this restaurant shares more than just a corporate structure. The design is similar, with what appears to be an undulating cocoon of wood set off by dramatic high ceilings and lighting plus a simple, one-page American diner menu with fun twists. Appetizers include mini chili-cheese dogs or pigs in a blanket, and the main pickings here are a small selection of steaks and seafood, but everything is done with care and delightfully presented. The atmosphere can be raucous

BUFFET STRATEGIES

Yes, you could just walk up to a buffet at 12:30 on a Saturday afternoon, but do you really want to stand in line for an hour? This is just one of the things to think about when heading to one of the city's all-you-can-eateries.

Timing Is Everything: The buffets in this town are popular, to say the least, and the lines at peak times can be ridiculous. Going early is better than going late because the food is fresher. To get in and out a lot more quickly, hit the breakfast buffets as soon as they open, the lunch buffets around 11 A.M., and the dinner buffets by 5 P.M.

Man, I'm Thirsty: Most buffets have a wait-staff serving the drinks and, unfortunately, most of them do not take orders until after guests have gotten back from their first trips to the food stations. This can mean you'll get halfway through your plate before you get something to wash your food down with. Either wait a couple of minutes before running off for that first helping and order your drinks beforehand, or leave a note for your server (the keno sheets are handy for this) so you can have the drinks waiting for you on your return.

A Tip on Tipping: As mentioned above, you may be serving yourself when it comes to food, but in most places there are actual, live human beings who bring the beverages. They depend on tips, so be sure to leave something on the table when you leave. A couple of bucks are sufficient.

Pace Yourself: Those big stacks of plates are there for a reason. You can use as many of them as you want, so there's absolutely no need to load everything on one. Start with a trip to the salad bar, then move on to selections from the main courses, trying to keep some semblance of food cohesiveness (mashed potatoes and pizza on the same plate? No.). Not only will this help your digestion and keep the items you've selected warm, but you can pretend the extra trips back and forth are burning calories.

Saving Dough: If you have transportation, the buffets away from The Strip are uniformly cheaper and often better. Go exploring and you can save a few bucks. Also, if you are a member of a players' club, be sure to check to see if you have earned enough points to merit a discount or even a free meal. The buffets are the first places where dropping money in the casino can earn you rewards.

with the bar in front full of noisy partygoers and the nightclub-worthy sound system making quiet dinner conversation impossible, but the energy and cuisine more than make up for it.

ASIAN

MING $

3535 Las Vegas Blvd. S. (in Imperial Palace),
888/777-7664, www.imperialpalace.com
HOURS: Daily 5-10 P.M.

You have to hunt to find this place, but it's well worth the effort. Located on the fifth floor, this tiny slip of a place serves up traditional Chinese dishes that are affordable, generously proportioned, and delicious. There are no revelations on the menu, but there's nothing wrong with the tried-and-true, like orange chicken

or the spectacular Mongolian beef. Prices are bargain-basement and there's enough on every plate that sharing is almost mandatory.

SOCIAL HOUSE $$

3300 Las Vegas Blvd. S. (in Treasure Island),
702/894-7223, www.socialhouselv.com
HOURS: Daily 5-11 P.M.

Taking over the space overlooking the "Sirens of T.I." pirate battle once occupied by the staid Buccaneer Bay Club, Social House has set the bar high for the trendy restaurant-as-nightclub concept that is sweeping the city. Its deliriously high-energy atmosphere features a live DJ and an interactive sushi bar that has been luring famous faces left and right. The food, mostly pan-Asian cuisine, is very good, but it's the environment

COURTESY MGM MIRAGE

Social House at Treasure Island

that seems to get the most attention here. So if it's not your style at first glance, either chug a Red Bull to keep up or spend a great deal of time with the extensive sake selections and you just won't care.

BRAZILIAN

PAMPAS BRAZILIAN GRILLE $$

3663 Las Vegas Blvd. S. (in the Miracle Mile Shops), 702/804-4646, www.pampasusa.com

HOURS: Daily 11:30 A.M.-10 P.M.

If you're looking for something different in your dining excursion, Pampas offers a terrific option to the high-priced buffets and traditional steakhouses. The traditional Brazilian grill concept starts with an open chilled foods station filled with meats, cheeses, and veggies (better than your average salad bar) and then continues with the waitstaff bringing skewers of grilled meats to your table—pick the ones you want and they hack you off a hunk. The sirloins are delectable, so focus on those, but don't miss the sausages, lamb, chicken, pineapple, and especially the bacon-wrapped turkey.

BUFFETS

BALLY'S STERLING SILVER BRUNCH $$$

3645 Las Vegas Blvd. S. (in Bally's), 702/967-7999, www.ballyslv.com

HOURS: Sun. 9:30 A.M.-2:30 P.M.

At around $65 a head, this is not a simple, cheap Sunday brunch. Instead, it's a lavish spread unlike any other in Vegas. The elegant dining room is outfitted like a traditional restaurant, complete with waiters happy to assist with selections. And what selections! Endless caviar, lobster, and champagne are just the starters here, and everything is so far above the typical buffet quality that the $65 starts to seem like a bargain.

THE BUFFET AT BELLAGIO $$

3600 Las Vegas Blvd. S. (in Bellagio), www.bellagio.com

HOURS: Sun.-Thurs. 8 A.M.-10 P.M., Fri.-Sat. 8 A.M.-11 P.M.

Blame this place for the $20-and-up prices on most dinner buffets on The Strip. Before its arrival in 1998, $15 seemed like a lot. But a meal here will explain why they are justified in charging these kinds of rates. The quality and selection are among the best in town, forgoing the pedestrian chicken variations found elsewhere and replacing them with duck and game hens. Regional cuisines (Mexican, Chinese, Japanese, etc.) offer endless choices, and wood-fired pizza, fresh sushi, and traditional dim-sum are just a few of the bonuses.

CRAVINGS BUFFET AT THE MIRAGE 💲💲

3400 Las Vegas Blvd. S. (in The Mirage), 702/791-7111, www.mirage.com

HOURS: Mon.-Fri. 7 A.M.-10 P.M., Sat.-Sun. 8 A.M.-10 P.M.

Cravings is the logical next step in the buffet evolution, amping up the restaurant quality and interaction even if you are holding your plate and saying "More, please." Serving stations offer live-action cooking displays and made-to-order menu items, and instead of a salad bar, diners tell the staff at the salad station what they want and it's tossed for them. There's plenty to choose from, including freshly baked pizza, pastas, sushi, fresh seafood, Mexican, Chinese, and other regional cuisines, plus a dessert station that truly impresses with delicate pastries, créme brûlée, and hand-scooped Italian ice cream. The dining room is warmly decorated, but is a bit visually busy and noisy at times.

FLAVORS BUFFET AT HARRAH'S 💲💲

3475 Las Vegas Blvd. S. (in Harrah's), 702/697-2880, www.harrahs.com

HOURS: Daily 7 A.M.-10 P.M.

As buffets move as relentlessly upscale as their hotel hosts, they often become a little too snobby for their own good—I don't care how much foie gras you put on the plates, it's still a buffet, people! But Flavors does a good job of elevating the concept without becoming inaccessible. Their regional stations all have festive names (Olé for the Mexican, Fresh for the seafood, etc.) and their carving station is one of the most complete I've seen, with roast beef, chicken, ham, turkey, sausage, lamb, roasted vegetables, and more. And unlike many buf-

Le Village Buffet at Paris Las Vegas

fets, their dessert station satisfies. Chocolate fountain. That's all I'm saying.

LE VILLAGE BUFFET AT
PARIS LAS VEGAS ⑤⑤

3665 Las Vegas Blvd. S. (in Paris Las Vegas), 888/266-5687, www.parislv.com

HOURS: Sun.-Thurs. 7 A.M.-10 P.M., Fri.-Sat. 7 A.M.-11 P.M.

It's hard to tell which is more enjoyable: the French countryside village design motif or the French-inspired menu items. The former is a visual delight, making it appear like an outdoor dining area in a rustic town square. The latter includes everything from beef bourguignon to handmade crepes, with enough "safe" American dishes (salads, carving station, chicken and fish dishes) in between to keep the crowds happy. Pray they have the bananas Foster on the menu when you visit. You won't be disappointed.

SPICE MARKET BUFFET ⑤⑤

3667 Las Vegas Blvd. S. (in Planet Hollywood), 702/785-5555, www.aladdincasino.com

HOURS: Daily 7 A.M.-10 P.M.

A perennial favorite in the local paper's readers' poll, the Spice Market Buffet has survived its host hotel transition from Aladdin to Planet Hollywood intact. It is the only remaining bit of Moroccan-inspired design in the building, and although the decor of the windowless room was freshened and the menu was slightly updated, it's still pretty much the same, since you don't fix what wasn't broken. A huge variety of food, including specialties from the Middle East and Mediterranean on top of the usual buffet suspects (American, Chinese, Mexican, Italian), makes this buffet stand out in a very crowded field. Decent prices, too!

FRENCH
BOUCHON ⑤⑤⑤

3355 Las Vegas Blvd. S. (in The Venetian), 702/414-6200, www.venetian.com

HOURS: Mon.-Fri. 7-10:30 A.M. and 5-11 P.M., Sat.-Sun. 8 A.M.-2 P.M. and 5-11 P.M.

Chef Thomas Keller of Napa's famed The French Laundry is the genius behind the elegant yet simple French cuisine served here, offering

dine street-side at Mon Ami Gabi

up delicate legs of lamb, perfectly seasoned beef bourguignon, fresh Snow Creek oysters, and a variety of equally fantastic seafood, game, beef, and poultry dishes. It's all presented and served with artistic precision, turning what was already a great meal into a true experience. When someone came up with the term "fine dining," they were envisioning a place like this.

MON AMI GABI ⑤⑤

3655 Las Vegas Blvd. S. (in Paris Las Vegas), 702/944-4224, www.monamigabi.com

HOURS: Mon.-Thu. 11:30 A.M.-3:30 P.M. and 5-11 P.M., Fri. 11:30 A.M.-3:30 P.M. and 5-midnight, Sat. 11 A.M.-3:30 P.M. and 5 P.M.-midnight, Sun. 11 A.M.-3:30 P.M. and 5-11 P.M.

Technically, this is French food, but really, *pommes frites* are just french fries with a foreign name, so you should give the place a chance. The casual bistro atmosphere (complete with a Strip-level sidewalk-dining section) and the wide-ranging menu are delightful. Yes, there are snails and paté, but there's also a fantastic French onion soup to even things out. The steak

COURTESY MGM MIRAGE

Picasso at the Bellagio

RESTAURANTS

selection is definitely attention-worthy, seeing as how the French thing provides an excuse to pour rich sauces on top (peppercorn and blue cheese are two of my faves). Lunch offers lower prices and plenty of sandwich and salad selections.

PICASSO $$$
3600 Las Vegas Blvd. S. (in Bellagio), 702/693-7223, www.bellagio.com
HOURS: Wed.-Mon. 6-9:30 P.M.
This is widely considered to be one of the best restaurants in the city, and one of the best in the country. Original masterpieces by Pablo himself adorn the walls. Having tens of millions of dollars' worth of art could cause lesser joints to fold under the pressure, but the cuisine from chef Julian Serrano is worthy of a museum display of its own. The menu of French specialties changes nightly, with four- or five-course prix fixe prices ranging from "Ouch" to "Oh my God" (that's $105–115 in numerical terms). If you can afford to throw around that kind of dough for a meal, you'd have a hard time finding a better reason to do so.

ITALIAN
ONDA $$$
3400 Las Vegas Blvd. S. (in The Mirage), 702/791-7223, www.mirage.com
HOURS: Daily 5-11 P.M.
Forget the red-checked tablecloths—this Italian restaurant from chef Todd English is a much more elegant affair, both in atmosphere and menu selection. Start with the antipasti platter or the delicious minestrone soup packed with tender noodles and beans, then move on to the main events with pastas, like lobster ravioli or traditional lasagna with sweet Italian sausages. A full selection of chicken, veal, and seafood offers more great options and a fine selection of sinful desserts is a great capper.

PENAZZI $$
3475 Las Vegas Blvd. S. (in Harrah's), 702/369-5084, www.harrahs.com
HOURS: Wed.-Sun. 5:30-10:30 P.M.
Italian transplant Gabriele Penazzi has created one of the best purveyors of his home-country cooking on The Strip in this fun and afford-

COURTESY HARRAH'S ENTERTAINMENT

Penazzi at Harrah's

able bistro at Harrah's. The multilevel dining room cascades down to an open kitchen, providing an intimate experience, and the food, traditional Northern Italian of all stripes, is a pure delight. Some dishes, like the delightful penne alla vodka with shrimp and prosciutto, is cooked tableside for a dramatic flair. It'll make you never want to eat at Olive Garden again. The table captains are all old-world Italians, lending an even more authentic flavor to the already delicious proceedings.

MEDITERRANEAN
OLIVES $$

3600 Las Vegas Blvd. S. (in Bellagio), 702/693-7223, www.bellagio.com
HOURS: Daily 11 A.M.-10:30 P.M.

Todd English strikes again with this casual restaurant offering a stunning variety of dishes, all with a Mediterranean influence (basically, Italian with a twist). The flatbread pizzas are almost legendary, done with a thin, crispy crust and piled with decadent toppings, like spiced lamb and feta cheese or fiery chicken sausage.

The pastas and risottos are satisfying (especially the ricotta ravioli), but go directly for the entrées, like the slow-braised lamb shank or the grilled sirloin on a crunchy Tuscan bruschetta and topped with caramelized onions. Although still pricey, many of the same dishes are offered for less money at lunchtime.

SANDWICHES
EARL OF SANDWICH $

3667 Las Vegas Blvd. S. (in Planet Hollywood), 702/785-5555, www.earlofsandwichusa.com
HOURS: Sun.-Thu. 10:30 A.M.-11 P.M., Fri.-Sat. 10:30 A.M.-midnight

According to legend, in 1762 a British earl named John Montagu was so busy being an earl, commanding the British Navy, and playing cards all day that he couldn't find time to stop to eat the usual hunks of meat that were served. So he slapped the meat between two pieces of bread and named it after his title, the Earl of Sandwich. Now, a few hundred years later, the descendents of that man run a small chain of restaurants devoted to turning sandwiches back into an art form. They use their own baked artisan bread with no preservatives and stuff it with anything from slow-cooked roast beef and horseradish sauce to ham with French Brie, Caribbean jerk chicken, Hawaiian barbecue (because they were originally called the Sandwich islands), and more. Salads, smoothies, and a wide variety of desserts (ice cream sandwiches!) round out a full and interesting menu.

SEAFOOD
JOE'S SEAFOOD, PRIME STEAK & STONE CRAB $$

3500 Las Vegas Blvd. S. (in the Forum Shops at Caesars Palace), 702/792-9222, www.icon.com/joes
HOURS: Sun.-Thu. 11:30 A.M.-10 P.M., Fri.-Sat. 11:30 A.M.-11 P.M.

A descendent of the famed Miami eatery (the history of which goes back 90 years or so), this Vegas seafood staple does not merely re-create its more widely known ancestor—it honors and expands on the tradition with a vast selection of fresh offerings flown in daily, just to make sure it is of the highest quality. The scallops are divine creations, tasting like they just crawled out of the ocean and, of course, the stone crabs are probably the best you'll find in Vegas, but even non-seafood eaters will find plenty to eat here, including steaks, poultry, pork chops, lamb chops, and more. Prices are high, but fish aficionados will not be disappointed. If the cost intimidates you, try the slightly cheaper lunch menu.

SOUTHWEST
BOBBY FLAY'S MESA GRILL $$

3570 Las Vegas Blvd. S. (in Caesars Palace), 702/731-7731, www.bobbyflay.com
HOURS: Daily 11 A.M.-2:30 P.M. and 5-11 P.M., Sat.-Sun. brunch 10:30 A.M.-3 P.M.

Food Network staple Bobby Flay could've coasted on his laurels (and huge bank account) and let someone else run the Vegas branch of his famed Mesa Grill. But he took a hands-on approach to everything from the design to the food preparation, and it shows. The quesadillas, cooked in a specially constructed oven, are perfect, period. Really, just order one, trust

me. Sixteen-spice rotisserie chicken is another favorite, whether on its own or over a salad. A zillion different margaritas and some truly spectacular desserts, like the raspberry cheesecake, put the feather in Mr. Flay's cap.

STEAKHOUSES
BOA $$$

3500 Las Vegas Blvd. S. (in The Forum Shops at Caesars Palace), 702/733-7373, www.boasteak.com
HOURS: Sun.-Thurs. noon-10 P.M., Fri.-Sat. noon-midnight

High-priced steakhouses are not terribly original in this town, but Boa has taken the concept and knocked it up a few notches with a stunning, ultra-lounge–inspired design (moody colors, dramatic lighting, and low-slung furnishings) and a range of traditional and not-so-traditional dishes. Take the BLT salad, for instance, packed with bacon and tomatoes, which manages to take the concept of salad and make it interesting and pointless at the same time (aren't they supposed to be a healthy alternative?). Steak, seafood, and poultry round out the menu, and it is all very well prepared with dramatic sauces and seasonings turning tradition on its ear.

DELMONICO STEAKHOUSE $$$

3355 Las Vegas Blvd. S. (in The Venetian), 702/414-3737, www.emerils.com
HOURS: Daily 11:30 A.M.-2 P.M., Sun.-Thurs. 5-10 P.M., Fri.-Sat. 5-10:30 P.M.

Yes, Emeril is back, and this time he's bringing the cow with him. But this isn't just any ordinary steakhouse. Instead, Lagasse throws in his native New Orleans influences to turn ordinary cuts of meat into special affairs. Try the grilled sirloin with blue crab or the grilled pork chops with bacon-wrapped shrimp (everything is better when it's wrapped in bacon). Portions are huge and most come with delicious sides (ask for the bourbon smashed sweet potatoes if your dish doesn't automatically come with it). And don't forget the desserts. Butterscotch créme brûlée and traditional banana cream pie are two of many good choices.

THE RANGE $$$

3475 Las Vegas Blvd. S. (in Harrah's), 702/369-5084, www.harrahs.com

HOURS: Daily 5:30-10:30 P.M.

Start your experience by gazing out the enormous windows overlooking The Strip (come after dark—it's spectacular). When you're done sightseeing, look at the menu and start salivating. This is a traditional steakhouse, with giant cuts of meat served best with baked potatoes and all the fixings. Simple, straightforward cholesterol-ingestion devices—that's what they specialize in here, with prices that are still on the high side but several bucks cheaper than those at other steakhouses in the neighborhood. The creamy five-onion soup, served in a giant hollowed-out onion, should start the meal. It's not to be missed.

North Strip | Map 3

BUFFETS
◖ THE BUFFET AT WYNN LAS VEGAS $$

3131 Las Vegas Blvd. S. (in Wynn Las Vegas), 702/770-7100, www.wynnlasvegas.com

HOURS: Sun.-Thurs. 8 A.M.-10 P.M., Fri.-Sat. 8 A.M.-10:30 P.M.

The breadth of food offerings here is almost shocking—to the point that it conjures those Sally Struthers infomercials about hungry children. Cuisines from virtually every region on earth, made-to-order omelets, freshly squeezed juices, and a dessert station with amazing hand-scooped ice cream are just starters. It is one of the most expensive buffets in town, but the food is of the highest quality and the dining rooms, with tons of natural light, gardens, and intimate spaces, make it feel worth the cost.

STRATOSPHERE COURTYARD BUFFET $

2000 Las Vegas Blvd. S. (in the Stratosphere), 702/380-7711, www.stratospherehotel.com

HOURS: Daily 7 A.M.-3 P.M. and 4-10 P.M.

Finally, proof that a good buffet doesn't have to cost a lot of money. With weekday brunch under $10 and a nightly dinner just a couple of bucks over, this is one of the most economical buffets on The Strip. But eat here and you can walk away feeling like you didn't give anything up just to save a few bucks. An American Bounty section offers a selection of comfort foods (mac and cheese, fried chicken, etc.) and regional cuisines range from English fish and chips to Swedish meatballs.

CHINESE
RED 8 $$

3131 Las Vegas Blvd. S. (in Wynn Las Vegas), 702/770-3380, www.wynnlasvegas.com

HOURS: Sun.-Thurs. 11 A.M.-11 P.M., Fri.-Sat. 11 A.M.-1 A.M.

Most restaurants at Wynn are prohibitively expensive for the average hungry person, so the moderate prices and quite delicious cuisine at this small Asian bistro are a delight. I demand you try the vegetable spring roll appetizers, with flaky crusts (is that a hint of vanilla, perhaps?) and delectable veggie stuffing, but from there you can go in almost any direction: noodles (in broth or wok-fried), rice dishes (steamed, porridge, or again with the wok), barbecue and roasted meats, vegetarian selections, or traditional favorites like Mongolian beef (excellent!) or sweet and sour pork. Almost everything is under $20 and, while maybe not the cheapest Chinese in town, it's definitely one of the best.

DESSERTS
ETHEL'S CHOCOLATE LOUNGE $

3200 Las Vegas Blvd. S. (in the Fashion Show mall), 702/796-6662, www.ethelschocolates.com

HOURS: Mon.-Sat. 10 A.M.-9 P.M., Sun. 11 A.M.-6 P.M.

I guess it had to happen. Everything else in Vegas is becoming trendy and cool (and expensive), so why not turn Ethel M. Chocolate stores into Ethel's Chocolate Lounges? I snark,

RESTAURANTS

NAME-BRAND DINING

As you go through the regular listings in this book, you may be thinking some usual suspects are missing. Where are the name-brand restaurants from those celebrity chefs that get all the space in other guidebooks or loving tributes on Travel Channel specials? Well, for the most part, I think that these restaurants are not as great as they have been billed to be or that you can find better examples of the types of cuisine they serve at the places I did list, often at better prices. These restaurants are undeniably popular, though, and didn't become name brands by serving bad food, so below you'll find some of the more noteworthy of the bunch.

SOUTH STRIP

Fans of sushi insist that you can't do better than **Shibuya** (3799 Las Vegas Blvd. S., 877/793-7111, Sun.-Thurs. 5:30-10:30 P.M., Fri.-Sat. 5:30 P.M.-1 A.M.), and since I'm not a fan, I have a hard time arguing, although I will say that the prices are shocking to the casual observer. Renowned French chef Alain Ducasse created **Mix** (3950 Las Vegas Blvd. S., 702/632-9500, daily 6:30-10:30 P.M.) high atop THEhotel's tower, and the champagne bottle decor and views are stunning, but the food is merely good and you can do better elsewhere. **Stripsteak** (3950 Las Vegas Blvd. S., 702/632-7414, daily 5:30-10:30 P.M.) is Michael Mina's entry into the steakhouse arena, and while certainly a competitor, it is overshadowed by other, better restaurants of its type in town.

CENTER STRIP

Spago (3500 Las Vegas Blvd. S., 702/369-6300, daily 5:30-10 P.M.) is Wolfgang Puck's most famous restaurant, and while the Vegas version is not as laudable as the justifiably praise-worthy Beverly Hills original, you can get the general idea here without having to go to California. Puck's **Chinois** (3500 Las Vegas Blvd. S., 702/737-9700, Sun.-Thur. 5-10 P.M., Fri.-Sat. 5-11 P.M.) is an Asian-inspired bistro also imported from the Los Angeles area and also not as good as the original. **Le Cirque** (3600 Las Vegas Blvd. S., 877/234-6358, daily 5:30-10 P.M.) is definitely a famous name, imported from the almost-historic New York establishment to Bellagio and losing something in the translation food-wise, although service and location (overlooking the Bellagio fountains) are world-class. Meanwhile, James Beard Award-winning chef Luciano Pellegrini brings his mastery of Italian cuisine to **Valentino** (3355 Las Vegas Blvd. S., 702/414-3000, daily 11:30 A.M.-11 P.M.), another example of good but probably overrated and definitely overpriced food. You can definitely find better steaks at better prices than at the famed **The Palm** (3570 Las Vegas Blvd. S., 702/732-7256, daily 11:30 A.M.-11 P.M.), but you may spot a celebrity or two among the caricatures that line the walls, so that could make it worth it for you. Another import is **Rao's** (3570 Las Vegas Blvd. S., 877/346-4642, daily 6 A.M.-3 P.M. and 5-11 P.M.), a version of the 110-year-old Harlem eatery famed for its classic Italian comfort-food fare that is probably better when the prices aren't marked up like they are here in Vegas. And, of course, it would be silly not to mention **Restaurant Guy Savoy** (3570 Las Vegas Blvd. S., 702/731-7731, Wed.-Sun. 5-10:30 P.M.), although silly is a word I'd also use to describe the check that is delivered at the end of this fine French meal, which can easily exceed $300 per person.

JUST OFF THE STRIP

There are a couple of restaurants near The Strip that you may have heard of, both worth knowing about but not necessarily great enough to be high on your list of dining options. **Morton's** (400 E. Flamingo Rd., 702/893-0703, Mon.-Sat. 5-11 P.M., Sun. 5-10 P.M.) is a branch of the steakhouse chain that got its start in Chicago and has been pushing the cow here for years. While undeniably good, the steakhouse market is full of better examples, so you should only choose this one if you can't resist the brand. **Little Buddha** (4321 W. Flamingo Rd., 702/942-6815, Sun.-Thur. 5:30-11 P.M., Fri.-Sat. 5:30-midnight) is a popular Asian restaurant and sushi bar that is worth visiting if you happen to be in the neighborhood, but isn't worth going out of your way for.

but the end result is fairly cool, with a couple of plush velvet seats, cool chocolate-inspired drinks (of both the alcoholic and nonalcoholic varieties), desserts including chocolate fondue, and, of course, plenty of their delicious chocolate candies, which fall on upper end of the scale in both quality and cost. If all lounges served chocolate, you might find me at them more often!

FRENCH
DANIEL BOULUD BRASSERIE $$

3131 Las Vegas Blvd. S. (in Wynn Las Vegas),
702/352-3463, www.wynnlasvegas.com
HOURS: Daily 5:30-10:30 P.M.

Boulud gained fame as a chef in New York, and while his Las Vegas restaurant probably doesn't live up to the justified hype surrounding his Big Apple endeavors, it still remains one of the best French restaurants in the city. The lovely patio views of the lake at Wynn Las Vegas enhance the dining experience, which can (and should) take hours to get through as you sample delicately constructed and exquisitely arranged masterpieces of the cuisine. Focus on the meat dishes—braised short ribs or crispy duck confit are perennial winners—or just say to heck with it and sign up for the three-course prix fixe menu and make it easier on yourself.

GOURMET
ALEX $$$

3131 Las Vegas Blvd. S. (in Wynn Las Vegas),
702/770-9966, www.wynnlasvegas.com
HOURS: Daily 6-10 P.M.

One of Steve Wynn's big "gets" was to lure renowned chef Alex Strada away from his award-winning Renoir at The Mirage to open a new eponymous restaurant at Wynn Las Vegas. The result is quickly garnering raves for its exquisite cuisine, a memorable blend of continental flavors with a delicate French touch. The menu changes regularly, with Chef Alex deciding what the evening's fare will be depending upon whatever fresh ingredients he can lay his hands on, but anything made in his kitchen is almost guaranteed to be a masterpiece of fla-

vor and presentation. Although almost mind-bogglingly expensive (expect at least $150 per person), true foodies say it's hard to do better in Las Vegas.

TOP OF THE WORLD $$$

2000 Las Vegas Blvd. S. (in the Stratosphere),
702/380-7711, www.topoftheworldlv.com
HOURS: Daily 11 A.M.-3 P.M., Sun.-Thurs. 6-11 P.M.,
Fri.-Sat. 6 P.M.-midnight

The ultimate room with a view is located at the top of the Stratosphere Tower, more than 800 feet above The Strip. As the restaurant slowly rotates, guests can gaze and dine at the same time. The menu here is gourmet-meets-continental-meets-steakhouse, with traditional selections (surf and turf, prime rib) alongside more daring dishes (quail, stuffed veal, Japanese pork chops). There are no mind-blowers here, but it's all solid, dependable, well-prepared food. The bill at the end will be higher than the fare warrants, but the price is for the view as much as it is for the meal.

ITALIAN
BARTOLOTTA $$$

3131 Las Vegas Blvd. S. (in Wynn Las Vegas),
702/770-9966, www.wynnlasvegas.com
HOURS: Daily 5:30-10:30 P.M.

Finally, an Italian restaurant on The Strip worthy of the high prices that others charge for dishes that aren't much better than what can be found at Olive Garden. Chef Paul Bartolotta flies his ingredients in daily from the Mediterranean, including a selection of fresh fish that will outdo any seafood found in this desert oasis. Pastas are creative wonders, with the ravioli being a winner on a menu full of winners. All this in a multilevel dining room overlooking a reflecting pond, complete with private dining cabanas. Eat here and realize why people sneer at the mention of the Olive Garden.

CORSA CUCINA $$

3131 Las Vegas Blvd. S. (in Wynn Las Vegas),
702/770-9966, www.wynnlasvegas.com
HOURS: Daily 5-10 P.M.

I have a food critic friend who has one of the most

refined palettes on earth and she proudly pro-claims herself to be a food snob, so the fact that she describes this as her favorite restaurant in Las Vegas is nothing to sneer at. New York chef Ste-phen Kalt has brought his Italian creations over to Wynn and elevated the cuisine to near artistic perfection. The lobster gnocchi, which actually doesn't have any pasta involvement, is divinity on a plate, while the things with actual pasta are, at the very least, worthy of devotion. This is not your mother's ravioli from a can—but don't let the somewhat intimidating ingredients stop you from savoring the experience.

FELLINI'S RISTORANTÉ 💲💲

2000 Las Vegas Blvd. S. (in the Stratosphere),
702/383-4859, www.fellinislv.com
HOURS: Sun.-Thurs. 5-11 P.M., Fri.-Sat. 5 P.M.-midnight
Tucked away in an almost forgotten corner of the casino is a branch of this local Italian favor-ite worth finding. High-ceilinged themed din-ing rooms (Venice, Rome, etc.) are the setting for traditional and authentic Italian cuisine. The minestrone is out of this world, with a perfect blend of fresh veggies and tangy seasonings; the tenderloin tips and potato gnocchi are slathered in a gorgonzola and mushroom cream sauce that begs for extra bread to soak it up with; and the lasagna with ricotta cheese and sausages is as close to perfect as you can get outside of your Italian mother's kitchen.

SANDWICHES

🅲 CAPRIOTTI'S 💲

324 W. Sahara Ave., 702/474-0229,
www.capriottis.com
HOURS: Mon.-Fri. 10 A.M.-5 P.M., Sat. 11 A.M.-5 P.M.
Warning: Eat one of the subs at Capriotti's and you'll never be able to have a sandwich at one of those chain places again. Everything has a "Mamma Mia" flair here—even the tur-key drips with provolone cheese and Italian dressing—so when you see ham and cheese on the menu, expect much more. The Cap's Specials are a wacky delight, with The Bob-bie (turkey, cranberry sauce, and stuffing) and

the Slaw-Be-Jo (roast beef, cole slaw, and Rus-sian dressing) being the most talked about. A nine-inch small runs $5–6 and a large goes for $10–11, but it's a crazy 20 inches long, more than enough to share.

STEAKHOUSES

THE STEAK HOUSE AT CIRCUS CIRCUS 💲💲💲

2880 Las Vegas Blvd. S. (in Circus Circus),
702/794-3767, www.circuscircus.com
HOURS: Sun.-Fri. 5-11 P.M., Sat. 5 P.M.-midnight.
Forget the light and bright, trendy decor. This is a steakhouse the way God intended it to be: dimly lit with candles and classic white cloths on tables, and a simple menu of back-to-the-beef basics to choose from. Plenty of warm bread to start, hearty salads to get things going, big cuts of meat and giant baked potatoes to kick things into overdrive, and decadent desserts to finish it off. There may be better steaks to be had in this town, but there's a lot to be said for the traditional, clas-sic, and timeless experience found here.

TAPAS

CAFÉ BA BA REEBA 💲💲

3200 Las Vegas Blvd. S. (in the Fashion Show mall),
702/258-1211, www.cafebabareeba.com
HOURS: Sun.-Thurs. 11:30 A.M.-11 P.M., Fri.-Sat.
11:30 A.M.-midnight
In case you're not familiar with the concept of tapas, it's a Spanish term for what basi-cally amounts to appetizers. Only here, in-stead of being a pre-meal treat, they *are* the meal as you delve through a huge selection of options including paella, cold and warm sea-food, beef and lamb, chicken and pork, and more, cooked with a Spanish flair and served in small portions. Order a bunch and share at the table to turn your meal into a com-munal feast, or get a couple just for yourself so you can eat a more sensibly sized lunch or dinner. Don't miss the mini-desserts—perfect and cheap cappers to a terrific dining experience.

Just Off The Strip   **Map 4**

AMERICAN

BOUGAINVILLEA CAFÉ $

4100 Paradise Rd. (in Terrible's Hotel & Casino),
702/733-7000, www.terribleherbst.com
HOURS: Open 24 hours

Just about every casino in town has some form of the 24-hour café, but you have to go about a mile from The Strip to find the one I think is the best. The menu includes good old American basics (sandwiches, burgers, soups, salads, rotisserie chicken), all-day breakfasts (terrific steak and eggs), Chinese specialties, and a huge Mexican section, all at prices that surprise and delight ($6 for a big sizzling plate of chicken fajitas!). Be sure to check out the late-night graveyard specials for some even better bargains.

HARD ROCK CAFÉ $

4475 Paradise Rd. (in Hard Rock Hotel),
702/733-8400, www.hardrockcafe.com
HOURS: Sun.-Thurs. 11 A.M.-11 P.M., Fri.-Sat. 11 A.M.-midnight

COURTESY OF HARD ROCK INTERNATIONAL

Hard Rock Café

RESTAURANTS

The Hard Rock Cafés around the world are usually overpriced tourist traps. But since Vegas is one big tourist trap (said with love), the Hard Rock doesn't seem as egregious here. The menu is a glorified version of what can be found at Applebee's—salads, sandwiches, burgers, pastas, beef and chicken entrées, fajitas, etc. While nothing's worth raving about for days, it's all good, and their hickory-smoked pulled-pork sandwich may leave you raving for at least a few hours. But the real draws are the displays of music memorabilia. Come on, who wouldn't want to eat next to Madonna's bustier?

M&M SOUL FOOD $

3923 W. Charleston Ave., 702/453-7685
HOURS: Daily 7 A.M.-8 P.M.

In 2006 I took an extended road trip through the American South and experienced some of the best down-home cooking anywhere, so I know of which I speak when I proclaim this to be the best example of the cuisine you're going to find in Vegas and pretty worthy even when compared to what you'll find in Mississippi. Try the smothered fried chicken, three pieces of juicy, slightly spicy meat covered in delicious gravy, or go traditional with the hot links, collard greens, gumbo, catfish, or short ribs. Their home-brewed barbecue sauce is revelatory and will make you wish they bottled it for you to take home. Sheltered suburban types may be slightly intimidated by the neighborhood, but get over yourself and go experience southern cooking at its best.

PT'S GOLD $

1651 E. Sunset Rd., 702/616-0723, www.ptspub.com
HOURS: Daily 24 hours

PT's Gold is part of a local chain of restaurant/bar/casino concepts that serve great low-cost food and throw in some drinks, games, and gaming to make it even more appealing. This particular edition of PT's has the bonus of being located right across the street from Mc-Carran International Airport, with big windows offering great views of the endless lines of planes taking off and landing. The menu is mainly pub grub—lots of appetizers, sandwiches, burgers, and pizzas. It's all hearty, with epic portions and ridiculously low prices, especially when compared with similar Strip establishments. A one-pound double-decker cheese and bacon burger with fries for around $10? Sign me up!

BUFFETS

GOLD COAST PORTS O' CALL BUFFET $

4000 W. Flamingo Rd. (in the Gold Coast), 702/367-7111, www.goldcoastcasino.com

HOURS: Daily 7 A.M.-9 P.M.

A big selection with small prices (without having to drive miles away), this is probably as close as it gets to a good old-fashioned buffet on The Strip these days. Located in a big, bright, airy room, a number of different cooking stations serve up salads and soups, American favorites, Mexican and Chinese selections, plenty of fresh seafood (love those crab legs), rotisserie chicken, and some fine desserts. Breakfast and lunch are in the $6–8 range, while dinners peak at around $16, but that's for all-you-can-eat seafood night with more finely prepared fresh fish and crustaceans than you can shake a halibut at.

ORLEANS FRENCH MARKET BUFFET $

4500 W. Tropicana Ave. (in the Orleans), 702/365-7111, www.orleanscasino.com

HOURS: Mon.-Sat. 7 A.M.-9 P.M., Sun. 8 A.M.-9 P.M.

Another bargain alternative to the high-priced Strip joints, the Orleans buffet provides breakfast and lunch for under $10, dinner for a few bucks more, and a Sunday brunch spread for $14 including champagne. The live-action cooking stations take guests around the world, with the typical Chinese and Mexican, but add Mongolian, Italian, American barbecue, and a big seafood spread to spice things up. It's all good to very good, and at these prices, diners can leave with a full stomach and a full wallet to boot.

RIO CARNIVAL WORLD BUFFET $$

3700 W. Flamingo Rd. (in the Rio), 702/252-7777, www.playrio.com

HOURS: Mon.-Fri. 7 A.M.-10 P.M., Sat.-Sun. 7:30 A.M.-10 P.M.

A favorite among locals and tourists alike, this enormous facility boasts more than 300 different menu items cooked daily, ranging from all-American favorites like hamburgers (plus fries and chocolates shakes, of course) to fresh sushi, cooked-to-order Mongolian barbecue, one of the best salad bars around, and a broad selection of pastries and pies for dessert. The fact that it's expensive (around $24 for dinner) shouldn't stop you from trying it. It certainly doesn't seem to stop anyone else. The popularity of this place means very long lines at peak mealtimes (up to an hour wait).

CHINESE

PF CHANG'S CHINA BISTRO $$

4165 Paradise Rd., 702/792-2207, www.pfchangs.com

HOURS: Sun.-Thurs. 11 A.M.-11 P.M., Fri.-Sat. 11 A.M.-midnight

I'm loathe to include chain restaurants since there are so many good restaurants that can only be found here, but when a meal is this good, why quibble about the corporate structure? A lively bistro setting (open kitchen, casual dining room) creates a fun environment in which to sample their California twists on Chinese cuisine. The lettuce wraps (crisp iceberg stuffed with zesty ground chicken) and the pan-seared Peking dumplings (pot stickers to you and me) are appetizer musts, and the orange peel chicken with chili peppers is a one-of-a-kind blend of sweet and spicy. Definitely worthy of inclusion in my book.

DELI

JASON'S DELI $

3910 S. Maryland Parkway, 702/893-9799, www.jasonsdeli.com

HOURS: Daily 8 A.M.-9 P.M.

The locals in town consistently rank this local chain as the best deli in Las Vegas and it's pretty clear why. The wide-ranging menu includes all sorts of delicatessen favorites (build your own subs, Reubens, clubs, tuna melts, etc.) plus salads, muffalettas, po'boys, paninis, pastas, and more, all cooked with a heart-healthy zero trans fats and generously proportioned. Personal faves include the Sergeant Pepper po'boy (hot roast beef with onions, bell peppers, and au jus) and the Smokey Jack panini (turkey, bacon, and jalapeño pepper jack cheese on olive oil–basted French bread). Yum! The fact that prices are a fraction of what you'd pay at the delis on The Strip is a bonus, really.

FRENCH
ⓒ ALIZÉ ⑤⑤⑤
4321 W. Flamingo Rd. (in The Palms), 702/951-7000, www.alizelv.com

HOURS: Daily 5:30-11 P.M.

Located on the top of The Palms hotel tower, the dining room has a stunning view of the entire Strip, romantic and thrilling at the same time. Those words could describe the cuisine as well, created by Las Vegas's master of French food, André Rochat, but more bold and daring than his namesake restaurant downtown (see *André's* in the *Downtown* section). The menu changes often, but look for delicacies like the foie gras with duck jus vinaigrette in the appetizer section or the green peppercorn–encrusted filet mignon among the main courses. Whatever the meal, it's sure to delight, despite the stratospheric prices (main courses are almost all above $40).

GERMAN
CAFÉ HEIDELBERG ⑤
610 E. Sahara Ave., No. 2, 702/731-5310

HOURS: Daily 11 A.M.-9 P.M.

Voted the best German food in Las Vegas every year by the locals, this small eatery just feels authentic, right down to its beer garden decor and kitschy Deutschland gift shop. The schnitzel, served on a grilled kaiser roll (naturally), is roughly the size of a hubcap, but much more tasty than one, while the turkey pastrami with sauerkraut comes on rye with tangy dressing and couldn't be more successful if it tried. Note the big map of Germany just inside the door, covered in pushpins identifying the hometowns

of visitors from the fatherland who came, saw, and enjoyed enough to make their mark. You can't buy that kind of endorsement.

HOFBRAUHAUS ⑤
4150 Paradise Rd., 702/853-2337, www.hofbrauhauslasvegas.com

HOURS: Daily 11 A.M.-midnight (bar open later)

Schnitzel, strudel, and braten of all shapes and ingredients make this descendent of the famed Munich Hofbrauhaus *wunderbar!* This carbon copy of the German version (in business since 1589!) includes a raucous beer hall and indoor beer garden (complete with a polka band). There's a lot to choose from on the big menu, but I recommend the *wurstplatte* (assorted sausages and franks) or the Hungarian stew. Oh, and don't forget the beer, flown in from Germany and still using the 400-year-old recipe. It's so good that in 1614 an invading horde agreed to stop plundering Munich in exchange for 344 buckets of the stuff. Now that's good beer.

INDIAN
GAYLORD INDIA ⑤⑤
3700 W. Flamingo Rd. (in the Rio), 702/777-7923, www.playrio.com

HOURS: Daily 5-11 P.M., Fri.-Sun. 11:30 A.M.-2:30 P.M.

A branch of the award-winning San Francisco restaurant of the same name (in business for more than 30 years), this warm den of a room specializes in northern Indian cuisine. Tandoori chicken is their trademark (and rightly so), but why not get a little daring with the *gosht vindaloo*, delicate chunks of lamb and potato in a fiery vinegar, or the mushroom *mattar*, with curried green peas. Or go totally crazy with the Indian-style feasts, massive multicourse meals fit for royalty.

SHALIMAR ⑤
3900 S. Paradise Rd., 702/796-0302

HOURS: Mon.-Sat. 11:30 A.M.-2:30 P.M. and 5-10:30 P.M.

Although their dinner courses are attention-worthy, it's really the lunch buffet that makes people sit up and take note. It's not fancy by any means, but the northern Indian dishes they serve are nothing short of a revelatory, especially if the traditional Las Vegas buffet has grown tiresome. Their tandoori and vindaloo are spicy and spicier, respectively, but there are plenty of tamer dishes, including lightly seasoned lamb, eggplant, and other vegetarian options, and some really fine flavored flatbreads. It not only beats The Strip buffets in flavor, but it beats them in price, with all you can eat for under $10.

ITALIAN
◖ CARLUCCIO'S TIVOLI GARDENS ⑤
1775 E. Tropicana Ave., 702/795-3236
HOURS: Tues.-Sun. 4:30-10 P.M.

Back before it became Carluccio's, it was Liberace's Tivoli Gardens. Yes, *that* Liberace. And he decorated the place himself. And they haven't changed it in 20 years. Do I need to keep going? Okay, beside the deliriously tacky decor (complete with one of his mirrored pianos), they serve up some really good Italian fare. It's all very straightforward, Americanized Italian (spaghetti, lasagna, pizza), but it's done with noticeably fresh ingredients and tantalizingly bold flavors, served in portions that will require doggie bags at the end of the meal. By the way, the Liberace Museum (see the *Arts and Entertainment* chapter) is right next door. Why not make it a theme outing?

JAPANESE
NOBU ⑤⑤
4475 Paradise Rd. (in Hard Rock Hotel),
702/693-5090, www.hardrockhotel.com
HOURS: Daily 6-11 P.M.

Chef Nobu Matsuhisa is a legend in the world of Japanese cuisine. His restaurants in New York, London, and Tokyo are often talked about in reverential tones. No wonder, then, that the Vegas version draws crowds full of famous faces. So if celebrity sighting is on your agenda, you may have luck here. Of course, the food should be the primary draw. Sushi is flown in daily from Tokyo, tempura and sashimi dinners are as close to perfect as they get, and the chicken and beef teriyaki are so flavorful and rich with exotic spices that you

can just smile when people make fun of you for ordering something so "safe."

MEDITERRANEAN
MEDITERRANEAN CAFÉ & MARKET ⑤
4147 Maryland Pkwy., 702/791-6030,
www.paymons.com
HOURS: Sun.-Thurs. 11 A.M.-1 A.M., Fri.-Sat. 11 A.M.-3 A.M.
(market open earlier)

Greek, Persian, and Middle Eastern cuisines all mix together into a richly original experience at this charming cultural complex. In the café, try the hummus or the *baba ghanoush* for a snack; the gyros pita is a must for a light lunch; and the *koobideh* (ground beef and veggies on a skewer with rice or hummus) is great for dinner. If your room has a fridge, stop by the market for takeout sandwiches or imported ingredients for your own Mediterranean feast back home. A hookah lounge stays open late, offering more than 20 flavored tobaccos to choose from and a light menu to go with them.

SEAFOOD
THE TILLERMAN ⑤⑤
2245 E. Flamingo Rd., 702/731-4036,
www.tillerman.com
HOURS: Daily 11:30 A.M.-2:30 P.M. and 5-11 P.M.

Finding fresh fish in the middle of the desert is challenging, but The Tillerman has been doing it (and doing it well) for more than 20 years. The menu is almost as enormous as the portions, so a light lunch is recommended. The lump crab or Australian lobster cocktails are a great way to start, but you may regret wasting the space when main courses like baked jumbo shrimp stuffed with crab or the Alaskan king crab entrée hit your table. For non-seafood fans, there are a couple of chicken- and cow-based dishes, but it's obvious the chef's attention is elsewhere.

STEAKHOUSES
DAN MARINO'S ⑤⑤
115 E. Tropicana Ave. (in Hooters Casino Hotel),
702/739-9000, www.danmarinosrestaurant.com
HOURS: Sun.-Thurs. 4 P.M.-11 P.M., Fri.-Sat. 4 P.M.-4 A.M.

Football star Dan Marino took advantage of

his post-game career to become a restaurateur, starting in Florida and then to Vegas in his eponymous eatery. The place is actually much classier than the Hooters hotel that it is housed in, with an upscale and modern design that is warm and comfortable. But the food here is the star on a wide-ranging menu of American classics, steaks, seafood, sandwiches, and more. Portions are huge, the food is terrific, and the prices are moderate at the high end and downright cheap for the more basic fare, so this one is a no-brainer alternative to the high-priced eateries on The Strip.

LAWRY'S THE PRIME RIB $$$

4043 Howard Hughes Pkwy., 702/893-2223
HOURS: Sun.-Thurs. 5-10 P.M., Fri.-Sat. 5-11 P.M., www.lawrysonline.com

Sure, you could go for the $6.95 prime rib specials at the cheap casinos on the east side of town, but the real deal can be found here. A Los Angeles institution since 1938, Lawry's serves up the best, most tender, most flavorful prime rib anywhere. The full meal comes in a variety of cuts (California for small stomachs and the stunningly huge Beef Bowl for the daring), plus their famous spinning bowl salad (tossed at the table with drama), mashed potatoes, signature whipped cream horseradish, and Yorkshire pudding. A classic dining event.

N9NE $$$

4321 W. Flamingo (in The Palms), 702/933-9900, www.n9negroup.com
HOURS: Sun.-Thurs. 5-11 P.M., Fri.-Sat. 5-11:30 P.M.

Done by the same Chicago family that created the classic Morton's, N9NE (pronounced nine) takes everything you think you know about a steakhouse and turns it on its ear. Unrelentingly upscale in a trendy way (cool blues, a water wall, and low-slung furnishings dominate), the room is anything but sedate, while the menu bolsters the finely prepared steaks and seafood with dishes like lobster fettuccini, roasted Colorado lamb chops, and a grilled salmon with Chinese mustard. The experience is more contemporary gourmet than traditional steak, but labels are unimportant with food this good.

THAI

LOTUS OF SIAM $

953 E. Sahara Ave., 702/735-3033, www.saipinchutima.com
HOURS: Mon.-Fri. 11 A.M.-2:30 P.M. and 5:30-9:30 P.M., Sat.-Sun. 5:30-10 P.M.

Tucked away in a dingy strip mall about a half mile from The Strip is what has been called (by no less than *Gourmet* magazine) the best Thai restaurant on the continent. The accolades are merited. There are the traditional dishes like pad thai—tender noodles with chicken and egg—all the way up to *pla doog yang,* a whole charbroiled catfish. Even more unusual are such delicacies as *nua nam tok* (charbroiled beef with green onions and chile) and *nam kao tod* (a grilled sour pork sausage with green onion and ginger with rice). The ingredients are amazingly fresh and everything is prepared with noticeable care. Rave reviews don't do this place justice.

RESTAURANTS

Downtown   Map 5

RESTAURANTS

AMERICAN

JILLIAN'S $

450 E. Fremont St. (in the Neonopolis Mall),
702/759-0450, www.jillianslasvegas.com

HOURS: Sun.-Thurs. 11 A.M.-10 P.M., Fri.-Sat. 11 A.M.-
11 P.M.

Most notable on the huge menu here are the
New Orleans favorites, like spicy jambalaya,
crawfish, and a terrific steak "po'boy," but
there's a little something for everyone, including huge burgers, sandwiches, salads, pizzas,
pastas, stir-fries, and even surf and turf. The
portions are enormous and the prices are significantly less than equivalent meals on The
Strip. To cap the meal, there's a big video game
arcade as well as bowling upstairs.

TRIPLE 7 RESTAURANT
AND BREW PUB $

200 N. Main St. (in Main Street Station), 702/377-1896,
www.mainstreetcasino.com

HOURS: Daily 11 A.M.-7 A.M.

Notice the hours—this is a terrific place to end
a night of Vegas debauchery with some fine pub
fare and maybe one of their terrific microbrews as
a nightcap. Burgers and sandwiches are the most
obvious menu choices—the Philly cheesesteak
deserves awards—but the options go way beyond
that with pasta, ribs, pizza, sushi, and enough appetizers (don't miss the onion rings) to qualify as
a meal of their own. The beer selections actually
have won awards, with the High Roller Gold and
the Market Pale Ale among the favorites.

◖ TRIPLE GEORGE GRILL $$

201 N. 3rd St., 702/384-2761,
www.triplegeorgegrill.com

HOURS: Mon. 11 A.M.-4 P.M., Tues.-Thurs. 11 A.M.-10 P.M.,
Fri. 11 A.M.-11 P.M., Sat. 4-11 P.M.

An homage to the 150-year-old Tadich Grill in
San Francisco, Downtown Las Vegas's Triple
George Grill is a delightful addition to a pretty
spare dining scene in the area. Done as a traditional early American diner with high-backed
wooden booths and a lunch counter, the res-

taurant serves up an array of American classics—comfort food like their signature chicken
noodle soup, beef Stroganoff, pot roast, and
meatloaf (wrapped in bacon, of course!) to
slightly more pricey fare like seafood pastas
and steaks of all varieties. The service is fantastic, and what they serve you will leave you
wanting to go back again and again. I have.

BUFFETS

GOLDEN NUGGET BUFFET $

129 E. Fremont St. (in Golden Nugget), 702/385-7111,
www.goldennugget.com

HOURS: Mon.-Fri. 7 A.M.-10 P.M., Sat.-Sun. 8 A.M.-10 P.M.

Once an also-ran in the buffet competition
in this town, the buffet at the Golden Nugget received a top-to-bottom makeover in
2006 that transformed it into a major contender. The big wall of windows overlooks
a stunning pool area, and the gold, copper,
and earth-tone hues of the dining room are
delightful. The food ain't too shabby, either,
with a large (although not as epic as some)
selection of cuisines from American to Chinese, salads to desserts, a carving station, and
more. Weekend brunch adds made-to-order
omelets and champagne for prices that are significantly cheaper than what you'll pay at the
big buffets on The Strip.

◖ MAIN STREET STATION GARDEN
COURT BUFFET $

200 N. Main St. (in Main Street Station), 702/387-1896,
www.mainstreetcasino.com

HOURS: Daily 7 A.M.-10 P.M.

The best buffet in town. There, I said it. The
dining room is the first clue, a beautiful garden setting with big windows letting in lots of
natural light. The food backs up that promise
with a huge variety of dishes, including pizza
cooked in their very own brick oven, a carving station with spicy sausages in addition to
the more traditional turkey, plenty of regional
cuisines (Hawaiian specialties are a unique oc-
currence), and even hot dogs with all the fix-

ings. Not convinced? How about the prices: $8 for lunch, $10 for Saturday and Sunday brunch, and $11–16 for dinner, the higher being an all-you-can-eat seafood night. What are you waiting for?

FRENCH

ANDRÉ'S $$$

401 S. 6th St., 702/385-5016, www.andrelv.com
HOURS: Mon.-Sat. 6-10 P.M.

André Rochat opened his fine French restaurant in Downtown Vegas more than 25 years ago and the awards have been piling up ever since. The menu changes regularly, but be on the lookout for mouthwatering pan-seared duck foie gras, smoked salmon and caviar, sautéed duck, or mustard-crusted Colorado lamb. This is one of those places where diners should just close the menu and let the knowledgeable waitstaff lead the way to gastronomic heaven. A massive wine list offers something for every palate. Two-person checks of well over $100 are common, but well worth it.

GOURMET

HUGO'S CELLAR $$$

202 E. Fremont St. (in the Four Queens), 702/385-4011, www.fourqueens.com
HOURS: Daily 5-10 P.M.

Ladies are given a red rose upon being escorted to the table, just the first of many fine touches at this elegant (but totally relaxed) restaurant. The fare has a continental flair with traditional steakhouse touches to keep things from getting too fancy (this is in the basement of a casino, after all). The herb-crusted rack of lamb is a fine selection, as are any of the fine cuts of beef (the thick filet in a béarnaise sauce is a standout). Palate cleansers buffer courses, served with care by a very attentive staff.

MEXICAN

DONA MARIA TAMALES $

910 Las Vegas Blvd. S., 702/382-6538, www.donamariatamales.com
HOURS: Mon.-Fri. 8 A.M.-10 P.M., Sat.-Sun. 8 A.M.-11 P.M.

There are two groups of people who should run here immediately: those who love taco stand–style Mexican food and those who want to have a great meal but not pay a lot of money for it. Tacos, burritos, and tamales are the unassuming shack's specialties, but everything on the menu is terrific, spicy, and packed with flavor. I've had meals at sit-down Mexican restaurants that cost three times what I've paid here and were nowhere near as good. Great food at a low price. What a concept!

EL SOMBRERO CAFÉ $

807 S. Main St., 702/382-9234
HOURS: Mon.-Sat. 11 A.M.-9 P.M.

In business since 1950(!), El Sombrero is the kind of place you might drive by without giving it a second glance. It's a bit of a dive in a slightly dodgy neighborhood, but don't judge a book by its cover. There's nothing on the menu over $10 and most of the items are half that, with burritos, tacos, enchiladas, and tamales served in portions that require take-home containers. Everything is deliciously flavorful and spicy, making this an unexpected treat for a simple lunch or hugely satisfying dinner.

SEAFOOD

SAN FRANCISCO SHRIMP BAR & DELI $

One Fremont St. (in the Golden Gate), 702/385-1906, www.goldengatecasino.net
HOURS: Daily 11 A.M.-2 A.M.

There's only one reason to include this small eatery in this guidebook: the 99-cent shrimp cocktail. The famous one. The Golden Gate is the oldest hotel in the city (since 1906) and they've been serving their trademark shrimp cocktail in a classic tulip glass with a "secret" sauce since 1959. This gets featured on television specials, written about in magazines, and highlighted in guidebooks, and whether it's actually worth all the hype is probably beside the point. It's more about the history. If you like shrimp cocktail, you'll like this one. The restaurant also serves snacks and sandwiches for remarkably low prices.

RESTAURANTS

STEAKHOUSES
CENTER STAGE $$

One Main St. (in the Plaza Hotel), 702/386-2110,
www.plazahotelcasino.com

HOURS: Wed.-Sun. 5-11 P.M.

The outside of this place has been in count-less Vegas movies. It's located inside the smoky glass dome at the head of Fremont Street in front of the Plaza Hotel. The reason that's important is because, in addition to its fine steakhouse fare, Center Stage offers a fantastic seating position from which to watch the Fremont Street Experience (see *Downtown* in the *Sights* chapter). Meals are satisfying and surprisingly affordable—if two can't do it for $75, you've eaten too much. Of course, that's pretty easy considering the Queen Cut prime rib is the size of a small Japanese car and there's a King Cut that's even bigger. Come hungry.

THE PULLMAN GRILLE $$

200 N. Main St. (in Main Street Station), 702/387-1896,
www.mainstreetcasino.com

HOURS: Wed., Thurs., Sun. 5-10 P.M., Fri.-Sat.
5-10:30 P.M.

Filled with lovely early 1900s antiques, ornately carved woodwork (check out that fireplace), and even a full Pullman railroad car acting as the cigar lounge, this fine dining experience is one of the few in Downtown worth going out of the way for. The steaks are tender and dripping with flavor, accompanied by a variety of sauces that aren't necessary, but are enjoyable all the same. There are some stumbles here and there—stick with the finer cuts (filet, rib eye, etc.) instead of the cheaper New York Strip.

ROBERTA'S $$

600 E. Fremont St. (in El Cortez), 702/385-5200,
www.elcortezhotelcasino.com

HOURS: Daily 4-10 P.M.

Eating at Roberta's is like slipping on a comfortable dinner jacket. The antithesis of the trendy, expensive, and loud restaurants on The Strip, this place is a traditional steakhouse in a room that still manages to be casually lovely without turning into a cliché. The menu will not surprise you—steaks, seafood, lamb chops, and a few other dishes, plus salads and soups—but the presentation, portions, and especially the prices will satisfy all but the pickiest of food snobs. The atmosphere is charmingly friendly and familial—our server was celebrating her 16th anniversary as an employee at the hotel.

ENTERTAINMENT

There's a lot to do in Las Vegas besides gambling. Some of the best shows, the hottest nightclubs, and most respected museums are located here. That wasn't always the case. Entertainment in Vegas used to be limited to magic shows, female impersonators, and (of course) topless showgirls. Shows were just a way to get people inside the casino, and if they weren't very good, who cared? People leaving the showrooms early got into the casinos faster.

But then a little hotel called The Mirage came along and changed all that forever. Siegfried and Roy had been around for years, but when Steve Wynn put them into their own multimillion-dollar showroom and threw many, many more millions of dollars at their show, they created a spectacle that set the standard for what Las Vegas entertainment could and should be.

Today, visitors can see not one, but five productions from world-renowned avant-garde circus and theater company Cirque du Soleil (with more on the way); several shows direct from the bright lights of Broadway; and major music acts setting up residence in their own showrooms. Of course, there are still magicians, female impersonators, and showgirls for a more traditional Vegas experience.

Nightlife has undergone a similar transformation. A decade ago, there were only a few nightclubs of any note on The Strip. Now you can't throw a Manolo Blahnik without hitting someone standing in line to get into the latest, hottest, hippest club. Every hotel has one and sometimes two or three. Add in all the lounges,

PHOTO BY AL SEIB; COSTUMES BY DOMINIQUE LEMIEUX © CIRQUE DU SOLEIL INC.

HIGHLIGHTS

LOOK FOR ◖ TO FIND
RECOMMENDED ENTERTAINMENT.

◖ **Most Mind-Blowing Special Effects:** A seemingly untethered floating stage is only the beginning of the eye-popping visuals in *KÀ* by Cirque du Soleil (page 111).

◖ **Best Broadway Transplant:** They've tried many successful Great White Way productions here, but none have been as absurdly entertaining as *Monty Python's Spamalot* (page 112).

◖ **Best Production:** Awe-inspiring. Evocative. Emotional. Spooky. Funny. Erotic. There aren't enough adjectives to adequately describe *Mystère* by Cirque du Soleil, still the best show all-around in Vegas (page 112).

◖ **Best Comedy Show:** Elvis may have been King, but **Rita Rudner** is the Queen of comedy in Las Vegas (page 114).

◖ **Best Bargain Show:** You'll get better illusions and more laughs at **Mac King's** show than you will at magic shows five times the price elsewhere (page 115).

◖ **Best Party Scene: Pure** is the biggest nightclub on The Strip, offering no fewer than four distinct environments to find your party groove (page 125).

◖ **Best Place to See and Be Seen:** Anybody who is anybody moves heaven and earth to dance the night away at **Tao** (page 127).

◖ **Best Blast from the Past:** Duck and cover at the **Atomic Testing Museum,** a fun, informative, and emotional look at the days of the Nevada Nuclear Test Site (page 138).

◖ **Best Kitsch Museum:** It's not *all* about the rhinestones and fur at this wacky homage to the late, great showman – but that's a big part of the **Liberace Museum** (page 139).

◖ **Best Gallery:** There are bigger, more high-profile galleries in town, but the simple pleasures of the **Guggenheim Hermitage Museum** are a tonic to the soul (page 140).

PHOTO BY CAROL ROSEGG, COURTESY WYNN LAS

the cast of *Monty Python's Spamalot* in the Grail Theater at Wynn Las Vegas

bars, and strip clubs around town and there's an almost endless array of places to party.

But beyond the showrooms and trendy clubs, Vegas actually has a good representation of the "arts" side of arts and entertainment. Some of the finest galleries in the world are located here, showcasing works of art that can usually only be seen in major museums. There are a bunch of notable museums as well, from the serious to the silly and everything in between.

This chapter will help you navigate the arts and entertainment choices in Las Vegas, showcasing the best of what the city has to offer to keep you amused, inspired, or inebriated.

Shows

Unfortunately, it's not always simple to get tickets to the Vegas productions. Before we get into the details of the best and most popular shows in Las Vegas, there are a few things you should be aware of to help you get tickets so you can actually see those shows.

First, understand that many of the big productions (most of the Cirque shows, for instance) sell out every single performance, often weeks or months in advance. Booking early and having options is key.

To obtain tickets, call the venues directly (almost all have toll-free numbers) or go through the hotel or show website. Do not, under any circumstances, no matter how desperate you are, use one of those ticketing agencies either in person or online. They charge significantly more for tickets (anything from $10 extra to twice the price) and, quite frankly, ticket prices in Vegas are high enough. If the show you want to see is sold out, there are 18 other options that will be just as entertaining.

Tickets2Nite (3769 Las Vegas Blvd. S., at the Showcase Mall, 888/4-TIX2NITE, www.tickets2nite.com), a same-day, half-price ticket agency, is a good option for anyone planning things last-minute. The big-name shows never have tickets here—as mentioned previously, they sell out every performance, so they don't need places like this—but often tickets for some of the B- and most of the C-list shows are available. The specific shows change on a daily basis and you have to be there in person to find out what they are. Hours are noon–9 P.M., but they start posting ticket availability at 11:30 A.M., so get there early to get the hottest bargains.

Tix4Tonight is a similar service that has four locations; three on The Strip and one Downtown. For more details, contact them at 888/849-4868 or online at www.tix4tonight.com.

Finally, most showrooms these days have preassigned seating, but a few still use the old-school maître d' system. You can tell the difference in one of two ways, either by checking your ticket (if it has a seat number on it, you're preassigned) or by noticing the guy in the tux at the front door. If there is such a guy (or gal, on occasion), you can score yourself better seats by slipping him (or her) a few bucks. How much depends on the ticket price of the show and how close you'd like to be to the front, but figure anything from $5 to $20.

PRODUCTION SHOWS
BLUE MAN GROUP
3355 Las Vegas Blvd. S. (at The Venetian), 888/641-SHOW, www.bluemen.com
HOURS: Sun.-Mon., Wed.-Thurs. 8 P.M., Tues., Fri.-Sat. 7 and 10 P.M.
COST: $76-126
Map 2

Part comedy, part musical, part performance art, and all gloriously weird, the Blue Man Group show is a unique oddity. The conceit is simple: Three men paint their heads blue and do strange stuff like shoot marshmallows into each other's mouths or play PVC pipe instruments. I said it was weird. But it's also a riot and is one of the best shows in Vegas. Their new-ish digs at The Venetian are perhaps not as comfortable as the old showroom at Luxor, but

UPCOMING SHOWS

As this book was going to press, there were several big shows coming down the pike that, unfortunately, weren't open by the time my editor snatched the manuscript out of my hands. The good news is I know enough about most of them to at least provide readers with a heads-up about something they may want to check out. One of them is a proven performer on Broadway and the other two are from the masters of the Vegas show scene, but whether or not they become must-sees is yet to be seen (so to speak).

Jersey Boys is the Tony Award-winning musical based on the lives, and featuring the music of, Frankie Valli and the Four Seasons. It's scheduled to open in a new theater at The Venetian's sister hotel, Palazzo (3325 Las Vegas Blvd. S.), in early 2008. It will be shorter than the standard Broadway version (at a sleek 90 minutes, reportedly) and will be performed without an intermission like most of the other Broadway transplants. As of press time there is no contact information for the hotel or the show, but you should be able to find informa-

tion through The Venetian's website at www.venetian.com or by calling 877/883-6423.

Continuing their trek toward total Strip domination, **Cirque du Soleil** is prepping two more shows, which will bring their total in Vegas to seven. The first will be a magic-themed spectacular featuring illusionist **Criss Angel** (of A&E's *Mindfreak*), set to open at Luxor Las Vegas (3900 Las Vegas Blvd. S., 800/288-1000, www.luxor.com) in 2008. Very few details are available as I type this, but the very thought of Angel's mind-bending magic with Cirque's mind-bending theatricality puts this one in the "highly anticipated" column.

Their other new production is even more highly anticipated by some quarters and will follow the template of a marriage of Cirque aesthetics and iconic music so successfully done with The Beatles and *Love* at The Mirage. But instead of John, Paul, George, and Ringo, this new show will feature music by none other than the King himself, Elvis Presley. It is due to open in 2009 at CityCenter (3780 Las Vegas Blvd. S., 866/722-7171, www.citycenter.com).

it really doesn't change the wonderfully wacky experience a whit.

LE RÊVE: A SMALL COLLECTION OF IMPERFECT DREAMS

3131 Las Vegas Blvd. S. (at Wynn Las Vegas), 888/320-7110, www.wynnlasvegas.com
HOURS: Thurs.-Mon. 7:30 and 10:30 P.M.
COST: $99-159
Map 3

Created by the same guy who did *O* by Cirque du Soleil, the comparisons are inevitable—artistic avant-garde theater mixed with aerialists and aquatic performers in, above, and under a giant pool. Here, though, the focus is on the theater part, with dramatic imagery of a nightmarish world of angels and demons that is evocative in surprisingly emotional ways. Constant revisions to the show since it opened have made it much more entertaining, including a simplification of the

storyline (such as it is) and a remodeled theater with bigger, plusher seats (some even come with gratis champagne, chocolate, and video monitors).

MAMMA MIA!

3950 Las Vegas Blvd. S. (at Mandalay Bay), 877/632-7400, www.mandalaybay.com
HOURS: Sun.-Thurs. 7:30 P.M., Sat. 6 and 10 P.M.
COST: $49-110
Map 1

Light bubble-gum pop with a featherweight of a story, it's a miracle this Broadway sensation doesn't just float up off the stage and disappear. Shakespeare it ain't, but it's also impossible to deny that it's a lot of fun. Songs from the classic 1970s super-group ABBA provide the structure for a story about a woman, her daughter, a long-lost love, and oh, who cares? They sing "Dancing Queen" and "Take a Chance on Me!" Let go of your

ENTERTAINMENT

Le Rêve at the Wynn Las Vegas theater-in-the-round

theater-snob pretensions and just have a good time, but you should note that if this is your cup of sugary tea, then you'll want to get there soon; the show is slated to close in mid-2008.

☾ KÀ BY CIRQUE DU SOLEIL

3799 Las Vegas Blvd. S. (at MGM Grand), 877/880-0880, www.mgmgrand.com
HOURS: Tues.-Sat. 7 and 9:30 P.M.
COST: $69-150
Map 1

It's almost impossible to believe you're seeing what you're seeing. A massive stage floats, spins, tilts, stands on its end, and disappears entirely, creating an almost unlimited setting for the kinds of aerial and acrobatic feats Cirque is known for. Unlike other Cirque shows, this one has a linear storyline about a pair of twins, separated by war, trying to find their way back to one another through storm-tossed oceans, sandy beaches, snowy mountain ranges, and vine-strewn jungles. Packed

with awe-inducing martial arts battle sequences and touching tenderness, *KÀ* is a spectacle in the best sense of the word.

LOVE BY CIRQUE DU SOLEIL

3400 Las Vegas Blvd. S. (at the Mirage), 800/963-9634, www.mirage.com
HOURS: Thurs.-Mon. 7 and 10 P.M.
COST: $69-150
Map 2

It's hard to imagine a more brilliant collaboration: the magic and artistry of Cirque du Soleil all set to the music of The Beatles. And like all Cirque shows, this one is an eye-popping visual delight, filled with dance and elaborate staging with a nonstop mix of John, Paul, George, and Ringo's best. But for non-Beatles fans (or for those who merely like the music instead of love it) seeking more Cirque in their Soleil (so to speak), the show disappoints with less of the aerial derring-do we have come to expect from the troupe. Beatles devotees, buy your tickets now, but for those seeking a more pure Cirque experience, try one of the other four shows playing within a few blocks.

◖ *MONTY PYTHON'S SPAMALOT*

3131 Las Vegas Blvd. S. (at Wynn Las Vegas), 888/320-7110, www.wynnlasvegas.com
HOURS: Sun.-Mon., Wed. 8 P.M., Tues., Fri.-Sat. 7 and 10 P.M.
COST: $49-99
Map 3

This Tony-Award winner based on the movie *Monty Python and the Holy Grail* is a deliriously silly and endlessly entertaining bit of madness about the knights of King Arthur's court on a mission to find the Holy Grail. Most everything you remember from the movie is there—the flying cows to the killer beast that guards the cave (don't want to ruin it for those who haven't seen it), the puns, the jokes, the pratfalls, and the absurdist, almost surreal humor all set to an eminently hummable score. Although shortened to 90 minutes or so and tweaked with some Vegas-specific gags (think Excalibur), it doesn't suffer in the translation at all. By far the best Broadway transplant playing in Vegas.

◖ *MYSTÈRE* BY CIRQUE DU SOLEIL

3300 Las Vegas Blvd. S. (at Treasure Island), 800/288-7206, www.treasureisland.com
HOURS: Sat.-Wed. 7 and 9:30 P.M.
COST: $60-95
Map 2

Cirque du Soleil's first Vegas show is still the best (by just a hair over *KÀ*). Packed with visual wonder, it brings together aerialists, acrobats, dancers, and stuntpersons performing amazing circus-style acts that no human being should be able to do (the trapeze artists and human sculpture segments are especially noteworthy in a show filled with noteworthy moments). It'll leave you slack-jawed. Wrapped up in an avant-garde performance theater aesthetic, the show pushes every button, making you laugh, gasp, and even maybe cry a little as the performers seem to fly through the air (with the greatest of ease) in an allegory for spiritual and emotional freedom.

O BY CIRQUE DU SOLEIL

3600 Las Vegas Blvd. S. (at Bellagio), 888/488-7111, www.bellagio.com
HOURS: Wed.-Sun. 7:30 and 10:30 P.M.
COST: $99-150
Map 2

Many proclaim this to be the best Cirque show in town, but the central conceit—the "stage" is a giant water tank—is often more limiting than freeing. Performers dive into, swim through, or float above the tank in a series of aquatic and aerial stunts that become a bit repetitive after a while. Having said that, it's still a remarkable show. The theatrical visuals are stunning, kicking off with a tender segment as carousel horses slowly fly in from the wings, land in the water, and float away.

PHANTOM: THE LAS VEGAS SPECTACULAR

3355 Las Vegas Blvd. S. (at The Venetian), 866/641-7469, www.venetian.com
HOURS: Mon., Thurs.-Fri. 7 P.M., Tues. 7 and 10 P.M., Sat. 6 and 9 P.M., Sun. 5 and 8 P.M.
COST: $75-150
Map 2

Yes, this production is different from the long-running Broadway musical *Phantom of the Opera* by Andrew Lloyd Webber, but not by much. The show is essentially the same—a tragic love story about a budding diva and a mysterious masked man—but they trim it down to about 90 minutes and attempt to justify the "spectacular" part with bigger staging and special effects. If you're a fan of *Phantom,* you'll probably want to see this no matter what I say, but everyone else should know that it's not exactly what you'd call a "feel-good" time at the theater. It's big, dramatic, operatic, and certainly worthy of the term spectacle, but "spectacular"?

THE PRODUCERS

3665 Las Vegas Blvd. S. (at Paris Las Vegas), 888/727-4758, www.parislv.com
HOURS: Mon.-Fri. 8 P.M., Sat. 6 and 9 P.M.
COST: $69-145
Map 2

The Tony Award–winning Broadway hit is based

on the Mel Brooks movie of the same name about a pair of producers conspiring to get rich by putting on the worst musical in history. It's great silly fun, but its long run on the Great White Way plus touring shows and a movie version means that a lot of people have seen it, and this production adds nothing new. In fact, it subtracts, running at a sleek 90 minutes. If you haven't seen the show in any of its forms, this one is worth going to. If you have, it isn't.

STOMP OUT LOUD

3667 Las Vegas Blvd. S. (at Planet Hollywood), 702/785-5055
HOURS: Sun.-Fri. 8 P.M., Sat. 7 and 10 P.M.
COST: $42-97
Map 2

The "Out Loud" portion of the title indicates that this is a bigger, bolder, and "badder" (in a good way) version of the long-running *Stomp* series. In truth, it's not much different in concept from its origins, with a cast of people creating music from found objects like brooms, dust pans, boxes, newspapers, water jugs, pipes, lighters, and, of course, the signature trash can lids. It's inspiring to watch these people create intricately crafted symphonies out of little more than trash, and the fact that the cast is a melting pot of races, genders, ages, and body types makes this feel like art the way it was meant to be: inclusive.

TOURNAMENT OF KINGS

3850 Las Vegas Blvd. S. (at Excalibur), 800/933-1334, www.excalibur.com
HOURS: Wed.-Mon. 6 and 8:30 P.M.
COST: $49.95 (includes meal)
Map 1

Medieval pageantry is the theme here as gallant knights joust on their trusty steeds while their fair maidens cheer. There's no real drama (the good guys win, the bad guys lose), but if you can leave your ironic detachment at the door and get into the spirit of things, you may actually have a good time (will it kill you to boo the dark wizard?). A full meal (usually something like glorified chicken, aka Cornish game hen) is included in the price and, while it won't get

the place listed in *Gourmet* any time soon, it's better than might be expected.

ZUMANITY BY CIRQUE DU SOLEIL

3790 Las Vegas Blvd. S. (at New York-New York), 866/606-7111, www.nynyhotelcasino.com
HOURS: Tues., Wed., Fri.-Sun. 7:30 and 10:30 P.M.
COST: $69-129
Map 1

This is the least successful Cirque show in town. (It's the LaToya. Or maybe the Tito. Whatever.) Here, the theme is also the problem: sex. It still has the circus-style acts, but instead of wrapping them in the usual ethereal performance-theater vibe, they go for a strip club feeling, with nudity (of the topless female variety), raunchy humor, and a deep exploration of every kink you can think of. It tries to be sexy and mostly isn't, but for those looking for a little T with their Arts, this is an option. Not for kids or prudes.

COMEDY
LOUIE ANDERSON

3850 Las Vegas Blvd. S. (at Excalibur), 702/597-7600, www.excalibur.com
HOURS: Sat.-Thurs. 7 P.M.
COST: $45
Map 1

Anderson has had a wildly varied career as a stand-up, host of game shows, star of sitcoms, and inspiration for animated children's shows, but it is here, on stage, that he is most comfortable and most inspired. Nothing in his comedy is terribly cutting-edge, often relying on old workhorses like the differences between men and women, the joys of relating to parents as an adult, and, of course, his ongoing weight issues, but his midwestern good nature and keen observances will more than satisfy your funny bone.

THE IMPROV

3475 Las Vegas Blvd. S. (at Harrah's), 800/392-9002, www.harrahs.com
HOURS: Tues.-Sun. 8:30 and 10:30 P.M.
COST: $27.95
Map 2

There are several traditional stand-up comic

ENTERTAINMENT

joints around town, but this branch of the legendary Improv is by far the best of them. The room is nicer (better sight lines, more comfortable furniture), the drinks are better, and the quality of the comedians is higher than what can be found at the less high-profile joints. They don't get big-name stand-ups here—don't expect to see Jerry Seinfeld—but the ones they do get are usually very talented working comics who do this sort of thing for a living. No open-microphone nights here.

◖ RITA RUDNER

3475 Las Vegas Blvd. S. (at Harrah's), 800/392-9002, www.harrahs.com
HOURS: Mon.-Sat. 8 P.M.
COST: $54
`Map 2`

The First Lady of stand-up comedy took a chance by eschewing the often more profitable theater circuit and making a permanent stand here in Vegas and in 2006 doubled down with a move to a bigger, more high-profile showroom at Harrah's. Thank goodness she did, because her endlessly entertaining observations on everything from marriage to shopping to Sin City itself leave audiences rolling in the aisles. Her delivery is endearingly loopy, but it's just a smoke screen—her comedy is sharp, sophisticated, and immediately relatable, never stooping to crassness or going after easy targets, so the audience can laugh and not feel guilty about it later.

SECOND CITY IMPROV

3555 Las Vegas Blvd. S. (at the Flamingo Las Vegas), 800/732-2111, www.flamingolv.com
HOURS: Mon., Tues., Fri. 8 and 10 P.M., Thurs., Sat.-Sun. 8 and 10 P.M.
COST: $39.95
`Map 2`

The Canadian sketch and improvisational group has bred such comedic legends as Gilda Radner, Mike Myers, and Martin Short, so there's a lot to live up to here. Luckily for them, and us, the Vegas troupe is more than up to the challenge. The intimate, nightclub-style theater gets the audience up close to the rapid-thinking five-person team, which blasts through

Rita Rudner at Harrah's

both scriptless and pre-scripted (but ever-evolving) sketches ranging from five minutes to five seconds long. But it's their improv skills that leave people breathless. Shout out a couple of words and the next thing you know the team's created an opera out of them. Genius.

ILLUSIONS AND MAGIC
LANCE BURTON

3770 Las Vegas Blvd. S. (at Monte Carlo), 877/386-8224, www.montecarlo.com
HOURS: Tues., Sat. 7 and 10 P.M., Wed.-Fri. 7 P.M.
COST: $66.50-72.50
`Map 1`

When Siegfried and Roy were still doing their show, Lance Burton served quietly in their spectacle-sized shadow down the street. Now that they are gone (but never forgotten), it's time to discover Burton, whose show I've always rated as so much better. Instead of the dramatic tomfoolery of some illusionary magic (will he escape the Whirling Blades of Death!?), Burton turns on his down-home charm and brings the audience up close for tricks both big (disappearing cars) and small (appearing ducks). It's a terrific show and a comparative bargain, to boot.

ENTERTAINMENT

☾ MAC KING

3475 Las Vegas Blvd. S. (at Harrah's), 800/392-9002,
www.harrahs.com
HOURS: Tues.-Sat. 1 and 3 P.M.
COST: $24.95
`Map 2`

Who'd-a-thunk the best (and certainly funniest) magic show in town would be found in the middle of the day and cost a fraction of the price of a really good meal, much less a show ticket? Forget about those grandiose "illusionists" and their disappearing helicopters, Mac King will reaffirm your faith in the genre with nothing-up-his-sleeve card tricks and other up-close magic you won't believe you're seeing. It's all wrapped up in King's genial backwoods hick shtick, with enough laugh-out-loud humor to make this seem like more of a comedy show than a magic show. Whatever you want to call it, just don't miss it.

NATHAN BURTON: COMEDY MAGIC

3667 Las Vegas Blvd. S. (at the Miracle Mile Shops),
702/932-1818, www.nathanburton.com
HOURS: Sat.-Thurs. 2 P.M., Fri. 4 and 6 P.M.
COST: $28-38
`Map 2`

Burton (no relation to Lance) has been toiling the magic circuit for a while now, but it was his series of appearances on the NBC series *America's Got Talent* that turned him into a hot property here in Vegas. His show is filled with all manner of illusions both small and big(ish), and while none of it is stuff you haven't seen before, he does put enough fun and funny twists on things to make this one a good option for those seeking a little bit of magic in their Vegas vacation.

PENN & TELLER

3700 W. Flamingo Rd. (at the Rio), 888/746-7784,
www.pennandteller.com
HOURS: Sat.-Thurs. 9 P.M.
COST: $75-85
`Map 4`

This is not a magic show. It's the deconstruction of a magic show—an almost university-level course in how the human psyche can be fooled into believing almost anything with

Penn & Teller at the Rio All Suite Hotel & Casino

COURTESY HARRAH'S ENTERTAINMENT

the right amount of smoke and mirrors. Your "professors" for the evening are Penn (the big one) and Teller (the silent one), master illusionists who do everything wrong by telling the audience what they are doing and how they are doing it. And then darned if they don't go ahead and amaze you anyway. It's remarkable, intelligent stuff that doesn't ruin anything, but instead provides a deeper appreciation for the craft.

IMPERSONATORS
DANNY GANS

3400 Las Vegas Blvd. S. (at the Mirage),
800/963-9634, www.mirage.com
HOURS: Tues.-Wed., Fri.-Sat. 8 P.M.
COST: $100
`Map 2`

I used to enjoy this show more when tickets were about half what they cost now, but even at these high rates Gans puts on a one-man

ENTERTAINMENT

cavalcade of stars that has to be seen to be believed. Taking on everyone from George Burns to Macy Gray, Gans is an incredible vocal mimic and an accomplished singer on top of it. Every evening is a little different, but usually includes as many as 100 different impressions, almost all of them eerily on target.

AN EVENING AT LA CAGE

2901 Las Vegas Blvd. S. (at the Riviera), 877/892-7469, www.rivierahotel.com
HOURS: Wed.-Mon. 7:30 P.M.
COST: $55
Map 3

Female impersonators used to be all the rage in Vegas, but these days La Cage is one of a rare breed for the kind of campy fun not found in a "straight" impersonator show. Hostess Joan Rivers (as done by renowned drag performer Frank Marino) keeps things moving with funny (if a bit predictable) audience bits and smart introductions of everyone from Diana Ross to Barbra Streisand. The performers lip-sync to the originals' music, so this is more about physical illusion than vocal impersonation, but fans of the genre won't be disappointed.

LEGENDS IN CONCERT

3535 Las Vegas Blvd. S. (at Imperial Palace), 888/777-7664, www.legendsinconcert.com
HOURS: Mon.-Sat. 7:30 and 10 P.M.
COST: $50-60 adult, $40-50 child (12 and under)
Map 2

The sets are cheesy (like something out of a bad 1970s variety show), the performers are uneven, and the showroom is uncomfortable for long shows, but *Legends,* in business for more than 20 years here, still reigns supreme as the premier celebrity impersonation show in town. The lineup varies. You may see Dolly Parton and Janet Jackson or you may see Cher and Charlie Daniels. You'll always see Elvis. Apparently, it's a rule. The singing is live—no lip-synching here—and not always successful, but you can usually find at least a couple of true standouts at every show.

MUSIC AND VARIETY

BETTE MIDLER IN CONCERT

3570 Las Vegas Blvd. S. (at Caesars Palace), 877/723-8836, www.caesarspalace.com
HOURS: Tues.-Wed., Fri.-Sun. 7:30 P.M.
COST: $95-250
Map 2

Seeing the Divine Miss M live on stage is a transformative experience, forever ruining your chance of enjoying concerts ever again. Okay, maybe that's a little over the top, but Midler does put on one hell of show with nonstop singing, dancing, joke-telling, and lay-it-all-on-the-line emotion. Hits like "The Rose" are standard, but it is the deeper dives into her rich catalogue of American music that will leave you raving for days. Or maybe you just want to see her in a mermaid costume or tell the Sophie Tucker jokes, dirty enough to make a sailor blush. Note: This show does not play every week, so be sure to call ahead for a schedule.

ELTON JOHN IN THE RED PIANO

3570 Las Vegas Blvd. S. (at Caesars Palace), 888/435-8665, www.caesarspalace.com
HOURS: Mon.-Tues., Thurs.-Sat. 8 P.M.
COST: $100-250
Map 2

"Bennie and the Jets," "Don't Let the Sun Go Down on Me," "Candle in the Wind," "Crocodile Rock," "Daniel." I could take up the entire space allotted here just listing the game-changing hits created by the legendary singer who puts his greatest hits catalogue to great effect at Caesars. Fronting a small band and a giant LED screen with video vignettes that enrich the experience, Elton sits at his big red piano and rocks the way God intended it to be. Note: This show is not performed every week, so call ahead or check the website to see if he will be playing when you are in town.

MANILOW: MUSIC AND PASSION

3000 Paradise Rd. (at the Las Vegas Hilton), 800/222-5361, www.lvhilton.com
HOURS: Tues.-Sat. 8 P.M.
COST: $95-225
Map 4

He writes the songs, ya know. Following in

Bette Midler in Concert at Caesars Palace

Celine's footsteps, Barry Manilow, the Dean of American Pop Music has taken up residence on the Vegas stage with this glorified greatest hits concert. He still sounds fantastic and looks good, so fan(ilow)s of his music certainly won't be disappointed. Everyone else should find something else to do with their $225. Note: The show is not performed every week, so anyone building their vacation around this should be sure to check the schedule before booking hotel rooms.

THE PRICE IS RIGHT LIVE

3645 Las Vegas Blvd. S. (at Bally's), 800/237-7469, www.ballyslv.com
HOURS: Tues.-Thurs., Sat. 2:30 P.M., Fri. 7:30 P.M.
COST: $49.50
Map 2

It is exactly what the title implies: a live stage show version of the long-running game show hit. Only here, the entire audience gets to participate by using an electronic device to answer simple pricing games that may earn you a trip on stage to play one of the classic TPIR games like Plinko, Hole-in-One (or Two!), Cliffhangers, and more. They give away real prizes (everything from washers and dryers to trips to, occasionally, a car), but your odds of earning your $50 back are just as slim as if you were dumping it into a slot machine out in the casino.

TONI BRAXTON: REVEALED

3555 Las Vegas Blvd. S. (at The Flamingo), 800/222-5361, www.flamingolv.com
HOURS: Tues.-Sat. 7:30 P.M.
COST: $69-109
Map 2

Toni Braxton has defied extremely negative early reviews to become quite the draw at The Flamingo, and for good reason. She's got a great voice, looks fantastic, and is a hell of an entertainer even if you don't know her music. But it is her performance attitude that really seals the deal, seizing the mantle of Vegas sex kitten from Ann Margret and reinventing it for the new millennium. Don't worry, there's nothing even R-rated in this show—instead, it is Toni as vamp, vixen, and naughty girl who likes to

ENTERTAINMENT

COURTESY HARRAH'S ENTERTAINMENT

the cast of Chippendales at the Rio All Suite Hotel & Casino

croon from laps of handsome male audience members, after politely asking permission from accompanying females, of course. On the night I was there, she even got the mayor of a major southern city up on stage for a little hip shaking and the whole thing was delightful.

SHOWGIRLS AND SHOWGUYS
CHIPPENDALES

3700 W. Flamingo Rd. (at the Rio), 888/746-7784, www.playrio.com

HOURS: Sun.-Tues., Thurs. 8 P.M., Fri.-Sat. 8 and 10:30 P.M.

COST: $40-50

Map 4

In a town filled with bare breasts as entertainment for the guys, it's good to see the ladies getting a measure of equality. Toned, tanned, and buffed within an inch of their DNA-blessed lives, the men of Chippendales whip the 99-percent female crowd into a frenzy with their bumps, grinds, teases, and taunts. Seriously, if men behaved like this at female strip shows

they'd get arrested. But it's all part of the fun, with the dancers providing a series of fantasy-fulfillment vignettes (the construction worker, the cowboy, etc.) and a big serving of beefcake.

CRAZY HORSE PARIS

3799 Las Vegas Blvd. S. (at MGM Grand), 877/880-0880, www.mgmgrand.com

HOURS: Wed.-Mon. 8 and 10:30 P.M.

COST: $59

Map 1

A relative of the famed burlesque house of the same name in France, this show turns the experience of looking at mostly naked women into something slightly less crass with highly-choreographed numbers, intricate staging, and dramatic lighting effects. Its existence and ongoing popularity has always confused me a little. I mean, really, if you want to look at breasts, do you want it to be this highfalutin? Okay guys, maybe your girlfriends will be a little more patient with the concept if you insist that it's art.

ENTERTAINMENT

Showgirls are inextricably associated with Las Vegas entertainment – past and present.

FOLIES BERGERE

3801 Las Vegas Blvd. S. (at Tropicana),
800/829-9034, www.tropicanalv.com
HOURS: Mon., Wed., Thurs., Sat. 7:30 and 10 P.M.,
Tues. and Fri. 8:30 P.M.
COST: $45-55
Map 1

A Vegas institution since 1959, this is a classic example of the kind of entertainment that used to rule the roost around here. Big headdresses, big sets, topless beauties, singing, dancing, and a little variety all presented in a straight-out-of-the-'70s showroom complete with the curved leather booths and long rows of tables. There's nothing the slightest bit edgy or daring here—this is the Donny and Marie of topless shows—but it's a timeless throwback to the days when people didn't need Canadian acrobats to liven up an evening. It should be noted that the host hotel will be undergoing some major changes in the next couple of years that will probably

spell doom for this show. Be sure to call ahead to make sure it is still playing.

JUBILEE!

3645 Las Vegas Blvd. S. (at Bally's), 800/237-7469,
www.ballyslv.com
HOURS: Sat.-Thurs. 7:30 and 10:30 P.M.
COST: $48-110
Map 2

Although this show has "only" been around since the early '80s, it has earned landmark status as one of only two remaining traditional showgirl extravaganzas (and perhaps the only one by the time you read this). Here the headdresses are larger, the sets bigger, and the production values higher, but whether you choose this one or *Folies Bergere* is really a matter of taste. A seemingly random series of vignettes (Sampson and Delilah followed by the sinking of the *Titanic*) is just an excuse to parade beautiful women around topless, so don't look for a deeper, hidden meaning here. It's just big Vegas fun the way it used to be.

THUNDER FROM DOWN UNDER

3850 Las Vegas Blvd. S. (at Excalibur), 800/933-1334, www.excalibur.com

HOURS: Sun.-Thurs. 9 P.M., Fri.-Sat. 9 and 11 P.M.

COST: $40-50

Map 1

Yes, there are male strippers at the "family-friendly" Excalibur. Do you need any more proof that the days of Vegas as a family destination are over? Less polished than their Chippendales counterparts, this troupe of Australian hunks makes up for the lower production values with higher energy and a general tone of "anything could happen" naughtiness not seen at that other male strip show. They're just as good (if not better) at working the ladies into a lather—something about the accents, I guess—but, ultimately, which you choose depends on your worldview: Do you prefer the beef at Ruth's Chris or Outback?

CONCERT VENUES
PLANET HOLLYWOOD THEATRE FOR THE PERFORMING ARTS

3667 Las Vegas Blvd. S. (at Planet Hollywood), 877/333-9474, www.planethollywood.com

Map 2

When they tore down the original 1966-era Aladdin, they saved the big theater and built the new hotel around it. Despite a major revamping of the rest of the property as it transitioned to Planet Hollywood, the new owners wisely left well enough alone with this place. The 7,000-seat auditorium is renowned for its concert-hall–level acoustics, making it a terrific place to see a show. These days, it hosts all manner of concerts (Prince, Mary J. Blige, and Sting are a few recent examples), plus a Broadway series highlighting the best road companies of big-budget musicals.

THE COLOSSEUM AT CAESARS PALACE

3570 Las Vegas Blvd. S. (at Caesars Palace), 888/702-3544, www.caesarspalace.com

Map 2

On about 100 days out of the year, the Colosseum is home to Bette Midler's show while Elton John takes another 100 or so (see *Production Shows* in this chapter), but on their days off, a lot of big-name acts take the stage, including Jerry Seinfeld and Gloria Estefan, to name a couple. Done as an homage to the Roman Colosseum, it's really nothing like that at all except for maybe some detail work on the outside of the building. Inside is a state-of-the-art, 4,000-seat theater, where no seat is more than 120 feet from the stage.

DANNY GANS THEATRE

3400 Las Vegas Blvd. S. (at The Mirage), 800/374-9000, www.mirage.com

Map 2

When impressionist Danny Gans (see *Impersonators* in this chapter) is taking some much-deserved days off, an impressive roster of talent uses his theater. Missing *Everybody Loves Raymond?* Well, when Ray Romano performs in Vegas, he usually does it here. Jay Leno has stopped by to test out material for *The Tonight Show,* and a variety of other comics and music stars have been on the schedule. The 1,250-seat theater is nothing special, but you didn't come here to look at the walls, did you?

HOUSE OF BLUES

3950 Las Vegas Blvd. S. (at Mandalay Bay), 702/632-7600, www.hob.com

Map 1

The acts are slightly lower in stature than those found at the bigger venues (and, in fact, than those found at many other HOBs around the country). Anthrax, Sum 41, Johnny Lang, and Al Green are a few recent performers. But if you see somebody you like on their schedule, this is a pretty good place to see them. The audience gets up close—depending on the act and the seating arrangement, patrons are usually no more than about 40 feet from the stage—and the place has great acoustics and sound, especially for rock shows.

THE JOINT

4455 Paradise Rd. (at the Hard Rock), 800/473-7625, www.hardrockhotel.com

Map 4

The owners of the Hard Rock have announced

The Colosseum at Caesars Palace

plans to build an all-new Joint that can accommodate up to 2,000 people for the roster of big-name acts that play here. The existing Joint—an 8,000-square-foot barn of a room with really uncomfortable banquet seats brought in for shows—is being converted into more casino space. Whichever place is in business when you visit, this is the venue to see acts like David Bowie, Green Day, Metallica, and the Black Eyed Peas, all of whom "rocked the joint."

MANDALAY BAY EVENTS CENTER

3950 Las Vegas Blvd. S. (at Mandalay Bay), 877/632-7400, www.mandalaybay.com

Map 1

There's almost nothing exciting to say about this place except that it hosts some really great acts. The 12,000-seat arena is like most other sport and concert arenas in America, meaning it's huge and totally inappropriate acoustically for a music venue. But that's what concertgo-ers have to put up with when they want to see the kinds of huge, spectacle-sized concerts that play places like this. Then again, if the performance is good enough, that airplane hangar effect won't matter so much. I saw Bette Midler's millennium concert here and I don't remember complaining about the acoustics. They also regularly host big-time boxing and other arena sporting events here.

MGM GRAND GARDEN ARENA

3799 Las Vegas Blvd. S. (at MGM Grand), 877/880-0880, www.mgmgrand.com

Map 1

See Mandalay Bay Events Center above, only across the street and with 17,000 seats. Seriously, it's a big arena that hosts huge concerts (Barbra Streisand, Cher, The Rolling Stones, Britney Spears, etc.) and equally huge sporting events (boxing, motocross, etc.). What else do you really need to know?

ENTERTAINMENT

MGM GRAND HOLLYWOOD THEATRE
3799 Las Vegas Blvd. S. (at MGM Grand),
877/880-0880, www.mgmgrand.com
Map 1

When David Copperfield is in town, this is where he usually sets up shop. The 740-seat theater is an intimate affair, smaller even than most showrooms in town, so you can get up closer. A favorite with stand-up comics and smaller-draw acts (Dennis Miller, Howie Mandel, Carrot Top, Chris Isaak, Tom Jones), the theater features a variety of seating choices, including traditional round booths and long tables plus regular theater-style seating and round buffet-style tables.

ORLEANS ARENA
4500 W. Tropicana (at the Orleans), 800/675-3267,
www.orleanscasino.com
Map 4

About the only difference between this arena and the ones listed previously is the number of seats, in this case 9,000. Oh, and this is the home to the local minor-league hockey team, so anyone desperate for some semblance of a live sporting event can check that out. Otherwise, the standard fare includes mostly B-level and below concert acts (they have a lot of country-western stars here), other types of sporting events, and, occasionally, Ringling Bros. and Barnum & Bailey.

ORLEANS SHOWROOM
4500 W. Tropicana (at the Orleans), 800/675-3267,
www.orleanscasino.com
Map 4

With just over 800 seats in standard theater-style rows, this showroom is the primary destination for performers who are lovingly referred to by some as "nostalgia acts." Others call them has-beens, but that's probably just being mean. Now, this doesn't mean they don't put on a heck of a show, but anyone hoping to see Beyoncé will be disappointed. Because I made that has-been comment, I'll refrain from naming names, but generally the roster includes singers from the 1950s, '60s, '70s, and '80s.

THE PEARL
4321 W. Flamingo Rd. (at The Palms), 702/942-7777,
www.palmspearl.com
Map 4

Opened in 2007, this 2,500-seat theater is done with a classic opera house layout (rounded main seating section, mini-balconies) but the decor is as distinctly modern as you would expect from this hotel, purveyor of all things hip and cool for Vegas. It was the main location for the MTV Music Awards in 2007, and had its grand opening with a concert by Gwen Stefani and more than 200 sky-tracker lights (good enough for the record books).

THOMAS & MACK CENTER
4505 S. Maryland Pkwy, 702/895-3900,
www.thomasandmack.com
Map 4

This venue is a typical, big barn-like arena (up to 19,000 seats, depending on the event) that hosts a wide variety of sports (University of Nevada Las Vegas athletics, boxing, etc.) and concerts (big spectacle shows). Its biggest event of the year is the National Finals Rodeo in December.

Nightlife

Navigating the treacherous waters of the Vegas nightlife scene is not always easy. There are a lot of sharks and riptides along the way, so here are a few things to keep in mind before you put on your dress-to-impress duds.

Cover charges are virtually impossible to keep track of. Instead of putting prices that will most likely be out-of-date or not applicable on the day you visit, I've put a notation in each listing to give you a guidepost. **Cover** indicates there is almost always a cover charge at the establishment. How much it is depends on the night and/or the event, but be aware that most popular clubs and bars charge at least $20 just to get in the door (and often significantly more). **Cover Varies** means that there may or may not be a cover, depending on what day of the week or what time of day you arrive. These are the places that usually charge something on the weekends or after, say, 11 P.M., but may not on other days of the week or earlier in the evening. The charges themselves also vary, anywhere from $5–40 per person. **No Cover** means that they usually don't charge a cover, but may on special occasions. Call or visit the websites to find out specifics for the particular day you want to visit.

Because this is a 24-hour town, most nightclubs don't get really busy until late, often after midnight. But that doesn't necessarily mean you should show up that late. Getting there early means shorter waits in line and a better chance that the surly doormen will let you in without a hassle. Most clubs also keep going until the last person drops with no set closing time. That's why many of the listings indicate things like "Opens at 10 P.M." instead of a formal open and close time.

All of the high-profile (and many of the smaller) clubs have some form of a dress code. Sometimes it's not set in stone and is more up to the discretion of the doormen, but, in general, stay away from shorts, tank tops, baseball caps, wallet chains, flip-flops or open-toed sandals, and any kind of ratty jeans unless they are really expensive ratty jeans. This mostly applies to men. Women, especially if they are con-

sidered "hot," can get away with wearing just about anything they darn well please.

Finally, a note about personal safety: Be aware. While it may be true that "What Happens in Vegas, Stays In Vegas," it doesn't give you license to throw every inhibition and care to the wind. There are as many, if not more, predators here in Las Vegas as there are in any other major city, so don't let that hot stranger hand you a drink (get it directly from the bartender), keep your drink in your hand the entire time, don't leave the club with people you don't know, and don't be too shy to tell the security staff if someone is bothering you. These are simple, basic rules that don't mean you can't have a good time, but will keep you safe while you are.

DANCE CLUBS
BODY ENGLISH
4455 Paradise Rd. (at the Hard Rock), 702/693-5000, www.bodyenglish.com
HOURS: Opens Fri.-Sun. at 10 P.M.
COST: Cover Varies
Map 4

Patrons descend a dimly lit staircase toward the pumping house beat to enter into another world—one where all the women are beautiful, the men are *GQ* models, and things like reality are checked at the door. This is the kind of nightclub seen in spy movies, done with an over-the-top gothic decor that doesn't feel at all over the top. It's two levels of hedonism, so grab a drink and head to the dance floor. Lines to get in are usually hours long and cover can go upwards of $30.

EMPIRE BALLROOM
3765 Las Vegas Blvd. S., 702/737-7376, www.empireballroom.com
HOURS: Opens Tues.-Wed. at 10 P.M., Thurs.-Sat. at 1 A.M., Sun. at 10:30 P.M.
COST: Cover
Map 1

Unlike most of the hot nightclubs, this one is not located inside a multibillion dollar hotel and

POOL IS THE NEW COOL

Going to a nightclub in Las Vegas can be a pressure-filled experience. You have to find the right outfit to wear, the right accessories to set things off, the right people to hang out with, and the right attitude to compete with. Now imagine all of that pressure in a bathing suit. Normal-bodied people like me are shuddering all over the globe.

But in Vegas, the hottest new trend is to turn the pools at the hotels into daytime nightclubs, complete with lounge-like seating, bars, live DJs, and, in at least one case, dance floors that float in the water. Unlike the normal business hours when the pools are restricted to only hotel guests, these so-called Pool Clubs are open to anyone willing to pay the cover charge and take their chances with the other hard-bodies.

I'm probably exaggerating a little on the clientele, but only a little. You have to trust me when I tell you that most of these places are populated by people who look like they stepped right off the pages of *Vogue* and onto a lounge chair near you. If you are even the slightest bit insecure, save yourself some angst and go have a drink somewhere less populated with supermodels.

The most successful of the bunch extends the brand of the very popular nightclub with **Tao Beach** (The Venetian, 3355 Las Vegas Blvd. S., 702/492-3960, www.taolasvegas .com). With private cabanas, lounge chairs, a DJ, and lots of alcohol, this daytime party spot is blowing all the others out of the water as of this writing. It's open daily from 10 A.M. to sunset and later on Saturday and Sunday nights when the pool area transforms into an outdoor nightclub complete with that floating dance floor I mentioned. Cover ranges from $20 to 30.

Bare Pool Club (The Mirage, 3400 Las Vegas Blvd. S., 702/791-7442, www.mirage. com) is similar in theme to Tao except it's only open Thursday through Monday from 11 A.M. to 7 P.M. It's a small chunk of The Mirage's beautiful pool area, so it's not quite as cool as getting to use the whole thing, and it will cost you between $10 and $40 to get in.

Bare Pool Club at The Mirage

COURTESY MGM MIRAGE

The **Venus Pool Club** (Caesars Palace, 3570 Las Vegas Blvd. S., 702/731-7110, www. caesarspalace.com) is a little more classy than Tao or Bare, but no less entertaining, with the requisite dance music, comfy furnishings, and lots of fun in the sun. It's open Wednesday through Sunday from 9 A.M. until 6 P.M., and the cover is $20.

The last two clubs are once-a-week affairs, but probably take the cake for the highest concentrations of the genetically blessed (and a few famous faces, to boot). **Ditch Fridays** (The Palms, 4321 W. Flamingo Rd., 702/938-9999, www.palms.com) takes over The Palms' always-grooving pool area on Fridays from noon until 7 P.M. (cover $20) while you can nurse your hangover with a tropical drink poolside at **Rehab** (Hard Rock Hotel, 4455 Paradise Rd., 702/693-5000, www .hardrockhotel.com, Sun. 11 A.M.-7 P.M., cover $15 to 30).

casino. So, of course, that means that the cover charges and drink prices are lower, the crowds are less fiercely competitive and intimidating, and the surroundings are slightly less pretentious, right? Well, no. But what you do get at the Empire is a slightly more eclectic lineup of guest DJs and the occasional concert that, depending on who is playing, make it worth the few extra steps outside of your hotel. The Thursday through Sunday "after hours" parties (is there such a thing as "after hours" in Vegas?) are crazy popular.

HOUSE OF BLUES: LATE NIGHT

3950 Las Vegas Blvd. S. (at Mandalay Bay), 702/632-7600, www.hob.com
HOURS: Opens Fri.-Sat. at 11 P.M.
COST: Cover Varies
Map 1

After they put away the southern fried food and all of the chairs and tables are tucked safely in a closet somewhere, House of Blues turns into a fun festival of a night spot. Live DJs crank the tunes (often retro in flavor) and the crowd (often a few years older than the usual club-goers) starts to shake whatever their mama gave them. There is virtually zero attitude here—a welcome relief from the obnoxious "I'm prettier than you are" places up the street.

JET

3400 Las Vegas Blvd. S. (at The Mirage), 702/693-8300, www.mirage.com
HOURS: Opens Fri., Sat., and Mon. at 10:30 P.M.
COST: Cover
Map 2

After suffering for years without a trendy nightclub while the rest of The Strip sneered at them in much the same way that certain nightclub-goers will sneer at you if you aren't wearing the right brand of jeans, The Mirage finally stepped up to the plate in 2006 and introduced Jet. The multiroom facility is not as over-the-top design-wise as some of the other dance clubs (muted browns and reds, soft lighting, low-ish ceilings), but the fact that you can wander around and experience a variety of musical styles (from deep house to hip-hop) makes this the mini-mall of dance halls. And I actually mean that in a good way.

MOON

4321 W. Flamingo Rd. (at The Palms), 702/942-6832, www.n9negroup.com
HOURS: Opens Thurs.-Sun. at 11 P.M.
COST: Cover
Map 4

Because two super-popular nightclubs weren't enough, The Palms added Moon in 2006 on top of their second hotel tower and triumphed yet again in this hyper-competitive market. The place is done with a moon theme, supposedly, but it looks more like a shiny disco ball exploded with mirrors, white surfaces, and silver bling everywhere you look. They even give you an opportunity to view the club's namesake with multiple outdoor balconies and a retractable roof! The music varies from current to retro, even in the same set, making the vibe distinctly party-like in a mix-tape kind of way.

POLLY ESTHER'S

2000 Las Vegas Blvd. S. (at the Stratosphere), 702/889-1980, www.pollyestherslv.com
HOURS: Opens Wed.-Sat. at 10 P.M.
COST: Cover
Map 3

So you say you like Donna Summer, Madonna, Destiny's Child, and Kelly Clarkson? Have I got a club for you! Polly Esther's combines four time-traveling themed rooms in one space. The namesake room features a bar shaped and painted like the Partridge Family bus while '70s hits blast on the light-up dance floor; a giant Pac-Man screen hangs over the '80s-themed Culture Club room; a replica of OJ's Bronco spices up Nerve Ana, the '90s room; and a modern, ultra-lounge flavor surrounds Suite 2000 with more current music.

◀ PURE

3570 Las Vegas Blvd. S. (at Caesars Palace), 702/212-8806, www.purelv.com
HOURS: Fri.-Tues. 10:30 P.M.-4 A.M.
COST: Cover Varies
Map 2

At more than 36,000 square feet, this is the biggest nightclub in Las Vegas, and on most weekend nights every square inch of it is

ENTERTAINMENT

packed with people. There are four sections: the main club portion with a huge dance floor and huger bar; a quieter but still fun ultra-lounge section; a gigantic outdoor patio with a separate DJ, bar, and private cabanas overlooking The Strip; and the Pussycat Dolls Lounge, covered separately in this chapter. Most of it is done in glaring white, but it's not as stark as it sounds. Besides, you'll be having too much of a good time to care about the wall color.

RAIN

4321 W. Flamingo Rd. (at The Palms), 702/942-6832, www.n9negroup.com

HOURS: Thurs. 11 P.M.–5 A.M., Fri.–Sat. 10 P.M.–5 A.M.

COST: Cover

Map 4

The Palms is home to many of this city's hottest hot spots and Rain, located on the ground floor, is just one of high-energy nightclubs on-site. If you watched MTV's *Real World: Las Vegas,* you may remember the place. The design is stunning, with water walls and flames making the room almost as much fun to look at as the people who are partying there. Speaking of which, this is a crazy-popular club and the competition to get in and get noticed is fierce. Be prepared to wait in line and pay for the privilege.

RUMJUNGLE

3950 Las Vegas Blvd. S. (at Mandalay Bay), 702/425-8981, www.mandalaybay.com

HOURS: Opens daily at 11 P.M.

COST: Cover Varies

Map 1

If George of the Jungle had his own nightclub, it might look something like this hot spot. Fire effects on the walls light up the safari, which is not as cloying as it sounds in print—"subtle" probably isn't the right word for a place with walls of fire, but it's not as heavy-handed as you might expect. And what about the other wildlife? It's all here with a super-hot dance floor and live DJ (often accompanied by percussionists), dancers, video screens, and fashionable attendees. There's something slightly more

Studio 54 at the MGM Grand

laid-back about this place, perhaps because it doubles as a restaurant, so people looking for less of the nightclub-type pressures should put this one on their to-do list.

STUDIO 54

3799 Las Vegas Blvd. S. (at MGM Grand), 702/891-7254, www.studio54lv.com

HOURS: Opens Tues.–Sat. at 10 P.M.

COST: Cover

Map 1

Some people (like me) dislike this club for its high prices, too-small dance floor, long lines, and "Look at those shoes, what were you thinking?!" attitude. But I have to admit, while I enjoy a good club, I am not a devotee of the genre and there are people who swear this is *the* best dance club in the city. I swear there are other places that do it better, but 54 is always packed, so they must be doing something right. I did like the great old photos of the original New York Studio 54's glory days. That was cool. God, I'm old.

◖ TAO

3355 Las Vegas Blvd. S. (at The Venetian),
702/388-8338, www.taolasvegas.com
HOURS: Opens Thurs.-Sat. 10:30 P.M.
COST: Cover
Map 2

The mantle of "hottest club" is passed around like plates at a buffet, but as of this writing, this is *the* place in a town filled with them. The post-apocalyptic Asian decor evokes a feeling of Chairman Mao's bunker with a dance floor that's dark and moody, with caverns scattered along a maze-like layout. The lines to get in are insanely long, the prices at the door and the bar are painfully high, and the crowd is the epitome of nightclub chic in ways both good and bad. So, of course, for the appreciators of the genre, this is the number one spot for partying until dawn.

TRYST

3131 Las Vegas Blvd. S. (at Wynn Las Vegas),
702/770-3375, www.wynnlasvegas.com
HOURS: Opens Thurs.-Sun. at 10 P.M.
COST: Cover
Map 3

When Wynn Las Vegas first opened, this club was called La Bete, French for "the beast," complete with big beasty statues and a vaguely hell-inspired design. It didn't do well (surprise), so they redid the joint, getting rid of the devil-may-care decor and turning it into a more luxurious, dramatic, and romantic spot that could live up to its new moniker. What you'll find here is not significantly different than most other nightclubs, except it seems to draw a more well-heeled crowd, owing mostly to the upscale hotel in which it is located. You'll also find a more well-heeled price tag, with cover charges around $30 for men.

ULTRA-LOUNGES

DOWNTOWN COCKTAIL ROOM

111 Las Vegas Blvd. S., 702/880-3696,
www.downtowncocktailroom.com
HOURS: Opens daily at 5 P.M.
COST: No Cover
Map 5

As part of the effort to bring a wide variety of bars, clubs, and honky-tonks to the Downtown area, this place fills a hole that may not have necessarily needed to be filled. It is, by design, a trendy ultra-lounge concept with rich, plushy furniture and cool lighting that would not be at all out of place on The Strip. The good news is with cheaper prices and a much friendlier atmosphere, this is the ultra-lounge for people who don't like ultra-lounges. The question is whether that's a big enough market to turn this cool club into a hot spot.

GHOSTBAR

4321 W. Flamingo Rd. (at The Palms), 702/942-6832,
www.n9negroup.com
HOURS: Opens daily at 8 P.M.
COST: Cover
Map 4

When people like Janet Jackson and Britney Spears go to hang at a cool ultra-lounge, this is the one they often pick, although you shouldn't let that scare you away. Located on the top floor of The Palms tower, it's got a stunning view of The Strip from a giant outdoor patio while, inside, the cool blues and low-slung furnishings offer an intimate place to get your groove on. Cover and drink costs are very high and those not wearing the latest couture will get sneered at, but exclusivity comes at a price.

IVAN KANE'S FORTY DEUCE

3950 Las Vegas Blvd. S. (at Mandalay Bay),
702/632-9442, www.fortydeuce.com
HOURS: Opens Wed.-Sun. at 10 P.M.,
Shows 11:30 P.M.-4 A.M.
COST: Cover Varies
Map 1

One of several burlesque clubs, Ivan Kane's Forty Deuce is probably the most fun. It's a tiny spot tucked away in an almost unnoticeable corner, but inside, the hip-hop–influenced sounds and cool, clubby vibe are thrilling. Four times a night, the DJ stops his turntables and the live jazz combo breaks out into retro-smooth music (*The Pink Panther* theme is a fave) to back up the lithe dancers who strut their stuff on a narrow walkway stage and the bar. A lingerie boutique just outside lets patrons embrace their inner striptease artist.

MIX

3950 Las Vegas Blvd. S. (at Mandalay Bay),
702/632-7777, www.mandalaybay.com
HOURS: Opens daily at 5 P.M.
COST: Cover Varies
`Map 1`

The main appeal of this lounge is the unparalleled scenic opportunities. Located more than 40 stories up at the top of Mandalay Bay's newer tower, the outdoor patio is a stunner and the floor-to-ceiling windows inside extend all the way into the bathrooms (toilets with a view!). Done in varying shades of black (that's a joke, by the way), the few colorful details (a red VIP balcony, a white martini bar) really pop, and the crowd of mostly moneyed, young business types seems to be having a good time. Be warned: Prices almost hurt—$8 for a bottle of water?

THE PLAYBOY CLUB

W. Flamingo Rd. (at The Palms), 702/942-7777,
www.palms.com
HOURS: Opens daily at 8 P.M.
COST: Cover
`Map 4`

It seems only fitting that the rebirth of the Playboy Club brand should happen in Vegas. Taking Hef's original concept and reinventing it for the new millennium means the club-like mansion details are modernized by stacked-stone fireplaces with flat-panel TVs above them and contemporary takes on things like leather winged-back chairs. The result is a perfect blend of Vegas and Playboy cool, especially with the bunny-tailed waitresses and dealers in the boutique casino.

PUSSYCAT DOLLS LOUNGE

3570 Las Vegas Blvd. S. (at Caesars Palace),
702/731-8323, www.purelv.com
HOURS: Opens daily at 5 P.M., Shows Tues.-Sat.
8:30 P.M.-midnight
COST: Cover Varies
`Map 2`

Direct from their hugely successful Los Angeles club (and a frighteningly successful recording career), the Pussycat Dolls have their own hot spot inside the Pure nightclub at Caesars. It's a whimsical space with two stages: one traditional and one in the round with a Pussycat-sized martini glass at the center. Unlike at other burlesque clubs, the Dolls throw in some singing on top of their dance moves, making it a much less prurient experience and more like naughty cabaret.

REVOLUTION LOUNGE

3400 Las Vegas Blvd. S. (at The Mirage),
702/693-8383, www.mirage.com
HOURS: Opens daily at 6 P.M.
COST: Cover Varies
`Map 2`

Created as an accompaniment to the Beatles-themed "Love" show playing at the hotel, this tribute to all things Abbey Road does not limit itself by merely throwing up a few posters of the lads and playing music by Ringo and the gang. Instead, the British Invasion details are modernized and turned retro-hip with go-go–clad servers and psychedelic-era design themes accompanying a wide mix of musical styles, from old school to new wave and just plain old new. You don't have to love (or even like) The Beatles to have a good time here.

TABÛ

3799 Las Vegas Blvd. S. (at MGM Grand),
702/891-7183, www.tabulv.com
HOURS: Opens Tues.-Sun. at 10 P.M.
COST: Cover Varies
`Map 1`

In my humble opinion, this is the best of the Las Vegas ultra-lounges, offering a big enough room to allow some freedom of movement, but broken up into intimate spaces allowing for up-close-and-personal encounters. There's a certain uninhibited spirit here that seems to be lacking at other "I'm too cool for the room" lounges, resulting in a higher fun quotient overall. The staff is one of the nicest I've ever experienced at a trendy club, so guests don't walk into it all intimidated by the surly doormen. Great music, too!

VOODOO LOUNGE

3700 Las Vegas Blvd. S. (at the Rio), 702/777-7777,
www.riovegasnights.com
HOURS: Opens nightly at 10 P.M.
COST: Cover Varies
Map 4

This swank bar/lounge offers dramatic views
from atop the hotel tower, complete with a
giant, multilevel outdoor patio and a sweeping exterior staircase that had to be airlifted
onto the building. That patio is fun as long as
it isn't windy, in which case you'd better hope
you brought extra-strength hairspray to keep
the 'do in check. Inside is another large bar,
lots of plushy booths and chairs, and live entertainment to keep the party rocking. There's
generally a more grown-up crowd here—but,
as usual, you better be dressed to impress or
risk the wrath of snooty doormen.

BARS

ART BAR

1511 S. Main St., 702/437-2787
HOURS: Daily 2 P.M.–6 A.M.
COST: No Cover
Map 5

The neighborhood is not the best in town
and the bar itself offers nothing terribly special in terms of the things a bar usually does,
but it is the Art part of its name that makes
this one noteworthy. Located in the eternally
burgeoning (but never quite burgeoned, it
seems) Arts District, the walls are adorned
with paintings by local artists, providing
an interesting opportunity for them and a
unique environment for you. The installa-
tions rotate often, so you never know if you
are drinking under a future masterpiece or
something destined for a yard sale.

BAR AT TIMES SQUARE

3790 Las Vegas Blvd. S. (at New York–New York),
702/740-6969, www.nynyhotelcasino.com
HOURS: Open 24 hours
COST: No Cover
Map 1

Dueling pianos are the big-ticket draw here,
turning what could've been just another

place to sit back and lounge into a boister-
ous party spot nightly. The place is tiny, so
personal space is at a minimum, and cigars
are omnipresent, so those with an aversion
to that particular aroma may want to stand
outside and listen. Those willing to put up
with the downsides, though, will have a lot of
fun. The entertainers are not only great pianists, but terrific at working the crowd into a
sing-along frenzy.

BEAUTY BAR

517 Fremont St., 702/598-1965, www.beautybar.com
HOURS: Opens Wed.–Fri. at 6 P.M., Sat.–Tues. at 9 P.M.
COST: Cover Varies
Map 5

The super-cool Beauty Bar brand got its
name in New York and Los Angeles, so with
a pedigree like that, it could have easily found
its way into any hotel on The Strip. Instead,
they chose a location on Fremont Street
Downtown, which in many ways hews
more closely to the hipster vibe the place is
known for. Done as a beauty parlor gone
mad, the atmosphere is congenial and more
intelligent than your average bar, with actual
conversations heard regularly that go beyond
"Dude, check out the (insert offensive term
here) on her!"

BLONDIE'S LAS VEGAS

3663 Las Vegas Blvd. S. (at The Miracle Mile Shops),
702/737-0444, www.blondiesvegas.com
HOURS: Daily 9 A.M.–2 A.M.
COST: No Cover
Map 2

Because the casinos would prefer you do your
football watching in their race and sports
books, preferably while making sizeable wagers, the sports bar concept in Vegas is a relative rarity. But the venerable Blondie's chain
of just such establishments will allow you to
catch up on the sport of your choice on more
than 30 television screens backed up by a full
bar, plenty of pub grub, and lots of convivial
hooting and hollering to go along with whoever scored whatever in whichever game you
happen to be watching.

ENTERTAINMENT

ENTERTAINMENT

CARAMEL

3600 Las Vegas Blvd. S. (at Bellagio), 702/693-7111,
www.caramelbar.com

HOURS: Daily 5 P.M.–4 A.M.

COST: No Cover

Map 2

For anyone tired of the boring gin and tonic or rum and coke, Caramel has the antidote, with a menu of out-there concoctions that combine drinking and dessert. The Oreo Shake has Van Gogh Vanilla, Godiva White Chocolate liqueur, and the namesake cookies whipped into a frothy mixture that's like spiking your Dairy Queen Blizzard with booze. Other cocktails come with caramel- or chocolate-coated glasses or dressed with jawbreakers, rock candy, and other sweet temptations. A small menu of appetizers adds a good touch of sour to the sweet, and the room sparkles with a warm, caramel color scheme to accompany that sugar and alcohol buzz.

CARNAVAL COURT

3475 Las Vegas Blvd. S. (at Harrah's), 702/369-5000,
www.harrahs.com

HOURS: Daily noon–2 A.M.

COST: No Cover

Map 2

Located just outside the main entrance to Harrah's along The Strip is this al fresco party spot in the middle of a small shopping gallery. There's a big bar under a merry-go-round canopy where the "flair" bartenders toss bottles with the best of them, plus a dance area and stage that features some great local bands. If you're lucky, you may catch Carnaval regular Cook E. Jarr, a wacky hybrid of lounge lizard and '70s reject who seems to be in on the joke, but you're never quite sure. Best on spring or fall nights since it's outdoors.

CORAL REEF LOUNGE

3950 Las Vegas Blvd. S. (at Mandalay Bay),
702/632-7777, www.mandalaybay.com

HOURS: Open 24 hours

COST: No Cover

Map 1

For more grown-up crowds and entertainment, people often head to hotel lounges, and the Coral Reef Lounge at Mandalay Bay is one of the best of the breed. It's near the back of the casino, adjacent to restaurant row, and features a fully stocked bar and live entertainment nightly for the small dance floor. Usually, the crowd is thirtysomething and up, all just looking for a place to have fun that doesn't involve hour-long waits in line with intimidating, thin model types. The cover bands are not name-brand, but are almost unfailingly talented.

COYOTE UGLY

3790 Las Vegas Blvd. S. (at New York–New York),
702/212-8804, www.coyoteuglysaloon.com

HOURS: Daily 6 P.M.–4 A.M.

COST: Cover Varies

Map 1

Which came first, the movie or the bar? As in the film, this place has a roadhouse saloon–style environment and lots of pretty female bartenders who can drink, dance, and quite possibly fight better than every guy in the place. They spray water on the crowd, jump up on the bar to do some boot-scootin' boogie moves, and generally take the concept of a quiet drink and shred it to pieces. Most men will probably love this place, while most women will probably alternate between being amused and horrified, but it really can be a kick for those in the right frame of mind.

CROWN AND ANCHOR PUB

1350 E. Tropicana Ave., 702/739-8676,
www.crownandanchorlv.com

HOURS: Daily 24 hours

COST: No Cover

Map 4

American versions of British pubs are often poor excuses to drink dark beer, throw some darts, and scream at a soccer match. So God bless the Queen for a place like the Crown and Anchor, which has all of that but somehow manages to be much less obnoxiously Yankee about the whole thing. The crowd is generally local and young (owing to its location near UNLV) and while things can get rowdy, they remain civilized just like the best Brits always do. Grab a Newcastle, order some fish and chips, and see what those hooligans at Manchester United are up to now.

DOUBLE DOWN SALOON

4640 Paradise Rd., 702/791-5775,
www.doubledownsaloon.com
HOURS: Open 24 hours
COST: No Cover
Map 4

Aggressively anti-trendy, the Double Down has one primary rule: You puke, you clean. Seriously, it's on a sign. Although not quite as rowdy and anti-Vegas establishment as they say, it's still more real than any of the over-processed boxes on The Strip. There's a big bar with video poker, pool tables, pinball machines, and a jukebox that doesn't carry Sinatra or Spears (think The Clash or Rancid instead). Since it's close to the UNLV campus, a lot of alternative college-age types come here, but despite the sometimes intimidating atmosphere, it's a friendly place to get away from the Vegas hype.

FONTANA LOUNGE

3600 Las Vegas Blvd. S. (at Bellagio), 702/693-7111,
www.bellagio.com
HOURS: Sun.-Thurs. 5 P.M.-1 A.M., Fri.-Sat. 5 P.M.-2 A.M.
COST: Cover varies
Map 2

Jeans and T-shirts are frowned upon here, with most women wearing evening-out ensembles and guys wearing slacks. But that has more to do with the fact that this is not a destination bar; it's more of a pit stop on the road to fancy restaurants or high-priced shows. Which doesn't mean you can't enjoy yourself while you're here. Live entertainment keeps things going on the small dance floor, the bar is expensive but has everything imaginable, a small snack menu satisfies the munchies, and a big outdoor patio provides the best viewing spot in the entire hotel for the Bellagio Fountains show.

THE GRIFFIN

511 Fremont St., 702/382-0577
HOURS: Opens Mon.-Sat. at 5 P.M., Sun. at 9 P.M.
COST: No Cover
Map 5

Done with a cozy English castle motif, The Griffin is one of the coolest spots in town for its total lack of pretention, even though it probably deserves to have lots of it. There are comfortable nooks and crannies everywhere, allowing for a secret rendezvous or friendly conversation plus a blazing fireplace and lively common areas encouraging the mingling and mixing. Live entertainment spices up the proceedings even further on some nights, but the crowd of mostly young, urban professionals seems satisfied without it.

HOGS AND HEIFERS

201 N. 3rd St., 702/676-1457
HOURS: Daily 1 P.M.-4 A.M.
COST: No Cover
Map 5

Coyote Ugly on The Strip took its name from the movie, but took its concept from Hogs and Heifers, the rowdy working-class bar in New York with take-no-prisoners female bartenders who prove they can be just as tough (if not tougher) than the men downing the shots. The Vegas version is less raucous than either the Gotham original or the Ugly offshoot, but is a perfect antidote to the falseness that is often found, well, everywhere in this town. Strong drinks, tough chicks, biker guys, and a gift shop—now that's a bar.

HOOKAH LOUNGE

4147 S. Maryland Pkwy., 702/731-6030,
www.hookahlounge.com
HOURS: Mon.-Thurs. 5 P.M.-1 A.M., Fri.-Sat. 5 P.M.-3 A.M.
COST: No Cover
Map 4

Take a seat in their dark den of a room (rich tapestries and Arabian details abound) and you'll be greeted by the Hookah Master, who will patiently explain what a hookah is to the uninitiated (a large, water-filled tobacco pipe). Next, he'll guide you through the fine Egyptian tobacco selection, including more than 20 on the menu (from traditional Turkish blend to strawberry or pistachio). Then you light up, dude. No, it's not like that at all. Since there's no paper burning, it's less like smoking and more like taking a deep breath of scented air. Oddly enjoyable, even for open-minded nonsmokers. A full bar accompanies.

LORRAINE'S BOOTLEGGER LOUNGE
7700 Las Vegas Blvd. S., 702/736-4939, www.bootleggerlasvegas.com
HOURS: Open 24 hours
COST: No Cover
Map 4

On most nights, this is just another low-key lounge with a bar, video poker, and live entertainment nightly. But on Mondays, this is one of the most raucous places in town, drawing both Vegas celebrities and regular people in droves. What, you may ask, brings them out? Karaoke. Local entertainer Kelly Clinton hosts the night and apparently she knows everyone in the Vegas showrooms, so a lot of them come here to unwind. Sheena Easton and Clint Holmes are semi-regulars, but some much bigger names show up on occasion. It's like an im-promptu Rat Pack show without Frank and Sammy, but still fun.

NAPOLEON'S
3655 Las Vegas Blvd. S. (at Paris Las Vegas), 702/946-7000, www.parislv.com
HOURS: Sun.-Thurs. 6 P.M.-2 A.M., Fri.-Sat. 5 P.M.- 3 A.M.
COST: No Cover
Map 2

Way back at the end of the shopping arcade is this small gem of a bar made even more appealing by the addition of dueling piano entertainment. The space is all Parisian bordello red, with plenty of comfy seating either at the bar or in lounge spaces around the room. The full bar serves up all the standard cocktails and plenty of specialty drinks at prices that aren't exactly cheap, but aren't as expensive as more trendy places in town. And, of course, the pianists spice up the at-

Napoleon's at Paris Las Vegas

mosphere nightly with a fun show designed for audience involvement.

PEPPERMILL'S FIRESIDE LOUNGE
2985 Las Vegas Blvd. S., 702/735-7635
HOURS: Open 24 hours
COST: No Cover
`Map 3`

One look around at the dark, clubby atmosphere straight out of the 1960s and you can almost envision the Rat Pack sitting around, swapping stories, and getting into trouble. The lounge is filled with low leather booths and a funky fire-pit conversation area that makes you want to put on a leisure suit and just go, baby, go. Big tropical drinks are the specialty here, but you may find yourself longing for something more classic—a martini, perhaps, or whiskey on the rocks. Yeah, that's cool.

PETE & SHORTY'S BOOK & BAR
115 E. Tropicana Ave. (at Hooters Casino Hotel), 702/739-9000, www.hooterscasinohotel.com
HOURS: Open 24 hours
COST: No Cover
`Map 4`

Acting as the race and sports book for Hooters, Pete & Shorty's is really just a small bar where you can sit, have a beer and some high-cholesterol snacks, watch a game, and maybe, if you feel like it, place a wager. It's that low-pressure atmosphere combined with affordable prices that make this one worth visiting if you're looking for a comfortable place to watch some sports. One warning for my fellow Iowans: They may bill their sandwich as being just like a Maid-Rite, but sadly, it isn't. Those who have no idea what a Maid-Rite is will have to trust me.

PETROSSIAN BAR
3600 Las Vegas Blvd. S. (at Bellagio), 702/693-7111, www.bellagio.com
HOURS: Open 24 hours
COST: No Cover
`Map 2`

There's a certain breed of people who elevate the consumption of alcohol to an art form—people who don't order anything as gauche as a "drink," allowing only "cocktails" to pass their lips. Those people consider Petrossian a Mecca of sorts. The bartenders here have won awards for their almost scientific construction of the finest liqueurs and freshest ingredients, turning mere alcohol into masterpieces. Afternoon tea (2–5 P.M. daily), caviar and other elegant eats, and premiere vodka tastings add to the exclusive allure. The prices are staggering, but connoisseurs should definitely come here.

SAND DOLLAR BLUES LOUNGE
3355 Spring Mountain Rd. (at Polaris), 702/871-6651
HOURS: Open 24 hours
COST: Cover Varies
`Map 4`

Once legendary as one of the few places in Vegas for listening to authentic blues bands, Sand Dollar was also widely known as a slightly scuzzy hangout for the biker-gang crowd. After closing it for a while, new owners spruced up the place and got rid of the "bad" element, but kept the "joint" flavor with a rotating schedule of blues acts playing nightly. For fans of the music, there's no better place in town—and it now feels a lot safer. The cover almost never rises above $5 and the drink prices are shockingly low.

SIDEBAR
201 N. 3rd St., 702/259-9700
HOURS: Sun.-Thurs. 5 P.M.-midnight, Fri.-Sat. 5 P.M.-2 A.M.
COST: No Cover
`Map 5`

The struggling Downtown area is pinning its hopes on places like this—casual little bars that make you want to sit down and relax for a while and maybe, just maybe, forget about all of that commotion down on The Strip. All of the new watering holes play their own roles and Sidebar's is as the connoisseur of the bunch. Classic and contemporary mixed drinks in stemmed glasses are the direction you should go in, or maybe choose from the satisfying wine list. Whatever your poison, savor it here instead of paying twice as much for a watered-down version on The Strip.

TOBY KEITH'S I LOVE THIS BAR & GRILL

3475 Las Vegas Blvd. S. (at Harrah's), 702/369-5000, www.harrahs.com

HOURS: Sun.-Thurs. 11:30 A.M.-2 A.M., Fri.-Sat. 11:30 A.M.-3 A.M.

COST: No Cover

Map 2

Despite the ever-increasing popularity of country music, you won't find a lot of it on The Strip. Maybe that's why there are often lines out the door to get into country superstar Keith's honky-tonk at Harrah's. With gigantic posters and memorabilia from the singer, the place is as heavily themed as the Hard Rock, but more focused, I suppose. Live country bands perform often and there is a small dance floor for boot-scoot-boogying, if you are so inclined. A full bar keeps the good times rolling, but my experience with the restaurant portion of the program has been less than stellar. Stick with the boozin' and the croonin'.

TOP OF THE WORLD

2000 Las Vegas Blvd. S. (at the Stratosphere), 702/380-7711, www.topoftheworldlv.com

HOURS: Sun.-Thurs. 10 A.M.-12:30 A.M., Fri.-Sat. 10 A.M.-1:30 A.M.

COST: No Cover

Map 3

There's absolutely nothing special about what they serve or how they serve it here. It's a lounge. Thing is, it's a rotating lounge at the top of a 1,000-foot tower with floor-to-ceiling glass windows offering dizzying views of all of Las Vegas and most of southern Nevada. There's nothing quite like sipping a cocktail while watching the world slowly turn by underneath. It's also a great place to go while your crazy sister is making herself sick on the thrill rides nearby. Note: There is no cover, but there is a $10 tower admission charge.

GAY AND LESBIAN

Las Vegas does not have the kind of vibrant gay, lesbian, bisexual, and transgender scene that other major cities do. There is no West Hollywood, Castro, or Chelsea here, settling instead for loose groupings of bars and nightclubs scattered around the city. Because gay and lesbian culture, for good or ill, seems to center around the bars and clubs, the few good ones listed here aren't the only ones to choose from. There are more than a dozen around town, each offering a slightly different experience and each catering to a slightly different audience. Although there are no strictly lesbian bars as of this writing, women are most welcome at **Krave,** which draws a very eclectic crowd. Transgendered folks, drag queens, bears, leather aficionados, and other sub-segments of the GLBT community can find places that are more comfortable for them by doing a little research (please see *Gay and Lesbian Travelers* in the *Essentials* chapter).

A primary area of interest is **Paradise Road at Naples Drive,** a couple of blocks south of the Hard Rock Hotel. Several of the major clubs plus a cafe/bookstore are here. Since they are the closest to The Strip, these businesses draw a much heavier percentage of tourists than locals, which can be a good or bad thing. Just don't expect to get lots of insider Vegas advice from the person standing next to you; it's more likely than not that he or she is visiting just like you.

Alternatively, the **Sahara Commercial Center** (953 E. Sahara Ave.) is a strip mall of sorts with several gay businesses, including bars, a bookstore, and a couple of, ahem, "gentlemen's clubs." This is a decidedly more low-rent (but not dangerous) section of town and the establishments here reflect that, drawing a bigger local crowd without a lot of the pretentious attitude endemic to the fancier places.

June and July are the traditional months for Pride celebrations, but it's just too hot in Vegas to put on leather or drag and go marching down the street. No, there's a pool and cocktails to be had during those months, so instead, the much more sensible Las Vegas GLBT community hosts the annual pride events in May, when temperatures are more moderate. Activities and parties vary from year to year (as do the specific dates), but expect a series of Vegas-centric celebrations, dances, and a parade and festival, usually in early to mid-May. For more information, visit the **Southern Nevada Association of Pride** website at www.lasvegaspride.org or call 702/615-9429.

There are also periodic circuit parties in Las Vegas, often in May or October (again, it's all about the weather, people). Check with **Atlantis Events** (800/6-ATLANTIS or 800/628-5268, www.atlantisevents.com) or circuit party impresario Jeffrey Sanker (310/860-0101, www.jeffreysanker.com) to see if there's anything interesting happening when you're going to be in town.

BADLANDS SALOON
953 E. Sahara Ave., 702/792-9262
HOURS: Open 24 hours
COST: No Cover
Map 4

Line-dancing fans really only have one choice in Las Vegas: here at the Badlands. It's not much to look at, but it gets the job done with a decent-sized dance floor, a full bar (with several weekly beer and liquor busts), video poker, pool tables, and a really friendly atmosphere. Note there are several other gay establishments in the Sahara Commercial Center where this is located, including a few other bars, a small cafe, and some adult entertainment. None are really worth going out of the way for, but if you're in the neighborhood, you might pop your head in to see what's going on.

BUFFALO
4640 Paradise Rd. 702/733-8355
HOURS: Open 24 hours
COST: No Cover
Map 4

This is Las Vegas's attempt at a leather bar, but it's really just a place that draws the kinds of crowds who usually frequent leather bars in their hometowns. It's a little on the dingy side, which is to be expected in this genre, but not sleazy in any way (which may be disappointing to some). The smallish bar serves up drinks that are cheaper than those found almost anywhere in town and there's video poker, pool tables, dart boards, and other amusements to keep patrons entertained, but no dance floor. Regular beer busts are a big draw.

GIPSY
4605 Paradise Rd., 702/731-1919, www.gipsylv.net
HOURS: Opens daily at 9 P.M.
COST: Cover Varies
Map 4

For years, this has been the premier gay nightclub in Vegas, drawing mostly tourists to its high-energy dance floor. They've toned down the silly archeological-dig theme that used to draw giggles and concentrated on making the place more plush, with a VIP area overlooking the dancers and a separate, glassed-in lounge for more intimate conversations. Lots of shows (from drag to strip) liven various nights, but it's primarily the dancing, the drinking, and the pretty people that draw the crowds.

GOOD TIMES
1775 E. Tropicana Ave., 702/736-9494
HOURS: Open 24 hours
COST: No Cover
Map 4

This place has a bit of a split personality, with one side of the establishment acting as a friendly neighborhood lounge (lots of conversation areas, big bar, video poker) and the other as a high-energy dance club (dance floor, loud music, sweaty people). Since it's a bit off The Strip, more locals frequent this place than tourists and the overall attitude is a lot friendlier than in some of the bigger clubs. It's located in the same strip mall as the Liberace Museum.

KRAVE
3667 Las Vegas Blvd. S. (at the Miracle Mile Shops), 702/836-0830, www.kravelasvegas.com
HOURS: Opens Tues.-Sun. at 8 P.M.
COST: Cover Varies
Map 2

Co-created by gay circuit club impresario Jeffrey Sanker, Krave is the city's first "alternative" club on The Strip. The inside is stunning, with a huge dance floor, go-go platforms, lots of booths and conversation areas, and an overall design that looks like somebody spent too much time with their Cher catalogue (gothic touches abound). This is the see-and-be-seen gay club in town (mostly gay, some lesbian, a few curious or

ENTERTAINMENT

just tolerant), so dress to impress and maybe stop at the hotel gym beforehand. Note: While it's attached to the mall, the entrance is on Harmon Avenue about half a block east of The Strip.

PIRANHA

4633 Paradise Rd., 702/379-9500,
www.piranhalasvegas.com
HOURS: Opens daily at 8 P.M.
COST: Cover Varies
Map 4

There are actually two nightlife options here including Piranha, the high-energy dance club, and 8½, the cool ultra-lounge. The former is as glam as any of the straight clubs with a walk-through aquarium, VIP booths and tables, a killer sound system for the dance floor, and plenty of men (mostly tourists) to invite onto it. The naughtily titled ultra-lounge portion heads the other direction, all swank and laid-back with plenty of cushy places to sit and groove to a more mixed set of beats. There are several other gay bars just steps away (Gipsy, Buffalo, etc.), so you have a plenty of options even if you never leave this building.

STRIP CLUBS

When it comes to strip clubs, misconceptions and misinformation abound. If you're planning a trip to one, here are a few things you should know.

While the dancers may touch customers in certain, highly restricted ways, it is forbidden for customers to touch them. Doing so will get you a new best friend called a bouncer who'll quickly show you to the curb.

The strip clubs inside Las Vegas city limits operate under a different set of rules than the ones outside its boundaries (most of The Strip and surrounding neighborhoods are *outside* of city limits), which are regulated by Clark County. The Vegas clubs are a little less restrictive, allowing more dancer-to-patron contact than the Clark County clubs. Let's just say there are people to whom that difference is important. A quick call to the strip club of your choice will tell you if they are beholden to Vegas rules or Clark County ones.

If a strip club serves alcohol, by law the dancers can only go as far as topless and a G-string. If the club doesn't serve liquor, they can get totally nude. The only exception to this rule is a club up on the north side of town that has been around so long it was grandfathered into the laws that came later, but that club is so far away and so sleazy that I can't recommend it.

Despite what you may have read or heard, prostitution is illegal in all of Clark County, including Las Vegas. That means two things: Don't offer more money for more than a lap dance and, if suggested, say no thanks. Making or accepting such an offer will get you a free room for the night, but there is no maid service and the beds are much less comfortable.

CHEETAH'S

2112 Western Ave., 702/384-0074, www.cheetahslv.net
HOURS: Open 24 hours
COST: Cover
Map 4

Multiple stages both large and small liven what is considered by most to be one of the friendliest strip clubs in town. Couples are welcome and the crowd tends to skew younger, so there's more of a party vibe than a sit-around-and-leer one. A full bar charges too much for drinks, but that's typical. Because of the booze, dancers can only go as far as topless and, as a general rule, there's a more "wholesome" brand of stripper here. Lap dances start at $20. And, by the way, yes, this is the place used in the movie *Showgirls*.

DÉJÀ VU SHOWGIRLS

3247 Industrial Rd., 702/894-4167, www.dejavu.com
HOURS: Mon.-Sat. 11 A.M.-6 A.M., Sun. 6 P.M.-4 A.M.
COST: Cover
Map 3

Fantasy is the watchword here, with the ladies doing more than just a bump and grind. These are full-on choreographed and costumed bits. It's sort of like *Flashdance*, only they take off all of their clothes. Yes, the strippers strip all the way here, so nary a drop of alcohol is served. The atmosphere is a little on the sleazy side, which may be a good thing or a bad thing, depending upon your point of view. Lap dances start at $20.

GIRLS OF GLITTER GULCH
20 Fremont St., 702/385-4774, www.glittergulchlv.com
HOURS: Daily 1 P.M.-4 A.M.
COST: No Cover
Map 5

In 2007, the Downtown stalwart got a million-dollar makeover, turning what had been a simple and relatively tasteful little club into a more glam experience. The good news is they kept the things that made them worthy of inclusion in the first place. First, there's no cover. There is a two-drink minimum, with drinks starting around $8, but it still costs less to get in this place and have a couple of cocktails than elsewhere. Second, it's located right on the Fremont Street pedestrian mall, so its high-profile location forces them to be a little less tacky. Dancers are topless, and lap and table dances start at $20.

LITTLE DARLINGS
1514 Western Ave., 702/366-0145, www.dejavu.com
HOURS: Mon.-Sat. 11 A.M.-6 A.M., Sun. 6 P.M.-4 A.M.
COST: Cover
Map 4

More than just a strip club, Little Darlings offers a wide variety of entertainment. There's an adult store stocked with videos, private booths, fantasy rooms, and, of course, the more traditional stages and stripper poles. It's all very naughty and yet not as deviant as it sounds. Dancers are fully nude, and both lap and private dances start at $20. There is no alcohol served, but the cover (usually $20) includes soda and juice.

PLAY IT AGAIN SAM
4120 Spring Mountain Rd., 702/876-1550
HOURS: Open 24 hours
COST: Cover Varies
Map 4

If there is such a thing as a respectable strip club, it's probably this one. Done more as a restaurant than a den of iniquity, it offers a full menu for dinner and an all-you-can-eat lunch buffet, the latter free with a two-drink minimum (the drinks are not cheap). Because of the less prurient surroundings, Play It Again draws larger groups, including a lot of women with their husbands and boyfriends in the crowd. This can provide a much less threatening experience for strip club newbies. VIP rooms allow for private dances, starting at $20. There's a full bar, so the dancers can only go topless.

SAPPHIRE
3025 S. Industrial Ave., 702/796-0000, www.sapphirelasvegas.com
HOURS: Open 24 hours
COST: Cover Varies
Map 3

It only makes sense that if they were going to build the world's largest strip club, it would be in Las Vegas. With more than 71,000 square feet in a converted athletic club, the facility has three huge stages in the main area, a separate 400-seat showroom, 13 skyboxes, private party rooms that can accommodate up to 1,000 people, several lounges, and private VIP booths and rooms. Epic is a good word for it. It's very classy and modern, so the sleaze factor is practically zero. Stages host both women (topless) and men, with lap dances starting at $20.

SEAMLESS
4740 S. Arville St., 702/227-5200, www.seamlessclub.com
HOURS: Open daily 24 hours
COST: Cover
Map 4

Deciding which category to put this place in was a tough call. During the day and early evening, it's a classic and very classy strip club, complete with multiple stages, catwalks, full bar, and plenty of topless women on display. But late at night into the wee hours, the stages disappear, the tops go on, the dance floor comes out, and the whole place becomes a high-energy nightclub. Since the lines between the city's night and strip clubs has been blurring lately (witness burlesque dancers and an anything-goes ethos), perhaps this was the next logical step. The good news is that they do both things very well here, so you should enjoy yourself no matter which experience you choose.

ENTERTAINMENT

TREASURES
2801 Westwood Dr., 702/257-3030,
www.treasureslasvegas.com
HOURS: Mon.-Thurs. noon-6 A.M., Fri.-Sun. 24 hours
COST: Cover
Map 4

Well, of course, if they have the biggest strip club in Vegas, they have to have the most expensive one also. Done like a palatial Beverly Hills country club, the place is packed with marble, intricately carved wood balustrades and trim, sculpture and paintings, and deep, plushy furnishings. A full restaurant (that could be at home at Bellagio) serves everything from shrimp cocktail to filet mignon, and champagne and caviar flow with abandon. Oh yeah, there are strippers, too. Dancers go topless and employ every theatrical trick in the book to class up the shows (dry ice?). Warning: It's usually crazy expensive here.

The Arts

MUSEUMS
◖ ATOMIC TESTING MUSEUM
755 E. Flamingo Rd., 702/794-5151,
www.atomictestingmuseum.org
HOURS: Mon.-Sat. 9 A.M.-5 P.M., Sun. 1-5 P.M.
COST: $12 adult; $9 child (7-17), senior, military, student with ID; free for children under 7
Map 4

In the 1950s, the Nevada Test Site (NTS) was the primary U.S. location for above-ground nuclear testing (complete with mushroom clouds) and it all happened about 60 miles from Vegas. This marvelous facility examines the impact of the NTS, both on Vegas and the world, with an exhaustive collection of photographs, videos, interactive displays, timelines, memorabilia, and more. It's endlessly fascinating from both a scientific and human standpoint, celebrating the achievements while acknowledging their toll on mankind. Many of the people who run the facility worked at the NTS, so their passion for the subject is tangible. An art gallery, a research library, and a gift shop are also on the premises.

Liberace Museum

AUTO COLLECTIONS
3535 Las Vegas Blvd. S. (at Imperial Palace),
702/794-3174, www.autocollections.com
HOURS: Daily 9:30 A.M.-9:30 P.M.
COST: $6.95 adult; $3 child (3-12), senior; free for children under 3
Map 2

Car enthusiasts will love it, but even those who can't tell a Lincoln from a Hyundai can still appreciate gorgeous automotive art. Exhibits change often, but they usually have a wide range of collectibles—1930s Duesenbergs are a specialty, classic '50s tail fins, hot '60s muscle cars, and so on. Many of these beauties are for sale, so if something catches your fancy, you can whip out your checkbook and take it with you. Be sure to check the website for free admission coupons.

LAS VEGAS NATURAL HISTORY MUSEUM
900 Las Vegas Blvd. N., 702/384-3466, www.lvnhm.org
HOURS: Daily 9 A.M.-4 P.M.
COST: $7 adult; $6 senior, military, student with ID; $3 child (3-11); free for children under 3
Map 5

Most people think of Las Vegas as strictly slot machines and showgirls, but in doing so, they overlook the rich ecological, zoological, and geological details of the area. This fine, if decidedly un-fancy, facility examines the history, present, and future of the ground, the plants, and the animals that have inhabited the area since well before the first Elvis impersonator. A permanent overview of local natural history (from dinosaurs on up) is accompanied by rotating exhibits. Everything is done well, so anyone interested in such topics will enjoy it.

◖ LIBERACE MUSEUM
1775 E. Tropicana Ave., 702/798-5595, www.liberace.org
HOURS: Mon.-Sat. 10 A.M.-5 P.M., Sun. noon-4 P.M.
COST: $12.50 adult; $8.50 senior, student; free for children under 10
Map 4

The giant tile wall of sheet music ("Beer Barrel Polka") and the even more giant neon pink piano outside are just the first clues of how absolutely, deliriously wacky this shrine to the late, great Liberace is. Anyone who remembers him should know he was in on the joke, so the wink factor here is appropriately high yet totally respectful. Visitors can see his mirrored pianos, fur- and rhinestone-covered costumes, furnishings, cars, and a host of other memorabilia, most of which is bejeweled within an inch of its existence. Look to see if they have the Riviera Hotel opening night menu on display. I donated that! A full gift shop and small café complete the package.

LIED DISCOVERY CHILDREN'S MUSEUM
833 Las Vegas Blvd. N., 702/382-3445, www.ldcm.org
HOURS: Tues.-Sun. 10 A.M.-5 P.M.
COST: $8 adult; $7 child (1-17), senior, military
Map 5

This is a great place for parents to bring their kids for several reasons. First, and most importantly, are the educational opportunities to be had. Young ones can learn about everything from healthier eating to how tornadoes form. Second, the exhibits are all hands-on, providing the exact kind of interactive experience that engages children. Last, there's so much to see and do here and so many places to run around and play, the kids will wear themselves out and parents might get a little peace and quiet on their Vegas vacation. But you didn't hear it from me.

MADAME TUSSAUD'S CELEBRITY ENCOUNTER
3355 Las Vegas Blvd. S. (at The Venetian), 702/862-7800, www.madametussaudslv.com
HOURS: Daily 10 A.M.-10 P.M.
COST: $24 adult, $18 senior, $15 student, $14 child (6-12), free for children under 6
Map 2

Note they don't call it a wax museum anymore. Part of that is marketing, but the old moniker certainly didn't do this Vegas version justice. Several rooms house rotating exhibits of the eerily lifelike creations, divided into themes (movie stars, sports stars, Las Vegas entertainers, etc.). Interactive exhibits (Marry George Clooney! Play poker with Ben Affleck! Get judged by Simon Cowell!) are often a hoot. I find it hard to justify the more than $20 ticket price, but I'm really creeped out by these things anyway. Others should feel like they got their money's worth.

GALLERIES
BELLAGIO GALLERY OF FINE ART
3600 Las Vegas Blvd. S. (at the Bellagio), 702/693-7871, www.bgfa.biz
HOURS: Sun.-Thurs. 10 A.M.-6 P.M., Fri.-Sat. 10 A.M.-9 P.M.
COST: $15 adult; $12 senior, student with ID
Map 2

Steve Wynn may have moved his collection to his eponymous hotel up the street, but the Bellagio has continued to draw crowds and raves among the art set for mixing up its schedule with old masters and new favorites. Exhibits change regularly, but there's as much chance of seeing Monet as Martin (as in Steve, the actor

ENTERTAINMENT

VEGAS GOES TO THE MOVIES

Vegas has long been a favorite of moviemakers, and why not? It's one of the most extravagant backdrops ever created and offers an almost instant atmosphere of excitement and sinful decadence.

But not all movies that feature Vegas as a setting are created equal. Many movies have failed to capitalize on the unique energy the city has to offer, making it seem like nothing more than a neon-lit studio-lot set.

So I sat down and developed the following list of movies that I think best showcase Vegas in all of its glory, debauchery, seediness, or wacky fun. In alphabetical order:

Bugsy (1991) – Warren Beatty, Annette Bening

Barry Levinson's epic about mobster Benjamin "Bugsy" Siegel, the man widely (and incorrectly) credited with creating Las Vegas, was nominated for 10 Academy Awards and won two. Although some of the historical details are a little fuzzy at best – the Flamingo was not the first hotel on The Strip, as the film would have you believe – it still offers a stunning portrait of the early days of Vegas in a way that no other movie has ever done.

Casino (1995) – Robert De Niro, Sharon Stone

Another renowned director, Martin Scorsese, with another stunning cast, examines the mob's effect on Las Vegas, this time in the fabulous 1970s, before all of the big corporations came to town and kicked all the "goodfellas" out. Check out the amazing period detail (shag carpeting and smoky mirrors), and if you look closely, you'll see Vegas Mayor Oscar Goodman in a small role.

Diamonds Are Forever (1971) – Sean Connery, Jill St. John

Sean Connery's last turn as James Bond puts him on the trail of a Howard Hughes–like billionaire bent on ruling the world, but that's not really important for this list. What is important is the fact that much of the film was shot in and around Vegas, with classic shots of old-glory hotels, such as the Tropicana, Las Vegas Hilton, and Circus Circus, among others. This is a fantastic time capsule of the city.

Honeymoon in Vegas (1992) – James Caan, Nicholas Cage

Much of this film was shot at Bally's, and it's interesting to see the neighborhood pre-Bellagio and Paris. But it's really the end scene, featuring Cage as one of a group of skydiving Elvis impersonators parachuting in over the city that establishes this as one of the best uses of Vegas in the movies ever. Plus, it stars Sarah Jessica Parker, and you just have to give extra credit for that.

Leaving Las Vegas (1995) – Nicholas Cage, Elisabeth Shue

Cage returned to Vegas a few years later and left with an Oscar for his turn as an alcoholic reaching the very depths of despair while finding some measure of redemption with a prostitute played by Shue. It's certainly not

---

who is also an accomplished painter). The room is nicely done, if a bit overly dramatic at times (the focus should always be on the art and not the walls that it hangs upon).

ⓒ GUGGENHEIM HERMITAGE MUSEUM

3355 Las Vegas Blvd. S. (at The Venetian), 866/484-4849, www.guggenheimlasvegas.org
HOURS: Daily 8:30 A.M.–7:30 P.M.
COST: $19.50 adult, $15 senior, $12.50 student with ID, $9.50 child (6–12), free for children under 6
Map 2

Of the two major art galleries on The Strip, this is by far the most impressive. The heritage of both New York's famed Guggenheim and Russia's equally impressive Hermitage mean that the power of those institutions is behind these exhibits. Many of the artworks on display here (they change regularly) have never been seen outside of St. Petersburg, lending an air of exclusivity and providing a rare privilege for true art lovers. Sure, entry is expensive, but it's a lot cheaper than finding a good connecting flight through Moscow. The hall is simple, elegant, and totally fades into the background, allowing the masterpieces to speak for themselves.

one of the more cheery movies ever made, but the way the filmmakers captured the undercurrent of desperation that runs through the city is astonishing.

Mars Attacks (1996) – Jack Nicholson, Annette Bening

You'll note this list is about the best representations of Vegas in the movies, which doesn't necessarily mean that they're good movies – a point proven by this entry. Although this Tim Burton comic book-inspired film about Martians attacking the Earth has a certain camp appeal, it's the Vegas settings – including a battle in the Neon Graveyard – that earn it a place on this list. After all, what other film includes the implosion of a real Vegas hotel (the Landmark)?

Ocean's 11 (1960) – Frank Sinatra, Dean Martin

I know I'm risking the ire of Vegas movie buffs by saying this, but you all secretly know it's true: The original Ocean's 11 is a pretty terrible movie. As evidence, I point to the part where Sammy Davis bursts into song with a group of garbage men. 'Nuf said. But from a time-capsule perspective, no other film comes close to capturing the mood, the vibe, and the sheer spectacle that was Vegas during the Rat Pack era. Plus, seeing current and long-gone classics, like the Sahara, the Desert Inn, and the Flamingo, at the height of their swinging glory is an absolute joy.

Ocean's 11 (2001) – George Clooney, Brad Pitt

In 40 years will we look back on this remake with the same fondness with which we view the original? Hard to say, since none of us can imagine hotels like Bellagio, The Mirage, and the MGM Grand not being there the way that the Desert Inn and Sands have disappeared since the Frank and Dino version. But this is still sheer popcorn-movie fun and features some of the coolest, most glamorous, sexiest shots of Las Vegas ever committed to film. Here, the city becomes another character, almost as entertaining as the rest of the star-studded cast.

Showgirls (1995) – Elizabeth Berkley, Kyle MacLachlan

Remember what I said about bad movies? Yes, Showgirls is widely considered to be not just a bad movie, but one of the worst movies ever made. The good news is that it's so bad it almost becomes good again – a campy, catty, and lewd look at the supposed life behind the headdresses. This is a terrific example of the seamy side of Vegas.

Viva Las Vegas (1964) – Elvis Presley, Ann-Margret

Shot mostly on location in and around Las Vegas, this is another trifle of a film that managed to capture the city like a moving postcard. The cotton-candy colors and vibrant energy of the 1960s are in full view here, along with what has become the unofficial theme song of the city: "Bright light city gonna set my soul, gonna set my soul on fire..."

CINEMA
CENTURY ORLEANS 18
4500 W. Tropicana (at the Orleans), 702/227-3456, www.orleanscasino.com

HOURS: Daily, showtimes vary
COST: $9.50 adult; $6 senior, child (3-11)
Map 4

It puzzles me why any tourist would want to go see a movie while they are in Las Vegas, but if you happen to be visiting the weekend that the next *Spider-Man* opens, the theaters at the Orleans could be a good place to see it. This complex features 18 screens showing first-run movies with stadium seating and THX and Dolby Digital surround sound, and was recently upgraded for digital movie projection capability.

LUXOR IMAX THEATER
3900 Las Vegas Blvd. S. (at Luxor), 800/288-1000, www.luxor.com

HOURS: Daily, showtimes vary
COST: $10 and up
Map 1

This big-screen movie format has been around for years, but it has only started gaining mass acceptance in the last few, with 3-D

ENTERTAINMENT

versions of things like *Polar Express* drawing in crowds. The Luxor IMAX Theater has been upgraded many times to keep up with technology advancements and shows a variety of 2-D and 3-D films on its seven-story screen. The chances of seeing 3-D *Star Wars* films here are pretty low, but they've still got some amazing stuff, like a trip down the Nile or an up-close encounter with some hungry sharks.

Note: At press time the Luxor was undergoing an extensive remodeling and this attraction may be closing.

UNITED ARTISTS SHOWCASE 8

3769 Las Vegas Blvd. S. (at the Showcase Mall), 702/740-4511, www.uatc.com

HOURS: Daily, showtimes vary

COST: $9.50 adult; $8.50 military, student; $5.75 senior, child (under 12)

Map 1

Located on the upper level of the Showcase Mall right next to the MGM Grand, this is the only first-run theater complex on The Strip. There are only eight screens and ticket prices are as high here as they are anywhere in Las Vegas, but if you don't feel like going over to the Orleans (where the theaters are nicer), this is your only option. Screens are smaller, seating and sound systems aren't as good, but, hey, you're the one who couldn't wait a couple of days to see the next *Spider-Man*.

SHOPPING

Las Vegas may not have the biggest mall in the world (Canada still has that honor), but it has one of the most successful. The Forum Shops at Caesars Palace earns more money per square foot of retail space than just about any other mall in the country. The industry average is around $350 per square foot. The Forum Shops takes in more than $1,400 per square foot.

It's obvious that people come to Vegas to spend, and not just on slot machines and buffets. According to research from the Las Vegas Convention and Visitors Authority, shopping often outranks gambling as a primary reason for people to visit Las Vegas. The average visitor to Las Vegas spends about $140 per trip on shopping alone, about twice as much as they do on sightseeing and shows.

Some of the biggest names in retail can be found on or near The Strip, with stores such as Nordstrom, Saks Fifth Avenue, Lord & Taylor, Tiffany, Gucci, and more. Of course, like most things in Las Vegas, shopping is not cheap. The T-shirt you pick up at The Gap or the pajamas you want from Victoria's Secret will probably cost you more here than they will at the same stores in your local mall. But when you step out of The Gap in your hometown, you won't see the Grand Canal in Venice running through the center of the plaza. Shopping is an experience in this town and that kind of experience is going to cost you extra. But you can save some money if you visit the shops located away from the heart of The Strip.

But whatever you might want, from the stratospheric-priced items of Rodeo Drive–style boutiques to the 99-cent Elvis key chain, from the latest in high-tech gadgetry to antiques, Vegas has it all—and then some.

LAS VEGAS NEWS BUREAU/LVCVA

HIGHLIGHTS

LOOK FOR  TO FIND
RECOMMENDED SHOPPING.

[Best Brain Food: Take a break from all of the Vegas inanity with a literary side trip to **The Reading Room** (page 145).

[Best Gifts: Your mother-in-law doesn't want an "I kissed Elvis" T-shirt. She wants chocolate. Bring her back something from **The Chocolate Swan** and you'll be in her good graces forever (page 145).

[Best Shop for Your Pup: Make a stop at the decadent pet supply boutique **Lush Puppy** and your favorite pooch will be your best friend for life (page 145).

[Best Mall: Malls without canals and singing gondoliers just aren't as fun. Get in the shopping spirit at the **Grand Canal Shoppes** (page 151).

[Best Imports: From biscuits to bangers, the shelves and freezers at **British Foods, Inc.** are packed with delights from across the pond (page 154).

[Best Music Store: Record stores are disappearing faster than you can say iTunes, so enjoy the old-school delights of **Zia Records** (page 154).

[Best Place to Buy a Piece of Vegas: Come on! You know you want your very own blackjack table. Get one at **Gamblers General Store** (page 156).

[Best Bargains: Name-brand merchandise at significantly reduced prices is the draw at the **Las Vegas Premium Outlets** (page 156).

The Reading Room

COURTESY OF MGM MIRAGE

South Strip | Map 1

BOOKS
❚ THE READING ROOM
3930 Las Vegas Blvd. S. (at Mandalay Place),
702/632-9374
HOURS: Daily 8 A.M.-11 P.M.

It's rare to find an independent bookstore, well, anywhere these days. Most have been eaten up by the big chains. So what a delight to see this fantastic little store tucked into a corner of a mall in a Vegas casino. Go figure! This is not the place to pick up the latest John Grisham novel (although they probably have it); instead, the selection here veers more toward the harder-to-find, including a big selection of limited editions and rarities. Get something good to read on the plane home! They also have a speaker series, author appearances and signings, discussion groups, and other special events.

CHOCOLATES
❚ THE CHOCOLATE SWAN
3930 Las Vegas Blvd. S. (at Mandalay Place),
702/632-9366, www.chocolateswan.com
HOURS: Daily 8 A.M.-midnight

It's hard to buy stuff from here and not eat it before reaching the door. After all, their fine chocolates, pastries, and Italian ice cream are the best in Las Vegas—and among the best in the world, in my humble opinion—and considering how much chocolate I eat, you need to listen to me. But those with willpower should consider some of their really great take-home and gift ideas. Choices include a wide variety of prepackaged items or an individual selection of sweets (the milk-chocolate caramels are out of this world) that they'll package in an elegant box, complete with a ribbon.

M&M WORLD
3785 Las Vegas Blvd. S. (at the Showcase Mall),
702/736-7611, www.mymms.com
HOURS: Sun.-Thurs. 9 A.M.-11 P.M., Fri.-Sat. 9 A.M.-midnight

So you say you're looking for an M&M bank where you pop in a coin and it pops out a hand-ful of rich, candy-coated chocolates, huh? Have I got news for you. The M&M World is more than just a store, it's a full-fledged experience, complete with interactive displays, a museum, short films, and more, but it's the gift shop area that makes this place most intriguing. You can find M&Ms in every color of the rainbow, a huge selection of M&M logo items, and a big selection of parent company Ethel M. Chocolates. Watch your waistline.

PET CARE
❚ LUSH PUPPY
3930 Las Vegas Blvd. S. (at Mandalay Place),
702/740-2254, www.lushpuppyonline.com
HOURS: Daily 10 A.M.-11 P.M.

You know that look your dog gave you when you walked out of your house to go to the airport to come to Vegas? I know you feel guilty, but a stop at Lush Puppy will take care of any hurt feelings at home. This extravagant boutique features the kind of over-the-top pet accessories that you'd normally associate with Paris Hilton's dog, including bejeweled collars, leather and animal print clothing, fancy bowls and treats to put in them, beds that are more comfortable than mine, and even dog-themed art. It's all silly expensive, but if the pets are going to PETCO, it's only because they don't know about this place.

SHOPPING MALLS
MANDALAY PLACE
3930 Las Vegas Blvd. S. (at Mandalay Bay),
702/632-9333, www.mandalayplace.com
HOURS: Sun.-Thurs. 10 A.M.-11 P.M., Fri.-Sat. 10 A.M.-midnight (store hours may vary)

There aren't a lot of stores in this unimaginatively designed (at least compared to other Vegas shopping malls) gallery, but what it lacks in quantity (a couple dozen stores, tops) it more than makes up for in quality. In addition to The Chocolate Swan, The Reading Room, and 55 Degrees wine store (highlighted in this chapter), you'll also find an art gallery, a Nike Golf store, a Davidoff cigar emporium, an upscale men's barber shop, a few restaurants, and a variety of apparel, jewelry, and gift boutiques. Bigger is not always better.

SHOWCASE MALL
3785 Las Vegas Blvd. S., 702/597-3122
HOURS: Vary by store

Calling this a mall is probably exaggerating things. There are really only a few outlets here, but they are notable enough to make the overall package worthy of inclusion. Plus, it's the place with the giant Coke bottle on the outside. That's the entrance to Everything Coca-Cola, a huge gift shop with pretty much anything with the Coke logo on it. Besides M&M World (detailed in this chapter), it houses the big video game arcade GameWorks, movie theaters, the half-priced, same-day Vegas show ticket service

Tickets2Nite, a food court with several fast-food–style outlets, and more.

WINE AND SPIRITS
55 DEGREES
3930 Las Vegas Blvd. S. (at Mandalay Place), 702-632-9373
HOURS: Sun.-Thurs. 10 A.M.-11 P.M., Fri.-Sat. 10 A.M.-midnight

Fifty-five degrees is apparently the temperature at which wine should be chilled. Okay, I'm not going argue with these folks because one step into their stunning store and it's obvious they know more about the subject than I do. Every type of wine and wine accoutrement (bottle openers, glasses, buckets, etc.) is available here, and their staff of experts can help guide clients to the perfect bottle. *Sideways* fans will love it here.

Center Strip   Map 2

ART
ENTERTAINMENT GALLERIES
3377 Las Vegas Blvd. S. (in the Grand Canal Shoppes), 702/866-6813, www.entertainmentgalleries.com
HOURS: Sun.-Thurs. 10 A.M.-11 P.M., Fri.-Sat. 10 A.M.-midnight

Pop culture is the celebration here with entertainment-themed art that may include a series of "Peanuts"-inspired prints, hand-painted movie posters, and even collections from famous names like Frank Sinatra. This is the place that Andy Warhol probably would have loved and despised at the same time, but his Campbell's Soup and Marilyn Monroe works would fit in perfectly here. Most of the works are very expensive, but there is a little something for almost every budget.

IMAGES OF NATURE
3667 Las Vegas Blvd. S. (in the Miracle Mile Shops), 702/731-0503, www.imagesofnaturewebstore.com
HOURS: Sun.-Thurs. 10 A.M.-11 P.M., Fri.-Sat. 10 A.M.-midnight

I'm a sucker for nature photography, so this store, filled with some fantastic examples of

the genre from Thomas D. Mangelsen, is a delight. Whether it's a grizzly bear cub nuzzling a signpost, a pod of bottle-nosed dolphins leaping as one out of the crystal blue water, or the majestic landscape of Africa, these rich pictures seem to open up and invite the viewer into the moment. Originals, prints, calendars, books, and more make the line accessible to everyone.

THE METROPOLITAN MUSEUM OF ART STORE
3663 Las Vegas Blvd. S. (at Miracle Mile Shops), 702/691-2506, www.metmuseum.org/store
HOURS: Sun.-Thurs. 10 A.M.-11 P.M., Fri.-Sat. 10 A.M.-midnight

It doesn't take a trip all the way to New York for a taste of what the famed Met Museum has to offer. True, they don't offer real Van Goghs, but the reproductions on sale here are of the highest quality. Framed prints and sculpture are the main lures, but they also have jewelry, books, posters, and more, with the proceeds going to help support the museum. Tell your neighbors it's real. They'll never know.

ONLY IN VEGAS

Come on, you can go to a Gap anywhere. Don't you want to shop in a place that is uniquely Vegas? The following stores are the best examples of the breed.

The Atomic Testing Museum Gift Shop (755 E. Flamingo Rd., 702/794-5151, www .ntshf.org, Mon.-Sat. 9 A.M.-5 P.M., Sun. 1 P.M.-5 P.M.) has a big variety of books and souvenirs relating to the above-ground nuclear testing that used to happen just outside of Vegas at the Nevada Test Site. In addition to the serious (books, videos, photographs), there's also a healthy dose of wacky, including mushroom cloud mouse pads and ties, plus the ultimate Atomic Age souvenir: the Albert Einstein action figure. I couldn't make this stuff up.

More traditional Vegas souvenirs can be found at **Bonanza Gift & Souvenir Shops** (2460 Las Vegas Blvd. S., 702/384-0005, 24 hours), located just across the street from The Sahara hotel and casino. The sign on the front says "World's Largest Souvenir Shop," and while I don't know who actually keeps track of such things, I'm willing to believe them because they've got almost every Vegas-themed knickknack and doodad here. Almost all of it is overpriced, cheap, and tacky, but isn't that what a good souvenir should be?

Speaking of tacky in a good way, you can't forget about the **Liberace Museum Gift Shop** (1775 E. Tropicana Ave. 702/798-5595, www .liberace.org, Mon.-Sat. 10 A.M.-5 P.M., Sun. noon-4 P.M.). Not only do they stock every CD

Bonanza Gift & Souvenir Shops

© RICK GARMAN/VERN GARMAN

the flamboyant entertainer ever made, but they also have rhinestone-studded caps and clothing, Liberace-emblazoned handbags and collectibles, and, of course, candelabras. Tell me you don't want a Liberace candelabra! You know you do.

Finally, Las Vegas glamour *can* be bought at **Serge's Showgirl Wigs** (953 E. Sahara Ave., 702/732-1015, www.showgirlwigs.com, Mon.-Sat. 10 A.M.-5:30 P.M.). Most of the collection consists of traditional, everyday-use hairpieces, but the showgirl part of the program is apparent in some of the more elaborate offerings. Sorry, headdress not included.

OH MY GODARD GALLERY

3663 Las Vegas Blvd. S. (at Miracle Mile Shops), 702/699-9099, www.michaelgodard.com

HOURS: Sun.-Thurs. 10 A.M.-11 P.M., Fri.-Sat. 10 A.M.-midnight

Michael Godard is a local Las Vegas artist who has gained worldwide recognition for his push-the-envelope artwork, most with a rock-and-roll Vegas aesthetic. Martini glasses and the things that accompany them are the recurring whimsical theme—olives at the Last Supper, for instance—but his framed prints, calendars, coasters, plates, and assorted doodads also feature flaming dice, roulette wheels, cards, and neon. Art snobs will have heart palpitations, but everyone else will love this stuff.

AUTOMOTIVE
EXOTIC CARS AT CAESARS PALACE

3500 Las Vegas Blvd. S. (in The Forum Shops at Caesars Palace), 702/735-7700, www.ecacp.com

HOURS: Sun.-Thurs. 10 A.M.-11 P.M., Fri.-Sat. 10 A.M.-midnight

Car nuts should put this place at the very top of

SHOPPING

their list. A full store of exotic car gear including Ferrari-emblazoned shirts, Lamborghini-covered caps, Porsche models, and McLaren key chains might very well be the closest most people will ever get to actually owning a piece of the exclusive nameplates. But it doesn't just stop at a store—there is a full showroom of exotic cars, classic muscle cars (Camaro, Barracuda, Mustang), and super luxury brands (Rolls, Bentley), plus this is the only authorized Koenigsegg dealer in the entire United States. The showroom costs $5 to enter, but it's worth it, and afterward you can get a picture of yourself in a Ferrari or play on one of the racing simulators. Get yourself in gear now!

BOUTIQUES
VIA BELLAGIO
3600 Las Vegas Blvd. S. (at Bellagio), 702/693-7111, www.bellagio.com
HOURS: Hours vary by store

There are fewer than a dozen stores in the shopping arcade at Bellagio, but you'd be hard-pressed to find a more exclusive collection anywhere outside of Rodeo Drive. Armani, Chanel, Dior, Gucci, Hermés, Prada, and Tiffany are a few of the names hanging above the doors, and while they may be out of the average shopper's price range, people with the credit card limits to afford it head here in droves. The rest of us can window-shop and celebrity-spot—this is where Ben Affleck took Jennifer Lopez out for a little jewelry shopping. You remember "Bennifer," don't you?

CLOTHING & ACCESSORIES
AGENT PROVOCATEUR
3500 Las Vegas Blvd. S. (in The Forum Shops at Caesars Palace), 702/696-7174, www.agentprovocateur.com
HOURS: Sun.-Thurs. 10 A.M.-11 P.M., Fri.-Sat. 10 A.M.-midnight

This exclusive U.K.-based purveyor of lingerie is well-known for their scandalous fashions, designed to put a smile on an estimated 90 percent of the male population. There are the typically lacy undergarments, but then they branch out in unexpected directions like a bridal collection, a line of maternity lingerie,

hosiery, beauty products, and more. The store is done like an old-fashioned bordello—perfect to get you in the mood to feel sexy.

BEN SHERMAN
3667 Las Vegas Blvd. S. (in the Miracle Mile Shops), 702/688-4227, www.benshermanusa.com
HOURS: Sun.-Thurs. 10 A.M.-11 P.M., Fri.-Sat. 10 A.M.-midnight

Representing the cutting edge of the British Invasion since the '60s, Ben Sherman clothiers has been the fashionable choice for the Carnaby Street crowd throughout the decades. With both men's and women's attire, shoes, accessories, and more, the focus here is definitely on the trendy and modern (read: young), but manages to be surprisingly affordable considering its heritage. Yes, you'll pay more for a classic polo than you will at your local K-Mart, but the quality and style are worth the extra few pounds—er, dollars—you'll shell out.

BETTIE PAGE BOUTIQUE
3667 Las Vegas Blvd. S. (in the Miracle Mile Shops), 702/636-1100, www.bettiepageclothing.com
HOURS: Sun.-Thurs. 10 A.M.-11 P.M., Fri.-Sat. 10 A.M.-midnight

The pin-up queen of the 1950s now has her own boutique in Vegas where you can indulge your exterior naughty girl in a line of Bettie-inspired clothing, shoes, belts, T-shirts (for men and women), and more. It's all infused with the naughty spank-me vibe that Page turned into an art form, but owing to its Eisenhower-era origins, there's nothing here that'll get you kicked out of the grocery store. Speaking of art, there is also a line of paintings and prints from renowned pin-up artist Olivia DeBerardinis, just in case you prefer to decorate your home in addition to your body.

H&M
3663 Las Vegas Blvd. S. (in the Miracle Mile Shops), 888/800-8284, www.hm.com
HOURS: Sun.-Thurs. 10 A.M.-11 P.M., Fri.-Sat. 10 A.M.-midnight

When I told a female friend of mine that an H&M store was opening in Vegas, there was an audible gasp on the other end of the line. This clothing retailer got its start in Sweden in 1947 and has since gone global with more than 1,400 stores in 28 countries, but only a couple of dozen in the entire United States. So what makes this place so noteworthy? Their fashions are remarkable for both their trend appeal and their prices, making it basically the IKEA of clothing stores. You can stock your entire closet with hip choices for less than you'll pay for a couple of shirts at Gucci and probably look better doing it.

NANETTE LEPORE

3500 Las Vegas Blvd. S. (in The Forum Shops at Caesars Palace), 702/893-9704, www.nanettelepore.com

HOURS: Sun.-Thurs. 10 A.M.-11 P.M., Fri.-Sat. 10 A.M.-midnight

I'm going to make a bit of a fool of myself here (like I haven't already), but if I were a girl and I had a good body and I had money, this is the place I would shop. Lepore's flighty and fun fashions have adorned celebrities like Sarah Jessica Parker and Eva Longoria (to name a couple), with sunny floral dresses, boldly colored tops and pants, and funky-chunky shoes. The total effect is one that simply puts a smile on your face and, I don't know, makes you want to skip through a fountain or something. Prices are very high, but if you're going to spend this kind of money, you should at least get something fun out of the deal.

PLAYBOY

3500 Las Vegas Blvd. S. (in the Forum Shops at Caesars Palace), 702/851-7470, www.playboystore.com

HOURS: Sun.-Thurs. 10 A.M.-11 P.M., Fri.-Sat. 10 A.M.-midnight

No, not everything here has bunny ears on it. Instead Playboy has extended its brand to include a full line of women's and men's clothing, home accessories, books, calendars, and more, all conveniently located in one fashionably funky store. The overall ethos, with or without the bunny ears, is Playboy cool and sexy with the fashions definitely trending toward things that are best worn tight on gym-toned bodies, and

the home decor mostly appropriate for rooms with wet bars, or maybe a grotto.

GAMBLING

SHOWCASE SLOTS

3663 Las Vegas Blvd. S. (at the Miracle Mile Shops), 888/522-7568, www.showcaseslots.com

HOURS: Sun.-Thurs. 10 A.M.-11 P.M., Fri.-Sat. 10 A.M.-midnight

If you're one of those types who has to be dragged from the casino kicking and screaming (I can identify), why not bring the casino home to you with your very own slot machine? Their store feature authentic, restored machines—antiques all the way up to the most modern slots and video poker, so there's pretty much something for everyone. They aren't cheap—newer models run a couple of grand. Plus, be aware that each state has different laws on what residents can own in their own homes. But if you can get over the hurdles, you'll never have to get dragged out of a casino again.

GOLF

IN CELEBRATION OF GOLF

3355 Las Vegas Blvd. S. (at the Grand Canal Shoppes), 702/699-9600, www.celebrategolf.com

HOURS: Sun.-Thurs. 10 A.M.-11 P.M., Fri.-Sat. 10 A.M.-midnight

With a name like this, the contents of the store are not a great mystery. It's all about football. No, actually it's all about golf, with virtually everything related to the sport on display: art, baby wear, ball cleaners, balls, chess sets, clothes, club covers, clubs, glasses, jewelry. I mean, really, I've heard about golf fanaticism, but this is way out there. It's all a mystery to me (unless there's a windmill involved), but for fans of the sport, this place can be your new Mecca.

HEALTH AND BEAUTY

ACCA KAPPA

3377 Las Vegas Blvd. S. (in the Grand Canal Shoppes), 702/733-0225, www.accakappa.com

HOURS: Sun.-Thurs. 10 A.M.-11 P.M., Fri.-Sat. 10 A.M.-midnight

Founded in Italy in 1869, this small boutique

carries a full line of bath and beauty care products including soaps, skin and hair care products for men and women, spa accessories, deodorants, colognes, and everything else you could possibly want to pamper your epidermis. The thing that makes this line truly special, though, is the fact that everything is made from natural ingredients and the company upholds a high level of environmental awareness, refusing to do any animal testing of its products and employing ecologically sound manufacturing processes. Make yourself feel good both inside and out.

KIEHL'S COSMETICS

3500 Las Vegas Blvd. S. (in The Forum Shops at Caesars Palace), 702/784-0025, www.kiehls.com

HOURS: Sun.-Thurs. 10 A.M.-11 P.M., Fri.-Sat. 10 A.M.-midnight

Kiehl's got its start in 1851 as an apothecary in New York City. More than 150 years later, they are still going strong there and in stores around the country, carrying a full line of skin and hair products, fragrances, suntan lotions and protections (a must in Vegas), men's grooming accessories, and even shampoo for your dog or horse. They use natural ingredients and eschew animal testing, so you can rest a little easier when you're applying that cleansing cream. While the prices are not exactly cheap, they are not as expensive as you'd expect considering the exclusivity factor.

SEPHORA

3355 Las Vegas Blvd. S. (at the Grand Canal Shoppes), 702/735-3896, www.sephora.com

HOURS: Sun.-Thurs. 10 A.M.-11 P.M., Fri.-Sat. 10 A.M.-midnight

There are women I know who consider a visit to Sephora a holy pilgrimage instead of just an outing for cosmetics. It's like the Disneyland of eye shadow and lipstick. Packed with every conceivable bath, fragrance, hair, makeup, and skin item on the planet (okay, maybe an exaggeration, but close) for both women and men, Sephora focuses on the higher end of things, with top-quality name-brand and exclusive products. They'll even give you a makeover just

COURTESY HARRAH'S ENTERTAINMENT

The Forum Shops at Caesars Palace

for walking in the door, a cool trick if you want to look fab for your night of clubbing. This, of course, means that prices are almost shocking ($14 for lip liner?!), but as the commercial says, you're worth it.

TRUEFITT & HILL

3500 Las Vegas Blvd. S. (at The Forum Shops at Caesars Palace), 702/735-7428, www.truefittandhill.com

HOURS: Sun.-Thurs. 10 A.M.-11 P.M., Fri.-Sat. 10 A.M.-midnight

A London institution since 1805, Truefitt & Hill has been the men's grooming salon of choice for the Royal Family and countless other dignitaries and celebrities. This unique store is one of only four outlets in the entire world, so the exclusivity factor is off the charts. Inside the small space (done as a 19th-century English barber shop) are a couple of antique barber chairs for some "real man"-style care, plus a wide range of men's grooming products (shaving accessories, shampoos, colognes, and so on).

COURTESY THE VENETIAN LAS VEGAS

Grand Canal Shoppes at The Venetian

JEWELRY
HARRY WINSTON

3500 Las Vegas Blvd. S. (at The Forum Shops at Caesars Palace), 702/933-7370, www.harrywinston.com

HOURS: Sun.-Thurs. 10 A.M.-11 P.M., Fri.-Sat. 10 A.M.-midnight

At all of the big awards shows, the celebrities glisten with multimillion-dollar jewelry. Many of those creations come from Harry Winston, so anyone who wants to look like Nicole Kidman on the red carpet should start here. Of course, there's no "Under $10" bin here, but for fine jewelry, this is the place to go. Plus, even those who can't afford it will have fun going in for a look. Just wait until you get outside to scream "That bracelet costs how much?!"

TIFFANY & CO.

3600 Las Vegas Blvd. S. (at Via Bellagio), 702/697-5400, www.tiffany.com

HOURS: Daily 10 A.M.-midnight

Indulge your inner Audrey Hepburn with a trip to one of the world's most recognizable

names in jewelry. Yes, if you choose to buy something here, it will come in the signature blue-green box with a white ribbon and you can expect that what is inside the little box will cost roughly the same as a pretty decent used car. Diamonds are everyone's best friend and the specialty, but they also offer gold, silver, and platinum on everything from bracelets to necklaces to watches and even clocks and candlesticks. Come on, you were looking for a place to use that platinum card, weren't you?

SHOPPING MALLS
THE FORUM SHOPS AT CAESARS PALACE

3500 Las Vegas Blvd. S. (at Caesars Palace), 702/893-4800, www.caesarspalace.com

HOURS: Sun.-Thurs. 10 A.M.-11 P.M., Fri.-Sat. 10 A.M.-midnight

Less of a mall and more of an experience, The Forum Shops is done as a Roman street scene, complete with stone floors, a changing sky, talking statues (amusing but not worth going out of your way for), and a three-story great hall with fountains and a circular escalator (one of only two in the world). The 500,000-square-foot facility boasts more than 160 stores of everyday faves (Gap, Banana Republic) and exclusive boutiques (Judith Lieber handbags, Kiehl's cosmetics, Versace, Dolce & Gabbana, Taryn Rose shoes, Dior, Gucci, Juicy Couture, etc.). This is also where several high-profile restaurants can be found, including Wolfgang Puck's Spago, The Palm, and Joe's Stone Crab.

◖ GRAND CANAL SHOPPES

3355 Las Vegas Blvd. S. (at The Venetian), 702/414-4500, www.venetian.com

HOURS: Sun.-Thurs. 10 A.M.-11 P.M., Fri.-Sat. 10 A.M.-midnight

At first glance, it looks like a mall with an Italian street scene theme. Yawn. Then comes the Grand Canal, complete with singing gondoliers, running up the center of the thing. That's enough to produce a smile. Then there's the giant indoor replica of St. Mark's Square. And that's sure to induce gleeful laughter. It's wildly entertaining: shopping as an experiential adventure. Most of the stores are typical (Ann Taylor, Banana Republic) but there are a few not found in standard malls, including Jimmy Choo shoes, Movado watches and jewelry, and Davidoff smoking accessories.

MIRACLE MILE SHOPS

3663 Las Vegas Blvd. S. (at Planet Hollywood), 888/800-8284, www.miraclemileshopslv.com
HOURS: Sun.-Thurs. 10 A.M.-11 P.M., Fri.-Sat. 10 A.M.-midnight (store hours may vary)

Formerly The Desert Passage, this shopping mall received a makeover just like the host hotel did when it transitioned from The Aladdin to Planet Hollywood. Where the previous incarnation was a highly themed "Road to Morocco" design, the new one attempts to evoke a more upscale Rodeo Drive experience. It's really quite boring in comparison, but luckily they more than make up for it with a really interesting mix of stores both common and unique, restaurants, entertainment venues, and nightclubs. You'll find everything from The Gap to Urban Outfitters here, plus some more

trendy boutiques, but the overall price point is more moderate than upscale malls like The Forum Shops and Grand Canal Shoppes.

TOYS
FAO SCHWARZ

3500 Las Vegas Blvd. S. (in The Forum Shops at Caesars Palace), 702/796-6500, www.faoschwarz.com
HOURS: Sun.-Thurs. 10 A.M.-11 P.M., Fri.-Sat. 10 A.M.-midnight

The parent company of the famed toy emporium has had some financial difficulties, but the Vegas store is still going strong. A giant hobby horse guards the entrance to the wonderland of amusements for kids of all ages with toys and games of all stripes, including many that you won't find at your local Toys"R"Us. There are plenty of play areas designed to get the wee ones immersed in the fun, and while there may not be a giant jump-on piano like the one in the movie *Big,* there is a charming little café up front with ice cream, pastries, and beverages that you can enjoy while little Johnny is exhausting himself with glee.

North Strip   Map 3

AUTOMOTIVE
PENSKE-WYNN FERRARI/MASERATI

3131 Las Vegas Blvd S. (at Wynn Las Vegas), 702/770-2000, www.penskewynn.com
HOURS: Mon.-Sat. 10 A.M.-10 P.M.

So you're sitting there at the nickel slot machine in Vegas and you're thinking, "I have a few extra hundred thousand dollars lying around. I wonder what I can do with it?" How about picking up a fine Italian sports car for the drive home? A full-service Ferrari and Maserati dealership probably wouldn't be noteworthy anywhere else, but this one is located *inside* a hotel-casino, falling squarely into the "What will they think of next?" category. The showroom has turned into an attraction of its own, with tons of Kia drivers drooling on the voluptuous metal creations. If you can't afford the actual car, they also have a full store full of

logo merchandise so you can attempt to look cool while walking back to your minivan.

BOUTIQUES
THE ESPLANADE AT WYNN LAS VEGAS

3131 Las Vegas Blvd. S. (at Wynn Las Vegas), 702/770-7000, www.wynnlasvegas.com
HOURS: Vary by store

Similar in design and attitude to the Via Bellagio shopping arcade (both created by Steve Wynn), the Esplanade trumps its spiritual ancestor by throwing in even more high-priced stores. Chanel, Dior, Cartier, Gaultier, Oscar de la Renta, Judith Lieber, and (look out, Carrie Bradshaw) Manolo Blahnik are just for starters. If you're like me, you can barely afford to breathe the same air as people who can afford this stuff, but for expensive tastes and big bank accounts, this is more than just a shopping arcade—it's a destination.

SHOPPING MALLS
THE FASHION SHOW
3200 Las Vegas Blvd. S., 702/369-0704,
www.thefashionshow.com

HOURS: Mon.-Fri. 10 A.M.-9 P.M., Sat. 10 A.M.-8 P.M.,
Sun. 11 A.M.-6 P.M.

With more than three million square feet of retail space, this is the biggest mall in Las Vegas, located conveniently on The Strip. It's hard to miss. There's a giant metal spaceship-looking thing out front—that's "The Cloud," part of an outdoor courtyard with big TV screens and lighting special effects. Inside, there are more than 200 shops (mostly the usual suspects, like Victoria's Secret, The Gap, and Sharper Image), plus many high-end department store anchors, including Bloomingdale's Home, Dillard's, Macy's, Neiman Marcus, Nordstrom, and Saks Fifth Avenue. It's huge, so budget a lot of time to walk through the whole thing, and it's always crowded and a bit overwhelming, so budget some Zen time for afterwards.

Just Off The Strip   Map 4

ANTIQUES
Believe it or not, Las Vegas is actually one of the most popular antique-shopping destinations in the Southwest. Maybe it's the heat—does it help keep old stuff preserved? I don't know. But whatever the reason, serious or weekend antique shoppers can find some real treasures here.

There are stores all over town, but the bulk of them are located along Charleston Avenue between I-15 on the west and Eastern Avenue (appropriately) on the east. There are about two dozen stores along this stretch of road, and shoppers can either go exploring on their own (like a true antique hunter would) or they can stop at **Silver Horse Antiques** (1651 E. Charleston Blvd., 702/385-2700) for a map of local stores.

Each one has a little something different to offer and what constitutes the best totally depends upon what kind of treasures a shopper is looking for, but there are a couple of places that are especially noteworthy in my opinion.

ANTIQUE SQUARE
2014-2034 Charleston Blvd., 702/471-6500
HOURS: Individual store hours vary

The Antique Square is a collection of musty stores that have none of the polish and sheen of fancier places. Most people into finding true antique bargains know that these are the kinds of stores to be visited first.

THE ANTIQUES MALL
1495 E. Flamingo Rd., 702/270-9910
HOURS: Daily 10 A.M.-7 P.M.

The Antiques Mall offers 24,000 square feet of "stuff" with 80 independent vendors showing off furniture, clothing, jewelry, toys, books, electronics, and even some Vegas memorabilia. There is a lovely tearoom for a pause if all the shopping is just too exhausting.

NOT JUST ANTIQUES MART
1422 Western Ave., 702/384-2334,
www.notjustantiquesmart.com
HOURS: Mon.-Sat. 10 A.M.-6 P.M., Sun. noon-6 P.M.

A visit to Not Just Antiques Mart will leave you saying "This is what an antique store should look like." They have more than 12,000 square feet of stalls and booths displaying a huge variety of collectibles, art, and plain-old old things from independent vendors and on consignment. Like The Antiques Mall, they also have a tea room, so if that was going to be the thing that tipped you in one direction or another, you're going to have to just go to both.

RED ROOSTER ANTIQUES
1109 Western Ave., 702/382-5253
HOURS: Mon.-Sat. 10 A.M.-6 P.M., Sun. 11 A.M.-5 P.M.

Red Rooster Antiques is sort of like a permanent flea market, a series of stalls and booths operated by different collectors and vendors all under one roof. It requires patience and fortitude to separate the gems from the junk, but it's often worth the effort.

BOUTIQUES
MASQUERADE VILLAGE
3700 Las Vegas Blvd. S. (at the Rio), 702/252-7777, www.playrio.com
HOURS: Hours vary by store

After navigating past slot machines and dancers (*Rio's Masquerade Village Show in the Sky*; see *Just Off The Strip* in the *Sights* chapter), the determined shopper will find a couple dozen boutiques and restaurants here at Masquerade Village. The standouts include Nawlins Authentic, with Big Easy–themed merchandise (Mardi Gras masks, voodoo candles, etc.), and the Harley Davidson store, with branded clothes and accessories. Other shops carry a satisfying array of clothing, jewelry, cosmetics, gifts, and more. Plus, if you time it right, you can catch the free show between stints of shopping.

CLOTHING AND ACCESSORIES
BUFFALO EXCHANGE
4110 S. Maryland Pkwy., 702/791-3960, www.buffaloexchange.com
HOURS: Mon.-Sat. 10 A.M.-8 P.M., Sun. 11 A.M.-7 P.M.

In a lot of the pricey boutiques on The Strip, they sell "distressed" (aka ripped up and ratty-looking) jeans for hundreds of dollars a pair. At Buffalo Exchange, they sell distressed jeans for $20. If you can tell the difference, you're a better person than I am. Of course, the clothes here are vintage (aka used), but they only stock the best-quality stuff, and prices are really reasonable. Fans of the alt-scene should take note that this store is a great place to find info on local bands, underground clubs, and the like.

GROCERS
◖ BRITISH FOODS, INC.
3375 S. Decatur, No. 11, 702/579-7777, www.britishgrocers.com
HOURS: Daily 10 A.M.-6 P.M.

Tucked away in an unassuming strip mall just east of The Strip is this delightful emporium of all things edible from across the pond. All of it is imported, so the prices are a bit higher than you'd normally pay for things like tea, but you can't find this stuff at your local grocery store. There are biscuits (cookies to you and me), custards and puddings, jams, and an entire display full of authentic British Cadbury chocolate, which is different—and in many people's opinion, better—than the American version. There's also a big freezer full of bangers, bacon, breads, sausages, fish, and more, which probably won't survive the plane ride home, but maybe you can stop somewhere and pick up a cheap grill.

OUTDOOR ACCESSORIES
BASS PRO SHOPS
8200 Industrial Rd., 702/730-5200, www.basspro.com
HOURS: Mon.-Sat. 9 A.M.-10 P.M., Sun. 10 A.M.-7 P.M.

Those into recreation—*any type* of recreation—should take an hour or two to visit this megastore of outdoorsy delights. To say this store is huge is a gross understatement. They have boats inside. Inside! There's also a shooting range, an archery range, camping supplies, fishing equipment, golf supplies, and so much more that I'd have to write a separate book. With waterfalls, trees, a big aquarium, and stuffed furry friends, the place is fun to look at, too. Despite stocking a variety of things with which to kill nature, they're surprisingly eco-friendly and offer a wide variety of workshops in all things outdoors.

RECORDS
◖ ZIA RECORDS
4225 S. Eastern Ave., 702/735-4942, www.ziarecords.com
HOURS: Mon.-Sat. 10 A.M.-midnight

In a world where the purchasing of music has turned into something you do from your computer at home, the fact that independent record stores like this one still exist is something to be celebrated. This is a classic record store, with bins full of new and used CDs of virtually every genre plus a full vinyl section, movies, games, posters, head shop gear, and even hula girls and Jesus statues to put on your dashboard. They have a full section of music from local bands, and on weekends they have concerts on a small stage in the corner emblazoned with signs asking patrons to eschew slam-dancing and hold hands instead.

SHOPPING MALLS
BOULEVARD MALL
3528 S. Maryland Pkwy., 702/732-8949
HOURS: Mon.-Sat. 10 A.M.-9 P.M., Sun. 11 A.M.-6 P.M.
The closest mall to The Strip that approximates the mall from home features more than 150 shops of traditional retail experience. Brookstone, The Gap, Hot Topic, Payless ShoeSource, and Victoria's Secret are just a few examples of the tried and true. Anchor stores include Dillard's, JCPenney, Macy's, and Sears, plus they have quite a few family-style restaurants on or around the property. It may not break any barriers, but if the Nordstrom's

on The Strip is too rich for your blood, come here and get what you need for less.

LAS VEGAS OUTLET CENTER
7400 Las Vegas Blvd. S., 702/896-5599, www.premiumoutlets.com
HOURS: Mon.-Sat. 10 A.M.-9 P.M., Sun. 10 A.M.-8 P.M.
Most people are familiar with the concept of an outlet mall, but just in case, they're filled with name-brand manufacturers and retail stores offering their over-stock, out-of-season, and irregular merchandise for less money than at the regular stores. At this particular outlet center, there are more than 130 stores—with names like Bose, Burlington, Casio, Casual Corner, Corningware, Jockey, KB Toys, Liz Claiborne, London Fog, Nike, Reebok, Tommy Hilfiger, Waterford, and Wilson's Leather—in an indoor, air-conditioned mall-like setting. A full food court and a fun indoor carousel add to the allure.

Downtown   Map 5

CLOTHING AND ACCESSORIES
THE ATTIC
1018 S. Main St., 702/388-4088, www.theatticlasvegas.com
HOURS: Mon.-Thurs. 10 A.M.-5 P.M., Fri. 10 A.M.-6 P.M., Sat. 11 A.M.-6 P.M.
Made semi-famous by an American Express commercial, this fun and funky boutique takes vintage clothes shopping to a Vegas extreme by offering a lot of outlandish getups, perfect for the office costume party. Need a boa? They've got 'em. They also have club-kid gear, hats, furnishings, wigs, shoes, souvenirs, and more; and, while they have some mainstream stuff, this is the kind of place where cool people shop for good bargains on fashions that will set them apart, not make them look the same.

D'LOE HOUSE OF STYLE THEN AND NOW
220 E. Charleston Ave., 702/382-5688, www.houseofstylethenandnow.com
HOURS: Mon.-Sat. noon-7 P.M.
This tiny store is packed to the doorjambs

with beautiful fashions and accessories from the 1930s to the 1970s. A full shelf of clutch handbags puts stunning 1940s-era beaded treasures next to sassy 1960s vinyl jobs with outlandish colors. Dresses for women and shirts and pants for men are equally time-travel–worthy, and everything is in terrific shape and reasonably priced for what you're getting. This is a terrific place to find one-of-a-kind vintage fashions that won't make you look like you're wearing used clothing.

GAMBLING
GAMBLERS' BOOK SHOP
630 S. 11th St., 800/522-1777, www.gamblersbook.com
HOURS: Mon.-Sat. 9 A.M.-5 P.M.
The *Gaming* chapter offers some basic overviews of various casino games, but anyone looking for the real lowdown on how to play should put this fantastic little bookstore on their itinerary. There are instructional manuals and strategy guides for every single game under the sun, plus other volumes on Las Vegas

and gaming history, casino management, sports (horse racing, etc.), travel guides, gaming-themed fiction, and more. They also carry computer software for practicing the games at home, DVDs and videotapes, and gambling-related memorabilia (chips, cards, etc.). A one-stop gaming resource.

(GAMBLERS GENERAL STORE

800 S. Main St. 702/382-9903,
www.gamblersgeneralstore.com
HOURS: Daily 9 A.M.–5 P.M.

If you're looking for something related to gambling and you can't find it here, it probably doesn't exist. Art, blackjack and other gaming tables, books, cards, dice, jewelry, photographs of historic Vegas, poker chips, roulette wheels, slot machines, software…the list goes on and on. This is a great place to pick up a gift for that casino fan back home or to bring back a little piece of Vegas for yourself. The staff is very knowledgeable and willing to hunt down any items they may not

have in stock, so be sure to ask for their advice along the way.

SHOPPING MALL
(LAS VEGAS PREMIUM OUTLETS

875 S. Grand Central Pkwy., 702/474-7500,
www.premiumoutlets.com
HOURS: Mon.-Sat. 10 A.M.–9 P.M., Sun. 10 A.M.–8 P.M.

A sister property to the Las Vegas Outlet Center listed previously, this one has two distinctions that give it the edge: It's closer to The Strip and the stores are more impressive. Regarding the latter, here are a few names: Armani, Calvin Klein, Crabtree & Evelyn, Dolce & Gabbana, Ralph Lauren, and Zales Jewelers. A lot of these places are not outlet-mall standards, and while the up-to-the-minute fashions are only in their regular stores, they do offer five-minutes-ago fashions at huge discounts. The only downside to this facility is the fact that some genius decided to make it an outdoor plaza, so don't go on hot summer days unless you're a fan of sunstroke.

RECREATION

I'm of the mind-set that a vacation means doing anything other than breaking a sweat, literally or figuratively. My idea of exercise is getting up to change the channel on the television instead of using the remote control. My idea of camping is a hotel without room service. You get the idea.

But there are lots of people out there who need to stay active and actually seek out forms of recreation when most right-minded people are sitting by the pool ordering drinks with lots of chunks of fruit hanging off the glass. For these types of visitors, Las Vegas offers plenty of opportunities for getting physical.

This is one of the premier golf destinations in the world, and while most of the really good courses are located far away from The Strip,

there are a couple right in the middle of town worth talking about.

There are also plenty of other diversions that fall into the recreation category, including tennis, bowling, family-friendly thrill rides and activities, and some professional sporting options.

And for the rest of us, there are some world-class spas and plenty of pools to lie around. And plenty of tropical drinks to be consumed.

Many more recreational activities, like bicycling, boating, camping, hiking, horseback riding, and skiing are found in areas outside the city limits. More information on these and other activities can be found in the *East and South of Las Vegas* and *North and West of Las Vegas* chapters.

HIGHLIGHTS

LOOK FOR ◖ TO FIND
RECOMMENDED RECREATION.

◖ **Best Spa:** Relax! You're on a vacation. Get treated like royalty at **The Bathhouse Spa at THEhotel** (page 159).

◖ **Best Golf Course:** With more than 1,200 trees, rolling greens, waterfalls, a challenging layout designed by Tom Fazio, and a $500-per-person fee, golf doesn't get any better or any more exclusive than at the **Wynn Las Vegas Golf Club** (page 165).

◖ **Best Place to Work Through Some Frustration:** Blast those invading alien hordes into oblivion at **GameWorks.** You'll feel better afterwards, I promise (page 167).

◖ **Best Roller Coaster:** Want a tour of New York-New York but don't have a lot of time? Ride the **Manhattan Express Roller Coaster** and see it fast *and* upside down (page 168).

◖ **Best Thrill Rides:** The three extreme **Stratosphere Tower Thrill Rides** include machines that will dangle you, drop you, and twirl you around the 1,000-foot-tall spire (page 169).

COURTESY MGM MIRAGE

The Bathhouse Spa at THEhotel

Spas

Las Vegas is a city of nonstop excitement for those who choose to take advantage of the 24-hour nature of things, but it also offers a terrific chance to rest and relax for those seeking a more low-key kind of vacation. Just because you're surrounded by nonstop-party people doesn't mean you have to be one of them.

All of the major resort hotels on The Strip have some form of spa featuring massages, facials, skin treatments, aromatherapies, and all manner of pampering designed to help guests de-stress, the best of which are listed on the following pages. No surprise they're also among the most expensive. Simple massages start at just under $100 and extravagant treatments can run three or four times that.

These are also the hotels that provide the best opportunity for lying around in a big, comfy room watching pay-per-view movies, ordering room service, and soaking in the tub. Yes, you can do that in just about any room, but the luxury level at hotels like this makes it a lot easier to justify.

In my opinion, however, the true rest and relaxation spots are away from the noise and hub-bub of The Strip, with spas at **The Ritz-Carlton Lake Las Vegas, Green Valley Ranch, Red Rock Resort,** and **The JW Marriott** among the best in the city. Check the *East and South of Las Vegas* and *North and West of Las Vegas* chapters for more details.

The remainder of your rest and relaxation

is really up to you, since everyone attains that bliss state in their own way. Some people will want to sit by the pool, others will want to take long walks in nature, while still others may want to do a food tour of the better restaurants to achieve some sort of nirvana. Whatever way you define it, you'll probably be able to find it in Las Vegas. Personally, I find a slot machine and a nice cold beer to be the height of Las Vegas calm.

◖ THE BATHHOUSE SPA AT THEHOTEL

3950 Las Vegas Blvd. S. (at Mandalay Bay), 877/632-9636, www.thehotelatmandalaybay.com
HOURS: Daily 6 A.M.–8:30 P.M.
COST: Gym/Spa Day Pass $30 guests, $35 non-guests
Map 1

Most spas in town are lovely affairs, but they tend to concentrate more on the services and less on the setting. The Bathhouse concentrates on both, with a full range of pampering served up in stunning surroundings. It's intimate, as twisting halls create a cocoon-like feeling with reflecting pools or a dramatic atrium tucked into corners in unexpected places. It's surprising and evocative, like walking through the forest and stumbling upon your very own waterfall. A full workout facility, whirlpools, wet and dry saunas, and a host of massage, facial, and personal care rituals make this a no-brainer.

CANYON RANCH SPACLUB

3355 Las Vegas Blvd. S. (at The Venetian), 800/742-9000, www.canyonranch.com
HOURS: Daily 5:30 A.M.–10 P.M.
COST: Gym/Spa Day Pass $35 (guests and nonguests)
Map 2

This enormous facility (69,000 square feet, bigger than many casinos!) boasts an unparalleled list of amenities. A health and wellness center focuses on nutrition, personalized fitness, and physical therapy; a workout facility has all the latest high-tech exercise equipment, a rock-climbing wall, and aerobics, kickboxing, meditation, spinning, and yoga classes; a full-service salon offers hairstyling, manicures, and pedicures; a store sells bath and beauty

products, clothes, candles, and more; and, of course, there are the treatments, including massages, wraps, aromatherapy, mud baths, and much too much to list all of it here. The fact that it is so big intimidates some, but prices are average for Strip spas, so that should help you relax.

NURTURE

3900 Las Vegas Blvd. S. (at Luxor), 800/258-9308, www.luxor.com
HOURS: Daily 6 A.M.–8 P.M.
COST: Gym/Spa Day Pass $25 guests, $35 non-guests
Map 1

Not only is this spa one of the most complete in terms of services, but often those services are cheaper than those found at the fancier places. A 50-minute signature massage will run around $125, anywhere from $5–50 less than competitors. Since the staff is just as good (if not better), it doesn't really matter that there's a little less marble and filigree. In addition to the wide range of massages, they also offer body treatments and scrubs, facials, wraps, tanning, personal training sessions (or do it yourself) in the well-equipped gym (machines and free weights), whirlpools, wet and dry saunas, and a full-service salon.

SPA BELLAGIO

3600 Las Vegas Blvd. S. (at Bellagio), 702/693-7472, www.bellagio.com
HOURS: Daily 6 A.M.–8 P.M.
COST: Gym/Spa Day Pass $30 guests only
Map 2

Remodeled and expanded in 2004, Spa Bellagio boasts nearly 40,000 square feet of space, making it one of the biggest spas on The Strip. It's also one of the most lovely. With its wide hallways, soft lighting, wood paneling, and green glass block highlights, the place feels like the embodiment of calm. They offer more than a dozen different types of massage (50-minute Swedish starts around $130), including Watsu (in water), an equal number of facials, body treatments and therapies, scrubs and wraps, a full-service beauty salon, waxing, tanning, and a fully stocked workout facility.

POOLING AROUND

Pools at all Las Vegas hotels are only open to the guests of those hotels. If you see something on this list that really strikes your fancy, you're going to have to book a room at that particular hotel to be able to enjoy it. They enforce this policy strictly, usually with security at the pool entrances asking for a room key to gain entry.

The only exceptions to this rule are the smaller, more exclusive, and seriously more expensive Pool Clubs that are springing up along The Strip. These are daytime versions of nightclubs, complete with all the good and bad things you may imagine from a concept like that (see *Nightlife* in the *Entertainment* chapter).

The locations of these pools can also be a bit of a pain. In many instances, guests must traipse through or near the casino to get to them, so just remember that before you put on that thong.

There are several pools that allow topless sunbathing in certain private, restricted areas, including those at Caesars Palace, Mandalay Bay, Wynn Las Vegas, MGM Grand, and Stratosphere, to name a few. This seems to be a growing trend, so by the time you read this, things may have changed at your hotel. If it's important to you, call ahead.

You should also be aware that while Las Vegas may be warmer than where you live during the winter months, it still gets chilly here, and most hotel pools are closed from roughly October–March. In some instances, the deck chairs may

the pool at the Bellagio

COURTESY MGM MIRAGE

still be out for sun worshippers, but the pools themselves are off-limits (and often drained).

During those summer months, be careful not to overdo things; this especially goes for those people who've spent the entire winter locked up inside an office somewhere. The sun in Vegas is brutal and, unfortunately, shade at most pool areas is at a premium. Bring plenty of sunscreen and limit your exposure. Nasty sunburns can ruin a vacation.

Below is a list of the pools that stand out in some way or another and the reasons why, with warnings about those downsides I mention.

Bellagio (3600 Las Vegas Blvd. S., Center Strip, 702/693-7111) offers a gorgeous area with multiple pools, plenty of deck chairs (with kicky little flags guests can raise for drink service), private cabanas for rent, and a much more grown-up attitude (meaning fewer kids). Downsides are the good spots get taken early, cabanas cost a fortune, and shade? Not so much.

Caesars Palace (3570 Las Vegas Blvd. S., Center Strip, 702/731-7110) has a typically over-the-top offering — what they call the Garden of the Gods Pool Oasis. It's 4.5 acres with four pools, two whirlpools, fountains, and enough columns and statuary to make *Gladiator: Part II*. The only real downside here is that the columns and statuary take up room that could be used for more badly needed deck chairs.

Flamingo Las Vegas (3555 Las Vegas Blvd. S., Center Strip, 702/733-3111) has 15 acres of tropical paradise with probably the most luxurious landscaping of any pool area in town, offering some much needed shade. Four pools (including the original oval from Bugsy's era), two whirlpools, waterslides, and private cabanas are available. The downside here is for adults who don't want to be around other people's kids. This place is very popular with families.

On the other hand, if adult is what you're looking for, the **Hard Rock Beach** (4455 Paradise Rd., Just Off The Strip, 702/693-5000) offers a totally grown-up party vibe that may be just your cup of suntan lotion. Packed with a crowd straight out of *Baywatch*, the pool area features sandy beaches, a lazy river, swim-up blackjack, and lots of palm trees for shade. Downside? People with body image issues should not apply.

Over at **Mandalay Beach** (3950 Las Vegas Blvd. S., South Strip, 702/632-7777) you'll find just what the name implies — a beach complete with their very own wave pool (originally designed for surfing, but let's just say that didn't work out), more traditional pools, a lazy river ride, and more. Downsides include the crowds (very, very popular place) and the crowds of kids if you're averse to the demographic.

The fabulous pool area at **The Mirage** (3400 Las Vegas Blvd. S., Center Strip, 702/791-7111) goes toe-to-toe with the Flamingo for lush landscaping and it's hard to pick a winner between the two. Here, they have two giant pools with a series of smaller lagoons, grottos, islands, waterslides, and three Jacuzzis. Unlike many pools in town, The Mirage's is open for most of the year (except December). No real serious downsides here to mention.

The only other major exception to the year-round rule can be found at **Tropicana** (3801 Las Vegas Blvd. S., South Strip, 702/739-2222) and that's because part of the pool area is indoors (the only one at a major resort in Vegas). This is also the place that invented (or at least perfected) the concept of swim-up blackjack, so traditionalists should come here. The downside to this pool is that guests have to stay at the Tropicana to use it, and as of this writing they will probably be closing it at some point as they rebuild a bigger, better Tropicana around it. Call ahead.

RECREATION

QUA BATHS & SPA

3570 Las Vegas Blvd. S. (at Caesars Palace),
866/782-0655, www.quabathsspa.com
HOURS: Daily 6 A.M.–8 P.M.
COST: Gym/Spa Day Pass $25 guests and non-guests
Map 2

The previous Caesars spa was no shabby affair, but this one takes the art of personal rejuvenation to a whole new level of sophistication. The facility offers 51 treatment rooms, but really stresses the concept of Social Spa-ing, naturally lit common rooms and baths including three dunking pools of varying temperatures, a warm (as in Fahrenheit) lounge, an ice room with snow falling from above, and a tea room accompanied by a sommelier. Who knew there was such a thing for tea? Treatmentss run the gamut from extravagant to really extravagant, and a basic massage starts at around $140. A fully equipped workout room and salon complete the package.

THE SPA AT THE GOLDEN NUGGET

129 E. Fremont St. (at The Golden Nugget),
800/634-3403, www.goldennugget.com
HOURS: Daily 6 A.M.–8 P.M.
COST: Gym/Spa Day Pass $20 guests only
Map 5

For those staying Downtown, this is really the only good option for spa services, but that doesn't mean it's sub-par in any way. Check out that gorgeous lobby, done as a garden veranda with an arched skylight. Inside is a satisfying spa menu, including facials, treatments, and massages that start around $120 for a 50-minute Swedish, and while that's not as much of a bargain as the prices they used to charge, it's still cheaper than most places on The Strip. A workout facility has machines and free weights and, of course, they have the usual whirlpool and sauna amenities. While they say they are only open to guests of the hotel, if they aren't busy they will allow non-guests to use it as well.

Wet spa at Treasure Island

COURTESY MGM MIRAGE

WET

3300 Las Vegas Blvd. S. (at Treasure Island),
702/894-7474, www.wetspati.com
HOURS: Sun.–Wed. 6 A.M.–8 P.M., Thu.–Sat. 6 A.M.–
10 P.M.
COST: Gym/Spa Day Pass $25 guests, $30 non-guests
Map 2

Much like the rest of the hotel, they went and sexed up their spa. No, not like that. What I mean is at most other places, the spa experience is one of quiet Zen reflection, which you can absolutely get here. But instead of the typical soothing earth tones you get cool, icy blues in the wall treatments, floors, and ceilings, often in a wavy pattern that evokes an undersea adventure. Despite the laid-back vibe, the place has an energy that is an interesting counterpoint to others in this neighborhood. And you can get some deals here as well. A standard 50-minute Swedish massage starts at $110, much cheaper than you'll find at most other spas of this quality.

Sports

For the past couple of years, Las Vegas has been in feverish negotiations to bring some sort of major-league sports franchise to the city. The Montreal Expos were rumored to be eyeing a move to Sin City that never came to fruition, and more than one major-league hockey team has considered skating in the desert, but so far nothing has come to pass.

There are a few reasons for it. First, there are no facilities that the major leagues feel are worthy of their franchises. The public stadiums and arenas in town just aren't up to snuff and, while the casino arenas are probably good enough, a pro team would never play at one. This brings us to the second major reason:

gambling. Most professional sports leagues are nervous about putting a team in a city where people are going to be betting on them a couple of blocks away.

So, in the meantime, sports fans have to settle for the two minor-league teams (51s baseball and Wranglers hockey, listed below) or hope one of the special-event sports is going to be in town during their visit.

Chief among the special events is **boxing,** with many of the sport's major title fights duked out here in Vegas. Venues vary, but they can usually be found at Mandalay Bay (3950 Las Vegas Blvd. S., 877/632-7400, www.mandalaybay.com), MGM Grand (3799

WORK UP A SWEAT

Spent a little too much time at the all-you-can-eat buffet, huh? I've been there. But I'm the kind of guy who will sit and whine about how full I am for a couple of hours and then say, "Oooh, is that chocolate?" If you, on the other hand, feel the need to burn off some of those calories, you've got lots of opportunities to do so in Las Vegas.

Recreation choices abound. This is one of the premier golf destinations in the country, with dozens of world-class courses designed by people with names like Nicklaus, Weiskopf, and Fazio. I'll admit up front that I know very little about golf, but I am told that those people are the best in the course-designing business. The top choices in the category include **Reflection Bay** at Lake Las Vegas, a 7,261-yard, par-72 course perched right on the shores of the glistening artificial lake; **Bali Hai,** a 7,002-yard, par-71 "luxury" course just south of The Strip with a gourmet restaurant and carts equipped with Global Positioning System software, just in case you drive off into the desert while looking for the back nine; and the epic greens at **Wynn Las Vegas,** as luxuriously designed as one would

expect the golf course for a $2.7-billion resort to be.

There's also bowling, tennis, bike riding, horseback riding, swimming, boating, and hiking at various locales around town.

Every major hotel (and many of the smaller ones) has some sort of gym facility, often with the latest in cardio-workout machines and weights. They usually require a fee, anywhere from $15-30 per day, but that usually includes access to the sauna, steam room, and Jacuzzi tubs if the spa facility has them (most do). Since the workout rooms are usually tied to the spa, the fee is often waived for people getting some sort of treatment, like a massage or facial.

But there are other ways to get the adrenaline pumping than by exercising. If your heart doesn't pound while riding one of the three "extreme" thrill rides high atop the 107-story **Stratosphere Tower,** then no amount of aerobics is going to do it. There are several high-energy roller coasters around.

And if none of that appeals to you, you could always walk up to a $100-a-pull slot machine and stick a crisp Ben Franklin in there. If that doesn't make you sweat, you might be dead.

RECREATION

LAS VEGAS NEWS BUREAU/LVCVA

Bali Hai Golf Club

Las Vegas Blvd. S., 877/880-0880, www .mgmgrand.com), or Caesars Palace (3570 Las Vegas Blvd. S., 888/702-3544, www .caesarspalace.com).

It is worth noting, however, that fight nights in Vegas draw huge crowds—and not always the safest ones. No one will talk about it on the record, but apparently many Los Angeles street gangs drive into Vegas for the big boxing matches and, occasionally, their rivalries spill out onto the streets. Witness the brawl in front of the MGM Grand after the Mike Tyson ear-biting incident and the infamous shooting of Tupac Shakur.

For a different type of gun-slinging, maybe you'd be interested in slipping into a pair of boots, chaps, and a cowboy hat. No, it's not a Village People audition, it's the **National Finals Rodeo,** an annual event that draws the best of the breed (and tens of thousands of fans) to Las Vegas in December. From bronco riding to barrel racing to calf roping and beyond, this two-week event is held at the Thomas and Mack Center (4505 S. Maryland Pkwy.,

702/895-3900, www.thomasandmack.com) on the UNLV campus about a mile and a half from The Strip. For more information, visit the NFR website at www.nfr-rodeo.com or call 888/NFR-RODEO.

There are occasional motocross events, monster truck rallies, exhibition football and basketball games, and other sporting events at the arenas listed previously. Check for schedules.

But if you're in the mood for a little do-it-yourself–style sports, here are some pointers on the best places to play something other than a game of chance.

GOLF
BALI HAI GOLF CLUB
5160 Las Vegas Blvd. S., 888/427-6678, www.balihaigolfclub.com
HOURS: Daily dawn-dusk
Map 1

Golf fans rave about this 18-hole, par-71 course located just south of Mandalay Bay, partly for the lush landscaping (more than 4,000 trees and 100,000 tropical plants) and the rest for the course itself, described as being challenging but not to the point of wanting to throw your clubs at people. This is more of a relaxed golf destination than a place to practice for the Masters. It isn't cheap—$99 for summer twilight up to almost $300 for peak-season weekends. That price does include a golf cart with GPS, though, to keep visitors from driving off into the desert. The facility includes a pro shop, driving range, snack bar, restaurant, and more, but alas, no windmill.

LAS VEGAS NATIONAL

1911 E. Desert Inn Rd., 702/734-1796,
www.lasvegasnational.com
HOURS: Daily 5 A.M.-dusk
Map 4

What a history this place has. Opened in 1961 as the Stardust Country Club, the course has been aligned over the years with The Sahara and the Las Vegas Hilton and has played host to countless PGA events. The 18-hole, par-71 course may not be as fancy as some, but those trees have been there for 40-plus years, not trucked in from a nursery last week. Plus, it doesn't have fancy prices. Tee-times cost as little as $59 and their peak is only around $159 (golf cart is extra). The facility has a driving range, pro shop, snack bar, and many other conveniences.

WYNN LAS VEGAS GOLF CLUB

3131 Las Vegas Blvd. S. (at Wynn Las Vegas),
888/320-7122 www.wynnlasvegas.com
HOURS: Daily 7 A.M.-dusk
Map 3

You have to seriously love golf to play here. First of all, players must be registered guests of the hotel—not even friends of registered guests can play. Second, players have to pay (are you sitting down?) $500 per person to tee up. Yee-ouch! But for those with the resources, this is truly one of the most stunning courses on earth. Designed by Tom Fazio, it's an 18-hole, par-70 challenger with lots of incredible landscaping (waterfalls, plants, and more than 1,200 trees rescued from the legendary Desert Inn course it replaced), a luxury clubhouse lounge, a pro shop, chipping and putting greens, a driving range, and all of the "I'm better than other golfers" attitude imaginable.

TENNIS

BALLY'S

3645 Las Vegas Blvd. S. (at Bally's), 702/967-4598,
www.ballyslv.com
HOURS: Hours vary seasonally
Map 2

Tennis used to be omnipresent on The Strip, but now there are only a few choices, with Bally's being the best. Why? Well, they've got eight "championship-caliber" courts (more than any other facility) that are illuminated for night play, equipment rental, a pro shop, and a professional staff on-site to help with instruction if need be. Guests and non-guests alike can use the courts, which start at around $10 per hour for hotel guests and $15 for non-guests.

FLAMINGO LAS VEGAS

3555 Las Vegas Blvd. S. (at Flamingo Las Vegas),
702/733-3444, www.flamingolv.com
HOURS: Mon.-Fri. 7 A.M.-7 P.M., Sat.-Sun. 7 A.M.-6 P.M.
Map 2

Although there aren't as many as at sister hotel Bally's, the four courts at the Flamingo are similar in just about every way. They are lit up for nighttime ball whacking, there's a pro shop for purchases and rentals, and professional tennis instruction for newbies. It's a little more expensive—guests pay in the neighborhood of $15 per hour and non-guests pay around $20.

BOWLING

GOLD COAST BOWLING CENTER

4000 W. Flamingo Rd. (at the Gold Coast),
702/367-7111, www.goldcoastcasino.com
HOURS: Open 24 hours
Map 4

This 70-lane facility features up-to-date (if not the latest, most cutting-edge) scoring equipment, a pro shop with every bowling-accessory need covered, coaching for those wanting to stay out of the gutters, a snack bar, a full bar and lounge, and a video arcade for young ones who find throwing balls at sticks of wood archaic. While the facility is not the most modern in town, it is the closest to The Strip and gets the job done.

RECREATION

ORLEANS BOWLING CENTER

4500 W. Tropicana Ave. (at the Orleans), 702/365-7111, www.orleanscasino.com

HOURS: Open 24 hours

Map 4

In a casino owned by the same company as Gold Coast, this is a veritable carbon copy of that facility: 70 lanes, a pro shop, meeting rooms, a video arcade, a full bar and lounge, and a snack bar. The primary difference is that this one is a little newer and a little fancier, with more comfortable furnishings, better score-keeping technology, and a generally higher level of sheen.

EXTREME SPORTS
FLYAWAY INDOOR SKYDIVING

200 Convention Center Dr., 877/545-8093, www.flyawayindoorskydiving.com

HOURS: Daily 10 A.M.–10 P.M.

COST: Flights $70 (packages available)

Map 3

Now this is more my speed. Ain't no way you're getting me to jump out of an airplane with a little piece of nylon on my back being the only thing between me and a really messy end, but here at Flyaway, they provide the sensation without the danger. Once suited up as if for a real jump, guests are loaded into a vertical wind tunnel with a giant turbine blasting straight up so they literally float on a current of air. It may not be exactly the same, but it's good practice for people who long to do the real thing and it's as close as wimps like me will ever get. Note there are height and weight restrictions and people with neck or back issues are discouraged since people get bumped around a lot in the process.

SPECTATOR SPORTS
LAS VEGAS 51S

850 Las Vegas Blvd. N. (at Cashman Field), 702/386-7200, www.lv51.com

HOURS: Schedule Varies

COST: Ticket Prices Vary

Map 5

There are no major-league sporting teams of any type in Las Vegas (although the mayor is trying desperately to change that), so people with a serious sporting jones are going to have to make do with either this AAA baseball team or the minor-league hockey team (see the Las Vegas Wranglers listing) to get their fix. The 51s (named after nearby Area 51) are like any other AAA team in that they work hard, they play well, and virtually no one pays any serious attention to them except for rabid baseball fans who don't have any other choice in town.

LAS VEGAS WRANGLERS HOCKEY

4500 W. Tropicana Ave. (at the Orleans), 702/471-7825, www.lasvegaswranglers.com

HOURS: Schedule Varies

COST: Ticket Prices Vary

Map 4

The Wayne Gretzkys of the world have to come from somewhere, so who knows? Maybe you'll see a future star of the ice (and not in a Capade kind of way) playing with this decent, if unspectacular so far, minor-league hockey team. That's not meant to be an insult to the Wranglers—they are settling nicely into a groove at the 9,000-seat Orleans Arena, and while they are still a relatively young team with no big championship trophies to show off, they've done well enough in season-ending tournament play to gain a healthy respect in the league.

UNIVERSITY OF NEVADA LAS VEGAS

4505 Maryland Pkwy., 702/739-FANS, http://unlvrebels.cstv.com

HOURS: Schedule Varies

COST: Ticket Prices Vary

Map 4

UNLV may not be one of those colleges that engender rabid fan bases who paint their bodies in wacky colors and get into fisticuffs over who has the better fight song, but they have generated enough winning teams in enough sports to make them a force worth reckoning with. They have a full range of athletics to choose from: baseball, football, softball, track and field, and volleyball, as well as men's and women's basketball, golf, soccer, and swimming. If your local college teams have been disappointing you lately, maybe you should see what the UNLV Rebels are up to.

Family Fun

ADVENTUREDOME AT CIRCUS CIRCUS

2880 Las Vegas Blvd. S. (at Circus Circus),
702/794-3939, www.adventuredome.com
HOURS: Mon.-Thurs. 10 A.M.-6 P.M., Fri.-Sat. 10 A.M.-midnight, Sun. 10 A.M.-9 P.M. (hours vary seasonally)
COST: Per-ride charge $4-7; all-ride pass $23 adult, $15 child
Map 3

The only amusement park in Las Vegas that is worth spending any real time at is this one, and that's because they put it indoors. The giant pink dome keeps things toasty in the chilly winter months and cool during the outrageously hot summers, when doing things like riding roller coasters can be painful. They've got one of those here, plus a water flume ride and several others that spin, flip, shake, and otherwise try to get riders to lose their lunches. There are a few tamer rides for smaller children, too. A full set of carnival-style midway games and arcade-style video games plus bumper cars and more make this a great place to take the kids.

◀ GAMEWORKS

3785 Las Vegas Blvd. S. (at the Showcase Mall),
702/432-GAME, www.gameworks.com
HOURS: Sun.-Thurs. 10 A.M.-midnight, Fri.-Sat. 10 A.M.-1 A.M.
COST: Free
Map 1

This monster entertainment facility is a great place for kids and people who act like kids. All of the latest video games are offered, including plenty of virtual reality wizardry, motion simulators, and hyper-violent shoot-em-ups (parents, you have been warned). There's also a host of more traditional games (air hockey, anyone?), a snack bar, and a rock-climbing wall for a little exercise between alien hunting. All this fun has a price. Each game or activity costs points, and you buy points that get loaded onto a debit-style card. Ten points cost $1, but that isn't going to get you much play, so it's best to focus on the bonus pack-

ages that cost $20 or more, but get you a lot more points and may help you feel like you're getting your money's worth.

JILLIAN'S

450 E. Fremont St. (in the Neonopolis Mall),
702/759-0450, www.jillianslasvegas.com
HOURS: Sun.-Thurs. 11 A.M.-10 P.M., Fri.-Sat. 11 A.M.-midnight
Map 5

The setup is not quite as elaborate and the offerings are not quite as extensive as at GameWorks, but the overall concept is the same: video games, carnival-style attractions (skee-ball!), table games (air hockey, not craps), and the like. This is a popular place for parents to drop off the kids while they having a nice meal or drink in the restaurant/bar area. Upstairs are a nine-table billiard hall and a 12-lane bowling alley with multimedia displays and disco lighting to amp up the excitement of throwing balls at pins.

LAS VEGAS CYBER SPEEDWAY

2535 Las Vegas Blvd. S. (at the Sahara Hotel),
702/737-2111, www.saharacasino.com
HOURS: Opens daily at 10 A.M., closing times vary
COST: $10 (packages available)
Map 3

Fans of racing should make a beeline for this cool motion-simulator ride that puts "drivers" behind the wheel of a seven-eighths scale NASCAR replica. The motion actuators give the sense of going, slowing, turning, and (all too often) crashing. Drivers even have the ability to fine-tune the experience by fiddling with simulated tire pressure, torque, and horsepower variables. The Las Vegas Motor Speedway course is okay for going around in circles, but try the more amusing road course up and down The Strip, past (and, in some cases, through) the hotels and casinos. Note: Pricing packages are available that combine this attraction with Speed: The Ride (listed later in this section).

RECREATION

RECREATION

COURTESY MGM MIRAGE

Manhattan Express Roller Coaster at New York-New York

LUXOR IMAX RIDEFILM

3900 Las Vegas Blvd. S. (at Luxor), 702/262-4000, www.luxor.com

HOURS: Sun.-Thurs. 9 A.M.-11 P.M., Fri.-Sat. 9 A.M.-midnight

COST: $6.50-10 (depending on film), all-day attractions pass $25

Map 1

This theater-style motion simulator features several different films, all with the same basic concept: fast-paced chases that send viewers up, down, and around in nonstop, 3-D, virtual-reality madness. The films change periodically but, at press time, they were offering *In Search of the Obelisk,* a wild dash through a pyramid (get it?) in search of ancient treasure; *Reboot,* a *Tron*-like adventure inside a computer mainframe; and *Dracula's Haunted Castle,* where all manners of ghosts and ghouls chase the viewer through a spooky lair. Warning: Just because the motion is simulated, people who know what Dramamine is for should skip this.

Note: At press time the Luxor was undergoing an extensive remodeling and this attraction may be closing.

MANHATTAN EXPRESS ROLLER COASTER

3790 Las Vegas Blvd. S. (at New York-New York), 702/740-6969, www.nynyhotelcasino.com

HOURS: Sun.-Thurs. 11 A.M.-11 P.M., Fri.-Sat. 10:30 A.M.-midnight

COST: $12.50 per ride (packages available)

Map 1

There's something just so incredibly right about riding a roller coaster around the New York City skyline. Done to look like the maddest taxicabs imaginable, this thrilling ride takes passengers up more than 200 feet (great view for a second for those not too terrified to look at it), drops them almost 150 feet, and propels them to speeds of up to 70 mph through loops, twists, and turns. While others have copied it, this was the first coaster to feature the "heartline" twist-and-dive maneuver, a stomach-churning bit that turns the car upside down before it dives toward the ground. Not for the faint of heart.

SPEED: THE RIDE

2535 Las Vegas Blvd. S. (at the Sahara Hotel),
702/737-2111, www.saharacasino.com

HOURS: Opens daily at 10 A.M., closing times vary

COST: $10 (packages available)

`Map 3`

Okay, how's this for a thrill ride? It starts out inside, but then accelerates to 70 mph in two seconds flat, blasts through an underground tunnel, zooms above ground into a full loop, needles through the hotel's marquee, and then climbs straight up (more or less) a 224-foot tower. Then it does the whole thing backward! It's a short (and relatively expensive) trip, but coaster fans say it's one of the coolest. Note: Packages are available that include unlimited rides on this and the Las Vegas Cyber Speedway (see previous listing).

STAR TREK: THE EXPERIENCE/ BORG INVASION

3000 Paradise Rd. (at the Las Vegas Hilton),
888/GO-BOLDLY, www.startrekexp.com

HOURS: 11:30 A.M.–9:30 P.M. (hours vary seasonally)

COST: $38

`Map 4`

You don't have to be a *Star Trek* fan to enjoy this, but it helps to have at least a passing knowledge of things like Klingons and Borgs. The two-part attraction features the original "Experience," a motion-simulator ride that puts "passengers" in a shuttle-craft running from alien ne'er-do-wells, and the newer

"Borg Invasion," with the same basic concept, only in a motion-simulator theater (complete with blasts of water and air surprising the heck out of viewers). Both parts feature live actors attempting to immerse guests in the "experience," but mostly just kind of coming off as silly. Video of beloved *Next Generation* and *Voyager* characters is integrated into the experiences and there is a Trek museum as well as gift shops and a bar to top things off.

STRATOSPHERE TOWER THRILL RIDES

2000 Las Vegas Blvd. S. (at the Stratosphere),
702/380-7777, www.stratospherehotel.com

HOURS: Sun.-Thurs. 10 A.M.-midnight, Fri.-Sat. 10 A.M.-1 A.M.

COST: $4-8 plus $10 tower access fee (packages available)

`Map 3`

Explain to me why anyone would want to do this. Seriously, it makes no sense. More than 900 feet in the air, at the tippy-top of the Stratosphere Tower, there's the Big Shot, a sit-in-a-seat-and-get-blasted-straight-up-a-tower kind of thing; X-Scream, a giant teeter-totter that straps riders in a seat, shoots them up a ramp at 30 mph, and then tilts them off the side; and Insanity: The Ride, a spinning octopus of a monstrosity that whirls passengers around in a circle while they're hanging out in midair 100 floors up over The Strip. I've said it before, I'll say it again: You have fun. I'll be at the bar.

RECREATION

HOTELS

One of the first things potential Vegas visitors do is try to choose a hotel, a Herculean task that depends mainly on a traveler's budget, their intentions, and their taste. Yes, of course you want to stay in the places that get all those stars and diamonds in other travel guides, but can you really afford $300 a night and up? And if you can, do you want to? Are you looking for a wild party weekend or a relaxing getaway? Do you fret about things like thread count or are you happy with a pillow and a shower?

The good news is that with so many options (there are more hotel rooms here than in any other city in the world), there's a little something for everyone: outrageously expensive or reassuringly cheap, opulent luxury versus basic accommodations, hip and trendy or grown-up and sedate, big sprawling resorts or slightly less big sprawling resorts (they don't do small here). It's possible to find something to suit every need.

While it is true that the days of a bargain Vegas vacation are pretty much a thing of the past, there is one way to keep things affordable, and that's to stay somewhere other than The Strip. If you're looking for a budget hotel, be sure to pay special attention to the hotels located just off The Strip or Downtown, many of which rival the accommodations you'll find on Las Vegas Boulevard but at substantially lower rates.

The selection in this chapter focuses on the best of the best, offering details on certain hotels that pale in comparison to their grander neighbors because they are the best option for their price, their location, or the demographic they serve.

COURTESY HARRAH'S ENTERTAINMENT

HIGHLIGHTS

LOOK FOR ☾ TO FIND
RECOMMENDED HOTELS.

☾ **Best Strip Hotel:** Huge rooms, high-tech amenities, great service, and dramatic public areas make **THEhotel** the best choice on The Strip (page 177).

☾ **Best Bargain: Bally's** is not necessarily the least expensive hotel on The Strip, but you'll save money without sacrificing comfort or amenities (page 179).

☾ **Best Classic Hotel:** Opened in 1966, **Caesars Palace** has reinvented itself but remains a classic example of old Las Vegas extravagance (page 180).

☾ **Best Retro Rooms:** The deliriously retro "Go" rooms at **Flamingo Las Vegas** are officially the coolest in all of Las Vegas (page 180).

☾ **Best New Hotel:** Turning the boring Aladdin into the fabulous **Planet Hollywood** was no easy task, but the new fun-and-funky, memorabilia-packed rooms here are tremendous (page 183).

☾ **Best Bathrooms:** Bigger and better appointed than some Vegas hotel rooms, the bathrooms at **The Venetian** are worth the price of admission (page 184).

☾ **Best Hotel for Families: Circus Circus** is the *only* serious hotel choice for families. The hotel features kiddie pools, games, circus-themed attractions, and family-friendly restaurants (page 185).

☾ **Best Hotel for Grown-Ups:** With prices like the ones they charge at **Wynn Las Vegas,** who can afford to bring the kids (page 186)?

☾ **Best Rooms with a View:** West-facing rooms in the north and south towers provide virtually unobstructed views of the entire Las Vegas Strip at the **Las Vegas Hilton** (page 189).

☾ **Best Downtown Hotel: Main Street Station** is less crowded, more friendly, less expensive, and more entertaining than any other hotel in the area (page 194).

COURTESY THE VENETIAN LAS VEGAS

a bathroom in a standard room at The Venetian

HOTELS

CHOOSING A HOTEL

The phrase "standard accommodations" means different things at different hotels. At a place like Excalibur, it's a simple motel-style room, while at The Venetian, their "basic" room is a 700-square-foot mini-suite. All hotels have upgraded rooms that may include more square feet, better views, one- or two-bedroom suites, and palatial high-roller digs that are bigger than most average homes—but, of course, those cost extra. Because the average Las Vegas visitor stays in the hotel's average room, that's what is focused on here.

Unlike other cities where the room rates are fairly stable, Las Vegas is a very volatile market with wild variations between weekdays and weekends and from week to week. Because of that volatility, there's every possibility in the world that when you call a $ hotel, they may be charging $$$ prices. A room that may cost $50 on a Tuesday may cost $250 the following Tuesday and even more on a weekend. It's all based on the demand, with the busiest times (weekends, holidays, conventions) bringing the highest rates.

The good news is that the reverse is also true, so don't rule out an "expensive" hotel automatically. During a slow time, they may be offering a bargain. Flexibility is the key. Not everyone has the luxury of being able to choose when they want to go (bosses can be so unreasonable, can't they?), but even having two possible options may save a ton of money.

When shopping for the best rates, be sure to check as many sources as possible. In general, the hotels' toll-free reservations numbers and websites are the best places to find the cheapest rates. Since Las Vegas averages 90–95 percent occupancy (while the rest of the country averages just over 60 percent), the hotels here don't need to go out of their way to work with travel agents or Internet travel booking sites like Expedia or Travelocity. Since the discounts they offer to such resellers are negligible, the markups those resellers put on the rooms to make a profit can actually mean a higher price than the one offered by the hotel directly. But that doesn't mean those outlets should be overlooked. Sometimes they do offer a better deal, so it's worth the effort to check.

WHEN TO BOOK YOUR HOTEL

Holidays are the busiest times of year in Las Vegas, bringing out big crowds and high room rates. And keep in mind it doesn't need to be a

PRICE-RATING SYMBOLS

The following price key should be used as a loose guideline only. Prices are what guests can usually expect to pay for standard accommodations, but there's every possibility that a $ hotel may charge $$$ prices and vice versa.

$ **less than $150 per night**
$$ **$150-250 per night**
$$$ **more than $250 per night**

The price ranges are for double occupancy (unless otherwise noted) and don't include room tax (11 percent Downtown, 9 percent elsewhere); resort or usage fees; energy, phone, or other surcharges; and, of course, all of those room-service and pay-per-view movie charges that rack up. Be sure to ask about these "hidden" fees (or read the Internet fine print) before handing over the credit card.

All of the hotels listed in this chapter are full-service resort-level accommodations, so expect to find a whole host of amenities that should make packing a little easier. (See *Planning Your Trip* in the *Discover Las Vegas* chapter).

These hotels come with a wide array of restaurants, shopping, entertainment, recreation, pools, spas, and workout facilities, the best of which are highlighted in other chapters. Each also has some form of casino, either in the hotel or just down a hallway.

major holiday for things to get busy. President's Day, Columbus Day, and even Martin Luther King Day usually create a three-day weekend, and that seems to be enough of an excuse for people in nearby cities like Los Angeles to jump in their cars and get away to the bright lights of The Strip.

Major holidays are even worse. Memorial Day, Fourth of July, and Labor Day are among the busiest weekends of the year. Thanksgiving used to be very slow for Vegas, but now people are taking advantage of that four-day weekend and turning out in droves to the all-you-can-eat buffets instead of Grandma's house.

Valentine's Day, especially if it falls on or near a weekend, brings out hordes of people who want to take advantage of the 24-hour wedding chapels to take the plunge. Considering that state law requires no blood test, no waiting period, and no proof that you actually even know the person you're marrying, getting hitched in Vegas holds an often irresistible allure.

But of all the holidays, New Year's Eve is the biggest. Over the past few years a big fireworks spectacular over The Strip at midnight has drawn hundreds of thousands of people to town. Most hotels sell out quickly and early and, no matter when the room was booked, it's likely to cost two to three times the normal room rate.

The only exception to the holiday rule is Christmas, with the week or two leading up to December 25th historically the slowest of the year. For the smallest crowds and cheapest room rates, forget Santa and come to Vegas.

But it isn't just holidays that need looking out for. Major sporting events, such as boxing matches or NASCAR races at the nearby Las Vegas Motor Speedway, have dramatic effects on room rates and occupancies. Although they're working on attracting one, the city doesn't have a major-league sports franchise, but it does have golf tournaments, bowling tournaments, and big pro-rodeo events each year, so vacation planners should pay attention to more than just football and baseball when looking for the busy times.

Lastly, major conventions can also cause major congestion here. Las Vegas is one of the top convention destinations in the world, and during peak periods there could be two or three trade shows or exhibitions happening at the same time, each drawing 40,000–50,000 people to town. Some of the biggest conventions draw well over 100,000 people, and when that happens, a normally cheap Tuesday night can become a sold-out nightmare.

The Las Vegas Convention and Visitors Authority maintains a calendar of major conventions that you can view online at www.lvcva.com, or you can call them at 877-VISIT-LV.

South Strip   Map 1

EXCALIBUR $$

3850 Las Vegas Blvd. S., 877/750-5464,
www.excalibur.com

With its cartoon castle theme (you keep expecting a certain mouse to jump out from behind a slot machine), Excalibur is still a popular choice for families, despite the more grown-up elements added in recent years (a male stripper show, for one). Yes, this place was built during the "Vegas is for parents and their kids" experiment, and since then the Sin City ethos has been reestablishing itself everywhere.

There are 4,000 rooms to choose from that, as of this writing, are making a transition. The older rooms are motel-basic in terms of layout, with a much more muted Camelot theme, small (for Vegas) bathrooms, and comfortable but simple furnishings. They are showing their age, so you should try to get into one of the newer rooms if you can. These are comparative palaces with more comfortable beds, oversized suede headboards, flat-panel televisions, nicer furnishings, and completely redone bathrooms. The plan is to eventually change all of

HOTELS

a room at Excalibur

the rooms to this new look, and it can't happen fast enough, in my opinion.

It's quite a hike, often through the crowded casino, from a guest room to, well, just about anywhere, although the good news is the trek to the pool lands you in a much nicer area, totally redone in 2007 with better landscaping, cabanas, a pool bar, and more.

The location, amid the busy South Strip, and lower-than-average prices make this a good choice for folks on a budget. Dump your bags here and go play at the fancier places across the street.

FOUR SEASONS $$$

3950 Las Vegas Blvd. S., 877/632-7800, www.mandalaybay.com

A true luxury resort hotel does not have 4,000 rooms, but in Vegas people usually forgo some luxury details (like personalized service) to get all of the perks of a bigger hotel. The Four Seasons offers the best of both worlds.

Their 400 beautifully appointed rooms are located on the upper floors of Mandalay Bay's

tower, offering separate check-in, elevators, and pool facilities. But the casino, restaurants, shows, nightclubs, shopping, and main pool area at the parent hotel and sister THEhotel are just a set of doors away.

The service is boutique-hotel attentive, and while rooms are essentially the same as those at Mandalay Bay, there are more upscale furnishings and amenities, including plushier beds and robes, minibars, and the usual flat-panels and high-speed Internet. The bathrooms are large enough to allow couples to share without wanting to kill one another.

Of course, none of this comes cheap. If you can get a room here for less than $300 a night, grab it. True luxury comes at a price, but for those willing to pay it, this may be the best place to do so.

LUXOR LAS VEGAS $$

3900 Las Vegas Blvd. S., 888/777-0188, www.luxor.com

There's something undeniably fun about staying at Luxor. Whether it's the wacky Egyptian exterior, the sloped walls of the Pyramid rooms, or the energetic zeitgeist of the place, this is a hotel that turns accommodations into entertainment. Even getting to the guest rooms is turned into a thrill ride, replacing elevators with inclinators that move up and sideways at the same time. Those and the dramatic open halls overlooking the pyramid interior make this a poor choice for phobics of many stripes.

Although all the Luxor rooms will be receiving a major makeover in the near future, the current Pyramid rooms are simple (note: most only have showers, no tubs), with furnishings that are "nice" but nothing to take pictures of that will make neighbors back home jealous. Meanwhile the Tower rooms, located in the blocky buildings just north of the Pyramid, have better decor and furnishings (and are a tad bigger). And if saving money is your idea of fun, Luxor qualifies there as well with rates that are often cheaper than similarly appointed hotels on The Strip.

There are five pools, a great spa, restaurants, and new features in the works with the hotel's current redesign.

MANDALAY BAY $$$

3950 Las Vegas Blvd. S., 877/632-7800, www.mandalaybay.com

The gleaming gold towers at Mandalay Bay are home to some truly lovely rooms with above-average square footage, above-average bathrooms (in both size and appointments), and above-average furnishings and amenities. While it may not exactly attain luxury level, it comes close and does it without the stuffy pretentiousness that mars the experience of staying at other hotels of this caliber.

The hotel's newer Gold rooms are even more noteworthy, with pillow-top mattresses, 42-inch plasma televisions, minibars, and retro-hip furnishings giving the space a clean and appealing vibe. The rooms are larger than the standard ones, so expect to pay more for the extra square-footage.

The service here is among the best in hotels of this size (more than 4,000 rooms if you count adjoining THEhotel and Four Seasons) and the

facilities (including one of the biggest and best pool areas in town) are top-notch. Prices are high, not surprisingly, with weekday rights often topping $200 and weekends almost always over $300 (and sometimes $400) per night. That puts it in a rarefied stratus against heavy-hitting competition, but whether or not it stacks up is more a matter of taste.

MGM GRAND $$

3799 Las Vegas Blvd. S., 877/880-0880, www.mgmgrand.com

With more than 5,000 rooms here, they certainly aren't lacking for options. The Grand Tower rooms are hotel-traditional in terms of layout, although the furnishings are quite a bit nicer than the average Holiday Inn. Comfy duvets and modern furnishings create a bit of glamour while the black-and-white marble bathrooms are generously proportioned.

Over in The West Wing (no, not the one with Martin Sheen), you'll find very small rooms (these were once part of the 1975-era Marina Hotel that the Grand replaced), but they are stunningly contemporary, with aggressively modern furnishings, lots of frosted glass and mirrored walls, and high-tech gizmos, including flat-panel TVs and DVD players.

The rest of the inventory includes spa suites, rooms with terraces, one- and two-bedroom suites, full-on "mansions," and $10,000-a-night Skylofts. Yikes. But if that's not enough, they've got nearly 1,800 additional places to park your luggage out back in the Signature at MGM Grand towers, each offering condominium-level accommodations with complete kitchens.

Navigating the enormous facility is a challenge, especially at busy times, but they offer so much to see, do, eat, and drink that guests never need to leave. Kids may enjoy the big pool area (with a lazy river ride) and everyone will appreciate the convenient Las Vegas Monorail stop right out back.

MONTE CARLO $$

3770 Las Vegas Blvd. S., 888/529-4828, www.montecarlo.com

The Monte Carlo is not quite as splashy as

HOTELS

FUTURE VEGAS

The face of Las Vegas is constantly changing, with new buildings going up seemingly every other week. While high-rise condominium towers are the latest rage (making up most of the new construction near The Strip), there's still a lot of action in the hotel market, with no fewer than a dozen major properties either under construction or in the planning phases as of press time. Here's the skinny on a few of the most notable:

CITYCENTER

MGM Mirage, the parent company of The Mirage, MGM Grand, and others, is building a 60-plus-acre development on land between their Bellagio and Monte Carlo hotels that is estimated to be costing in the neighborhood of $7.4 billion. Yes, $7.4 billion. And that's just an estimate, but even at that price tag, it is the largest privately funded construction project in American history. The project will feature a 4,000-room mega-resort (with a casino, of course), three smaller luxury hotels of around 400 rooms apiece, more than 1,600 condominium units, and an additional half million square feet of restaurant, shopping, and entertainment facilities, plus a high-tech people mover to connect the whole thing. The first phase is scheduled to open in late 2009.

THE COSMOPOLITAN

Although the hotel will be managed by the Hyatt chain, it will not be a Hyatt branded property and will not be a typically Hyatt low-key affair. No, the 2,000-plus-room hotel will be the centerpiece of a $2-billion development of casino, restaurant, entertainment, and condominium space going up just south of Bellagio. It is tentatively set to open by early 2009.

ENCORE AT WYNN LAS VEGAS

Before the $2.7-billion "first phase" even opened, Steve Wynn announced plans to build a $2-billion, 2,000-room expansion called Encore. More casino space, shopping, and restaurants are expected, and the hotel will likely be connected to, but run independently of, Wynn Las Vegas. Construction is underway and the building should be open by late 2008.

ECHELON PLACE

The legendary Stardust hotel was imploded in 2007 to make way for this $4-billion development of hotels, casinos, entertainment, and shopping. When complete, it will have more than 5,000 rooms in multiple towers, including a few independently run boutique hotels. Spread across more than 60 acres, the facility will rival CityCenter in its scope, but will not

its neighbors, resulting in an odd situation where people often overlook this 3,000-room hotel. That's too bad because behind that relatively bland exterior are rooms that are just as nice as most on The Strip, although not much more interesting than the outside of the building.

They are average in just about every way: size, layout, amenities—even the decor is "forget me right now" earth tones. Excitement is not their strong suit. But the room rates, often cheaper than comparable hotels, may bring the excitement quotient back up. I've seen off-season weekday rates as low as $59 here. That's a steal for any hotel in Vegas, much less one this nice. Bland, but nice.

One thing worth noting is that the epic CityCenter project is being constructed all around this hotel and they are working 24 hours a day to meet a target 2009 opening. If you stay at the Monte Carlo, be sure to ask for a room facing southeast to get as far away from any potential noise as possible.

NEW YORK-NEW YORK 🄳🄳
3790 Las Vegas Blvd. S., 888/693-6763, www.nynyhotelcasino.com
In a hotel as audaciously designed as this one (The Big Apple in half-scale with a roller coaster running through it), it would seem that the rooms should be just as entertainingly madcap. For good

have the residential component. It is expected to open in 2010.

FONTAINEBLEAU

If all goes according to plan, there should be a Vegas version of the famed Miami Beach hotel of the same name by 2009. The $2-billion development will feature 4,000 rooms, a casino, restaurants, shopping, entertainment, and all of the other things expected of a $1.5-billion hotel in Vegas. It's being built on land just north of The Riviera where the famed Algiers and Silverbird hotels used to be.

PALAZZO

By the time you read this, the new Palazzo resort will be open for business. If you count the more than 4,000 rooms at the adjoining Venetian hotel (and most do), the 3,000 or so being added at the Palazzo will make this the biggest hotel in the world. The Italian theme will continue, but more in spirit than through specific replicas. A 100,000-square-foot casino, 450,000 square feet of shopping including a branch of Barney's New York, 14 restaurants, another 65,000 square feet of spa space, a new theater to house the Broadway hit *Jersey Boys,* and more are included in the project, all housed at the base of a 50-plus-story tower. For more information, visit the Venetian's website at www.venetian.com.

THE PLAZA

In 2007, the owners of the famed Plaza hotel in New York, the Israeli based Elad Group, bought the aging Frontier Hotel and Casino across the street from Wynn Las Vegas for an estimated $1.2 billion. They closed the hotel and are building in its place a $4-billion version of the Plaza right on The Strip. It will feature more than 3,500 hotel rooms, 300 residential units (most likely for the super-rich), a casino, restaurants, entertainment, and much more – although no Eloise, apparently. It is scheduled to open in 2011.

THE TRUMP INTERNATIONAL

Yes, *that* Trump. The Donald makes his first foray into Vegas with not one, but two 64-story hotel/condominium towers, each containing more than 1,200 units. They supposedly sold out before the first shovel of earth was ever turned, but you know, it was Donald Trump saying that, so please let me know if you need some grains of salt. It's going up behind the former location of The Frontier Hotel, just north of The Fashion Show mall and across the street from Wynn Las Vegas. There will be no casino, but there will be restaurants and entertainment facilities. The first of the towers should open by early 2008.

HOTELS

and for ill, they're not. The good is that all that wackiness can be exhausting after a while, so perhaps it's best to have much more sedate rooms. The ill is that the wackiness is part of the fun.

Because rooms are located in the meandering NYC skyline buildings, they're not all plain boxes; depending on the section, they might be L-shaped, have entry halls, or feature other unique layout touches. They have most of the usual amenities found in Vegas hotel rooms these days including Internet, hair dryers, irons and boards, and the like. The only downside is that some (especially the Park Avenue Deluxe and Skyline rooms) can be very small. Ask for the Broadway Deluxe if there's no extra charge, but even there

is, you'll probably still be paying less than you will for a comparable room at nearby hotels.

The rest of the building gets us back to the wacky, and it is endlessly entertaining no matter how many times you've seen it. Plenty of restaurants keep you well-fed, and there are shows, an entire Coney Island–themed amusement area, a Greenwich Village–themed shopping area, and bar with a glittery big apple hanging over it. Sometimes it's the little things that sway you.

☾ THEHOTEL $$$
3950 Las Vegas Blvd. S., 877/632-7800, www.thehotelatmandalaybay.com
The best on The Strip? That's saying a lot

COURTESY MGM MIRAGE

a standard suite at THEhotel

flat-panel televisions in every room (a 42-inch in the living room, another in the bedroom, and a 13-inch in the bathroom). Wet bars, separate tubs and showers, and modern furnishings all chalk up bonus points.

Service, as you might expect, is luxury hotel-level at every turn, and so are the prices; expensive, to be sure, but no more so than the nicer hotels on The Strip and they offer more buck-bang here. Now if they could just do something about THEname.

TROPICANA $

3801 Las Vegas Blvd. S., 888/826-8767, www.tropicanalv.com

When it opened in 1957, it was almost an oasis at the south end of The Strip, taking more than 30 years for development to truly catch up to it. But as Excalibur, Luxor, the MGM Grand, and Mandalay Bay popped up around it, the Trop started to look a little dingy in comparison.

No big surprise, then, that the hotel is in the midst of a massive redevelopment effort, rumored to be costing several billion dollars and designed to feature more than 10,000 rooms. Everything in the old hotel, with the exception of the current high-rise towers, will be torn down in phases while they build new versions of everything from the lobby to the casino, showrooms, restaurants, and more.

Despite this massive undertaking, they are planning on keeping the hotel open while they tear down a chunk, build it back up again, and tear down the next chunk. What this means to you is that you will probably be facing a major construction nightmare if you choose to stay here, and predicting what you're going to find upon arrival is nearly impossible. But the cheap prices may be worth the inconvenience.

considering the competition, but THEhotel earns my accolades. Silly name aside, it operates independently of Mandalay Bay, but a walk down a long hall delivers guests to that property and all its casino, restaurant, and entertainment options.

Or, if you choose, ignore that entirely and it impresses with every square inch of the place. The sleek and dramatic public spaces, all soaring dark wood panels and dramatic lighting, are elegant without being fussy, while the beautiful one-bedroom, one-and-a-half-bath suites (standard) are fantastic departures from the boring box norm. There are sleek and modern furnishings plus three

Center Strip   Map 2

BALLY'S 💲💲
3645 Las Vegas Blvd. S., 888/742-9248,
www.ballyslv.com

Once the largest and most elegant hotel on The Strip, Bally's has worked hard to stay competitive and it has paid off. The 2,800 rooms are larger than average; they come equipped with all of the amenities you could need, including plush beds, high-speed Internet, irons and boards, and hair dryers; and on top of all of that, the furnishings are stylish and comfortable. If it weren't for places like Bellagio sitting across the street, this would be considered a luxurious resort and, in fact, it is.

But they don't charge luxury-resort prices. With off-season weekday rooms as low as $59 and peak-season rates a solid $100 lower per night than those fancier places next door, this is an unbelievable bargain.

Add in the fantastic location in the heart of the Center Strip and the monorail station out back ready to whisk guests to points north and south, and Bally's becomes an almost unbeatable combination of convenience, comfort, and economy.

All of that is good news, but there's bad news, too: The owners of this hotel are working on plans that may involve either demolishing it or substantially renovating it, so yet another decent and affordable hotel could bite the dust.

BILL'S GAMBLIN' HALL & SALOON 💲💲
3595 Las Vegas Blvd. S. 866/245-5745,
www.billslasvegas.com

This hotel has been going through some changes lately, but few that are obvious to the naked eye. The big one was the name, switched from Barbary Coast to the homey Bill's brand when it was purchased by Harrah's in 2007. Other than the signage, not much else was done to the place, and Harrah's fully intends to tear the

HOTELS

COURTESY HARRAH'S ENTERTAINMENT

a room in the Augustus Tower at Caesars Palace

joint down at some undefined point in the future, so if this has appeal to you, call to make sure it's still there.

And it does have its appeal. With only 200 rooms, Bill's is barely a blip on the radar next to the 3,000- and 4,000-room mega-resorts that surround it. That, of course, is its strength, giving guests the opportunity to make it from the front desk to their rooms without having to hire a Sherpa and leave breadcrumbs to find their way back. The rooms are fairly basic and the bathrooms are almost microscopic, though, so you're making a trade-off.

There's no pool or spa, the casino is tiny, and the on-site dining and entertainment choices are limited, but it's steps from more of all of that at neighboring hotels. The lower-than-average room rates may help you get over it.

BELLAGIO $$$

3600 Las Vegas Blvd. S., 888/987-6667, www.bellagio.com

There are two, and only two, downsides to this hotel. The first is the price, averaging around $400 per night on most weekends. The second is the sheer size (more than 4,000 rooms), making it nearly impossible to offer the kind of luxury resort service they want guests to believe they do. If you can afford it and don't care that the maids don't know your name, this is one of the finest hotels in the world.

Rooms are stunning (although certainly not the biggest in town), with elegant furnishings, all the latest high-tech gadgetry, and beds so comfortable they'll make you want to throw a match on your mattress once you get home. They are classically decorated with fabrics and textures that scream "look at me, I'm luxurious!" but don't exactly get the heart racing in terms of modernity. People looking for something hip should look elsewhere.

World-class restaurants and shows, swank clubs, shopping that you can usually only find on Rodeo Drive, a lovely pool, and a fantastic spa complete the package. Can you find similar for less elsewhere? Yes. But not the same.

CAESARS PALACE $$$

3570 Las Vegas Blvd. S., 877/427-7243, www.caesarspalace.com

Opened in 1966, Caesars is once again the Grande Dame of The Strip after years of neglect. More than $1 billion has been thrown at the place in the last decade and the result is an opulent masterpiece, perfectly balancing luxury hotel necessities with Las Vegas kitsch by way of its gaudy Roman decadence theme.

More than 3,000 rooms vary dramatically in style and function, with the older Forum, Centurion, and Roman towers providing small but complete accommodations; the Palace Tower (opened in 1997) offering larger, more extravagant surroundings including flat-panel televisions, richly modern decor, and plenty of personal space in the bathrooms; and the Augustus Tower (opened in 2005) laying out digs fit for an emperor, with more than 600 square feet of marble, fine furnishings, and multiple flat-panel TVs.

More than a half-million square feet of shopping is attached and, of course, there are tons of restaurant, nightclub, entertainment, and recreation opportunities, including the appropriately named Garden of the Gods pool area. It's pricey to stay here, with the basic accommodations easily surpassing $200 a night and the more upscale stuff regularly going over $400, but for a classic Vegas experience, it's tough to beat.

FLAMINGO LAS VEGAS $$

3555 Las Vegas Blvd. S., 888/308-8899, www.flamingolv.com

Bugsy's Folly is all grown up. As one of the oldest continually operating hotels on The Strip, the Flamingo aims squarely at the middle market and hits a bull's-eye with its terrific location, more than 3,600 hotel rooms, restaurants, entertainment, and moderate rates.

While guests may not write postcards gushing about the standard rooms, the furnishings and amenities are top-notch, the design is simple and functional, and they can save you some dough. But it's the newer "Go" rooms that are worth buzzing about as the official "coolest" rooms on The Strip.

Done with a big nod to the Bugsy Siegel era, the rooms feature decidedly retro decor with big white padded vinyl headboards, furnishings that look like they time-traveled from the 1940s, and full walls of white drapes (electronic, no less) offset by vibrant pinks and deep browns in the wallpaper, carpeting, and accents. Flat-panel televisions, CD/DVD players, high-speed Internet, and bathrooms with frosted glass walls keep it modern so the overall effect is very hip. Staying in one of them will cost you extra (about $50 more per night if the website is any indication), but it's totally worth it.

This isn't a budget hotel—busy weekends will push the $200-a-night barrier for a standard room, but that is almost guaranteed to be at least $100 a night cheaper than the more luxurious hotels in the area. If that's not enough, they also have one of the best pools in town.

HARRAH'S ⑤⑤

3475 Las Vegas Blvd. S., 800/392-9002, www.harrahs.com

Believe it or not, with about 2,500 rooms, Harrah's is one of the smaller of the major resorts on the Center Strip. It isn't small, mind you, but smaller can sometimes be a blessing, especially when you're late for dinner or a show. Navigating the rambling casino can be a challenge as usual, but with doors out front that lead directly to the bustling center Strip and doors out back that lead to a station on the Las Vegas Monorail route, your options once you see daylight are virtually limitless.

Rooms in the newer Carnival tower are larger than most of the hotels from this era, with an extra triangle of space at the end providing a nice area for a table and chairs. Renovations to the decor have produced a nicer environment in which to waste some time, but even with the new furniture these rooms are not so luxurious that you'd want to spend all day here. They do come standard with some niceties like high-speed Internet access for those of us who can't be away from our email for more than three hours without having seizures, minibars in most rooms, irons and boards, and hair dryers.

Rooms in the older Mardi Gras tower are smaller and darker, mostly with views of other buildings, so unless the price differential between the two is prohibitive, go with the Carnival.

Speaking of prices, they seem to fluctuate more wildly here than at other hotels, so be careful—it's a fine hotel, but not worth paying an arm and a leg for.

It's also worth noting that the parent company, Harrah's Entertainment, is developing plans that could bring major changes to this hotel, so be sure to ask about construction when you book your room.

IMPERIAL PALACE ⑤

3535 Las Vegas Blvd. S., 800/634-6441, www.imperialpalace.com

Cheap. That's what you get here. Cheap rates, cheap furnishings, cheap amenities, cheap restaurants, cheap shows...you get the idea. But if budget is your main concern and you absolutely, positively cannot survive unless you stay *right on The Strip,* this is one of your best options.

The 2,700 rooms are motel-basic and small, but they are clean and comfortable, and did I mention that cheap part? This is the place where people check in, throw their bags in the room, stay out until five in the morning, crash for a few hours, and then haul their bloodshot eyes down to the buffet to re-energize for the day ahead. Furnishings and decor is instantly forgettable, and there are no jazzy flat-panels and electronic drapes here.

Of course, cheap rates often draw cheap crowds (not a judgment, just a fact), and an extra $30 a night can get a much nicer room elsewhere. But if that $30 is more than you want to pay, the IP will do just fine.

Just like their other properties in the area, Harrah's Entertainment is working on plans that may involve tearing this hotel down at some point in the next couple of years, so don't be surprised if you call and find the number disconnected.

HOTELS

THE MIRAGE 💲💲

3400 Las Vegas Blvd. S., 800/374-9000,
www.mirage.com

Put simply, modern Las Vegas wouldn't exist if it weren't for this hotel. While newer, more palatial properties have made The Mirage less cutting-edge, it is still one of the best hotels on the planet, and a recent top-to-bottom remodel and renovation has made it competitive with hotels built a couple of years ago instead of a couple of decades ago.

The more than 2,700 elegantly appointed rooms whisper luxury instead of screaming it, offering fine furnishings, a muted South Seas theme, and a complete list of amenities including marble entryways, high-speed Internet, in-room safes, makeup tables, and more. Some may complain that the bathrooms are not as big as what has become expected in this town, but they are still larger than average and, really, do you need to park a car by the shower?

The renovations to the public area have made things darker and more glam, but in a good way. It's like a really hip but nonthreat-ening nightclub here now and it's great to see a more youthful energy infusing what had become staid.

Expensive (and meant to be), it's still a few bucks cheaper than the really high-cost places and just as good in all of the important ways. This is a masterpiece that is only growing lovelier with age.

PARIS LAS VEGAS 💲💲

3655 Las Vegas Blvd. S., 877/796-2096,
www.parislv.com

The nearly 3,000 rooms in this surprisingly charming hotel are all done with a tasteful French provincial design scheme, which is really only important because it's one of the few places where guests can open their eyes and immediately recognize where they are. Although nowhere near as luxurious as some of the other hotels in the area, the accommodations are several steps above pedestrian in every quantifiable measure.

There are no surprises when it comes to layout or amenities, but everything is of a quality that feels more substantial than what can

a standard room at Paris Las Vegas

be found at many other hotels in its price range. Bathrooms are large and offer a separate tub and shower for convenience, plus makeup mirrors, hair dryers, and plenty of outlets for your grooming-tool needs.

If possible, check to see if you can get upgraded to one of the petite suites located at the ends of each wing. They are a little larger than the standard rooms and are often offered at the same price just by asking or slipping the desk agent a tip upon check-in.

PLANET HOLLYWOOD $$

3667 Las Vegas Blvd. S., 866/919-7472, www.aladdincasino.com

The hotel formerly known as The Aladdin was purchased out of bankruptcy by the twice-bankrupt Planet Hollywood restaurant chain, who promptly announced they would redo the hotel from top to bottom and make it hip, modern, and competitive. No one believed them, including me, but I'm not ashamed to admit when I'm wrong, and boy was I wrong about this.

The new Planet Hollywood is a winner throughout, from the gorgeously funky lobby to the dramatic casino and the additions of new restaurants, nightclubs, shopping, and entertainment has created an energy and excitement here that I didn't think was going to be possible.

All of the more than 2,500 rooms have been Hollywood-ized (or should be by the time you read this), each coming with its own Tinseltown theme and memorabilia. While there may be more than one "Pulp Fiction" room, no two will have the same collection of glass-encased goodies in them, so staying here will be a unique experience every time. The funky furnishings (velvet headboards, leather lounge chairs) are both fashionable and functional, and every amenity you could probably need is covered.

Prices have gone up, but are still more affordable than what you'll pay at more staid hotels.

TREASURE ISLAND $$

3300 Las Vegas Blvd. S., 800/288-7206, www.treasureisland.com

I almost didn't include this hotel in this book

HOTELS

COURTESY PLANET HOLLYWOOD

the lobby at Planet Hollywood

COURTESY MGM MIRAGE

Treasure Island

because I'm so annoyed with what they've done to the place. In an effort to shed its family-friendly pirate theme, they decided to try to make the place "sexy," stripping out the fun elements and replacing them with tawdry ones. I'm no prude—I simply liked the old hotel better than the new one.

Having said all that, it's still one of the better hotels in town, with more than 2,800 very fine rooms all done in a much more tasteful manner than the rest of the joint. Color schemes are muted earth tones and the furnishings are simple but comfortable. And comfort abounds in the amenities list as well, including pillow-top mattresses, high-speed Internet, and much more.

The grown-up environs will almost be enough to make you forget about those scantily clad female pirates out front.

◖ THE VENETIAN $$$

3355 Las Vegas Blvd. S., 877/883-6423, www.venetian.com

The rooms at The Venetian are stunning

achievements of form and function. An enormous bathroom is just inside the door, offering a separate tub and shower, a private water closet, and enough marble to pave a driveway with. Towels sit on wooden shelves instead of hanging on metal racks and everything is plated in gold tones, giving it a *Lifestyles of the Rich and Famous* vibe.

If you ever decide to come out of the bathroom, you'll go past it and find the sleeping chamber with oversized padded headboards and miniature canopies over the plush mattresses, custom-loomed bedding, and a flat-panel television. Beyond *that,* the sunken living room features couches, chairs, a desk, a fax machine/printer, and another armoire with another flat-panel, all done in an Eastern European motif that is richly elegant without being obnoxious about the whole thing.

It's almost decadent from beginning to end—and, of course, so are the prices. Some Internet research might find you a mid-week, off-season rate of just under $200, but you almost never find anything less than $300 on the weekends. Worth noting is the fact that the place is attached to a big convention center, so it can sometimes make normally cheaper weekdays outrageously expensive.

But you know what? When you're luxuriating in the tub in that crazy-huge bathroom, you're not going to care.

VENEZIA $$$

3355 Las Vegas Blvd. S., 877/883-6423,
www.venetian.com

It's hard to image how a hotel built on top of a parking garage, almost as an afterthought, could be such a delightful combination of visually stunning design and pure luxury. The sister hotel to The Venetian, the place is connected both physically and spiritually, but could be worlds apart if you wanted it to be

that way. The gorgeous public areas are instant classics, intricately designed with an Italian Renaissance detail that will make this a landmark-worthy building in 100 years or so (if it, unlike other Vegas hotels, can last that long).

It has its own check-in desk and pool area, limited exclusively to guests staying in this portion of the building. But while the riff-raff staying in the "standard" rooms can't bother you, you can bother them with full access to all of the amenities The Venetian has to offer, including their larger pool area, spas, shows, casino, restaurants, and more.

The rooms here are nearly identical to those at The Venetian, so I won't spend a lot of time redescribing them here. Suffice it to say they're big, luxurious, and incredibly expensive.

North Strip   Map 3

☾ CIRCUS CIRCUS $

2880 Las Vegas Blvd. S., 877/224-7287,
www.circuscircus.com

For families with small children who insist upon staying on The Strip, Circus Circus is the only truly family-friendly option. Many other hotels offer certain facilities or entertainment offerings the kids will like, but they are too often right down the hall from a topless show or some painfully trendy bar full of obnoxious drunks. Here it's all about moderation, something that concerned parents may appreciate but may wind up boring them after the kids go to bed.

The circus theme is frenetic and tiresome after a while to most adults, but kids should eat it up, especially when they see the circus acts, the carnival midway, and the indoor theme park complete with a roller coaster. Lots of new construction in the area will bring more off-property entertainment options later this decade, but currently you'll have to walk about a mile to get to the really good stuff on the Center Strip, so bring a comfortable pair of shoes.

More than 3,700 rooms are found in one of two towers (fairly standard in every way, fewer

clowns on the walls) and the "Manor," a set of motel-style buildings out back that should be avoided unless budget is an issue.

Worth noting is the fact that the parent company, MGM Mirage, has purchased more than 60 acres of adjacent land and plans a massive new development for the area. This will include substantial renovations to Circus Circus, but none of this is likely to begin much before 2009. Just in case, ask about construction when you call to book your room.

THE RIVIERA $

2901 Las Vegas Blvd. S., 800/634-6753,
www.rivierahotel.com

Until the late 1980s, The Riv was considered to be one of the most elegant, most luxurious, and most desirable hotels on The Strip. Opened in 1955 (Liberace played host and entertained the crowds), it was the first high-rise on Las Vegas Boulevard—a towering nine stories. But then along came The Mirage, Bellagio, MGM Grand, and all of those other pricey hotels, and The Riv's star faded quickly.

Today, it is a shadow of its former glory, with

tacky topless shows, straight-out-of-the-'70s decor, and distinctly unappealing rooms that appear "used." Many thought the hotel would meet its end when Donald Trump bought a small interest in the parent company, but he has moved on and The Riv still stands. The future is murky. Rumors abound, and as of this writing several companies are in a bidding war to buy the place, but it is unclear about what the new owners will do with the joint when they get their hands on it.

THE SAHARA ●

2535 Las Vegas Blvd. S., 888/696-2121, www.saharacasino.com

Another classic Vegas hotel is facing an uncertain, although distinctly brighter, future. Opened in 1952, the hotel had become a bargain hunter's paradise with cheap rooms, cheap gambling, and pretty much cheap everything else. For what you were paying it was pretty good, but it was still cheap.

Now a Los Angeles–based hotel and nightclub impresario has purchased the place and plans to start a top-to-bottom overhaul sometime in 2008. The intended end result had not been revealed at press time, but public comments and private expectations lead me to believe it will try to compete with places like The Palms and Hard Rock for the hip and trendy market.

The status of those renovations will depend on when you're reading this book, so a phone call to the hotel's front desk couldn't hurt if they are willing to be honest with you about construction inconveniences.

STRATOSPHERE ●

2000 Las Vegas Blvd. S., 800/99-TOWER, www.stratospherehotel.com

For the record, the 2,400 or so rooms are not in the big observation tower that looms large over the city skyline. Instead, they are found in a 24-story building down below. Even though it's one long building, it's divided up between the older World Tower section and the newer Premiere Tower.

There is no real difference between the rooms in the two sections, offering a fairly limited list of amenities (no high-speed Internet?!), but there are beds, chairs, a TV, and a bathroom, so what are you whining about? The decor and quality of the furnishings in the standard accommodations is strictly Motel 6, but there is absolutely nothing wrong with Motel 6 as long as you weren't expecting The Ritz-Carlton.

Located at the northernmost edge of The Strip, closer to Downtown than to the southern end, the Stratosphere isn't as conveniently located as perhaps it could be, but for the bargain-basement rates usually available (as low as $80 on a Saturday, mid-week as low as $40?!), it could be worth having to walk a few extra blocks.

◖ WYNN LAS VEGAS ●●●

3131 Las Vegas Blvd. S., 888/320-9966, www.wynnlasvegas.com

Weekday rates are almost always above $200 (sometimes WAY above), weekends almost always above $300 (ditto), and busy times even higher, with one-night-stay rates in a standard room often eclipsing the $500 mark. This makes this one of the most expensive hotels in Vegas, which of course begs the question: Is it worth it?

Well, you get a lot for your money, with gorgeously decorated rooms, floor-to-ceiling windows with amazing views, plush bedding and furnishings, huge bathrooms with separate tubs and showers, super-soft towels and robes, and just about every high-tech gizmo, including electronically controlled draperies in case your arms are just too tired from pulling those slot machine handles all day.

In any other city, a room like this in a hotel like this would cost twice as much, but in Vegas it's still just plain old expensive—and not just for the rooms (a bottle of water in the sundry shop is $7). For a grown-up experience (they don't even allow strollers in the building) or just a leisurely day in bed ordering room service, it may be worth the dough, and if you have the dough, this is undoubtedly the place you should spend it. For everyone else, there are very nice rooms elsewhere for significantly less.

Just Off The Strip   Map 4

GOLD COAST $

4000 W. Flamingo Rd., 888/402-6278,
www.goldcoastcasino.com

I'm going to make this relatively simple: as low as $45 a night weekdays, $99 weekends. Need more? Okay: more than 700 simple but clean and comfortable rooms, all of the standard amenities, plus a few perks like high-speed Internet (for a fee) and coffee makers, free access to the workout facility (small but more than adequate for most people), a nice pool, a big casino, and plenty of high-quality, low-cost restaurants for as low as $45 a night weekdays!

I'm sorry to keep harping on that factoid, but people whine all the time about how expensive Las Vegas has gotten and they are absolutely right. However, if you don't need an extravagant luxury suite right on The Strip, there are ways of still having an affordable vacation in the city, and staying in a place like this is one of the keys.

For those who want to be close to The Strip but can handle not being right on it; who don't care that the parking lot is filled with Fords and Hondas instead of Ferraris and Mercedes; and are perfectly content opening their own drapes instead of having some electronic doohickey do it for them, then the Gold Coast is one of the best bets.

HARD ROCK HOTEL $$$

4455 Paradise Rd., 800/HRD-ROCK,
www.hardrockhotel.com

This is not for people who want a quiet, relaxing Las Vegas getaway. No, this is a place for partying. I'm talking stay up all night drinking and gambling, scream at the top of your lungs, cannonball into the pool, wake up the next morning wearing someone else's underwear partying. I'm not encouraging this, mind you.

The hotel draws a younger, almost impossibly pretty crowd (and the people who chase them), which can be intimidating for those of us who aren't either. Although it is possible for the Average Joe to enjoy staying here, the Hard Rock really isn't built to accommodate moderate budgets or tastes. But for those who aren't easily intimidated and don't mind the high prices that come with such a popular place, the nearly 700 rooms are fantastic, with lots of comfy, very contemporary furnishings, French doors and a balcony, and upgraded amenities like Bose CD radios and high-thread-count linens.

As I write this, the new owners of the hotel are kicking off a massive renovation and expansion campaign to the tune of about $750 million. What that will mean is two new hotel towers, nearly 1,000 new rooms including 400 VIP suites, an expanded casino, a new concert venue, and more restaurants and entertainment, plus design refinements to their existing rooms and public areas. Asking about construction impacts is key if you decide to book a room here.

HOOTERS CASINO HOTEL $

115 E. Tropicana Ave., 866/584-6687,
www.hooterscasinohotel.com

So it's come to this, has it? Admit it: In the back of your head you knew that someday Las Vegas would have a Hooters Casino Hotel, didn't you? Yes, because apparently you can't find scantily clad women anywhere else in town, the Hooters brand has graduated from restaurants to full-fledged destinations.

I make fun of the place because it's easy, but when you get right down to it, they have created something not as socially or morally repellent as you might expect when you see the name on the outside of the building. They turned the dumpy old San Remo into a Florida-themed beach retreat, threw in some decent restaurants, redid the pool, upgraded the casino, and revamped all the rooms to match. They couldn't get past some of the limitations involved in not tearing the old building down and starting over—rooms are small with low ceilings—but all things considered, the place is fine, especially if you can get some of the

HOTELS

HOTELS

NON-CASINO HOTELS

You can stay in a non-casino hotel anywhere in the world. Why do it in Vegas?

Well, to be fair, there may be a couple of reasons. First, non-casino hotels are much better alternatives for families. Parents don't have to worry about the little ones walking up to a slot machine or asking what "Crazy Girls" means, and these places are smaller and easier to navigate.

Second, many of the big hotel-casinos sell out their 4,000-plus rooms on a regular basis, so those who don't plan far enough ahead may not have a choice in the matter.

What follows is a list of dependable chain hotels and motels plus a few independent operators close enough to The Strip to make it worth knowing they are there in a last-minute emergency. Visit their websites for more details about the hotels, but know that they are all in fine shape in fine locations and can provide a thoroughly "fine" Las Vegas vacation.

- **Alexis Park Resort,** 375 E. Harmon Ave. (near the Hard Rock), 800/582-2228, www.alexispark.com

- **Ambassador Strip Inn Travelodge,** 5075 Koval Lane, 800/578-7878, www.lvtravelodge.com

- **Amerisuites,** 4520 Paradise Rd. (near the Hard Rock), 877/877-8886, www.amerisuites.com

- **Atrium Suites,** 4255 S. Paradise Rd. (near the Hard Rock), 866/404-5286, www.atriumsuiteshotel.com

- **Best Western Mardi Gras,** 3500 Paradise Rd. (near Flamingo Rd.), 800/634-6501, www.mardigrasinn.com

- **Candlewood Suites,** 4034 Paradise Rd. (at Flamingo Rd.), 877/874-6542, www.candlewoodsuites.com

- **Carriage House Suites,** 105 E. Harmon Ave., 800/221-2301, www.carriagehouselasvegas.com

- **Clarion Hotel & Suites,** 325 E. Flamingo Rd. (near Paradise Rd.), 877/424-6423, www.clarionhotel.com

- **Courtyard by Marriott,** 3275 Paradise Rd. (near the convention center), 800/321-2211, www.courtyard.com

- **Embassy Suites,** 3600 Paradise Rd. (near Wynn Las Vegas), 800/EMBASSY, www.embassysuites.com

- **Fairfield Inn,** 3850 Paradise Rd. (near Wynn Las Vegas), 800/228-2800, www.fairfieldinn.com

- **Hampton Inn,** 4975 Dean Martin Dr. (near Excalibur), 800/HAMPTON, www.hamptoninn.com

- **Hawthorn Suites,** 5051 Duke Ellington Way (near the airport), 888/777-7511, www.hawthorn.com

- **La Quinta,** 3970 Paradise Rd. (near Flamingo Rd.), 866/725-1661, www.laquinta.com

- **Marriott Suites,** 325 Convention Center Dr. (near the convention center), 800/228-9290, www.marriottsuites.com

- **Motel 6,** 195 E. Tropicana Ave. (near the airport), 800/466-8356, www.motel6.com

- **Platinum Hotel & Spa,** 211 E. Flamingo Rd., 877/211-9111, www.theplatinumhotel.com

- **Renaissance by Marriott,** 3900 Paradise Rd. (near the convention center), 866/352-3434, www.renaissancelasvegas.com

- **Residence Inn,** 3225 Paradise Rd. (near the convention center), 800/331-3131, www.residenceinn.com

- **Super 8,** 4250 Koval Lane, 800/775-8463, www.super8.com

cheaper rates they offer. I've seen rooms go for as low as $40 during the week, although closer to $100 is more common, and the weekend rates higher still.

Considering that it is literally steps from the South Strip hotels like MGM Grand, New York-New York, and Luxor, that's a pretty good deal, if for no other reason than the location.

☾ LAS VEGAS HILTON ❸❸

3000 Paradise Rd., 888/732-7117, www.lvhilton.com
You know how you have to take a step back from a work of art to get a full appreciation of its beauty? That's sort of what the view of The Strip is like from the west-facing rooms at the Las Vegas Hilton. There are absolutely no other rooms in town that provide this kind of panoramic view of what makes this city so spectacular.

Popular with business travelers due to its location right next to the Las Vegas Convention Center, it's also a great choice for tourists now that the Las Vegas Monorail stops right out front, ready to carry guests over to The Strip for about $5. Cheapskates in good shape can easily make the one-mile (give or take) trek to The Strip, although I wouldn't recommend doing it in August unless you're a fan of heatstroke.

More than 3,000 rooms offer better-than-average everything including flat-panel televisions, silky duvets on billowy beds, high-gloss wood furnishings, high-speed Internet access, and more. The recently remodeled public areas are lovely also, with a classy lobby, plenty of restaurants, entertainment, and Klingons. (It's a *Star Trek* thing. Read the *Recreation* chapter.)

Unless there's a big convention in town, prices are remarkably affordable, as low as $65 during the week and often under $200 on weekends. If this hotel was located about a mile west, right in the thick of The Strip action, prices would be double that.

ORLEANS ❸

4500 W. Tropicana Ave., 800/675-3267, www.orleanscasino.com
Close enough to The Strip to be convenient,

this hotel, with its more than 1,800 rooms, is still far enough away to be considered a locals' joint, meaning they offer lower rates on rooms, meals, entertainment, and gaming. There's certainly enough of all of the above with a 135,000-square-foot casino, a dozen restaurants, movie theaters, bowling, a showroom, an events arena, two pools, a health club, a spa, and more.

The rooms themselves are larger than average, with an extra square of space near the windows for a table and chairs or a sofa. Bathrooms are small, so make sure you're on good terms with whomever you're sharing yours with. The in-room amenities list is long and the prices are usually around $140 a night on weekends and as low as half that during the week. Quite a deal.

PALACE STATION ❸

2411 W. Sahara Ave., 800/634-3101, www.palacestation.com
The Station Casinos chain is famous in this area for their local appeal. With more than a dozen properties around Las Vegas, they specialize in high quality and low prices with tons of amenities at relatively affordable prices. Until recently, though, their first hotel, and the one closest to The Strip, had been overlooked in favor of spending money at other hotels in their corporate structure.

But the Palace is back on the map with a major room renovation, new restaurants and entertainment offerings, new casino games, and much more. Whereas before I would've only suggested people stay here if they couldn't afford anything else, now I'd recommend people stay here regardless.

The new rooms are elegant: sleek and modern with flat-panel televisions, clean lines on the furnishings, and a tastefully muted earth-tone decor. They come well equipped with Internet service, safes, hair dryers, irons and boards, and more, so you can save some room in your suitcase. The fact that you can get them for as low as $40 a night means that you can fill up that extra room in your suitcase with all the souvenirs you can buy with the money you save.

HOTELS

COURTESY HARRAH'S ENTERTAINMENT

a standard suite at Rio All Suite Hotel & Casino

THE PALMS $$

4321 W. Flamingo Rd., 866/942-7777, www.palms.com

Battling for control of the young party set with the Hard Rock, The Palms has become a haven for celebrities, celebrity worshipers, and "pla-yas" of every stripe. I find the crowd around the trendy nightclubs and restaurants to be tiresome, but the really fantastic rooms provide enough reason to ignore them.

There are more than 800 rooms in two towers, all done in a low-key, contemporary style. They are packed to the doorframes with every convenience imaginable and are supremely comfortable, especially the glorious, fluffy clouds they call beds. "What's that? There's a big wild city to explore? But I'd have to get out of bed!" Seriously, they are that nice.

Those with buckets of disposable income or a recording contract may want to consider the fantasy suites, apartment-size accommodations that feature, variously, a basketball court, a bowling alley, a miniature nightclub with its own DJ booth, or a stripper pole on a stage. Yeah, it's that kind of place.

Rates range from surprisingly cheap to shockingly expensive. Leap on them if they are the former; check around elsewhere if they are the latter.

RIO ALL SUITE HOTEL & CASINO $$

3700 W. Flamingo Rd., 888/752-9746, www.playrio.com

Other writers have gotten into trouble for insinuating that the rooms here are not really suites but are more like overgrown standard rooms. Call them what you will; just be aware that while very large (more than 2,500, all more than 600 square feet), they are each one big open room—no wall between the sleeping and sitting areas—meaning there's no door to shut for a bit of privacy.

All rooms have a couch, chair, and tables, plus floor-to-ceiling windows (great views from the east-facing rooms), an in-room mini-fridge, and a vanity and dressing area outside of the bathroom (very convenient for roommates). These are not super-luxury accommodations, but the general vibe is definitely one of a higher order than you'll find at most chain hotels.

Downstairs there are enough amusements to ensure that you'll never need to hop the free shuttle to The Strip if you don't want to, including restaurants, nightclubs, several shows, a bowling alley, shopping, pools, a spa, and a couple (thousand) slot machines.

SILVERTON $

3333 Blue Diamond Rd., 866/946-4373,
www.silvertoncasino.com

In 2005, the folks who own this place threw tens of millions of dollars at it, turning what was a slightly dingy glorified motel with a Gold Rush–era theme into a really nice glorified motel with an Adirondack Lodge theme. It's stunning inside, with stone, wood, and copper accents creating a warm environment that is much less hectic and stressful than hotels on The Strip.

The 300 rooms are filled with first-rate furnishings, tons of handy amenities like high-speed Internet access and minibars, and free access to the well-equipped gym. The walls are a bit thin here and there's quite a bit of nearby freeway noise at the pool, but with rates as low as $79 a night on the weekdays, who cares?

As of this writing, there aren't enough diversions here to keep you on the property your entire stay, with only a handful of restaurants, a small pool, a casino, a couple of bars, and a big outdoor recreation store. A planned expansion will add more of just about everything by 2009, so be sure to listen for the sound of jackhammers in the background when you call for reservations.

In the meantime, there is a free shuttle to The Strip and the airport that will help guests get the couple of miles to where they'll want to spend most of their time.

TERRIBLE'S $

4100 Paradise Rd., 800/640-9777,
www.terribleherbst.com

The name comes from founder Ed Herbst, a man apparently so proudly ruthless in business (gas stations, originally) that he enjoyed the nickname Terrible and put it on his company. Decades later, they have expanded from convenience stores to a chain of small, low-cost hotel-casinos, including this one, located about a mile from The Strip.

There are only 325 rooms, most in low-rise motel-style buildings and the rest in a newer six-story tower. While they are perfectly decent accommodations, guests won't want to spend a lot of time inside doing anything other than sleeping. You get better than motel-basic with plasma televisions and a few other niceties, but for the most part, these are what you'd expect to get for the prices you pay.

And that's where we get into the meat of why you might want to consider staying here. Are you sitting down? Rooms can go for as low as $29 during the week. That is not a typo. Even when they aren't that cheap, you're talking about well under $100 weekdays and just under or slightly over on weekends. In a town where $300-a-night rooms are common, that's an almost unbelievable bargain.

There are a couple of restaurants, a smallish casino, and a nice pool area, plus a free 24-hour gym facility and a free airport shuttle for guests.

TUSCANY SUITES $

255 E. Flamingo Rd., 877/887-2263,
www.tuscanylasvegas.com

This rambling complex features more than 700 rooms in three-story buildings instead of a bazillion in a giant tower. Good or bad? Your call. Rooms have a sofa (convertible on request), work desk, full-size dining table, and a kitchenette with a sink, coffee maker, and mini-fridge (some even have small stovetops). There are also large televisions with in-room movies and Nintendo-style games for the kids (or grown-ups, I suppose). But to be clear, this is all in one big room, not a traditional suite with separate living and sleeping areas. The bathrooms are large, with separate tubs and showers and plenty of vanity space to spread out those hair care products. A small casino, on-site restaurants (with some really terrific ones within walking distance), and a nice pool area complete this often affordable package.

HOTELS

WESTIN CASAURINA 💲💲

160 E. Flamingo Rd., 866/837-4215, www.westin.com

The Westin brand has a certain caché to it, and while the Las Vegas hotel may not live up to its promise, it's worth knowing about. They took a derelict hotel (The Maxim) and tricked it out, redoing the entire place in cool slates and browns that offer a professional vibe, if not necessarily a fun one. This is more about serious business than Vegas fun, so if you're looking for a party spot, you may want to check out the Hard Rock or Palms instead.

The 825 rooms aren't as large as most in this price range (owing to the fact that they didn't tear down the old building, just retrofitted it), but they are stunningly furnished, sleek, and modern, and feature their trademark "Heavenly" beds and baths. The level of appointments is as good, if not better, than 75 percent of the hotels on The Strip, so despite the small size, they manage to pack a lot into it.

There is a tiny casino, a big spa facility, a couple of restaurants, and a bar, and that about covers it. I think that more can be had for similar or even cheaper rates, but there's something to be said for brand-name products like Westin.

Downtown   Map 5

THE CALIFORNIA 💲

12 Ogden Ave., 800/634-6255, www.thecal.com

Popular with tourists from Hawaii, The California has a Polynesian flair throughout the building, including the nearly 800 rooms. Give up some of the perks of staying at a fancy Strip resort—furnishings are more basic, TVs are smaller, and the list of amenities, while fine for most travelers, is not as extensive as elsewhere—in exchange for a much more friendly environment and much lower rates. Weekdays can be as low as $50 and weekends may broach the $100 mark, but usually not by much.

It's also conveniently small and just steps away from the classic Vegas experience of Fremont Street, otherwise known as Glitter Gulch, so if the few restaurants and lack of entertainment aren't doing it for you, you have options nearby. A rooftop pool, regardless of how small it is, is a rarity for Downtown properties.

EL CORTEZ 💲

611 E. Fremont St., 800/634-6703,
www.elcortezhotelcasino.com

Built in 1941, the El (as she is affectionately known) had never really been a hotel worth considering until recently. Mostly appealing to the retirement crowd and located several seedy blocks from the Fremont Street Experience, it was just too, well, old to be of interest. But the old gal has been reborn and now I'd put it up high on my list of choices if I were considering Downtown Las Vegas.

The public spaces and casino have gotten a complete makeover, eliminating the crowded smokiness of the former incarnation and putting in its place a friendly, casually elegant design scheme of dark wood and copper plating. Even the neighborhood surrounding it has gotten an upgrade with a new porte cochere accessible by a plaza of trees and fountains from Las Vegas Boulevard and the Fremont Street frontage filled with funky bars, wide sidewalks, landscaping, and fewer prostitutes.

The rooms got upgraded as well, all with flat-panel televisions, high-speed Internet access, and better furnishings. Nothing here will win any design awards and the rooms themselves are on the small side, but for rates as low as $40 during the week and rarely above $100 on weekends, you won't even notice the bedspreads.

FITZGERALD'S 💲

301 E. Fremont St., 800/274-LUCK,
www.fitzgeraldslasvegas.com

Upgrades over the last few years have transformed this hotel from an also-ran into a serious contender in the Downtown area. They added a pool (unfortunately located adjacent to the street and the valet parking area, so not exactly a tropical paradise), redid the public areas and hallways with significantly upgraded appointments, and made over the more than 600 rooms with better furnishings and decor.

All of the basic amenities are included, but it's worth noting that since the rooms are on the small side, the choices include a king or two double beds, not two queens. Roomies should be on good terms. The surroundings will never cause it to be mistaken for The Ritz-Carlton, of course, but neither will the bill.

FOUR QUEENS $

202 E. Fremont St., 800/634-6045,
www.fourqueens.com

The 690 rooms at the Four Queens got a serious upgrade in 2007, and while they couldn't do anything about their smallish size, they are much more well-appointed than they were. Flat-panel, 32-inch, high-def televisions are a great start with high-speed wireless Internet, coffeemakers, hair dryers, irons and boards, and comfortable (if not particularly interesting) furnishings complete the package.

There is no pool, spa, gym, or showroom with big headliner entertainers, but the casino is one of the friendliest in town and all of the entertainment and nightlife options that come along with Fremont Street right outside the doors tend to make up for the lack of other amusements.

So why would I include this fairly run-of-the-mill hotel on this list of what is supposed to be the best in the city? How does $44 a night sound? Weekday rates can go that low and weekends will almost never go over $100. People on a budget should put this one pretty high on the list of options.

FREMONT $

200 E. Fremont St., 800/634-6182,
www.fremontcasino.com

Another great low-cost alternative. Like most of the rooms in the Downtown area, these rooms (447 in all) are very small, and while they come with the basics, like irons, boards, and hair dryers, there isn't a lot else. Staying here is like staying at any respectable chain motel with a 6 or an 8 in its name, except that downstairs is a casino and just outside the front door is the spectacular light and sound show of the Fremont Street Experience. Weekday rates can go as low as $39, with weekends approaching the $100 mark but rarely going over it. Guests also get that unique Downtown experience of much more friendly, personal service. Expect to be called "sweetheart" and "hon" a lot.

THE GOLDEN NUGGET $

129 E. Fremont St., 800/846-5336,
www.goldennugget.com

Once the premier Downtown Las Vegas hotel (when Steve Wynn ran the place), the Nugget passed through a series of owners, each diluting its appeal somewhat. It was the epitome of faded glory, but now yet another new owner, the Landry Restaurant corporation, has tossed tens of millions of dollars at the place and it is, once again, the Grande Dame of Downtown.

All of the public areas received a major makeover, turning the property into something that wouldn't be out of place on The Strip. A big new pool area has a fun outdoor bar and water slide that passes *through* the shark-infested aquarium. New restaurants from the corporate parent, cool lounges and bars, revised entertainment offerings, and an upgraded spa have now been completed, with more on the way including more hotel rooms in a new tower.

As it stands, it is the biggest hotel in Downtown with nearly 2,000 rooms, all done in a comfortably modern design scheme with plenty of amenities to keep you satisfied: high-speed Internet access, hair dryers, irons and boards, in-room safes, full-sized desks, and furniture that you can actually sit in for an extended period of time without wanting to cry.

Although certainly the most expensive Downtown hotel, it is still a huge cost-saver over comparably appointed Strip hotels. Weekday rates are usually below $100 a night and weekend rates not too much above it, so this may be the

HOTELS

place to stay if you're looking for a better class of hotel but don't want to pay for it.

🄲 MAIN STREET STATION 🅢

200 N. Main St., 800/465-0711,
www.mainstreetcasino.com

I'm not one to throw around words like "gem" easily, but it definitely applies to this charming place. Done with an early 20th–century San Francisco theme, lovely touches (including antiques, stained glass windows and skylights, and stamped tin ceilings) abound in the public spaces. The effect is gorgeous, from the classic wood detail of the old-world lobby to the lazy ceiling fans above the casino bar.

There are three really good (to great) restaurants on-site and a nice casino, and while they don't have their own pool, the one next door at The California is available to Main Street guests, and the entertainment of Fremont Street is just a block away. Terrific all the way around.

The 430 rooms are bigger than many in the area but be warned that one of the two double beds will be right up against the wall, so "bigger" is relative. Each room was remodeled in 2005 with new, very comfortable (and quite stylish) furnishings, all-new bathroom fixtures, plantation shutters on the windows, and a substantial list of in-room amenities that will make vacation packing a little easier.

The only caveat to throw in here is that the hotel is located right next to railroad tracks. I personally never heard it during any of my stays here, but others I know have complained about it. Bring earplugs.

EAST AND SOUTH OF LAS VEGAS

With a few notable exceptions, the communities on the east and south sides of the Las Vegas Valley are devoid of the glitz and glamour one normally associates with the city. Instead, they're made up of mostly working and middle class neighborhoods filled with people who rarely venture to The Strip unless they happen to work there or have friends visiting from out of town.

It's tempting to say that this is the "real" Las Vegas, but it's difficult to ascribe the word "real" to just about anything in this town, so let's just call it "average" and move on with our lives, shall we?

Heading out of Downtown Las Vegas, Fremont Street runs into Boulder Highway, a major thoroughfare that used to carry people from Glitter Gulch to Hoover Dam before they got all modern and threw in a freeway. Along this stretch of road is everything from used car lots and strip clubs to some really nice and affordable hotels, including one with the second biggest casino in the entire city. It's the hotels that make the area worth noting, especially for people on a budget.

Between the Boulder version of The Strip and Hoover Dam is the bedroom community of Henderson. Packed full with just about every national-brand department and discount store, chain restaurant, and fast-food joint, this is the part of town that most resembles where the majority of visitors come from. But tucked away in unexpected places are a few of the area's most notable hotels and casinos—including one made famous by a Discovery Channel reality show.

COURTESY LAKE LAS VEGAS RESORT

HIGHLIGHTS

LOOK FOR ◖ TO FIND RECOMMENDED SIGHTS, ACTIVITIES, DINING, AND LODGING.

◖ **Best Casino:** Green Valley Ranch in Henderson is a beautiful resort hotel offering an equally stunning casino with surprisingly affordable and rewarding games (page 201).

◖ **Best Excuse to Forget Your Diet:** If you can walk into **The Cupcakery** and resist their sinfully delicious treats you are a better person than I am (page 202).

◖ **Best Nightclub:** Whiskey Bar/Whiskey Beach is a trendy (but not too trendy) ultra-lounge from Rande Gerber and Cindy Crawford, and while they don't actually hang out there all that often, it's still cool (page 206).

◖ **Best Beds:** Five minutes in the beds at **Green Valley Ranch** and you'll never want to get up again (page 208).

◖ **Best Place for a Respite:** The playground encircling the 320-acre **Lake Las Vegas,** surrounded by multimillion-dollar homes, world-class golf courses, a beautiful

Italianate shopping village, and some high-end resort hotels, is a genuine vacation from the go-go garishness of The Strip (page 210).

◖ **Best Golf Course:** Perched right on the shores of Lake Las Vegas, **Reflection Bay Golf Club** is as much a scenic destination as a sporting one (page 213).

◖ **Best Hotel:** The Ritz-Carlton Lake Las Vegas is not only the best hotel in the area, but it may be one of the best hotels in the country (page 214).

◖ **Best Manufactured Wonder:** Located about 45 miles southeast of the city, **Hoover Dam** (originally called Boulder Dam) soars more than 700 feet from its base and quite literally changed the course of history for the western United States (page 219).

◖ **Best Recreation:** Lake Mead is one of the top recreation destinations in the country for swimming, paddling, and power-boating yourself into a frenzy (page 220).

Lake Mead National Recreation Area offers outdoor enthusiasts year-round opportunities for swimming, waterskiing, camping, boating, fishing, tours, and cruises.

LAS VEGAS NEWS BUREAU/LVCVA

Lake Mead Drive, a scenic highway that eventually leads to the Lake Mead National Recreation Area (hence the street name), crosses Boulder Highway. Situated along this road is Lake Las Vegas, a smaller synthetic natural wonder surrounded by residential, entertainment, and recreation opportunities that absolutely shouldn't be missed, along with a couple of the finest hotels within a 300-mile radius. Lakeshore Scenic Drive leads to Lake Mead's creator and the area's top sight: Hoover Dam.

For those visiting Las Vegas for the first or even second time, this region can provide some serious bargains or a welcome respite from the overwhelming neon glitz. It's surprising what can be found by venturing away from The Strip.

PLANNING YOUR TIME

Deciding how much time to spend in the communities east of Las Vegas really depends on why you're going.

It's possible to hit all of the high points, including the casinos and shops, and even get a little bit of rest and relaxation all in one day, but to see it all or to concentrate on one specific agenda, it may be best to budget an extra day. Rabid golf fans aside, visitors really have no reason to allocate more than that to the area.

If you have one day, get up early and head down to **Hoover Dam** for a morning tour. The access to the dam has been limited since 9/11, so it's possible to see and do everything and still make it back to the **Lake Las Vegas** area by lunchtime. Spend the afternoon wandering through the Italian village shopping complex at MonteLago Village, maybe squeeze in a round of golf at one of the world-class courses in the area or get a facial at The Ritz-Carlton spa, and stop by Casino MonteLago to try your hand at the games of chance. In the evening, head over to Green Valley Ranch for dinner at any of their fantastic restaurants and then party the night away at the super-trendy Whiskey nightclub.

If you have two days, explore some of the other local casinos, including Boulder and Sunset Station and/or Fiesta Henderson. There's a lot to see and do here, including some very fine, very inexpensive restaurants, movie the-aters, and even bowling at Sunset Station and Sam's Town. The recreation-minded may want to spend the second day at **Lake Mead,** back on the links at Lake Las Vegas, or, if the weather is cooperating, on a hike to work off those all-you-can-eat buffet indulgences.

Keep in mind that there are some low-rent neighborhoods sprinkled throughout the Boulder Highway and Henderson areas, and with them come some typical problems. Most of the things to see and do aren't within walking distance of each other, but just in case, it needs to be said: It's probably not a good idea to hoof it at night. When driving, stick to the main thoroughfares and don't park in the dimly lit far reaches of the lots or parking garages.

HISTORY

A lot of the areas east of Las Vegas sprung up because of the massive requirements of labor needed for two significant projects: the building of Hoover Dam in the 1930s and the manufacturing of magnesium in the 1940s for World War II.

In the early 1900s, a series of devastating floods along the Colorado River accelerated a project first suggested by President Teddy Roosevelt in 1902: Find a way to harness the power of the river to fuel the growth of the American West.

Some 20 years after Roosevelt issued the edict, the recommendations were in place to build in Boulder Canyon—about 40 miles southeast of Las Vegas along the Nevada/Arizona border—what was then the world's tallest dam. Another decade of planning went by, but in 1932, the work to divert the river around the dam site began and an epic battle of man against nature ensued. Over the next five years, more than 21,000 workers laid enough concrete to pave a road from San Francisco to New York City—more than 4.3 million cubic yards of the stuff—forming a structure soaring more than 70 stories from its base. Even by today's standards, the Hoover Dam (as it was renamed from Boulder Dam in 1947) is an architectural and engineering marvel, but its impact goes far beyond the rocky walls of Boulder Canyon.

In many ways, it was responsible for the explosive growth of the western United States after the Great Depression. By helping to control the supply of water, generating massive amounts of electricity, and providing stable irrigation for valuable farmland, the dam helped create the major population centers of the Southwest, including, in no small measure, Las Vegas.

Many of the people who worked on the project chose to live in the company town, known as Boulder City, constructed near the dam, but it also drew lots of workers from Las Vegas.

Keep in mind that during the 1930s, the action in Las Vegas was centered in Downtown—The Strip didn't really exist yet, with the first major resort hotel not going up until 1941. So, with the bulk of the action and the bulk of the people coming from the Fremont Street area, a new highway was built to link Las Vegas and the construction site, angling from fringes of the city southeast to the state line. Since it was heading to Boulder Dam, it became known as Boulder Highway.

Entrepreneurs seized on the opportunity and several businesses opened along the route, eventually becoming the eastern border of Las Vegas as it grew and expanded over the following decades.

Henderson, located just southeast of Las Vegas, was another company town, mostly filled with workers from the Basic Management, Inc. (BMI) plant making magnesium for munitions and airplane parts in the latter days of World War II. At one point, as many as 14,000 people lived in the area solely to work at the plant.

But after the war, the need for magnesium dried up and so did the town. By 1947, half of the town-site's homes were vacant and the United States War Asset Administration even put it up for sale as surplus property. Locals and state legislators stepped in to save the area and, by 1953, the town had been incorporated.

These days, Henderson acts as a suburb of Las Vegas, which virtually surrounds it on all sides. It is a diverse community offering low, moderate, and extremely wealthy housing tracts, sprawling mainstream commercial developments, and a few very popular resorts and casinos.

Lake Las Vegas, on the other hand, was built not as a home for the common worker but as a playground for the rich and nearly rich. Developed in the 1980s by a real estate company, the lake was created in a barren desert valley by constructing an 18-story dam on a tributary feeding into Lake Mead. Not wanting to spoil the pristine essence of the area they were trying to create, the engineers had to find a way to divert the Las Vegas Wash, a glorified drainage ditch carrying the detritus of the city to ecologically unstable places unknown. The solution came in the form of two 84-inch diameter pipes, which now flow under the lake.

More than a decade after its completion, the lake is only partially developed with very expensive homes and a few high-end resorts. The full master plan will add an island in the lake with more resorts, more golf courses, more houses, and just more.

Henderson   Map 6

If there is a representation of middle America around Las Vegas, it is probably Henderson, the bedroom community located just south and east of the city. Acres of indistinguishable tract homes mingle with acres of nondescript commercial developments to form a comfortable, safe, middle-of-the-road town that lacks the kind of over-the-top pizzazz most people come to Vegas for.

But that in and of itself makes the area noteworthy. A lot of people get overwhelmed by Las Vegas and find themselves aching for the restaurants and shopping experiences they are familiar with and can more easily afford. Henderson is the place to find those comforts of home with enough Las Vegas–style twists to keep it truly interesting.

SIGHTS

CLARK COUNTY HERITAGE MUSEUM

1830 S. Boulder Hwy., 702/455-7955, www.co.clark
.nv.us/parks/clark_county_museum.htm
HOURS: Daily 9 A.M.-4:30 P.M.
COST: $1.50 adult, $1 child (3-15), $1 senior

A good option on the way back from Hoover Dam, this fun, inexpensive, and very informative look at the area covers everything from the dinosaur era through the Rat Pack days. Displays, interactive exhibits, full-scale replicas, relocated and restored homes and buildings from throughout the area, and old buildings from the Gold Rush years make this a lively way to spend a few hours.

The highlight is Heritage Street, a block-long go-at-your-own pace exhibit of authentic homes and businesses from throughout Las Vegas's history, moved here and restored to their former glory. Each is done in loving detail, from an early Henderson town-site house to an example of Las Vegas lodging from days gone by (forget high-speed Internet—guests were lucky to have air-conditioning). Each building contains period furnishings and other exhibits from a particular era, so it's more than just looking at an old house. Be sure to take some time to read the signs posted by various objects—they provide some really fascinating glimpses into the past.

It's worth noting, however, that many of the exhibits are outdoors. So, if it's one of those common summer days when temperatures exceed 110°F, a morning visit may be best.

ETHEL M. CHOCOLATE FACTORY

Two Cactus Garden Dr., 888/627-0990,
www.ethelm.com
HOURS: Daily 8:30 A.M.-7:30 P.M. except Thanksgiving and Christmas Day
COST: Free

This place is something akin to Mecca for those of us who consider the four basic food groups to be milk chocolate, dark chocolate, white chocolate, and truffles. A free, short but informative self-guided tour empties out into a very well-stocked gift shop where they give out free samples! And this is good chocolate, not the processed stuff found at the grocery store.

Outside the factory is a Botanical Cactus Garden, a four-acre collection of more than 300 species of drought-tolerant plants, cacti, and other succulents. It's really a beautiful and quite serene spot in which to soothe those casino-jangled nerves, especially with a box of chocolate just purchased inside. In December, they gussy up the place with thousands of lights and decorations to celebrate the holidays. Like the factory tour, the garden is open from 8:30 A.M.–7:30 P.M. and is also free of charge.

GAMING

As I've done throughout the book, now comes the time when I impart the most important thing there is to know about these casinos: Which one has given me the most winnings? Hands down, it goes to Green Valley Ranch, which over the years has rewarded me with some of the biggest video poker and slot machine jackpots I've ever won. It is rare that I

EAST AND SOUTH

LOCALS' CASINOS

When the Nevada Gaming Commission releases its reports about how many billions of dollars the casinos in the state have raked in, there are some interesting numbers buried deep inside. It's in the section where numbers are broken out geographically, showing how much money was taken in by casinos on The Strip versus those in Downtown Las Vegas versus those in the outlying areas.

These so-called neighborhood, or locals', casinos make a lot of money off the slot and video poker players for sure, but the amount of money they keep versus the amount of money they give back in winnings is quite interesting: They actually pocket less of a percentage from their players than do the casinos on The Strip or Downtown.

This figure is called the payout percentage. Under state law, all slot and video poker machines must pay back no less than 75 percent of what they take in over a set period of spins, known as the machine cycle. The exact numbers and machine-cycle details are not released because that would allow smart math types to cheat, but here's an example of how it works.

Let's say a slot machine's cycle is 1,000 spins. Over those 1,000 spins, the machine takes in $2,000 of your hard-earned money. Under state law, the machine must give back $1,500 somewhere during the 1,000 spins. This could be in small amounts here and there spread out over the cycle to multiple players, or it could be in one big jackpot to one player. When it's all said and done, the casino has made $500 off that machine during the cycle.

The payout percentage for casinos on The Strip is the lowest of any concentrated geographical area in the state, averaging 80-85 percent. The Downtown Las Vegas area pays a little better, averaging in the 85-90 percent range. But the Las Vegas neighborhood casinos as a whole are where players can find the best odds, with payout percentages averaging above 90 percent.

Why would they do this? It's simple: to lure people into their casinos. These smaller locals' joints can't compete with the glitz and glamour of The Strip and it's never easy to get people out of the pedestrian- or monorail-friendly tourist areas to places that require driving. So they take less money off their slot machines to make players feel like they're winning more money more often.

Of course, this is no guarantee that you're going to actually win more in a locals' casino. Yes, the odds are slightly more in your favor when compared to Strip or Downtown gaming halls, but the overall odds are still in the casinos' favor.

By the way, sprinkled throughout the town are scores of small, independent casinos without hotels attached to them. For the most part, these aren't worthy of your time unless you are itching to see how the "other half" lives. They mostly draw lower-income locals, and an air of desperation seems to hang over the low-limit slots, reducing what should be an entertaining diversion to an almost sad exercise in futility. Gambling should be fun, and it usually isn't at these small casinos, so avoid them.

walk out of the place with less money than I walked in with. Sunset Station has treated me fairly well, and while many people say they win all the time at Fiesta Henderson, I'm not one of them.

Scattered around town are dozens of smaller, independently run, non-hotel casinos. Generally speaking, they are not worth the time or effort of the car ride, with many of them straying way into dingy territory. Stick with the bigger places and you'll be happier.

FIESTA HENDERSON

777 W. Lake Mead Dr., 702/558-7000,
www.fiestacasino.com
HOURS: Open 24 hours

The hotel was originally called The Reserve and done with an African jungle theme, but when Station Casinos bought the place and gave it the Fiesta moniker, they revamped it into a Mexican jungle. What's the difference? Fewer elephants, perhaps.

Nowadays, that too-heavy-for-its-own-good

COURTESY STATION CASINOS

the casino at Sunset Station

theme is fading away in bits and pieces as the hotel is being redone, expanded, and moved up-scale. The new look is more of a southwestern cantina, all earth tones setting off the adobe. Generally speaking, it's a much more enjoyable space in which to gamble since you may no longer feel the need to keep an eye out for hungry pumas.

All that aside, the Fiesta Henderson casino does have a lot to offer: more than 1,900 slots and video poker machines, a couple dozen table games, keno, a bingo parlor, a poker room, and a small sports book. As with the other neighborhood joints, the limits on the machines and tables are lower and the payouts are purported to be higher.

GREEN VALLEY RANCH
2300 Paseo Verde Pkwy., 702/617-7777,
www.greenvalleyranchresort.com
HOURS: Open 24 hours
Different people have different ideas regarding what makes a casino comfortable, but high ceilings, plushy furniture, wide spacing between machines and tables, and soft lighting seem to appeal to the widest demographic, and Green Valley has all of that in spades. Its bronze and copper accents meld with luxurious stone and woodwork to create an inviting and cozy room, despite its 50,000-square-foot size.

Video poker and slots dominate the casino floor, with denominations ranging from pennies to dollars in the main room and a separate section with $5–100-a-pull slots. All of the machines are equipped with the latest ticket-in, ticket-out technology, meaning there is no more jingle-jangle of coins in the slot machine tray. Some decry this as blasphemy, but the convenience and ease of use is undeniable.

Surrounding the hip Drop Bar, a ring of table games comprises all the usual suspects (blackjack, roulette, craps) plus trendy games like Let It Ride, Caribbean Stud, 3-Card poker, Pai Gow poker, and much more. A big sports book, with all the latest high-tech gadgetry, rounds out the offerings.

EAST AND SOUTH

SUNSET STATION
1301 W. Sunset Rd., 702/547-7777,
www.sunsetstation.com
HOURS: Open 24 hours

A sister property to Green Valley Ranch, this was the most upscale in the Station Casinos portfolio until Green Valley came along and stole that crown. But that doesn't make the casino at Sunset any less appealing.

A Spanish Mission style with polished Mexican stone flooring and an elaborate stained-glass ceiling make this one of the most lovely casinos in town. The meandering twists and turns of the layout offer some unexpected and intimate spaces, but there's plenty of room throughout to claim a place of your own.

As with Green Valley, slots and video poker of all denominations rule the roost, with a similar array of table games grouped under the aforementioned stained-glass display. Bonus features here include a race and sports book, a 12-table live poker room offering Texas Hold 'Em and other games with very reasonable limits, a bingo parlor, and a keno lounge.

RESTAURANTS
BONEFISH GRILL ●
10839 S. Eastern Ave., 702/228-3474,
www.bonefishgrill.com
HOURS: Mon.-Thurs. 4–10:30P.M., Fri.-Sat.
4–11:30P.M., Sun. 4–10P.M.

Famous on the East Coast and especially in Florida, there are few branches of this chain of seafood restaurants out West, and this is the only one in Las Vegas (as of this writing). Several notches above your average Red Lobster in terms of food quality and presentation, Bonefish specializes in freshness with all of their selections flown in daily and never frozen. This is typical for much more expensive seafood restaurants on The Strip, but a refreshing surprise out here in the hinterlands. The wide-ranging menu will satisfy any seafood aficionado, and there are even some pasta, chicken, pork, and beef options for those who insist that all fish tastes fishy no matter what anyone says. Service is spectacular and the prices are moderate at their upper range.

CAPRIOTTI'S ●
1146 Sunset Rd., 702/558-9111, www.capriottis.com
HOURS: Mon.-Fri. 10 A.M.-7 P.M., Sat. 11 A.M.-7 P.M., Sun. 11 A.M.-6 P.M.

This place eclipses every other submarine sandwich shop in existence, including those with the little toasty ovens and the guy who lost all the weight. This local chain of family-run stores serves up hearty subs, from the traditional meatball, roast beef, salami, tuna, and turkey (all with an Italian flair) to Capriotti's specials, like The Bobbie (turkey, cranberry sauce, and stuffing—making it Thanksgiving on a roll) or the Slaw Be Jo (roast beef, cole slaw, provolone cheese, and Russian dressing). The prices seem high at first—$6 for a small, $11 for a large—but the small is 9 inches and the large is 20 inches, easily enough for two people.

There are locations all over the Las Vegas Valley, with a second Henderson location at 11155 S. Eastern Avenue (702/257-3354).

◖ THE CUPCAKERY ●
9680 S. Eastern Ave., 702/207-2253,
www.thecupcakery.com
HOURS: Mon.-Fri. 8 A.M.- 6 P.M., Sat. 10 A.M.-6 P.M.

Designer cupcakes have been the rage in major and minor cities across the country, but of all the ones I have sampled—and you have to trust me that I've sampled a lot—these are the best. Period. The choices of flavors may leave you quivering with indecision (something I usually solve by just getting a dozen), but if you have to narrow it down, go for the Red Velvet or the Oh My Gosh, Ganache, the latter a silky vanilla cake with a chocolate truffle baked inside, piled high with chocolate buttercream frosting.

FATBURGER ●
2300 Paseo Verde Pkwy. (at Green Valley Ranch),
702/617-2209, www.fatburger.com
HOURS: Open 24 hours

This chain has found its way into about half of the states in the union, and America is a better place for it. They serve burgers the way God intended them to be—big, greasy, juicy, loaded with cholesterol and calories, and dripping with fixings both traditional (fresh tomatoes, onions, etc.) and fun (fried egg?). They cost a few bucks more than the average McDonald's burger ($4–7, depending on the fixings), but man, is it worth it. In addition to the Green Valley Ranch location listed here, there are additional outlets at Sunset Station (1301 W. Sunset Rd., 702/450-7820, open 24 hours) and at 4633 E. Sunset at Mountain Vista (702/898-7200, 9 A.M.–10 P.M. daily).

FEAST AROUND THE WORLD BUFFET 💲💲

2300 Paseo Verde Pkwy. (at Green Valley Ranch), 702/617-7777, www.greenvalleyranchresort.com
HOURS: Daily 8 A.M.–10 P.M.

The "Feast Around the World" buffet is a popular staple at Station Casinos around town, but this one is by far the best—and the most expensive. Designed as an elegant bistro, the room is opulent for an all-you-can-eatery, but still lively and well laid out for those second and third helpings (dare I say fourth?). The serving stations offer a wide variety of ethnic cuisines—American, Chinese, Italian, Mexican, etc.—and all of the food is prepared and served with care. This feast costs a couple bucks more than some of the others (breakfast $9, lunch $11, dinner $18–19, brunch $19), but it seems worth it.

FIESTA HENDERSON FESTIVAL BUFFET 💲

777 W. Lake Mead Dr. (at Fiesta Henderson), 702/558-7000, www.fiestacasino.com
HOURS: Mon.-Fri. 11 A.M.–9 P.M., Sat. 10 A.M.–9 P.M., Sun. 9 A.M.–9 P.M.

Take a look at these prices: lunch around $7, dinner $9–10, brunch $12. It's the same basic concept as most other buffets in town—serving stations featuring different regional cuisines—but did I mention the most you're ever going to pay here is $12, and you get free mimosas with brunch?! The quality of the food may not be worthy of culinary awards, but it's

absolutely fine by just about any measure and darn good at these prices.

HANK'S 💲💲

2300 Paseo Verde Pkwy. (at Green Valley Ranch), 702/617-7777, www.greenvalleyranchresort.com
HOURS: Daily 5-10 P.M.

Most of Henderson is awash in a sea of chain-restaurant mediocrity. There's nothing wrong with eating at Outback, but you can do that at home. Instead, why not step out of the steakhouse box and put on some fine dining clothes for an evening at Hank's? This premier restaurant at Green Valley Ranch is patterned after their very successful Austins Steakhouse at Texas Station, but everything here is kicked up a notch with higher-quality surroundings (dig the crystal-beaded lighting fixtures and wall dividers), food, and service. The steaks are individual masterpieces while the Australian lobster tails are roughly the size of my head. The waitstaff is trained to synchronized-swimming levels, turning the presentation of the meal into a grand affair. Prices are higher than at Outback,

COURTESY STATION CASINOS

Hank's at Green Valley Ranch

of course, but instead of throwing another $20 in the slot machine, throw it at a good meal.

LUCILLE'S SMOKEHOUSE BAR-B-QUE $$

2245 Village Walk Dr., 702/257-7427, www.lucillesbbq.com

HOURS: Sun.-Thurs. 11 A.M.-10 P.M., Fri.-Sat. 11 A.M.-11 P.M.

Relocate this place to a dusty road in Mississippi and you'd have a nearly authentic Deep South barbecue roadhouse, complete with a hickory-wood smoker in the middle of the room. The selections here are vast, from simple pulled-pork sandwiches in Lucille's trademark sauce (more sweet than tangy) to ribs of all varieties to jambalaya and beyond. The spicy hot links live up to their name (have water available) and the New Orleans gumbo is probably the best found outside of Louisiana. Come hungry—portions are enormous and everything comes with two sides (the garlic mashed potatoes and macaroni and cheese are faves).

MEMPHIS CHAMPIONSHIP BARBECUE $

2250 E. Warm Springs Rd., Las Vegas, 702/260-6909, www.memphis-bbq.com

HOURS: Sun.-Thurs. 11 A.M.-10 P.M., Fri.-Sat. 11 A.M.-11:30 P.M.

Somewhat of a local legend, Memphis offers some of the best traditional smokehouse flavors west of the Mississippi. This small, family-run chain of a handful of restaurants got its start in Illinois, the base from which they fly out the apple wood for smoking the various cuts of meat they offer. Appetizers run the gamut, from a plate of stringy "Onion Straws" that is bigger than most hotel rooms to Memphis-style wings, crawfish tails, barbecue nachos, and southern fried dill pickles, to name a few. Entrées include baby back ribs (full or half rack), smoked barbecue chicken, smoked Memphis hot links, char-broiled shrimp, blackened rib eye steak, and a full range of sandwiches, links, and burgers. The pulled barbecue chicken sandwich has meat that almost falls apart when you touch it and is seasoned perfectly with their tangy, vinegar–based signature sauce and barbecue "dust." Portions

are enormous and prices are very reasonable—a hearty meal for less than $10 a person is easy.

PF CHANG'S CHINA BISTRO $$

101 S. Green Valley Pkwy., 702/361-3065, www.pfchangs.com

HOURS: Sun.-Thurs. 11 A.M.-11 P.M., Fri.-Sat. 11 A.M.-midnight

If PF Chang's hasn't made it to a "Big Box" shopping center near you, you owe it to yourself to check it out so you can be excited when they do come to town. These lively destinations offer absolutely terrific Chinese food knocked up a notch with California-style twists (the lettuce wraps deserve some sort of trophy) and enough traditional fare (orange chicken, perhaps?) to make just about anyone happy. With an average entrée price in the $8–15 range, it's also easy on the wallet.

THE SONOMA CELLAR STEAKHOUSE $$

1301 W. Sunset Rd. (at Sunset Station), 702/547-7777, www.sunsetstation.com

HOURS: Daily 5-10 P.M.

The fine steakhouse at Sunset Station is a more traditional experience than some, with a wine cellar motif offering lots of cozy dining spaces and a romantic vibe. The menu is steakhouse-basic with a variety of cuts of beef, several seafood dishes, and various poultry and game options. Nothing here stands out as an instant classic until you throw in one or more of the sauces available as accompaniments. Steeped in a béarnaise, bordelaise, hollandaise, truffles and veal demi-glacé, whole-grain mustard, or a deceptively tangy blue cheese au poivre, the steaks are enhanced immeasurably. Prices are more modest than most casino steakhouses—in the $18–30 range—and, factoring in that the price includes a salad, vegetable, and choice of potatoes or rice, it's even more of a bargain.

SWEET WATER PRIME SEAFOOD $$

9460 S. Eastern Ave., 702/588-5400, www.sweetwaterprimeseafood.com

HOURS: Daily 11 A.M.-midnight

Along with the nearby Bonefish Grill, this area

is becoming an unlikely hot spot for fine seafood dining. Sweet Water is unique in a lot of ways, from their warmly upscale design to the fun chef's tables with views of the cooking facilities to the fish market up front in case you want to put a grouper in your suitcase for the trip home. The seafood selections are vast with salads, chowders, and create-your-own-shellfish-feasts, and many of the dishes have a vaguely Asian or French spin, but it's often the tried-and-true plates that win the day here—the pan-seared swordfish steak served with a choice of accompanying sauces is perfect. A few steaks and chicken dishes satisfy the non-seafood eaters, and everyone will love the cheesy garlic bread appetizer.

ENTERTAINMENT
GREEN VALLEY RANCH
2300 Paseo Verde Pkwy., 702/617-7777,
www.greenvalleyranchresort.com

The **Events Center** and the **Whiskey Outdoor Amphitheatre** are two relaxed entertainment venues at Green Valley Ranch. The former is essentially a converted ballroom, while the latter is a casual space near the stunning pool area. There are no regularly scheduled performers, but they do draw a slightly better class of entertainment than what can be found at most neighborhood casinos. Harry Connick, Jr., Smokey Robinson, Josh Groban, Seal, and Bill Engval were just a few of the names that appeared in the last couple of years.

They also have a **Regal Cinemas** (702/221-2283) 10-screen movie theater complex with stadium seating, private viewing suites, and more.

SUNSET STATION
1301 W. Sunset Rd., 702/547-7777,
www.sunsetstation.com

This hotel also has an amphitheater, but theirs tends to draw a list of entertainers who aren't exactly in what you might call their prime. Think Kenny Rogers, Rick Springfield, Willie Nelson, and the like. Not that they don't put on good shows and, to be sure, the nostalgia factor is off the charts, but don't come here looking for Britney or Justin. Give them ten years and then they'll be performing here.

COURTESY STATION CASINOS

EAST AND SOUTH

Whiskey Beach at Green Valley Ranch

Inside the hotel is **Club Madrid,** a lively casino lounge usually showcasing great local and touring cover bands. While you won't recognize any of their names, these workhorses of the Las Vegas entertainment scene don't get these gigs for nothing and the crowds at Club Madrid usually have a great time.

Also at Sunset Station is a **Regal Cinemas** (702/221-2283) 13-screen movie theater complex and a **Kids Quest** (888/319-4655) daycare center for parents who want to drop off the wee ones and party in the amphitheater like it's 1987.

◖ WHISKEY BAR/WHISKEY BEACH

2300 Paseo Verde Pkwy. (at Green Valley Ranch),
702/617-7777, www.greenvalleyranchresort.com
HOURS: Nightly from 6 P.M.
COST: Cover varies

While you're at Green Valley Ranch, you may want to check out this indoor/outdoor nightclub from Rande Gerber and Cindy Crawford. It's all done in that kind of retro 1960s mod that is very popular these days for reasons that escape me. For a trendy nightclub, though, this one offers a lot less attitude and much lower cover and drink prices than found elsewhere. The inside space falls squarely into the category known these days as ultra-lounge, meaning lots of low-slung seating areas plus a DJ, although unlike many ultra-lounges they do have a small dance floor. The outdoor area borders the pool and features what they call "opium beds," big comfy platforms for lounging under the stars.

SHOPPING
THE DISTRICT

2240 Village Walk Dr., 877/564-8595,
www.thedistrictatgvr.com
HOURS: Mon.-Sat. 10 A.M.-9 P.M., Sun. 11 A.M.-7 P.M.,
individual store hours may vary

Built in 2004, this retail, dining, residential, and office complex is conveniently located right next to Green Valley Ranch. Designed to evoke a street scene (they say Michigan Avenue, I say lower Halstead Street), the complex features more than 40 boutiques and stores, more than a dozen restaurants, office spaces, and loft-style

condominiums on the upper floors going for as much as $1 million. Visitors may recognize some of the mid-level to high-end retailers, such as Anthropologie, Aveda spa and salon, Bluestone Gallery, Cachet, Pottery Barn, and Williams-Sonoma, plus dining outlets like Elephant Bar, King's Fish House, and PF Chang's.

GALLERIA AT SUNSET

1300 W. Sunset Rd., 702/434-0202,
www.galleriaatsunset.com
HOURS: Mon.-Sat. 10 A.M.-9 P.M., Sun. 11 A.M.-6 P.M.

This typical suburban mall is anchored by Dillard's, Mervyn's, and Macy's, and features more than 140 stores and boutiques with familiar names like The Gap, Eddie Bauer, Ann Taylor, Lerner, and, of course, Victoria's Secret (is it a law or something that every mall has to have one of these?). There's probably nothing here that can't be found in the mall at home, but sometimes when you're far away from home, that can be comforting.

SPORTS AND RECREATION
BLACK MOUNTAIN GOLF AND COUNTRY CLUB

500 Greenway Rd., 702/565-7933,
www.golfblackmountain.com
HOURS: Daily dawn-dusk

Finally, a golf course that satisfies without charging rates that make a person want to sit down and cry (or at least before you keep continually slicing into the woods). There's an older 6,550-yard, par-71 course with 18 holes and a 9-hole addition that came in 2004. While it's not as dramatic or as elegant as Revere or Rio Secco, Black Mountain offers enough challenges and enjoyment to keep even the most avid golfer entertained, if for no other reason than tee times can be had for as little as $30 during the summer and usually less than $100 at peak times.

HENDERSON BIRD VIEWING PRESERVE

2400 B. Moser Dr., 702/267-4180
HOURS: Daily 6 A.M.-3 P.M.
COST: Free

Evidence exists that there are ways to spend time outdoors in Henderson without the frustration of smacking a little ball into a little hole. This 140-acre facility features thousands of migratory waterfowl and desert birds. There are nine ponds and numerous walking trails throughout the preserve, making this a nice way to relax and get a little exercise. If it's summertime, morning visits are best; otherwise, it'll be too hot to enjoy.

REVERE AT ANTHEM

2600 Hampton Rd., 877/273-8373,
www.revereatanthem.com
HOURS: Daily dawn–dusk

With a 7,143-yard, par-72 course built in the foothills at the southern end of town, Revere at Anthem offers some stunning views of the Las Vegas Valley. Designed by Billy Casper and Greg Nash, the course has a Revolutionary War theme, with its 18 holes called things like Old Ironsides and Midnight Ride (Revere, get it?). A putting green, pro shop, and on-site restaurant round out the amenities, with prices in the $110–250 range for tee times.

RIO SECCO

2851 Grand Hills, 888/867-3226, www.playrio.com
HOURS: Daily dawn–dusk

Rio Secco is the golf course run by the Rio Suites Hotel & Casino near The Strip, although tee times are available to people who aren't staying at that hotel. With broad plateaus overlooking the city on six holes and stunning desert and canyon terrain on the other 12, this 7,332-yard, par-72 course is one of the most popular and most expensive in town. For hotel guests, tee times start at $250; non-guests pay $300 or more. Golf fanatics say it's worth it.

STRIKE ZONE BOWLING CENTER

1301 W. Sunset Rd. (at Sunset Station), 702/547-7777,
www.sunsetstation.com
HOURS: Open 24 hours

If bowling is more your bag (sorry, it had to be done), Sunset Station opened this state-of-the-art center in 2005 with all of the latest scoring equipment plus a snack bar, a lounge, a pro shop, a video game arcade, and

more. Flat-panel televisions hang above every scoring area, and the one facing above the pins can also be used for video projections, turning this into a new-millennium multimedia event. Who knew bowling could be so high-tech?

WHISKEY BEACH AND GREEN VALLEY RANCH SPA

2300 Paseo Verde Pkwy. (at Green Valley Ranch),
702/617-7777, www.greenvalleyranchresort.com

If sitting by a pool or getting a massage are your ideas of recreation, this should be your primary destination. The stunning pool area, with a sandy beach and views of The Strip, is only open to guests, but their 40,000-square-foot salon and spa is open to the public. Done with a distinctly Zen feeling, complete with treatment rooms that have opaque ceilings under reflecting pools, the spa offers all of the pampering you could possibly need. Come on, admit it: Wouldn't you rather be inside getting a massage than outside in the heat in polyester golf pants?

HOTELS
FIESTA HENDERSON ⑤

777 W. Lake Mead Dr., 702/558-7000,
www.fiestacasino.com

For lower rates with the features of a sizeable resort-style hotel-casino, Fiesta is the best bet in the area. Their standard accommodations can go for as low as $40 a night (although weekends run about $100) and offer basic hotel-style lodging with simple furnishings, high-speed Internet, in-room coffee makers, Nintendo games and pay-per-view movies, hair dryers, and irons and boards.

The hotel has a complete casino; restaurants, including a fine and affordable buffet plus a food court; a lounge, featuring live entertainment on the weekends; movie theaters; and a heated pool and Jacuzzi. In no way does this compare to the swank places on The Strip, but for these prices, who cares? Fiesta Henderson provides a flavor of the Vegas experience, with enough savings for guests to enjoy a show or spend more time in the casino.

a standard hotel room at Green Valley Ranch

◖ GREEN VALLEY RANCH ⑤⑤

2300 Paseo Verde Pkwy. 702/617-7777,
www.greenvalleyranchresort.com

Most hotels in Henderson are mere alternatives to The Strip, but Green Valley is a worthwhile destination on its own. Made semi-famous from the Discovery Channel documentary series *American Casino,* Green Valley is one of the jewels in the Station Casinos crown. Done with an elegant, rambling southwestern resort style, the hotel is a stunner from just about every angle, inside and out. Elegant without being pretentious, luxurious without being intimidating, it offers more than 500 rooms with high-ticket amenities like high-speed Internet, robes, all-marble bathrooms, and what are, I would argue, the most comfortable beds in all of Las Vegas. Seriously, you'll never want to get up.

On-site is a 50,000-square-foot casino; a dozen restaurants, including many fast-food outlets; a trendy nightclub and other bars and lounges; a beautiful pool area with its own sandy beach; a 10-screen luxury movie theater complex; a 40,000-square-foot spa; an adjacent shopping complex; concierge service; and much more.

It's not cheap to stay at Green Valley Ranch—peak weekend rates can go for as much as $300 a night, but off-season weekdays are about a third of that, making an average stay here about $200 a night. Expensive, yes, but a similar level of comfort and service on The Strip is going to cost more, so this becomes a bargain by comparison.

SOUTH POINT ⑤

9777 Las Vegas Blvd. S., 866/796-7111,
www.southpointcasino.com

There's a boardroom intrigue story about this hotel that is decidedly lacking in intrigue, so I won't bore you with the details except to say that what was once corporately owned South Coast is now independently owned South Point, but beyond a change to a couple of letters on the signs, this hotel is pretty much the same as it was in ways both good and slightly less than good.

The facility is packed with diversions including restaurants, nightclubs, a pool and spa, a bowling alley, a movie theater, a giant equestrian center, and a barn-like casino. It's all geared toward the local market, so everything here is substantially cheaper than comparable offerings up the street.

That applies to the lovely guest rooms as well, which can go as low as $60 a night on the weekends and as low as $100 on weekends. They are large and beautifully furnished, with a simple Southern California spa feel, flat-panel televisions, high-speed Internet, coffee makers, iPod radios, and more. Change the view out the window and you would never know you weren't on The Strip.

But you aren't, and here that's a bit of a downside. The closest major casino at the southern end of The Strip is six miles away, so a car is necessary unless you want to try to depend on the free shuttle.

SUNSET STATION ⑤

1301 W. Sunset Rd., 702/547-7777,
www.sunsetstation.com

The sister property to Green Valley Ranch may

not be as luxurious, but it's also not as expensive. The hotel, done in an attractive Spanish Mission architecture scheme, features a 110,000-square-foot casino; more than a dozen restaurants, including (heaven help us) Hooters; a 13-screen movie theater complex; an outdoor performance amphitheater; several bars and lounges; a Kids Quest day care and activity center; a heated pool and Jacuzzi; a bowling alley; and 450-plus rooms and suites.

The accommodations here are more along the lines of a standard hotel room—the kind of thing found at a Holiday Inn. But with modern and comfortable furnishings, irons and boards, hair dryers, high-speed Internet access, in-room pay-per-view movies, and many more conveniences, Sunset Station offers more than you'll probably ever need in a hotel room. Peak season weekend rates rarely run more than $150 per night, with rooms often going for less than half that on slower weekdays.

PRACTICALITIES
Information and Services
For more information about the city of Henderson, visit the official city-sponsored website at www.cityofhenderson.com or contact the Henderson Chamber of Commerce at 702/565-8951 or online at www.hendersonchamber.com.

Many of the hotels, restaurants, and entertainment facilities mentioned in this section are featured on most Las Vegas tourism websites, including www.Vegas4Visitors.com, www.Vegas.com, and www.LasVegas.com, plus the Las Vegas Convention and Visitors Authority (877/VISIT-LV, www.visitlasvegas.com) has additional information.

Essential services are located throughout the city, including branches of all major banks (ATMs and check-cashing services are available at the casinos, of course). There is a full-service post office at 404 S. Boulder Highway (near Lake Mead Parkway, 702/558-7486) and several quick-serve locations scattered around the city. For more details, visit the United States Postal Service website at www.usps.gov.

St. Rose Dominican Hospital is located at 102 E. Lake Mead Drive (702/564-2622) for major emergencies, and there's a TLC Care Center at 1500 W. Warm Springs Road (702/547-6700) for lesser ones.

Getting There and Around
The best way to get to the stuff worth seeing and doing in Henderson is by car. It's only a 15-minute drive (depending on traffic) from The Strip to the major casinos and shopping areas, but once in Henderson, none of them are within easy walking distance of each other. Taking cabs is prohibitively expensive. You could try to navigate your way using the Las Vegas city bus system, but if that's your only option you may want to rethink going in the first place. As mentioned previously elsewhere, the bus system in this town is notoriously ineffectual. There are no other modes of mass transit.

So driving is it. From The Strip or Downtown, hop on I-15 South to I-215 East. Get off at Green Valley Parkway for Green Valley Ranch and the shops and restaurants of The District. Go a few more miles to Lake Mead Drive and I-515 for Fiesta Henderson. Continue north on I-515 to Sunset for Sunset Station, the Galleria at Sunset, and the bulk of the name-brand shopping outlets and restaurants mentioned.

If Green Valley Ranch is your sole Henderson destination, they do offer a free shuttle to and from Mandalay Bay from around 9 A.M.–10 P.M. on weekdays and 9 A.M.–11 P.M. on weekends. Check their website (www.greenvalleyranchresort.com) for the latest schedule.

Lake Las Vegas   Map 6

Created over a decade, Lake Las Vegas is a manufactured oasis in the middle of the desert. A short drive east of the city through small tract-style home developments delivers visitors to a stone archway, complete with waterfalls, that somehow manages to be understated considering what lies beyond it.

A long, winding road descends through lushly landscaped golf courses, and to the left is one of the most pure and scenic views of The Strip from anywhere in town. The lake lies just around a corner, tucked into a valley, surrounded by the graceful Italianate- and southwestern-style architecture of the homes, resorts, and commercial districts. It really is a stunning achievement of form and function, a testament to what can be accomplished with the right amount of vision and money.

Lake Las Vegas is the anti-Vegas: relaxed where the city is harried, calming where the city is overstimulating. Visitors come here to unwind, recharge, and affirm that a Las Vegas vacation doesn't have to mean staying up all night drinking and gambling. And even if it does, they can take a break from it here.

SIGHTS
◖ LAKE LAS VEGAS
1605 Lake Las Vegas Pkwy., 702/997-7347, www.lakelasvegas.com

Yes, it was manufactured, mostly as a playground for the wealthy folks who can afford to buy the big houses that overlook it, but that doesn't change the fact that this is still a lovely and very scenic place to get a little recreation under your belt.

Power boats are not allowed on the lake, but there are still a variety of ways to get out onto it, including kayaks, sailboats, sailboards, pedal boats, and canoes. Boating and fishing supplies are available at the **MonteLago Village Dockhouse** (702/568-6024), located at the shoreline of MonteLago Village.

The lake has been stocked with a diverse se-

lection of bass, bluegill, bonefish, sunfish, and trout to appeal to fly-fishing enthusiasts. Lessons, group outings, and equipment rentals are available through the **Outdoor Source** (702/499-8921, www.outdoorsource.net).

Hiking and mountain bike trails are scattered throughout the hills above the lake, although there are no formal programs offered to the general public at this time, so it's all do-it-yourself.

The Lake Las Vegas loop is a 3.5-mile trail skirting the fringes of the community with a dual scenic vista of beautiful desert landscape alongside some of the priciest real estate in the country. The Wetland Park trail goes down closer to the lake and all of the natural flora and fauna associated with it.

Guests of the hotels in the area can participate in group outings, so check with the front desk of either The Ritz-Carlton or Loews hotel for schedules and availability.

The Ritz-Carlton, in particular, offers a wide variety of outdoor activities for its guests, the most noteworthy of which include evening "Stars and S'mores" or "Stars and Cigars" adventures, complete with resident astronomers pointing out the constellations and attendants cooking over a campfire or lighting stogies.

GAMING
CASINO MONTELAGO
8 Strada Di Villaggio, 877/553-3555, www.casinomontelago.com
HOURS: Open 24 hours

The 40,000 square feet of gaming space here is designed to look like an old Italian winery. There are more than 600 slot and video poker machines, all coinless (they accept bills, but pay out in tickets that have to be redeemed by attendants or at the casino cage), a small sports book/lounge, and about a dozen table games, including blackjack, craps, and roulette, among others. It's a very friendly, relaxed space, usually much less intimidating and in-your-face than The Strip casinos. So, for a quiet place to gamble away your life savings, this is the place you should consider first. I've done very well at Casino MonteLago on all but one occasion, one time taking out about three times the rather substantial stake I walked in with.

RESTAURANTS
BISTRO ZINC $$

15 Via Bel Canto, 702/567-9462, www.bistrozinclv.com
The brainchild of Bistro Zinc is Joseph Keller, late of Josef's Brasserie on The Strip and brother of the celebrated Thomas Keller of Napa's French Laundry fame. Here, he takes his rather extensive knowledge of food and how to serve it and creates a lively bistro serving American food with French influences and looking a lot like New Orleans cuisine. Po'boys, designer pizzas, salads, and an oyster bar are among the offerings at lunch, while dinner is heavy on the seafood but rounded out with braised short ribs, duck confit, and other beef and poultry dishes. The location, virtually poised on the banks of the lake, couldn't be better for a lovely dinner.

COMO'S STEAKHOUSE $$

10 Via Brianza, Ste. 100, 702/567-9950,
www.comosllv.com
HOURS: Daily 11:30 A.M.-10 P.M.
Also by Joseph Keller, this one focuses on the beef portion of the program. With a whimsically colored decor mixing startling blues and yellows, the restaurant is a beautiful departure from the typically staid steakhouses that populate this town. The menu is sprinkled with the standard steak and seafood fare, all done with care and worth the elevated prices ($14–49), but dig a little deeper for the true standouts, like the prime rib wraps, tender pieces of beef and tangy bleu cheese dressing in a soft tortilla, or the rotisserie chicken, perfectly seasoned with a zesty flair and cooked to the precise point where it is neither too dry nor too moist, something few rotisserie chickens live up to. A flourless chocolate cake is the star of a deliciously tempting dessert selection.

MEDICI CAFÉ & TERRACE $$

1610 Lake Las Vegas Pkwy. (at The Ritz-Carlton), 702/567-4700
HOURS: Daily 7 A.M.-3 P.M. and 6 -10 P.M.
You'd expect the restaurant at The Ritz to be nice—and you won't be disappointed. It features an elegant dining room, with giant windows overlooking the gardens and lake, and an outdoor dining patio for warm evenings. For those planning a romantic dinner, it would be hard to find a better locale than this. The Mediterranean-influenced menu features a wide range of dishes to satisfy just about any mood, with entrées in the $15–30 range. Be sure to save room for dessert: Their pastry chef has won awards for his creations and you'll be hunting through your thesaurus for days trying to come up with enough superlatives to heap on them.

MONTELAGO VILLAGE EATERIES $

75 Strada Nathan, 866/752-9558,
www.montelagovillage.com
Scattered throughout the MonteLago Village entertainment complex are a bunch of small eateries worth knowing about. Simple fare may be found at **Caffe Positano** (702/567-1450, 7:30 A.M.–7 P.M. daily), a simple storefront-type cafe with drop-to-the-floor delicious pastries (go here for breakfast) and hearty sandwiches for lunch, most less than $10.

The **Tappo Bar** at Casino MonteLago (702/939-8888, 11 A.M.–10 P.M. daily) is a small bar/restaurant with amazing hot dogs and lots of great appetizers, all less than $10.

Tenuta, also at Casino MonteLago (702/939-8888, 24 hours) is a coffeehouse-style restaurant with an inexpensive, wide-ranging menu of steaks and seafood, sandwiches, pastas, and salads, most less than $10.

Visitors with an active sweet tooth have two must-stop locations: **Tutti Gelati** (702/564-5555, www.tuttigelati.com, 11 A.M.–8 P.M. daily) serves up the richest Italian ice cream outside of Tuscany and **The Rocky Mountain Chocolate Factory** (702/547-1000, 10 A.M.–6 P.M. daily) has signature caramel apples and homemade fudge that are out of this world.

Stars on the Lake concert series at MonteLago Village

ENTERTAINMENT
MONTELAGO VILLAGE
75 Strada Nathan, 702/564-4766,
www.montelagovillage.com
HOURS: Individual store hours vary

In keeping with its general laid-back vibe, Lake Las Vegas doesn't have the kind of high-energy entertainment scene found in town a few miles away. Although there are discussions under-way at press time to open a full-fledged night-club in MonteLago Village, at this juncture the nightlife is limited to the lobby lounge at **The Ritz-Carlton** (702/567-4700), the bar at **Casino MonteLago** (877/553-3555, www.casinomontelago.com), the lounge at **Como's Steakhouse** (702/564-9950), and the bar at **Sunset and Vines wine shop** (702/382-7900), all located within the village itself. Occasional live entertainment spices up the proceedings, usually on weekends, but for the most part these are better suited toward quiet drinks with friends or coworkers.

There is really nothing noteworthy about any of these spots. That's not to say they aren't nice; there just isn't a standout feature that would put one over another. Since they are all within walking distance of one another (and walking is mandatory in the pedestrian-only village), check them out and see which has the ambience suiting your mood on that particular night.

MonteLago Village does sponsor a variety of events throughout the complex, including concerts on a floating stage on the lake, ice skating during the winter, art shows, and peri-odic theme parties. During the late spring and summer months, they have Movies Al Fresco, an outdoor showing of classic films, plus jazz concerts every weekend. Check the website or call the hotline for details.

SHOPPING
MONTELAGO VILLAGE
75 Strada Nathan, 866/752-9558,
www.montelagovillage.com
HOURS: Individual store hours vary

This shopping and dining complex is done as a faithful replica of a seaside Italian village,

COURTESY LAKE LAS VEGAS RESORT

The Falls Golf Club at Lake Las Vegas

complete with cobblestone streets and candy-colored paint schemes. It's a lovely place in which to stroll and shop, even on warm days when misters provide some relief from the broiling sun. There are about a dozen boutiques, mostly of the high-end variety (gold cards, be ready), but shoppers can often find some wonderfully unique items at a bargain. Among the offerings are men's and women's apparel, perfumes and cosmetics, bath and body supplies, fine art galleries, jewelry, floral arrangements and gifts, home furnishings and accessories, and golf accoutrements.

SPORTS AND RECREATION
THE FALLS GOLF CLUB
101 Via Vin Santo, 877/698-4653,
www.lakelasvegas.com/golf_falls.asp
HOURS: Daily dawn-dusk
The Falls is a 7,250-yard, par-72 course designed by Tom Weiskopf, former PGA champ and now world-renowned links architect. Arranged on the hills above the lake, the course provides stunning vistas, including a postcard-

worthy view of The Strip in the distance. Golf fans say that while certainly a challenge, the holes here are more suited to a relaxing afternoon with a few buddies than a cutthroat game with pros. A clubhouse and an Italian restaurant are on-site. Greens fees range from $150–270 and include a fully stocked cart and range use prior to play.

REFLECTION BAY GOLF CLUB
75 Montelago Blvd., 877/698-4653,
www.lakelasvegas.com/golf_reflection.asp
HOURS: Daily dawn-dusk
Designed by golf superstar Jack Nicklaus, Reflection Bay offers a 7,261-yard, par-72 course winding its way through the desert terrain and along the shores of the lake. In addition to being a serious test for serious golfers, it provides some of the most breathtaking scenery found on any course in the region. Facilities include a full clubhouse, a terrific restaurant with fine Mediterranean cuisine, and the Golf Institute of Las Vegas, offering a variety of lessons. Greens fees range from $150–270 and include a fully stocked cart and range use prior to play.

HOTELS
LOEWS LAKE LAS VEGAS ⑤⑤
101 Montelago Blvd., 702/567-6000,
www.loewslakelasvegas.com
Prior to 2006, this building was the Hyatt Lake Las Vegas. Instead of building their own place as they originally intended, Loews bought the Hyatt and are slowly putting their imprint on the property through some mostly cosmetic remodeling. The 500 rooms in the hotel aren't quite as luxurious as those in The Ritz, but they also aren't quite as expensive. Each is done in an appealing Moroccan scheme with heavy wood furnishings and leather details wrapping up a full list of convenient in-room amenities. The property features a dramatic, multilevel lobby overlooking the lake, with nightly entertainment; two restaurants, including the stylish Asian-fusion Marssa and a relaxed cafe; two gigantic pools, one with a waterslide; and a full child day care

EAST AND SOUTH

and activity center (this is the better choice at the lake for families).

MONTELAGO VILLAGE RESORT ⑤⑤

30 Strada Di Villaggio, 866/564-4799, www.montelagovillage.com

The concept here is catching on across Vegas—buy a condo and rent it to strangers. The resort is two rambling complexes of condominiums that are placed into a rental pool by the owners. Viera is the original, located in the heart of the MonteLago Village complex, while Luna di Lusso is located on the other side of the lake across a pedestrian bridge. Ranging from studios to three-bedroom units, these fully furnished accommodations offer a more residential feel, with full kitchens and large patios or balconies, but still have all the conveniences of a hotel, including 24-hour guest reception, concierge services, housekeeping, two pools, a spa, a fitness room, a game room, and a media room with a big-screen television. A great option for families or people who want some of the comforts of home.

◖ THE RITZ-CARLTON
LAKE LAS VEGAS ⑤⑤

1610 Lake Las Vegas Pkwy., 702/567-4700, www.ritzcarlton.com/resorts/lake_las_vegas.com

The Ritz is a true luxury spa resort in a town that loves to throw words like that around even when they don't really apply. With only 350 rooms and suites, The Ritz has a world-class staff that's able to treat guests with the kind of care and devotion a true luxury destination should offer (instead of pretending they can do it when they have 4,000 rooms).

The entire place is a wonder of eye-catching sumptuousness, from the marble and wood-trimmed lobby overlooking gardens and the lake to the casually elegant rooms packed with every convenience imaginable, plus a few more. If the timing is right (and budget allows), try to get a room on the club level, a wing of the hotel built on a replica of the Pontevecchio Bridge stretching out *over* the lake. Not only do these rooms offer upgraded amenities and free food and beverage service, but they

also provide guests with the particular joy of being able to step out onto a balcony and look straight down at fish jumping below.

The hotel also features a full-service spa, ranked as one of the top in the United States; a lobby bar offering afternoon high tea; a fine restaurant called Medici; a gorgeous pool area and beach offering lake swimming; and a wide variety of activities, including fly-fishing, boating, and star-gazing. The whole thing is adjacent to the MonteLago shopping and entertainment village with lots of stores, restaurants, and a casino.

PRACTICALITIES
Information and Services

For more information on Lake Las Vegas, visit their official website at www.lakelasvegas.com. For more information on MonteLago Village and Casino, visit their official website at www.montelagovillage.com or call 866/752-9558.

Hotels around the lake can help guests with just about any need, including postal services, cleaning and laundry, transportation, business services, and more. Other visitors will most likely need to head into nearby Henderson to find similar services since the hotels primarily cater to their paying guests.

Wherever there are casinos, there are ATMs, so Casino MonteLago is conveniently located near cash machines. There are no banks or other financial services at Lake Las Vegas as of this writing—Henderson is the nearest place for that.

Getting There and Around

To get to Lake Las Vegas from The Strip, take I-15 South to I-215 East. That freeway ends at I-515, from which Lake Mead Drive heads east for about six miles to Lake Las Vegas Parkway on the left. There is no stoplight at that intersection and it's easy to miss if you aren't paying attention.

From Downtown, take I-93/95/515 South to Lake Mead Drive and follow the above instructions from there.

The Ritz-Carlton and MonteLago Village

and Casino are on the south shore of the lake, while the Loews is on the north shore (follow the signs). All destinations, whether they are the hotels, the casinos, the golf courses, or the shopping village, provide parking. Visitors can also take advantage of the various transportation modes. A free shuttle takes passengers along the winding lakeside drive from one side to the other, and a water taxi crosses the lake for a couple of bucks.

Boulder Highway   Map 6

The blue-collar bastion of Las Vegas is mostly a road of RV parks and cheap casinos, but towering above the relatively innocuous landscape (at least compared to The Strip) are three truly noteworthy hotel-casinos, each offering a ton of dining, entertainment, and accommodation options for rates that are usually substantially lower than just about anywhere else in town.

There are no "sights" per se—instead, this is the place for some low-limit gaming, cheap eats, and maybe a concert or two from people you haven't thought about in a couple of decades.

GAMING
ARIZONA CHARLIE'S
4575 Boulder Hwy., 702/951-5900,
www.arizonacharlies.com
HOURS: Open 24 hours
The casino here is roughly half the size of the one at nearby Boulder Station and feels like it. A smaller casino is not automatically a bad thing, but since it's all contained in one space with a miniscule upstairs addition, it seems like options run out quickly, especially for gamblers who aren't doing well. They have more than 1,100 coinless slots and video poker machines, blackjack, craps, roulette, Pai Gow poker, and

COURTESY STATION CASINOS

the casino at Boulder Station

EAST AND SOUTH

other table games; a 500-seat, 24-hour bingo parlor; and a small race and sports book.

BOULDER STATION

4111 Boulder Hwy., 702/432-7777,
www.boulderstation.com
HOURS: Open 24 hours

Boulder is one of those great, fun, casual locals' casinos that have absolutely zero snobbery and no pretentious airs. It has more than 75,000 square feet of gaming in a rambling, Victorian-era train station motif. With high ceilings and wood floors in some areas, it feels a lot less claustrophobic than nearby Sam's Town, even though it's half the size. More than 2,800 slot and video poker machines come in mostly nickel and quarter denominations, but they have penny, dollar, and higher-limit machines as well. Gaming options also include a live keno lounge, a 600-seat bingo parlor, a race and sports book, and a full array of table games, including blackjack, craps, roulette, 3-Card poker, Let It Ride, and mini-baccarat, among others. Of the three casinos in this area, Boulder Station stands out in my mind as the most consistently satisfying gaming experience.

SAM'S TOWN

5111 Boulder Hwy., 702/456-7777,
www.samstownlv.com
HOURS: Open 24 hours

The casino at Sam's is the second largest in the entire city, with more than 150,000 square feet of gaming on three levels. The cowboy theme gets a little tiresome after a while and they've managed to pack nearly every inch of that massive floor space with some sort of game, so personal space is at a premium, but the lower limits and theoretically higher payouts make it a popular destination for locals and visitors alike.

They have more than 3,000 slot and video poker machines. Limits range from pennies all the way up to $100, but nickel and quarter denominations are the most prevalent. There is also a full range of table games, including blackjack, roulette, Let It Ride, craps, Pai Gow poker, and more; a poker room with low-stakes

Texas and No-Limit Hold 'Em; a race and sports book and a keno lounge.

RESTAURANTS

SAM'S TOWN FIRELIGHT BUFFET ⓢ

5111 Boulder Hwy., 702/456-7777,
www.samstownlv.com
HOURS: Mon.-Fri. 7 A.M.-9 P.M., Sat.-Sun. 8 A.M.-9 P.M.

With a soaring ceiling and a wall of flames behind the serving station, the room is one of the most dramatic in town. One wall opens out onto the indoor park, allowing a little bit of faux nature inside for an overall lovely dining experience.

The food stations are arranged in a linear fashion, offering regional cuisines (Chinese, Mexican, Italian), salads, a carving station, and much more. Theme nights offer up all-you-can-eat barbecue, steak, and seafood. A terrific dessert station, with hand-scooped ice cream a worthwhile centerpiece, is separate from the main serving area.

Everything here is well prepared and flavorful, and while it may not be the gastronomic delight of places like the Bellagio buffet, it's also nowhere near as expensive. Weekday breakfast, lunch, and weekend brunch are less than $10, while dinner ranges from $11–18, depending on the theme.

THE WILD WEST BUFFET ⓢ

4575 Boulder Hwy. (at Arizona Charlie's),
800/632-4040, www.arizonacharlies.com
HOURS: Sun.-Thurs. 7 A.M.-9 P.M., Fri.-Sat. 7 A.M.-10 P.M.

This is a much smaller and simpler affair, but it doesn't change the fact that they offer some solid food choices at ridiculously low prices. A wide-ranging salad and fruit bar sits beside the all-American–style entrée selections, all done with cafeteria-type efficiency (and I mean that in a good way). Just keep your expectations in check by noting the prices: Breakfast is $5, lunch $7, Sunday brunch only $9, and dinner $9–12, with the higher end reserved for their all-you-can-eat steak and shrimp night. You'd expect little more than fuel here, but it's actually better than that.

ENTERTAINMENT
ARIZONA CHARLIE'S
4575 Boulder Hwy., 702/951-5900,
www.arizonacharlies.com

The Palace Grand Lounge is a glorified casino bar, but they have live entertainment every night (except for Monday) and afternoons on Friday, Saturday, and Sunday. Granted, the bands are not of the big-name variety, but these local acts are the backbone of the live entertainment scene here in Vegas and they earn their money and audiences' respect. You may be surprised by how much you enjoy some of these talented performances.

BOULDER STATION
4111 Boulder Hwy., 702/432-7777,
www.boulderstation.com

The Railhead at Boulder Station is the best place to catch a variety of live entertainment acts. Having won special venue awards from the Academy of Country Music, The Railhead is an intimate, multilevel space with a southern-roadhouse kind of vibe. With the right band, this is a terrific, fun place to see a show. Again, the groups that play here (and elsewhere on Boulder Highway) are not exactly A-listers. In fact, many could easily qualify for an E! *Where Are They Now?*–type special. Taylor Dayne, Morris Day and the Time, Foreigner, Toto, and John Cafferty and the Beaver Brown Band are just a few of the recent headliners. Now mind you, many of these acts still put on great shows and have their definite nostalgia appeal, but for current, top-of-the-charts–type groups, this is not the place.

Boulder Station also has a **Regal Theatres** (702/432-7777, www.boulderstation.com) 11-screen movie theater complex and a Kids Quest (702/432-7569) "playcare" facility for kids 6 weeks–12 years of age.

SAM'S TOWN
5111 Boulder Hwy., 702/456-7777,
www.samstownlv.com

Larger concerts are held at **Sam's Town Live,** a 1,100-seat showroom that represents the biggest venue on Boulder Highway. Unfortunately, bigger doesn't necessarily mean bet-

The Railhead concert venue at Boulder Station

ter. The acts that get booked into Sam's Town Live aren't of any significantly higher caliber than those at The Railhead. So wouldn't you rather be up close and personal?

Smaller acts can be found at **Roxy's,** a 100-seat nightclub/lounge at Sam's Town usually featuring country bands.

In addition, Sam's Town has a **Century Theatres** (702/456-7777, www.sams-townlv.com) 18-screen movie theater complex with stadium seating and digital sound.

SPORTS AND RECREATION
SAM BOYD STADIUM
7000 E. Russell Rd., 702/895-3900,
www.thomasandmack.com

Run under the aegis of the University of Nevada Las Vegas, this stadium is home to many of their athletic teams. Since there are (as of this writing) no professional sports teams of any kind in Las Vegas, college games will have to satisfy those who can't stand to be away from a scoreboard for an entire vacation. The stadium also hosts several special events, including concerts, monster truck rallies, motocross competitions, and extreme sports tournaments. Be warned, this is a big, open, and not terribly modern facility despite recent renovations, so seeing any type of event here can be a pain, especially if it's on a warm day. They usually don't schedule things during the hottest summer afternoons, but sometimes the heat can sneak up on you in Vegas, so keep that in mind. For schedules and tickets for UNLV sporting events, call 866/388-FANS or go online to www.unlvtickets.com.

SAM'S TOWN BOWLING CENTER
5111 Boulder Hwy., 702/456-7777,
www.samstownlv.com
HOURS: Open 24 hours
This 64-lane, state-of-the-art facility has the latest in automatic scoring, a snack shop, a cocktail lounge, and a day-care facility for league players. They also do Extreme Bowling on Friday and Saturday nights and, no, it doesn't mean you get throw the balls at each other. Instead, it uses lighting effects and music to turn the place into a nightclub with gutter balls. This is the one and only recreation option in the Boulder Highway area, so despite the fact that bowling is the only sport that provides cup holders for the players' beers, those who want to work up a sweat will have to do it here.

HOTELS
ARIZONA CHARLIE'S $
4575 Boulder Hwy., 800/632-4040,
www.arizonacharlies.com
The 300 guest rooms are located in motel-style (read: outdoor access) buildings and most function as mini-suites, with sitting and sleeping areas in separate rooms. The furnishings are simple but well maintained, which is not always easy to do in a budget-minded facility such as this. Amenities are sparse—irons and boards or coffee makers are available upon request—but everything other than air, a phone, and a TV need to be packed in advance. The rest of the hotel is also simple, but they do offer a lot of bang for the buck with a 37,000-square-foot casino; four restaurants; a casino lounge with live entertainment most nights

and weekends; a pool and spa; on-site do-it-yourself laundry facilities; and a 200-space RV park.

Price is the primary reason to consider staying here. Standard weekday rates are around $50 a night (although special offers will cut that in half on occasion), while weekends rarely exceed $100. That's a terrific bargain for a clean, comfortable room in a hotel-casino in Las Vegas.

BOULDER STATION $
4111 Boulder Hwy., 800/683-7777,
www.boulderstation.com
This is yet another link in the Station Casinos corporate chain, a company that knows how to do simple, neighborhood hotel-casinos better than just about anyone in town. The facility, done as an 1800s train station, features 300 tastefully decorated guest rooms in a 15-story tower offering some pretty cool views from higher floors; a 75,000-square-foot casino; more than a dozen restaurants, including a buffet and some fast-food staples; several bars and lounges offering live entertainment; a concert venue; an 11-screen movie theater; a Kids Quest child-care and activity center; and a small pool area.

The guest rooms are all a tad larger than standard accommodations with very lovely Victorian-meets-modern furnishings and most of the common amenities, such as irons and boards, hair dryers, coffee service, televisions with pay-per-view movies, and the like.

Boulder Station is nice enough to warrant room rates much higher than they normally charge. You can get weekdays here as low as $39 a night, with weekends in the $99–149 vicinity. As with most of the hotels in this neighborhood, if they are charging at the upper end of their price range, hotels on The Strip will definitely be significantly higher.

SAM'S TOWN $
5111 Boulder Hwy., 800/634-6371,
www.samstownlv.com
What started as a regular casino with a budget motel has grown into a sprawling complex with the second biggest casino in the city (more than 150,000 square feet on three levels); more

than 600 rooms; four traditional restaurants, a buffet, and a food court; an 18-screen movie theater; a 24-hour, 56-lane bowling center; two nightclub/concert venues; and two RV parks with 500 spaces.

The rooms are done simply, with a vaguely southwestern motif that I guess could be called Cowboy Lite. It's very understated in both execution and function, with forgettable but comfortable furnishings in the rooms. Amenities are limited—air-conditioning, satellite television, irons and boards, and hair dryers pretty much cover it—but at these prices, what are you complaining about?

Rooms at Sam's Town go for as low as $34 on off-season weekdays, with busier periods and weekends usually in the $100–140 range.

PRACTICALITIES
Information and Services
As alluded to throughout this section, some of the neighborhoods surrounding the Boulder Highway hotels and casinos are not the best in the city. They also aren't the worst, but those who don't know exactly where they're going probably shouldn't go out exploring. Therefore, I highly recommend allowing the major hotel-casinos to handle whatever service needs may arise. All of them offer postal and business services, cleaning, and basic banking through their ATMs or casino cashier cages (check-cashing, credit cards, etc.).

You can get more information on each of the hotels by visiting the websites or calling the numbers listed in the accommodations section.

Getting There and Around
The three main hotel-casinos on Boulder Highway are all within a couple miles of each other between Flamingo and West Desert Inn. To get there, take any of the major east-west streets from The Strip (Tropicana, Flamingo, Desert Inn, or Sahara) to Boulder Highway. From Downtown, take Fremont Street east and it becomes Boulder Highway at Sahara Avenue.

As of this writing, Sam's Town has a free shuttle running approximately 9 A.M.–midnight, ferrying passengers from Harrah's on The Strip and The California and Fremont hotels in the Downtown area. The schedule changes and is subject to availability, so check their website or call ahead.

None of the three major hotels on Boulder Highway are within walking distance of one another, less because of the actual mileage and more because of the less-than-stellar surrounding neighborhoods. Play it safe and drive or take cabs between destinations.

Lake Mead National Recreation Area Map 6

The Lake Mead National Recreation Area encompasses more than 1.5 million square miles, twice the size of the state of Rhode Island. It is divided into four sections: The Boulder Basin is the most popular area, located immediately adjacent to the Hoover Dam and closest to Las Vegas; The Overton Arm, just east of the Boulder Basin and stretching north to the Valley of Fire State Park, is significantly larger than the Boulder Basin, but much less developed; East Lake Mead is, appropriately, the easternmost area of the park, reaching all the way into Arizona to the fringes of the Grand Canyon National Park; and Lake Mohave is at the southern end of the park, below Hoover Dam.

I will be focusing on the Boulder Basin since, as mentioned, it's the closest and most convenient to Las Vegas. However, for serious naturists, the rest of the park is worth exploring.

SIGHTS
◖ HOOVER DAM
Lower Colorado Regional Office of the Bureau of Reclamation, P.O. Box 61470, Boulder City, NV 98006, 866/730-9097, www.usbr.gov/lc/hooverdam
HOURS: Daily 9 A.M.-6 P.M. (except Thanksgiving and Christmas Day)
COST: $11 adult, $9 senior, $6 child (7-16), free for children under 7
The dam was opened to the public in the 1970s,

EAST AND SOUTH

VALLEY OF FIRE STATE PARK

As the earth has reshaped itself over the last couple hundred million years or so, it has left behind some truly spectacular scenery, some of which can be found near Las Vegas in the Valley of Fire State Park. This 36,000-acre refuge is more than just desert and rock; it features towering spires, deep canyons, and bizarre-looking geological formations in varying fiery shades of red, all formed by the oxidation of the minerals in the rock as it was carved by wind, water, and time.

It's really quite a spectacular sight, evoking an almost alien landscape. Perhaps that's why Hollywood has come calling more than once, using the park in films like *Star Trek: Generations* as a stand-in for other planets.

The best, and easiest, way to see the park is from the comfort of an air-conditioned automobile. Besides the fact that it's a protected wilderness area, there's a reason why no one wants to build condos out here – it's not exactly what you might call hospitable terrain. To get there, take I-15 North out of Las Vegas approximately 40 miles or so to the Valley of Fire Highway (Nevada 169), which leads straight into the park. An alternate route would be to get off I-15 at Lake Mead Boulevard (just north of Downtown) and take that east all the way to Northshore Road (Nevada 167) near Lake Mead. Follow Northshore and it will connect with the Valley of Fire Highway on the east side of the Valley of Fire park. The second way is longer (add at least another 30 miles to the drive), but more scenic.

There's a $5-per-car access fee at the park entrance. Next, stop at the Valley of Fire visitors center (702/397-2088, 8:30 A.M.-4:30 P.M. daily), located on the Valley of Fire Highway about six miles west of Northshore Road. They've got maps for hiking and camping, plus they know the best viewing spots for simple sightseeing.

and visitors used to be able to put on a hard hat and actually descend into the bowels of the structure. The tragedies of September 11, 2001, changed all of that. Today, the tours mostly stay on top of the dam and provide exhibits and films to show guests what is going on underneath their feet. It's nowhere near as interesting as it used to be, but that's the reality of living in our post-9/11 world.

To get to Hoover Dam, visitors will need to rent a car or take a tour bus to the area. **Gray Line** (800/634-6579, www.graylinelasvegas.com) offers a good tour package that also includes Lake Mead, and most hotels will be able to arrange travel with any of a myriad of reputable companies that escort people to the attraction. For drivers, take I-15 (running parallel to The Strip) south to I-215 East. This will connect to 515 South, which eventually merges with Boulder Highway (also known as Highway 93/95). Go another 20 or so miles and you'll be at Hoover Dam.

Even though the distance is a relatively short one, this is a very popular destination, so during the peak tourism periods allow at least an hour to get there and an hour to get back. It's been known to take as long as two hours to get there on very busy holiday weekends.

Upon arrival, drivers are directed to a parking structure that charges $7 per vehicle to enter.

On the tour are murals, maps, and photos of the history of the dam, films about the construction and the dam's influence on the region, plus exhibits, scenic views (bring a camera!), and a look at the massive generators. An hour is all that's really necessary to see the high points, but anyone who's really interested in this kind of thing might allow an extra hour.

◖ LAKE MEAD

Park Headquarters, 601 Nevada Way, Boulder City, NV 98006, 702/293-8907, www.nps.gov/lame

It seems obvious when you think about it, but many people don't realize that Lake Mead was created when they built the Hoover Dam, making it the largest manufactured lake in the United States. Before that, this area was mostly barren desert and craggy outcroppings of rock with a few small towns scattered about, mostly settled by Mormon travelers in the 1800s.

When the dam was finished in 1935, the area began to fill, slowly burying the desert valleys and abandoned town sites with 9.3 trillion gallons of water at its highest level, or roughly what flows through the Colorado River over the course of two years.

Severe drought across the western United States for the past few years has reduced the lake to record low levels. Some of the marinas have actually had to be moved just to keep them floating, and many popular areas are now restricted. Heavy rains in 2005 didn't do much to help, so visitors should pay close attention to posted signs and do as much advance research as possible to know what they can and can't do.

The drought has also exposed some long-forgotten history. In 2003, the streets and foundations of buildings that were once the Mormon settlement of St. Thomas were uncovered by the receding waters. Another long-buried bit of history was discovered in 2001 when divers found the wreckage of a B29 Superfortress bomber that crash-landed in the lake in 1948. Although still deep under the surface, the bomber is almost entirely intact, preserved for more than five decades by the cold, dark waters of the lake.

RECREATION
Boating and Fishing

There are marinas scattered around the Boulder Basin, mostly grouped at Boulder Beach, Las Vegas Bay, and Callville Bay. Rental boats are available at any of the marinas—from Jet Skis to houseboats and everything in between. It is highly recommended that larger boats be reserved well in advance, since six-month waiting lists are not uncommon.

All of these marinas also offer fishing gear for rent and can supply clients with the necessary permits. Smaller bait-and-tackle shops dot the landscape and offer similar services.

THE LAKE MEAD RESORT

322 Lakeshore Rd., Boulder City, NV 89005, 800/752-9669, www.sevencrown.com

The Lake Mead Resort offers ski boats, fishing boats, personal watercraft, and patio boats for half-day, full-day, and seven-day rentals (Jet Ski rentals are half-day and full-day; no seven-day rentals). Prices range from around $60 for a half day with a fishing boat to more than $1,000 for seven days with a speed boat. Jet Ski rentals are surprisingly expensive at more than $100 for a two-hour rental.

THE LAS VEGAS BOAT HARBOR

490 Horsepower Cove, Boulder City, NV 89005, 702/293-1191, www.drydockboatsales.com

Also check out The Las Vegas Boat Harbor, offering Jet Skis, fishing boats, speed boats, and pontoon boats for hourly or daily rentals. Prices vary by the craft and when it's rented, but expect $30–60 per hour and $180–360 per day, plus deposits.

CALLVILLE BAY RESORT AND MARINA

HC-30, Box 100, Las Vegas, NV 89124, 800/255-5561, www.callvillebay.com

Callville Bay Resort and Marina is the furthest away from Las Vegas, but that can be a good thing since it's also the least crowded. They specialize in houseboat rentals, but be warned that they book up very early (six months or more) and aren't cheap. A three-day off-season rental on their smallest boat is $1,000, while a seven-day summer rental starts at $3,000 and goes up to $7,000 for their grandest boat.

LAKE MEAD CRUISES

702/293-6180, www.lakemeadcruises.com

If you want to do the water thing but don't want to do it yourself, Lake Mead Cruises offers a variety of sightseeing excursions on either the *Desert Princess,* a three-level Mississippi-style paddle wheeler holding up to 300 passengers, or the *Desert Princess Too,* a two-level side–paddle wheel boat holding up to 150 passengers.

Options include Breakfast Cruises with a small buffet (around $32 adult, $15 child),

Midday Cruises ($20 adult, $9 child), Dinner Cruises with a meal ($44 adult, $21 child), and Dinner/Dancing Cruises with a meal and entertainment ($54 adult, children not allowed). Each of the cruises takes passengers around the more scenic parts of the lake and includes water views of Hoover Dam.

Camping and Hiking

All of the campgrounds surrounding the Boulder Basin are administered by the National Park Service and offer restrooms, running water, dump stations, and picnic tables. The basic campsites are first-come, first-served, but guests must pay a $10 fee before setting up their tents.

Recreation vehicles are welcome at the campsites, but only two at the Boulder Basin portion of the lake have full hookups: one at the **Lake Mead RV Village** at Boulder Beach (702/293-2540) and one at **Callville Bay Resort** (702/565-8958). The same $10 fee applies, but rental of the hook-up spaces costs extra (usually around $20 per night). Call ahead to reserve them.

The Alan Bible Visitors Center (see *Practicalities* section below) has a map detailing the locations of all the campsites.

Also at the visitors center is a map of all the backcountry roads and marked hiking trails. It is highly recommended that you stick to the approved trails and paths; otherwise you're bound to become a headline.

PRACTICALITIES
Information

The best resource for up-to-the-minute information can probably be found at the **Alan Bible Visitors Center** (702/293-8907, 8:30 A.M.–4:30 P.M. daily except Thanksgiving and Christmas). In addition to maps, directions, and recommendations for all areas of the Lake Mead National Recreation Area, this informative and educational facility contains interactive exhibits and historical displays that will help visitors understand more about the region. It's located about four miles east of Boulder City at the junction of Highway 93 and Lakeshore Road.

Fees

Budgetary crunches in most states have affected the access fees at many national parks, including the Lake Mead National Recreation Area. I mention this primarily because they keep going up faster than anyone can keep track of them, so don't be surprised if you arrive and the fees are higher than what you're reading in this book.

Entrance fees for the park are $5 per vehicle (covers all passengers) or $3 per person for those on a motorcycle or bicycle, or on foot. The fee is assessed at the park entrances.

Lake fees are assessed upon every vessel touching the water at $10 for the first vessel and $5 for each additional vessel. That fee is often included in boat rentals, but be sure to ask before you whip out your credit card.

Fishing licenses are required before dropping a lure into the water. As of this writing, licenses run $18 for a day, plus $7 for each additional day, and are available at most of the marinas.

Camping permits are required at all of campsites around the lake. A fee of $10 per night is charged at each of them.

Getting There

To reach Lake Mead National Recreation Area, take I-15 South to I-215 East. Crossing Boulder Highway, continue onto Lake Mead Drive, which will eventually lead to the Lake Mead National Recreation Area. Alternatively, connect from I-215 to I-515 South, which eventually merges with Boulder Highway (also known as Highway 93/95).

NORTH AND WEST OF LAS VEGAS

The regions north and west of The Strip and Downtown Las Vegas are a study in contrasts. Some rough, low-income neighborhoods give way to some of the priciest real estate in the region. Row after row of tract homes and strip malls segue into the beautiful scenic vistas at Red Rock Canyon. Acres of concrete blend with rolling green hills at some of the finest golf courses in the country. And sprinkled throughout are some terrific hotels, casinos, restaurants, and recreation opportunities.

With the exception of the opportunities for nature lovers, there is little in these neighborhoods that can't be found in greater quantity closer to The Strip. But here the prices are lower, the attitude friendlier, and the pace a little slower, making an excursion to this side of town worthwhile for anyone in need of a break from the hyperactivity and high costs of the major tourist areas.

North on I-15 past Downtown is the community of North Las Vegas, a full-fledged town complete with its own mayor and city council. It functions primarily as a suburb of Las Vegas, not as ritzy as some of the communities further out, but filled with the kind of working-class folk who make the region run. It's more than just a backstage area for Vegas, though. In fact, it contains several of the best neighborhood casinos and hotels, one of the premier sporting facilities in the world (the Las Vegas Motor Speedway), one of the biggest malls in the area, and what I consider to be several of the best restaurants in the entire city.

Head west along I-95 to the Summerlin Parkway and you'll run into one of the biggest

HIGHLIGHTS

LOOK FOR (TO FIND RECOMMENDED
SIGHTS, ACTIVITIES, DINING, AND LODGING.

(**Best Steaks:** In my humble opinion, **Austins Steakhouse** not only serves up the best steaks in Las Vegas, but it's one of the best restaurants in the entire city (page 231).

(**Best Place for an Adrenaline Rush:** Fulfill your need for speed at the **Las Vegas Motor Speedway,** one of the top spots in the country for motor sports racing of all types (page 233).

(**Best Inexpensive Hotel:** Rooms at **Santa Fe Station** cost a fraction of what they cost on The Strip, and they'll make you wonder why anyone would ever want to pay those prices in the first place (page 234).

(**Best Casino:** With more than 80,000 square feet of every type of gaming option imaginable, the casino at **Red Rock Resort** serves up all your gambling needs in a stunning package (page 236).

(**Best Restaurant:** When I say **Hannah's** is the best restaurant, I don't mean the best just in this area of town. It's really that good (page 238).

(**Best Breakfasts:** The delightfully "twisted farm food" at **Hash House a Go Go** will serve up pancakes the size of pizzas and make you never want to eat those scrambled eggs at the breakfast buffets again (page 239).

(**Best Golf Course:** Arnold Palmer designed the fantastic links at the **Arroyo Golf Club at Red Rock,** but the designer of the surrounding scenery at Red Rock Canyon really deserves the credit for making this one stand out (page 242).

(**Best Resort Hotel:** The amenities, the rooms, the surroundings, and the level of service at **Red Rock Resort** rival anything found at the big fancy places on The Strip (page 245).

COURTESY STATION CASINOS

Austins Steakhouse at Texas Station

master-planned communities in the country at Summerlin, a 22,500-acre spread of thousands of homes, mainstream shopping centers, golf courses, parks and hiking trails, and a couple of upscale resorts that combine Strip elegance with neighborhood-casino amenities.

Summerlin acts as the western border of Las Vegas, but beyond it lies the Red Rock Canyon National Conservation Area, a 197,000-acre wilderness preserve highlighted by dramatic canyon geography and stunning desert flora and fauna. The recreation opportunities here are almost endless (provided they don't involve water), but hiking, biking, horseback riding, and nature sightseeing are the leading draws. The fact that this is only a 20-minute drive (if traffic is minimal) from The Strip is not only amazing, but also important for vacation planning.

Most visitors to Las Vegas won't venture off The Strip to explore the areas north and west of the city. Don't fall into that trap. Some of the city's best offerings, in just about every category, are located beyond the bounds of Las Vegas Boulevard. Serious nature lovers or golf fanatics, in particular, can find a plethora of sights and activities that should not be missed. Get out there and explore.

PLANNING YOUR TIME

Most visitors really only need one full day to hit the highlights of the north and west sides of Las Vegas, unless they decide to stay in the area. (And why not? It can save you some dough.) Serious naturists and the recreation-minded might want to budget two days to cover the best of the seemingly endless opportunities in these areas.

If you have one day, take a morning drive out to the **Red Rock Canyon National Conservation Area.** The earlier you go, the better, especially during summer when the afternoon temperatures make it prohibitive to explore the region outside the confines of an air-conditioned rental car. That's an option, too, with the 13-mile scenic drive providing a best-of-the-park overview—but the park deserves at least one stop, either for a little hiking

or a horseback ride, or just to snap some pictures of the scenery.

For lunch, visit a buffet (Red Rock Resort and Santa Fe Station have two of my favorites) and then spend the afternoon with a round of golf at the Arroyo Golf Club at Red Rock or a spa treatment at Aquae Sulis.

Hopefully you won't have eaten too much at the lunch buffet so you'll have room for the wonderful food at Austins Steakhouse or Hannah's; both are fantastic. Afterward, either sit around and happily complain about how full you are or gamble at one of the many casinos in the area, see a movie, throw a couple of gutter balls in one of the bowling alleys, or check the showroom and arena schedules to see who's performing.

If you have two days, go for the wild breakfasts at Hash House a Go Go and then spend some more time at Red Rock Canyon hiking or horseback riding to work off all the food you've eaten. A visit to Bonnie Springs or Spring Mountain Ranch State Park might also be in order. There are a number of ways to fill the rest of the time: more golf at one of the area's world-class courses, a drive out to the Las Vegas Motor Speedway to catch a race (or race something yourself), or maybe a chat with the animals at the Southern Nevada Zoological and Botanical Park. If it happens to be a Friday or Saturday evening, a visit to the CCSN Planetarium and Observatory is a great way to cap off the night.

It's worth noting that the neighborhoods immediately north and west of Downtown Las Vegas are some of the roughest in the city. Everything worth seeing and doing is further out, but getting to them requires traveling through or past these neighborhoods. Stick to the freeways or the major thoroughfares and it won't be a problem. Just in case your car breaks down or you decide to play Lewis and Clark out in the desert or up in the mountains, it's probably a good idea to bring a fully charged cell phone when venturing away from the safety of The Strip.

HISTORY

A couple of miles south, along dusty Fremont Street, Las Vegas had been rapidly developing for the better part of two decades when some folks, perhaps fed up by the rampant lawlessness of the early frontier town, decided to create their very own early version of a suburb, christened Vegas Verde (Green Meadows).

It was renamed North Las Vegas in 1932 and incorporated as a city in 1946, about the same time the Flamingo was making an opening splash on The Strip several miles away. The reason that's important is because as The Strip blossomed, development of Las Vegas moved south, leaving North Las Vegas a bit of an outpost for decades.

But someone got smart in the 1990s and the city began annexing adjacent desert tracts from the government. As available land to the south, west, and east began to fill up, the people began to move north. Today, the town of North Las Vegas is one of the fastest-growing in America.

Meanwhile, out west is the master-planned community of Summerlin. It's hard to believe that a relatively sedate place like this, filled with endless acres of tract housing and strip malls, could have an interesting history, but it does. In fact, no less than Howard Hughes himself is responsible for the development in a roundabout kind of way.

Hughes became enamored of Las Vegas in the 1940s, eventually turning his vast wealth toward the ownership and management of some of the city's premier casinos, like The Desert Inn. But in the early 1950s, Hughes was still an airplane man and his Culver City, California headquarters were bursting at the seams with all of the post–World War II and early Korean War contracts. Looking for a place to build a research facility, Hughes swapped another tract of land for the completely undeveloped, 36-square-mile parcel on the western fringes of Las Vegas.

The research facility was never built and the land sat empty for 30 years until Hughes's death in 1985. The Howard Hughes Corporation took over responsibility and, in the late 1980s, began work on the massive master-planned community known as Summerlin (Hughes's mother's maiden name). Today, it encompasses 22,500 acres of homes, shops, businesses, parks, and community features and is one of the most desirable neighborhoods in the area.

The Red Rock Canyon National Conservation Area has a much longer history, of course. Geologists believe this entire region was once under a salty sea (hence the limestone deposits) and later buried beneath a vast sandy desert. Eons later, the wind and water have carved deep canyons through the red rock, creating this scenic wonderland of desert vistas.

North Las Vegas   Map 7

The actual city of North Las Vegas is bounded by Decatur Boulevard on the west, Lake Mead Boulevard on the south (not to be confused with Lake Mead Drive on the south side of Las Vegas), I-15 on the east, and the Las Vegas Beltway on the north. But some of the sights and attractions fall outside of the actual city limits, so for the purposes of this section, I'm defining North Las Vegas as everything north and east of I-95 over to around Pecos Road, a few blocks west of I-15.

The area is a broad mix of residential, commercial, and industrial areas, most of which are not going to be of any interest to the average Las Vegas tourist. In fact, it's not of much interest to the average Las Vegas resident. But throughout the sprawling neighborhoods are a number of places worth knowing about, including lower-cost alternatives for hotels, dining, and entertainment.

SIGHTS
CCSN PLANETARIUM AND OBSERVATORY
3200 E. Cheyenne Ave., North Las Vegas, 702/651-4SKY, www.csn.edu
HOURS: Shows Fri. 6 and 7:30 P.M., Sat. 3:30 and 7:30 P.M.
COST: $6 adult, $5 senior and child (under 12)
Located just a couple of miles north of Down-

DESERT NATIONAL WILDLIFE REFUGE

Located a short 20 miles north of Las Vegas is the biggest national wildlife refuge in the lower 48 states, encompassing nearly 1.5 million acres and home to dozens of endangered and threatened species of animal and plant life. The refuge was established in 1936, primarily as a protection zone for the bighorn sheep, but today it's home to such endangered and threatened creatures as the desert tortoise, the Pahrump poolfish, the peregrine falcon, and the bald eagle.

Nature opportunities abound within the refuge but are of the do-it-yourself variety, with limited hiking and primitive campsites available, but the primary objective here is wildlife observation. Keep in mind that since this is a protected natural wildlife zone, development within the area is minimal and the very few roads are of the gravel variety. Anyone wanting to venture deep into the refuge will need a four-wheel drive vehicle and/or a hearty set of hiking legs.

To get there, take I-15 North to US 95 North out of Las Vegas approximately 25 miles. A brown sign points to the Corn Creek Field Station, about four miles down a dirt road. There are self-serve kiosks here that stock brochures detailing the main roads, hiking trails, and observation areas. There is no charge for entry or for the brochures.

For more information, visit the main DNWR office at 4701 N. Torrey Pines Drive, call 702/515-5450, or visit them online at http://desertcomplex.fws.gov/desertrange/index.htm.

town, the planetarium and observatory on the College of Southern Nevada campus is a unique experience for Las Vegas, focusing on an entirely different category of bright lights and heavenly bodies. What the facility lacks in size, it more than makes up for in presentation, offering a different experience on every visit.

Using the time of year and what might be happening up in the sky, the staff plots a course for their big telescope and then projects whatever it's looking at on the planetarium ceiling. It's sort of like watching a big movie about outer space, only these are no special effects. You might get a close-up view of the moon, neighboring planets, or stars outside of our galaxy.

After the 7:30 P.M. planetarium presentations, the observatory is open for informal public viewing sessions. Again, the focus depends on the time of year, although full moons seem to be a crowd favorite.

A couple of notes: Obviously, when skies are cloudy there are no viewings, and since the place is fairly small, it fills up quickly, so get there early to ensure admittance. No one is allowed into the planetarium once the showings have begun.

THE NEON BONEYARD

Las Vegas Blvd. and McWilliams Ave., 702/387-6366, www.neonmuseum.org

HOURS: Tue.-Fri. 11 A.M.-5 P.M., by appointment only

Behind a chain-link fence, in a vaguely rundown neighborhood near Downtown Las Vegas, sits what appears to be a giant silver slipper and—wait, is that a genie's lamp? This is one of the biggest treasure troves of Las Vegas history: the Neon Boneyard.

For decades, the Young Electric Sign Company (YESCO) has been creating the majority of the neon signage that has graced the fronts of the hotels and casinos in Las Vegas. Actually, it goes way beyond that—the neon signs on most gas stations, motels, convenience stores, and just about everything else in this city have been done by YESCO.

But as the The Strip moved upscale, the neon signs have fallen by the wayside, viewed by many as tacky and antiquated. Whether they were replaced by one of those gigantic TV screens (yeah, those aren't tacky) as a hotel remodeled or were rescued just before the implosion, neon as a design aesthetic has faded on Las Vegas Boulevard.

YESCO offered refuge to many of those

signs over the years, creating what was colloquially known as the Neon Boneyard (or Graveyard, to some), a big fenced-off lot located near their main facility where classic neon artwork was left to fade and rot in the unrelenting Nevada sun. These signs represented the last bits of the colorful history that Las Vegas has swept away in the name of modernity.

And there they probably would've stayed if it hadn't been for the efforts of The Neon Museum, a not-for-profit organization that rescued the signs and set out on an ambitious project to restore them to their former glory.

Just under a dozen of these glorious creations have been brought back to life and are currently on display on and around The Fremont Street Experience Downtown. But there are dozens more still waiting to be restored in a new Neon Boneyard operated by The Neon Museum.

Like their predecessor, these two dusty lots near Downtown Vegas are not open to the public except by special arrangement for groups. For a generous enough donation, though (at least $50), guests can get their own tour of the lots and get up close to fantastic old signs from The Stardust, Binion's Horseshoe, Sassy Sally's, the Silver Slipper, The Showboat, the Golden Nugget, and more.

The Neon Museum is in the process of raising money to build a permanent museum on the site where the Boneyard is located. It will include a visitors' center, restored signs, a cafe, and more.

OLD LAS VEGAS MORMON FORT STATE HISTORIC PARK

500 E. Washington Ave., Las Vegas, 702/486-3511, www.friendsofthefort.org

HOURS: Daily 8:30 A.M.-4:30 P.M.

COST: $3 adult, $2 child (6-12), free for children under 6

In 1855, Mormon settlers struck out from Salt Lake City with a mission to spread the word across the western part of North America. One group of about 30 men picked a creek amid a meadow in the middle of the desert as their stopping place, becoming the first early American residents of what would eventually become Las Vegas. They built a fort of adobe measuring about 150 square feet and began the process of turning the neighboring land into farms and corrals for animals.

A portion of that fort, including the oldest building in Nevada, still stands at this historic site. Visitors to the facility get an early view of the area through photographs, exhibits of artifacts found at the site, and re-creations of everything from army living quarters to covered wagons. They even re-created a portion of the creek, which dried up decades ago.

There's not much to the place and "exciting" isn't exactly the word I'd use to describe it, but that doesn't mean you shouldn't visit. It's hard to believe something like this even exists, especially in a town that seems to revel in imploding its history, so take a moment away from the slot machines and showgirls to step back to a simpler time in Las Vegas's past.

SOUTHERN NEVADA ZOOLOGICAL AND BOTANICAL PARK

1775 N. Rancho Dr., Las Vegas, 702/647-4685, www.lasvegaszoo.org

HOURS: Daily 9 A.M.-5 P.M.

COST: $7 adult, $5 senior, $5 child (2-12)

It's not the biggest or fanciest zoo in the world, but this well-run facility is still a great place to go to get up close to nature, especially for families. Spread out across three acres, the zoo features a wide variety of animal and plant life, much of which is indigenous to the southern Nevada desert. They claim to have at least one of every species of venomous reptile native to the area.

There are endangered large cats; reptiles of all shapes and sizes; a big aviary collection, including emus, ostriches, and flamingos; and a primate collection of chimpanzees and the very rare Barbary apes. In fact, this is reportedly the only zoo in the United States with this type of ape.

There's also a botanical garden filled with rare gemstones and endangered plants from the region.

Because it's a small facility, it's also a lot friendlier and less structured than most zoos. While visitors can't go up and pet a mountain lion, it does feel like the animals are closer to the visitors here, even if they probably aren't. The whole place is intimate and run by people who seem to have a true love for the animals. That alone makes it worth visiting.

Because most of the facility is outdoors, morning visits are recommended, especially during the hotter summer months. Not only is it cooler, but there's also a better chance of seeing the animals, since later in the day many of them go indoors to point and laugh at the idiots standing out in the hot sun trying to see them.

GAMING

Texas Station has been the most consistently profitable in my experience, especially on their video poker machines. I've even been late to a dinner or two at Austins Steakhouse because I've been doing so well in the casino—once you read the restaurant review you'll understand how big of a deal that is.

Santa Fe Station has been very kind to me on a couple of occasions, but on just as many I have walked out with less money than I started with.

I have never done well at the Cannery or the Fiesta, although, to be fair, I haven't spent as much time in either facility as I have at the others.

It's worth noting that Santa Fe Station, Texas Station, and Fiesta Rancho are all a part of Station Casinos Boarding Pass players' club (see the *Players' Clubs* sidebar in the *Gaming* chapter).

AREA 51

Looking for a close encounter of your very own? Some say the drive along Highway 375 about 100 miles or so north of Las Vegas is the best place to find it. Officially rechristened a few years ago as the E. T. Highway (there are signs and everything), this stretch of two-lane highway through the mostly barren Nevada desert approaches the infamous Area 51, a super-secret government installation that has long been rumored to be the place where the Feds keep all of the alien spaceships we've captured over the years. Or something like that.

Whether you believe (the truth is out there!) or not, this can be a mildly entertaining diversion, especially for those who need to get away from the hectic pace of Las Vegas. A nighttime jaunt may not net any actual UFO sightings, but it's hard to imagine a more peaceful place to view the majestic blanket of stars above.

It's a long drive (about 300 miles round-trip), so you have to be serious about doing this, whatever the reason – whether you believe you're going to see an alien spaceship or just because you have a healthy sense of ironic adventure. Start on I-15 heading north out of Las Vegas and exit at Highway 93 (about 20 miles north of Downtown). Take 93 North about 80 miles to Highway 375 and turn left. This is the

official start of the E.T. Highway and you can keep going for as long as you want, but the tiny town of Rachel, about 40 miles down the road, is the best place to stop. It's not much more than a collection of dusty buildings, but visit the **Little A'Le'Inn** (HC 61, Box 45, Hwy. 375, 775/729-2515, 8 A.M.–10 P.M. daily) for a quick bite to eat and to pick up a map of popular UFO-spotting zones. They also know the best spots for getting up next to the Area 51 fence, which won't allow you to actually see anything interesting, but at least you can say you were there.

It should go without saying (but I'm going to say it anyway) that this is mostly barren territory, so make sure the car has a full tank of gas (or you can refill in Rachel if need be), plenty of water, and a really good cell phone just in case (believe it or not, they do work sporadically even way out here).

For more information, contact the **Nevada Commission on Tourism** (401 N. Carson St., Carson City, NV 89701, 800/NEVADA-8, www.travelnevada.com). They have brochures available on E. T. Highway sights and services to help with trip planning. Also check out www.rachel-nevada.com for information about Rachel, Nevada.

CANNERY CASINO HOTEL

2121 E. Craig Rd., North Las Vegas, 866/999-4899,
www.cannerycasinos.com

HOURS: Open 24 hours

The more than 50,000-square-foot casino at the Cannery has a fun World War II theme, if things like a world war can be fun, that is. It's done up as a patriotic factory, with Rosie the Riveter–style posters and 1940s touches everywhere. While it may not be gambling in the middle of Central Park or 1890s Paris, it's still a pleasant and eye-catching environment.

They have more than 1,250 slot and video poker machines, all coinless. Because this is a neighborhood-style casino, the limits are generally lower here, with pennies, nickels, and quarters outnumbering the higher denominations. Nearly two dozen table games (blackjack, craps, roulette, etc.), a 130-seat race and sports book, a poker room, and a bingo hall round out the offerings.

FIESTA RANCHO

2400 N. Rancho Rd., Las Vegas, 702/631-7000,
www.fiestacasino.com

HOURS: Open 24 hours

Local gaming giants Station Casinos snapped up the Fiesta chain of hotel-casinos a few years ago and they have been upgrading this property ever since. The south-of-the-border theme continues, but everything here is nicer and newer, with all of the latest slots and video poker machines in a rambling 50,000-square-foot space.

Those video poker machines are a big draw here. They have a reputation for paying out well, with marketing phrases like "Royal Flush Capital of the World" thrown about like confetti.

They have a full range of table games (including highly touted $3-a-hand blackjack tables), a 394-seat bingo room (games every other hour, 11 A.M.–7 P.M.), a keno lounge, and a 100-seat race and sports book.

SANTA FE STATION

4949 N. Rancho Rd., Las Vegas, 702/658-4900,
http://santafe.stationcasinos.com

HOURS: Open 24 hours

Another Station Casinos purchase, the Santa Fe used to be a dump. And that's putting it kindly. What a difference tens of millions of dollars can make. Station has transformed this dingy gaming hall into a gorgeous facility with nice furnishings, upgraded games, beautiful stonework, and softer lighting. It has a similar look and feel to their flagship Green Valley Ranch, and while it may not be quite that nice, it's pretty darned close.

Spread out across more than 70,000 square feet, the casino has more than 2,200 slot and video poker machines (with lots of penny machines for the budget gambler), all of the standard table games, a 488-seat bingo room, a beautiful high-tech race and sports book with comfy furnishings and plasma TVs, a poker room, and more.

TEXAS STATION

2101 Texas Star Ln., Las Vegas, 702/631-1000,
www.texasstation.com

HOURS: Open 24 hours

The biggest casino in the northern part of town is also one of the most satisfying in terms of gaming options and return on investment. With more than 91,000 square feet of

Texas Station

space, they have a huge selection of slots and video poker machines (more than 2,400 total), most of which are of the more affordable penny, nickel, and quarter variety. Fans of video poker can pencil this place in on their casino hit list—they have *a lot* of machines to choose from.

Table games run the gamut and there's also a poker room (offering Texas Hold 'Em and Omaha Hi/Lo), a 220-seat race and sports book, a keno lounge, and a huge 495-seat bingo parlor with games every other hour, 9 A.M.–11 P.M.

Done up with a Lone Star State theme, the casino meanders and twists seemingly forever, offering a number of different areas for gambling, some quieter than others (try to avoid the machines near the food court and kids' activity center unless you're a fan of noise).

RESTAURANTS

AUSTINS STEAKHOUSE $$$
2101 Texas Star Ln., Las Vegas (at Texas Station), 702/631-1033, www.texasstation.com
HOURS: Sun.-Thurs. 5-10 P.M., Fri.-Sat. 5-11 P.M.

Almost every hotel in this city has a steakhouse, so it's almost shocking to discover the best of the bunch (and one of the best restaurants in the entire city) located in this neighborhood casino miles from The Strip. I've eaten here many times and it is no exaggeration to say that everything I've sampled has been amazing. Guests really can't make a mistake, but if I were to pick the perfect menu, I'd go with the bacon-wrapped shrimp appetizer, the Maui onion soup or the giant steakhouse salad, and the huge rib eye, rubbed in peppercorns and pan-seared in a garlic-butter-cilantro sauce. For dessert, close your eyes and point—they are all that good. All this plus stellar service, a beautiful dining room, and better food for less money than steakhouses on The Strip make this a winner from start to finish.

CANNERY ROW BUFFET $
2121 E. Craig Rd., North Las Vegas (at the Cannery), 866/999-4899, www.cannerycasinos.com
HOURS: Mon.-Thurs. 11 A.M.-9:30 P.M., Fri. 11 A.M.-10 P.M., Sat. 8:30 A.M.-10 P.M., Sun. 8:30 A.M.-9 P.M.

As with most of the newer buffets, the serving area here is divided into stations, mostly based upon regional varieties. Diners will find things like Italian pastas, sausages, and pizza; Chinese noodle and rice dishes, egg rolls, and orange chicken; and Mexican fajitas and tacos. But the big news here is the giant barbecue section, with everything from pulled pork to Kansas City spare ribs and more. Add the huge salad and fruit bar and a satisfying dessert station and this buffet has the makings of a really good meal. Prices are more than reasonable, with lunch at $8, dinner $12–18 (the latter for seafood night), and a Sunday Champagne and Seafood Brunch (with made-to-order omelets and big bowls of shrimp and crab legs) at a remarkable $10.

FEAST BUFFET $
4949 N. Rancho Rd., Las Vegas, 702/658-4900, http://santafe.stationcasinos.com
HOURS: Daily 8 A.M.-10 P.M.

Along with all of the other improvements they have made at this hotel, in 2006 Station Casinos brought in what I consider to be one of the best examples of their Feast Buffet. The dining room is sleek and modern, but still warm, while the food selections are almost paralyzing in their scope. Should you start with pulled pork at the barbecue station or the tender Pad Thai in the Asian section? Maybe you'll want made-to-order pasta or the fried chicken. A Tex-Mex area offers up tamales, enchiladas, and more. There's a great salad and soup bar, plus a very satisfying dessert station. All of this for very competitive prices that start at about $8 for breakfast and top out at $13 for dinner and the champagne brunch.

FIESTA FESTIVAL BUFFET $
2400 N. Rancho Rd., Las Vegas (at Fiesta Rancho), 702/631-7000, www.fiestacasino.com
HOURS: Mon.-Thurs. 11 A.M.-9 P.M., Fri. 11 A.M.-10 P.M., Sat. 9 A.M.-10 P.M., Sun. 9 A.M.-9 P.M.

The buffet here is virtually identical in presentation and pricing to the one at sister hotel Fiesta Henderson on the other side of town. Whether you choose that one or this one should totally be based on where you happen to find yourself when you get hungry. And bring your hunger with you—six stations offer a variety of ethnic and regional cuisines, all well prepared and satisfying to most palates (although food snobs may want to stick with the buffets that charge three times as much). Lunch goes for $8, dinner $10–11, and weekend brunch is only $11.

ENTERTAINMENT
CANNERY CASINO HOTEL
2121 E. Craig Rd., North Las Vegas, 866/999-4899, www.cannerycasinos.com

Unlike most casinos that have a traditional showroom, the Cannery offers a unique venue they call simply **The Club.** It's a giant black box of a room that can be reconfigured into a myriad of entertainment possibilities. Move the stage to one side, fly in a couple of collapsible walls, throw in some seating, and you've got a traditional proscenium-stage theater. Move the stage to the other side, add some tables, and open the big garage doors to the buffet and you've got an expanded dining area with entertainment. Set up the dance floor on a warm summer night and open the giant glass wall and you've got an indoor/outdoor club complete with a high-tech lighting and sound system. Or throw open that glass wall and set up some food booths and games in the adjoining outdoor courtyard, and you've got a street fair perfect for springtime festivals.

In 2006 the hotel added a **Galaxy Theater** 14-screen movie theater complex that has already garnered locals' awards for their plush seats, digital projection and sound, and really good popcorn, which you can smell all the way into the casino. Call 702/639-9779 for showtimes or visit the hotel's website listed above.

The Cannery also has the cute 1940s-themed **Pin-Ups Lounge** with nightly entertainment (except Mondays).

SANTA FE STATION
4949 N. Rancho Rd., Las Vegas, 702/658-4900, http://santafe.stationcasinos.com

There are three entertainment venues at Santa Fe worth noting: one for adults, one for kids, and one for all ages.

The Chrome Showroom is an interesting

Santa Fe Station

facility with flexible seating arrangements that can host a variety of concerts or shows, be converted into a full-fledged nightclub, or be opened to the adjoining casino as a lounge space. Call or visit the website to find out what will be going on when you get there.

Kids Quest (702/658-4966, www.kids quest.com) is a big "playcare" facility for children 6 weeks–12 years of age. It's filled with a variety of games, activities, and an indoor playground designed to keep the tykes busy while the parents are off gambling in the casino. It's run by a professionally trained and licensed staff that takes the care of children very seriously.

The **Century 16 Santa Fe Station** movie theater complex shows all of the latest blockbusters in theaters equipped with stadium seating, THX and Dolby Digital sound systems, and big screens for watching Spidey kick some evil henchman butt. Call 702/395-0222 or visit the main Santa Fe Station website for schedule and showtimes.

TEXAS STATION

2101 Texas Star Ln., Las Vegas, 702/631-1000, www.texasstation.com

The Dallas Events Center is a 2,000-seat ballroom with a big stage and banquet chair seating (which can be uncomfortable for long shows). Shows do include big names, but while the Willie Nelson and Merle Haggard types show up every now and again, the acts are more commonly on par with the ones featured regularly on those VH1 shows like *I Love the '80s*. Call 866/264-1818 or visit the main Texas Station website for tickets and schedules of performers.

Also at Texas Station is the **Regal Cinemas 18** movie theater complex. It's not quite as fancy as the newer facility at sister property Santa Fe, but they do offer stadium seating and the state-of-the-art projection and sound systems that modern moviegoers seem to demand. Call 702/221-2283 or visit www.regalcinemas.com for showtimes and movie selections.

There is another **Kids' Quest** facility at Texas Station that is virtually identical to the one at Santa Fe Station. Call 702/631-8355 for more information.

SHOPPING
MEADOWS MALL

4300 Meadows Ln., Las Vegas, 702/878-4849, www.meadowsmall.com

HOURS: Mon.-Sat. 10 A.M.–9 P.M., Sun. 10 A.M.–6 P.M.

You know that mall just down the road from you that has the Sears, the JCPenney, and the Foot Locker? This mall is just like that. The good news is that the lingerie at the Victoria's Secret here probably costs a couple of dollars less than that in the highly themed malls on The Strip. So if the airline lost your luggage, you can save a few bucks by coming here to replace things. Anchor stores include Macy's and Dillards, while the 140 or so other shops are mostly of the Bath and Body Works and Hot Topic varieties.

SPORTS AND RECREATION
FIESTA RANCHO SOBE ICE ARENA

2400 N. Rancho Rd., Las Vegas, 702/638-3785, www.fiestacasino.com

HOURS: Public skating hours vary daily

They tore down the beloved ice skating rink at Santa Fe Station (much to the dismay of local residents), but then built a new, better one at this sister property just down the street. It's got a full-size regulation rink offering public skating, instruction, hockey, figure skating, and other programs mostly geared toward people who live around here, but they have a full pro shop and rental counter for guests who'd like to express their inner Michelle Kwan. There's something odd about an ice rink in the middle of the desert, with slot machines blaring away just outside the doors, but hey—this is Las Vegas after all.

◖ LAS VEGAS MOTOR SPEEDWAY

7000 Las Vegas Blvd. N., Las Vegas, 800/644-4444, www.lvms.com

HOURS: Hours vary

COST: Prices vary

The $200 million (and counting) they've thrown at this facility has transformed a barren bit of the desert into one of the premier auto-racing complexes in the United States. Covering more than 1,600 acres, there's a 1.5-mile super-speedway, road courses, a drag strip, a dirt track, a short oval, and much more, ensuring that virtually every type of racing can be hosted here. Several NASCAR events, Craftsmen Truck Series races, NHRA funny car and drag racer showdowns, and FIA-sanctioned GT events are held every year. The grandstand seats more than 150,000 people (plus more in the air-conditioned luxury skyboxes) and there's a 4,500-space RV park overlooking the track.

TEXAS STATION BOWLING CENTER

2101 Texas Star Ln., Las Vegas, 702/631-8128, www.texasstation.com

HOURS: Open 24 hours

The 60-lane bowling center at Texas Station features the latest high-tech scoring equipment, a pro shop, a snack bar, and a lounge, plus it's open 24 hours a day if you get a hankering to bowl a few frames at five in the morning. Stranger things have happened. Weekends offer Cosmic Bowling; anyone unsure of what that means probably doesn't want to do it anyway (think disco-style lighting and loud music). At press time, they were offering a deal that would score you (sorry) a free game if you brought in your receipt from the movie theaters or the buffet.

HOTELS

CANNERY CASINO HOTEL $

2121 E. Craig Rd., North Las Vegas, 866/999-4899, www.cannerycasinos.com

The 200 rooms at the Cannery are nothing to write home about, but they do offer enough square footage and handy conveniences to make them worth knowing about, especially for the rates they charge. Rooms almost never cost more than $100 unless there's an event at the nearby Las Vegas Motor Speedway, and even then, they're still a bargain compared to rates everywhere else in the city. Furnishings are modern and comfortable, and in addition to the standard amenities they have 24-hour room service and on-site coin-operated laundry facilities.

FIESTA RANCHO $

2400 N. Rancho Rd., Las Vegas, 888/899-7770, www.fiestacasino.com

They only have 100 rooms, but the ones they have are surprisingly up to date in terms of

decor and amenities (there are still hotels on The Strip that don't have high-speed Internet access). The Station Casinos chain that owns this property knows how to do things right, and this is no exception. True, the drive back and forth to The Strip can be a pain, especially during rush hour, but for prices as low as $39 a night, it's really hard to complain.

SANTA FE STATION $

4949 N. Rancho Rd., Las Vegas, 866/767-7771, http://santafe.stationcasinos.com

Along with the rest of the property, the 200 rooms at Santa Fe Station got a makeover recently, turning what were basic, boring, motel-style accommodations into classy, almost stylish ones. They have a full range of amenities, including the standard (irons and boards, hair dryers) and not-so-standard (Nintendo, high-speed Internet, coffee makers). With comfy furnishings in each room and a host of facilities in the building (from a casino to movie theaters), this is a terrific hotel choice even before factoring in the room rates, which can be as low as $39 a night.

TEXAS STATION $

2101 Texas Star Ln., Las Vegas, 800/654-8888, www.texasstation.com

Upgraded a couple of years ago with new furnishings and amenities, the 200 rooms here may not swaddle guests in luxury, but they will absolutely keep guests comfortable. They have all of the standard conveniences, and while they don't beg to be lounged around in all day, that's not what a Vegas vacation should be about anyway. So who cares that they don't have 300-thread-count linens on the bed? There's a nice (if small) pool and an astounding number of on-site restaurants and entertainment options. Low room rates are almost a bonus.

PRACTICALITIES
Information and Services

For more information about the city of North Las Vegas, visit the official website at www.ci.north-las-vegas.nv.us or call the city offices at 702/633-1000.

RACING FOR DUMMIES

What's that? You say you want to be Jeff Gordon or Kurt Busch, tearing up the asphalt in a 600-horsepower NASCAR beast, aiming for the checkered flag and all the glory that comes with it? Well, here's your chance.

The **Richard Petty Driving Experience** (7000 N. Las Vegas Blvd., 800/BE-PETTY, www.1800bepetty.com) operates at more than 20 tracks nationwide, allowing normal folks like us the chance to slip behind the wheel of a Nextel Cup-style stock car and take it for a little jaunt. The company was founded in 1994 by Petty, driver of the legendary #43 in the NASCAR circuit with 200 career wins under his big belt buckle.

Although the programs and prices vary at each track, the Las Vegas Motor Speedway edition offers experiences ranging from a simple Ride Along, where visitors get to sit in the passenger seat of a professionally piloted car going about 165 miles per hour, all the way up to an Advanced Racing Experience that allows visitors to drive 40 laps of competition-style NASCAR combat. The most popular is the Rookie Experience, with eight laps.

An affable crew of instructors starts the program by showing a brief video about what to expect, reassuring everyone the entire way that the RPDE was built for fun, but with a great deal of safety in mind. In other words, "You're not going to be crashing our expensive cars into any walls while we're on duty."

Next, visitors get a hands-on tour of the car itself, which, with the exception of some additional safety equipment, is virtually identical to those driven by the pros. Lessons include how to climb in and out through the window (there are no doors) without making a fool of yourself, how not to get impaled on the steering wheel stalk, the manual shift patterns (sorry, no automatics here), the emergency fire system and engine kill switches, and a host of other minor details.

A tour of the track in vans, some pictures for posterity, and safety harness and helmet fittings later, and it's off to the races. In the Rookie Experience, drivers are led by a pace car but are encouraged to go as fast as they can possibly stand going and get as close to those concrete walls as they can get.

It's a thrilling experience, and although the car vaguely resembles a Ford Fusion, it isn't one – a fact that becomes readily apparent as you are pinned back against the driver's seat from the power of that 600-horsepower engine blasting you around the oval at speeds of around 140 mph. Adrenaline rush doesn't even begin to cover it.

A couple of things worth noting: Weekend sessions fill up months in advance, so visitors need to either sign up early or try to do it during the week if they have the flexibility. Also, the cars are not exactly what you'd call roomy or in the least bit comfortable, so people with claustrophobia or back or neck issues may want to pass this one by. Last, it ain't cheap. The Rookie Experience costs around $399, but it's an experience you'll remember for a lifetime.

Many of the hotels, restaurants, and entertainment facilities mentioned in this section are featured on most Las Vegas tourism websites, including www.Vegas4Visitors.com, www.Vegas.com, and www.LasVegas.com, plus the Las Vegas Convention and Visitors Authority has additional information; call 877/VISIT-LV or visit www.visitlasvegas.com.

Essential services, including branches of all major banks, are located throughout the city (ATMs and check-cashing services are available at the casinos). There's a post office at 1414 E. Lake Mead Boulevard in North Las Vegas (702/633-5087), but hotels can handle most mailing and shipping needs for their guests.

For major emergencies, the Lake Mead Medical Center is located at 1409 E. Lake Mead Boulevard in North Las Vegas (702/649-7711), and there are two UMC Quick Care facilities for walk-in treatment of minor emergencies. One is at 1760 Wheeler Peak Drive (702/383-2565) and the other at 2202 W. Craig Road (702/382-6270).

Getting There and Around

Most of the things worth seeing in the North Las Vegas area are close to the major freeways. Take I-15 north from The Strip and it runs right through the heart of North Las Vegas, with easy access to places like the Cannery at the Craig Road off-ramp or the Las Vegas Motor Speedway at the Speedway exit.

I-95 heads west away from Downtown Las Vegas, but then curves north, where a Rancho Road exit is located. This is where hotels like Santa Fe Station and, a little further down the road, Texas Station and Fiesta Rancho can be found. Alternately, take Sahara Avenue west from The Strip to Rancho Road, turn right, and head north for several miles until you see the bright casino lights.

There is city bus service throughout the area, but quite frankly, if you are depending on the bus for your transportation, you probably shouldn't bother coming out here. The only way to get around with any ease is to provide your own set of wheels.

West Las Vegas   Map 7

Although West Las Vegas is not its own city or even a formally used term, it is a fairly common nomenclature used by locals to describe pretty much anything west of The Strip. Many of the attractions, casinos, and hotels close to the tourist areas are covered in the *Just Off The Strip* neighborhood sections of each chapter, so this section focuses on things a little further out, starting at roughly Decatur Boulevard (about 2.5 miles west of The Strip) and heading all the way out to the Las Vegas Beltway (I-215).

The southwest section of the area is mostly undeveloped (but will be growing rapidly over the next few years), so most of the things worth going to see are due west and northwest of town. It's here that a few notable resort hotels and casinos (including one of the best in town), some restaurants and entertainment options, and quite a few recreation facilities are located.

GAMING

I've done very well at Red Rock Resort on multiple occasions, although the winning has not been consistent. I'm sorry to say that I've never done exceptionally well at either of the other casinos here, although I've also never done exceptionally poorly either. I did hit a moderate-sized jackpot at Suncoast once, which I then proceeded to gamble away almost immediately, but on most occasions, I have walked out of both with less money in my pocket than I came in with.

RAMPART CASINO

221 N. Rampart Blvd., 702/507-5900, www.rampartcasino.com

HOURS: Open 24 hours

Run independently of the JW Marriott Las Vegas hotel where it is located, the Rampart Casino seems smaller than it actually is. The 50,000 square feet of gaming space puts it on par with the neighborhood casinos in the north part of town, but it feels more intimate and ritzy. A full range of table games is arrayed in the center under a colorful glass dome, with more than 1,200 slots and video poker machines surrounding it in one big circle. All of the latest machines in all denominations are represented, but unlike most locals' places, there is a broader mix that doesn't focus quite as heavily on the pennies and nickels (although there are plenty of those for the budget gambler). A small race and sports book is also available.

RED ROCK RESORT

11011 W. Charleston Ave., 702/797-7576, www.redrocklasvegas.com

HOURS: Open 24 hours

It's almost impossible to adequately describe the visual accomplishment they have achieved

Rampart Casino at the JW Marriott Las Vegas

here in this resort, the newest of the Station Casinos chain of hotels. Everywhere you look throughout the gorgeous casino there is movement, texture, light, and space, with natural materials like sandstone, onyx, and the local red rock blending with teak, mahogany, and ebony woods and crystal appointments to create a room in which even the support columns become works of art.

The 80,000 square feet of gaming space is fully equipped for all of your needs with more than 3,000 slot machines and video poker of all denominations, 60 table games, a huge high-tech race and sports book, a poker room, a bingo hall, and keno. The space is well laid out with multiple sections offering a create-your-own-atmosphere ethos. Want a party-all-night experience? Hang out at the gaming tables. A high-stakes adventure? The poker room or high-limit slot areas are there for you. A casual, low-key, low-cost affair? There are plenty of penny slots near the food court. No matter what you're looking for, you can probably find it here.

SUNCOAST
9090 Alta Dr., 702/636-7111, www.suncoastcasino.com
HOURS: Open 24 hours

The appointments may be a little more fancy than the typical neighborhood casino, with rich sun-hued colors and lots of wood and mosaic-tile detail work, but underneath it all, this 80,000-square-foot facility is aimed squarely at the local market. This means lower limits on the slots and a lot more video poker machines than are found at the casinos on The Strip. There are more than 2,400 machines total, plus 50 of the most popular table games, a 600-seat bingo parlor, and a 150-seat race and sports book. This sister hotel of Orleans operates under the same Coast Casinos players' club, so members can earn points here and redeem them at either property.

RESTAURANTS
THE CARMEL ROOM ⑤⑤⑤
221 N. Rampart Blvd. (at the Rampart Casino), 702/507-5900, www.rampartcasino.com
HOURS: Sun.-Thurs. 5 -10 P.M., Fri.-Sat. 5-10:30 P.M.
Fine dining in the hinterlands of Las Vegas

is not always easy to find, but The Carmel Room does a good job of approximating the appointments of luxury steakhouses without the high prices. Kick off your meal with a very fine onion soup (very salty, just the way I like it) and then try a main course like the Veal á la Oscar (medallions crowned with blue crab) or one of the delicious chops (the filet with Roquefort cheese topping and the prime rib are winners here). For dessert, the white and dark chocolate crème brûlée is decadent, while the deep-fried strawberries and table-side cherries jubilee or bananas Foster are terrific cappers to a great meal.

FEAST BUFFET $

11011 W. Charleston Ave. (at Red Rock Resort),
702/797-7777, www.redrocklasvegas.com
HOURS: Sun.-Thu. 8 A.M.-10 P.M., Fri.-Sat. 8 A.M.-11 P.M.
The Station Casinos buffets are highly regarded in this town for their almost epic options of really good food, fine surroundings, and moderate prices. This one is no different, and yet better in a lot of ways. There are six live-ac-tion cooking stations offering made-to-order omelets during breakfast and brunch, hand-cooked pasta specialties at lunch and dinner, and slices of various fine cuts of meat from the carving station. Barbecue, sushi, American, Chinese, Italian, desserts, and one of the best salad bars in town make this buffet better than average, and the costs of around $9 for breakfast up to about $19 for the champagne brunch keep it competitive.

HANNAH'S $$

1050 S. Rampart Blvd., 702/932-9399,
www.hannahslv.com
HOURS: Daily 11 A.M.-11 P.M.
This incredible Pan-Asian bistro is from the same An family that created the renowned Crustacean in San Francisco and Los Angeles. Hannah's is more casual than that but no less important. The decor is whimsical with bamboo reeds as section dividers, water flowing down walls and through floors, and fun food-themed art everywhere. But the menu is what gets the juices flowing—a huge selection

Hannah's restaurant

of food, mostly Asian but with Vietnamese, French, and American influences. Start with one of the flatbreads, preferably the Caesar or barbecue, then move into the noodle dishes or sushi, and prepare to linger for a while on the entrée list featuring everything from steak to Vietnamese game hens. If I had to pick one winner, it would be the Shaken Beef—cubed tenderloin wok-fried in a red wine sauce with caramelized onions and peppers—but it's hard to find a loser here.

☾ HASH HOUSE A GO GO ⑤

6800 W. Sahara Ave., 702/804-4646,
www.hashhouseagogo.com
HOURS: Daily 7:30 A.M.-2:30 P.M. and
Mon.-Sat. 5-10 P.M.

Their mission is offering up what they call "twisted farm food" and these Indiana natives know what they're talking about. Pancakes come in varieties like brown-sugar banana and are roughly the size of a large pizza, while their bacon waffles come with actual strips of farm-fresh bacon baked right inside. A full selection of their signature hashes run the gamut from traditional corned beef to meatloaf with spinach and mozzarella, while the Farm Scrambles are like those skillets at Denny's, only bigger, better, and more interesting (smoked salmon and Brie). A full lunch and dinner menu is also available, but breakfast is really the star here. They've even got something called "O'Hare of the Dog," a 24-ounce Budweiser served in a paper bag with a side of bacon. How can you not love that?

RAMPART BUFFET ⑤

221 N. Rampart Blvd. (at Rampart Casino),
702/507-5900, www.rampartcasino.com
HOURS: Daily 11 A.M.-3 P.M. and 4-9:30 P.M.

The classy soft lighting and wood finishes give the dining room a distinctly restaurant-quality feel, more intimate than the usual barn-like atmosphere of similarly priced buffets. The food selections are vast, with a generous selection of American, Asian, Italian, and Mediterranean cuisines, plus a wood-burning pizza oven, a rotisserie grill, and a fine carving station. The

quality and overall presentation of the food is a step or two above what might be expected from a place charging these kinds of reasonable rates—around $9 for lunch, $13 for weekend brunch, and $12–18 for dinner, the higher price for the seafood night that also includes all-you-can-eat prime rib.

ROSEMARY'S ⑤⑤

8125 W. Sahara Ave., 702/869-2251,
www.rosemarysrestaurant.com
HOURS: Daily 5:30 P.M.-close and
Mon.-Fri. 11:30 A.M.-2:30 P.M.

New Orleans natives Michael and Wendy Jordan brought the lessons they learned in that city's fine dining circuit to the Las Vegas desert with this fun and fantastic bistro that has earned raves for its cuisine. It's chic nouvelle American, mostly with a noticeable Deep South zing. The Texas barbecue shrimp with Maytag blue cheese slaw is a definite for the starter list or, for fans of things like foie gras, the seared version here with a delicate orange brioche is stunning. Entrées run the gamut from roasted rack of lamb to goat cheese raviolis, all of which are fine choices, but the pan-roasted filet of beef in a kicky green peppercorn sauce or the honey Creole mustard-glazed salmon are the definite stars. Service and atmosphere are close to perfect and the prices, while high, are bargains compared to similar, and lesser, restaurants on The Strip.

SALT LICK BBQ ⑤

11011 W. Charleston Ave. (at Red Rock Resort),
702/797-5176, www.redrocklasvegas.com
HOURS: Sun.-Thu. 11 A.M.-10 P.M., Fri.-Sat. 11 A.M.-11 P.M.

Since 1969, the Salt Lick BBQ near Austin, Texas, has been something of a destination where barbecue devotees travel from near and far to get a taste of their famous secret recipe sauce, pork ribs, and high-octane sausages. To say that the branch here in Vegas is not as good as the original probably shouldn't come as a great galloping surprise, but that's sort of like saying that the tropical rainforest in The Mirage isn't as good as the real ones in South America. It's still the Salt Lick and it's still amazing barbecue and among the best you'll find in town. You must try their beer-battered onion rings and the slow-smoked pulled pork, and if you walk out without a piece of one of their delicious fruit cobblers, you only have yourself to blame.

ST. TROPEZ BUFFET ⑤

9090 Alta Dr. (at Suncoast Casino), 702/636-7111, www.suncoastcasino.com

HOURS: Mon.-Thurs. 7 A.M.-9 P.M., Fri. 7 A.M.-10 P.M., Sat. 8 A.M.-10 P.M., Sun. 8 A.M.-9 P.M.

As with the Rampart Buffet, the designers took a large space and divided it up into smaller sections, making the experience of eating here more like dining in a warm bistro environment than a big, impersonal buffet. A Mongolian barbecue station is one of the unique touches that set the food selection apart, and the wide-ranging seafood station offers higher quality selections than should be reasonably expected. The prices are neighborhood-casino reasonable, with breakfast around $6, lunch for $9, dinner $13–18, and Sunday champagne brunch only $13.

TERRA ROSSA ⑤⑤

11011 W. Charleston Ave. (at Red Rock Resort), 702/797-7576, www.redrocklasvegas.com

HOURS: Sun.-Thu. 11 A.M.-10 P.M., Fri.-Sat. 11 A.M.-11 P.M.

Fans of Fox TV's *Hell's Kitchen* may have wondered what happened to 2006 winner Heather West. Well, she wound up here as a senior chef, helping to define the Italian cuisine that this casual restaurant offers. The wine list is epic, so take some time to peruse (and feel free to ask for help), but you can also dive right into the menu options with a delicate prosciutto appetizer, zesty minestrone that could've come from your mother's kitchen, pizzas, raviolis, pastas, giant calzones, risottos, seafood, steak, osso bucco, and much more. Although not my favorite Italian restaurant in town, the offerings here are quite good, and when you factor in the moderate prices (most pastas are under $20 and most entrees under $30), you have more reasons to eat here than the possibility of seeing a reality television star.

ENTERTAINMENT

CHERRY

11011 W. Charleston Ave. (at Red Rock Resort), 702/797-7777, www.redrockstation.com

HOURS: Thu.-Sat. 10 P.M.-5 A.M.

If you're out in this section of town, you really only have one choice for nightclubbing, but the good news is that Cherry is just as cool, hip, and exciting as the hot spots down on The Strip. A glowing red tube delivers you to the space-age nightclub, complete with a slamming dance floor, VIP booths with bottle service, and a giant bar. Past that, you'll find a door that leads to an under-the-stars extension complete with another bar, VIP cabanas, and a shallow pool to lounge by and sip whatever trendy drink you are imbibing. Cheaper than average for this kind of experience and much less attitudinal, Cherry is worth a visit not just because there aren't any other good options.

GUSTAV MAULER GOURMET CIGARS

221 N. Rampart Blvd. (at the Rampart Casino), 702/896-6700, www.gustavmaulercigar.com

HOURS: Daily from 4 P.M. until the smoke clears

COST: No cover

For a more relaxed entertainment option, try this clubby little space run by a local celebrity chef who specializes in upscale accoutrement without the upscale snobbishness. They offer a wide range of fine cigars (Havana, Romeo-Julieta, Mayorga, and more) plus a full drink menu, specializing in cognacs and signature martinis. Cigar aficionados should definitely stop by, and if you're a true fan, you can even get your own personalized humidor that will have your name on it and be under your very own lock and key. Better than a Vegas coffee mug with your name on it any day of the week.

LAS VEGAS ART MUSEUM

9600 W. Sahara Ave., 702/360-8000, www.lasvegasartmuseum.org

HOURS: Tues.-Sat. 10 A.M.-5 P.M., Sun. 1-5 P.M.

COST: $6 adult, $5 senior, $3 student, free for children under 12

The art galleries on The Strip may get more attention simply because of their high-profile

Cherry nightclub at Red Rock Resort

location, but they can't hold a candle to this beautiful facility, part of a local fine art coalition that has been around for more than five decades. Built in 1997, the museum boasts three dramatic exhibition spaces that dwarf those puny galleries in The Strip's casinos. Their affiliation with the Smithsonian Institute means the shows here are of the highest caliber, but they seem to do a good job of knocking down the stuffy museum attitude in both presentation and among the personnel.

NEVADA BALLET THEATRE

1651 Inner Cir., 702/243-2623, www.nevadaballet.com
HOURS: Performance times vary
COST: Prices vary

This company's roots go back to 1972 when a dancer with *Folies Bergere* at the Tropicana gathered a group of like-minded Vegas performers to present a series of ballet performances. Now, more than 30 years later, the NBT offers a regular schedule of performances, operating as one of the few permanent, professional fine arts programs in the state. The 36,000-square-foot facility here in Summerlin

is primarily used for training and exhibitions, but the company puts on full-scale ballet productions at major theaters around the area, so call or visit their website for specific details.

RED ROCK RESORT

11011 W. Charleston Ave., 702/797-7777,
www.redrocklasvegas.com

Besides Cherry (listed above), Red Rock has a wide variety of entertainment options to keep you amused. **Lucky Bar** sits in the middle of the casino and is filled with stunning crystal light fixtures, lots of cozy lounge furnishings, and a fierce DJ on weekends to keep you grooving. Over at **Rock's Lounge** you'll find an equally hip environment (zebra print seating, lounge-like environs) with live bands on weekends.

Outside is the beautiful **Backyard** pool area, which features periodic concerts from some pretty big names in the entertainment world. Nelly Furtado, Lauryn Hill, Vertical Horizon, and Sting are just a few of the names who have performed here.

At the other end of the facility, they offer a

72-lane bowling alley (see **Red Rock Lanes** under *Sports and Recreation* in the West Las Vegas section of this chapter) and a **Regal Cinemas** (702/233-6948) 16-screen movie theater complex with stadium seating, high-back reclining chairs, digital sound, and even VIP viewing areas if you don't want to sit with "the common folks."

A **Kids Quest** (702/797-7646) "playcare" facility offers hourly packages to keep the wee ones distracted with a reading corner, a karaoke stage, games, climb-on playground equipment, and much more.

SUNCOAST
9090 Alta Dr., 877/636-7111,
www.suncoastcasino.com

The **Showroom at the Suncoast** is a 500-seat facility set up to mimic the classic Vegas showrooms that have mostly disappeared. This means that instead of theater-style seats, they offer rounded booths and long tables facing the large stage. If it weren't for the modern decor, you'd almost expect Wayne Newton to walk by with a rousing chorus of "Danke Schön." Most of the entertainers who perform here are in the "Where are they now?" category, but every now and then they get someone fun like Debbie Reynolds (who puts on amazing show, by the way).

The Suncoast also features a **Century Cinemas** 16-screen movie theater complex with stadium seating and the latest high-tech sound systems. Call 702/341-5555 for movie selections and showtimes.

SPORTS AND RECREATION
AQUAE SULIS SPA
221 N. Rampart Blvd. (at JW Marriott), 877/869-8777,
www.jwlasvegasresort.com
HOURS: Daily 5:30 A.M.-8 P.M.
COST: Gym/Spa day pass $20 guests, $35 non-guests

This facility is one of the nicest spas in town, offering a full range of treatments in their 36 comfortable rooms, a complete workout facility, a salon, and a boutique. But it's their unique Hydrotherapy circuit pools that really draw the attention. The experience begins inside in a hot or cold plunge, followed by the warm float pool,

and then moves outside to a series of six dipping pools with different temperatures and massaging jets, all surrounded by lush landscaping. It's an invigorating way to rejuvenate after too much Las Vegas-style partying.

◀ ARROYO GOLF CLUB AT RED ROCK
2250 Red Springs Dr., 866/934-4653,
www.arroyogolfclubatredrock.com
HOURS: Daily dusk-dawn

With a link design from golf legend Arnold Palmer, this 18-hole, par-72 course is most notable for its surrounding landscape on the edges of the Red Rock Canyon National Conservation Area. Ranging from craggy canyon surroundings to dramatic elevations with views of the nearby mountains and The Strip in the distance, golfers spend just as much time looking at the scenery as trying to hit the little ball in the little hole. Tee times start at around $159 during the week and $189 on the weekends, but twilight sessions are cheaper. There's also a restaurant and a pro shop on-site.

BEAR'S BEST GOLF COURSE
11111 W. Flamingo Rd., 702/804-8500,
www.bearsbest.com
HOURS: Daily dusk-dawn

Jack Nicklaus selected 18 of his favorite holes from the more than 200 courses he has designed around the world and put them all together in one spot here at Bear's Best. Players start at a dogleg par 4 from PGA West in Palm Springs, work their way through bunkers and water features re-created from courses in Arizona, Mexico, and Montana, and then finish up at a sloping green from La Quinta. A clubhouse restaurant features memorabilia from Nicklaus's career and a full pro shop stocks signature golf accessories. Tee times range from $205-255, with twilight pricing knocking a few bucks off that.

LAS VEGAS MINI GRAN PRIX
1401 N. Rainbow Rd., 702/259-7000, www.lvmgp.com
HOURS: Sun.-Thurs. 10 A.M.-10 P.M.,
Fri.-Sat. 10 A.M.-11 P.M.

For anyone with kids and a car at their disposal, this is a must-visit attraction. Inside, there's a big arcade with video and carnival-style games, plus a snack bar offering some shockingly good pizzas and sandwiches, but outside is where the real fun begins. They've got four go-kart courses, including a kids-only route, a high-banking oval, a competition road course (the longest in Las Vegas) where drivers battle against each other, and a timed road course where drivers battle against the clock. The karts themselves go from simple putt-putts to serious roadsters and are a blast to play around in.

RED ROCK LANES
11011 W. Charleston Ave., 702/797-7467, www.redrocklanes.com
HOURS: Open 24 hours

For people like me who still have their pins and patches from the bowling leagues they were in as children, the thought of "luxury" bowling alleys is a bit silly. But walk into this place and you'll never want to go back to the smoke-stained wretches that you grew up with. Seventy-two lanes feature the latest in bowling technology with 40-inch LCD scoring monitors and Brunswick Vector Plus scoring systems, 42-inch plasma televisions between lanes, giant projection screens, a snack bar, a pro shop, an arcade with pool tables and dart boards, and more. And that's just in the "regular folks" section. There are also VIP suites in 4, 8, and 12-lane configurations that come with bottle service, nightclub-level sound systems, and lounge-like furnishings for that super-luxury evening of bowling you've been dying for.

THE SPA AT RED ROCK/ ADVENTURE SPA
11011 W. Charleston Ave., 702/797-7878, www.redrocklasvegas.com
HOURS: Daily 5:30 A.M.–8 P.M.
COST: Gym/Spa included in resort fee for guests, $35 non-guests

Owing to its location near Red Rock Canyon, the spa here at the Red Rock Resort is not just a lie-around-and-be-pampered experience. Sure, they offer that in a beautiful facility with mas-

sages, treatments, salon facilities, and more. But it's the Adventure Spa portion of their offerings that really set this place apart. Sign up for hiking, horseback riding, rock climbing, kayaking, river rafting, mountain biking, and even off-road vehicle tours that will get your inner explorer revving. Rates vary from expensive to really expensive, but the program offerings and the instructors/guides are among the best in the business, so you can fully put your trust in the guy saying "Go ahead, jump off the side of that cliff, the rope will hold you."

SUMMERLIN PARKS AND TRAILS
Veteran's Memorial Leisure Services Community Center, 101 S. Pavilion Center Dr., 702/229-1100, www.summerlin.com
HOURS: Hours vary

Winding its way through the acres of tract housing in Summerlin are more than 100 miles of paved and unpaved trails linking parks, villages, and nature areas. Many sections of the system are along residential streets, but are wide and offer enough landscaping to keep them from being glorified sidewalks. Other trails wander through the natural arroyos of the area and the whole thing will eventually be linked to the adjacent Red Rock Canyon trail system.

Scattered along the route is a series of parks, many of which have public recreation (tennis and basketball courts) and entertainment facilities (amphitheaters and community centers). There is no formal program for the trail system—it's all do-it-yourself. The best starting points are at any of the 17 parks throughout the area. The community center and website can help guide visitors to the best locations.

SUNCOAST BOWLING CENTER
9090 Alta Dr. (at Suncoast Casino), 702/636-7400, www.suncoastcasino.com
HOURS: Open 24 hours

It's hard to come up with something interesting and unique to say about a bowling alley, but at this location, they actually do things a little differently. The layout is distinctive, with 32 lanes on each side of a big center aisle, and while that doesn't change the fact that it's still knocking down pins with a heavy ball, at least it makes the facility a little more visually interesting. There's a snack shop, a pro shop, and a lounge with a full bar, and they offer the popular Cosmic Bowling (jazzy lights and sound) on weekends.

TCP AT THE CANYONS

9851 Canyon Run Dr., 702/256-2000,
www.tpcthecanyons.com

HOURS: Daily dawn-dusk

Home to regular PGA events, TCP at The Canyons is an 18-hole, par-72 course winding its way through the arroyos and rolling, stony outcroppings of the natural desert landscape. As expected from a course that draws the pros, this is not an easy jaunt through the links—casual golfers looking for a relaxing back nine should not apply, unless frustration is high on their to-do list. They offer twilight tee times in summer for as low as $75, but the peak weekends cost around $275 for 18 holes. The facility also boasts target and driving greens, a full restaurant and a smaller snack bar, a full bar, and a pro shop.

HOTELS

JW MARRIOTT LAS VEGAS $$$

221 N. Rampart Blvd., 702/869-7777,
www.jwlasvegasresort.com

Perched on a rise at the west end of the Las Vegas Valley, this lavish resort offers some stunning views of the surrounding area from almost any angle. Two wings of more than 500 rooms stretch back from the center lobby and casino area (run independently of the hotel) with a graceful Spanish missionary design theme throughout. It's really a beautiful and peaceful place inside and out as a series of lushly landscaped lawns surround the pool and spa area, perfect for an afternoon respite. The rooms themselves are stunning as well with walk-in closets, minibars, waterfall showers in the giant bathrooms, balconies or patios, and all of the upscale resort amenities. It's not cheap to stay here, but you'll feel like you're getting your money's worth.

The lavish JW Marriott Las Vegas is worth the splurge.

(RED ROCK RESORT $$

11011 W. Charleston Ave., 866/767-7773,
www.redrocklasvegas.com

If you've been paying attention to this section of the book you'll notice that I've been rhapsodizing about the various pieces of this hotel, so it should be no great surprise that I'm going to do the same thing about the guest accommodations and the resort as a whole.

The rooms are huge and stunning, all sleek dark woods and textured walls, platform beds with deliriously comfortable mattresses, built-in desks, minibars, high-speed Internet (wired or wireless), robes, irons and boards, and breathtaking views of either Red Rock Canyon to the west or the Las Vegas Strip about 11 miles to the east. The bathrooms are equally stunning, large with all-marble dual-vanities and sunken tubs, separate walk-in showers, hair dryers, makeup mirrors, and a water closet. Even in here the textures continue with leather walls.

Prices are expensive, to be sure, but cheaper than similar accommodations on The Strip and more than worth what you're getting: one of the best hotel experiences in town.

SUNCOAST $$

9090 Alta Dr., 702/636-7111, www.suncoastcasino.com

The more than 500 guest rooms at the Suncoast are bigger than average at around 550 square feet, allowing for a unique layout in those with king beds. In them, a half-wall separates the sleeping and conversation areas, the latter with floor-to-ceiling windows overlooking nearby golf courses and The Strip or mountains in the distance. Furnishings verge on luxurious and the amenities list is resort-level complete. Prices include free access to the well-equipped fitness center, and there's also a free shuttle to The Strip and the airport to make the far-flung locations a little less inconvenient for those without a rental car at their disposal. Weekday off-season rates can go for as low as $70 a night, but expect to pay at least double that for a typical night's stay.

a standard room at Red Rock Resort

MOUNT CHARLESTON

One of the truly interesting things about the Las Vegas area is the wide range of recreation opportunities provided by the varying landscape. Want to go horseback riding or hiking in the desert? They've got that covered at Red Rock Canyon and Valley of Fire. How about swimming or waterskiing? Lake Mead and Lake Las Vegas offer those. And yes, there's even snow skiing and snowboarding at Mount Charleston, the nearly 12,000-foot-high peak about 40 miles west of town.

It's primarily a winter destination; the primary reason to come here is for the snow sports, most of which are centered around the **Mount Charleston Lodge** (1200 Old Park Rd., 800/955-1314, www.mtcharlestonlodge .com) and the **Las Vegas Ski and Snowboard Resort** (3620 N. Rancho Rd. (mailing only), 702/872-5462, www.skilasvegas.com).

The lodge is a rambling facility of rooms, cabins, and villas near the main skiing areas, complete with the roaring fireplace requisite to a place called a ski lodge. In addition to the full-service restaurant, there are some video poker machines at the bar for those who just can't be away from gambling for that long.

The resort features a number of runs with Vegas-centric names, like Blackjack, Slot Alley, and The Strip, plus a half-pipe and a snowboard park. The hills range in difficulty (yes, there is a bunny hill), but the big runs are mostly reserved for folks with a moderate-high skill level, so beginners may want to consider taking a few more lessons before attacking these slopes. Full ski instructions, equipment rentals, children's programs, and more are available.

The lodge is open year-round, but the ski resort is usually only in operation from November through the late spring, depending on snow conditions. Lift tickets run around $45 for an all-day adult pass and around $35 for a half-day pass, with discounts available for kids and seniors.

The lodge can assist visitors with additional information on hiking, camping, and horseback riding opportunities available during the non-ski times.

To get there, take I-15 North to US 95 North about 30 miles out of town. Highway 157 (also known as Kyle Canyon Road) comes first and goes directly to the lodge about 20 miles down the road. Keep going a few miles on US 95 to get to Highway 156, which goes to the resort, also about 20 miles off the main road.

PRACTICALITIES
Information and Services

For more information about the Summerlin area, visit the official website at www.summerlin.com. It's not an official city, so there are no offices or tourist bureaus to call or visit, but that website provides a broad overview of things to do in the neighborhood.

Many of the hotels, restaurants, and entertainment facilities mentioned in this section are featured on most Las Vegas tourism websites, including www.Vegas4Visitors.com, www.Vegas.com, and www.LasVegas.com, plus the Las Vegas Convention and Visitors Authority (877/VISIT-LV, www.visitlasvegas.com) can provide additional information.

Essential services, including branches of all major banks, are located throughout the city (ATMs and check-cashing services are available at the casinos). The closest post office is located at 6850 Spring Mountain Road (702/248-7027), but the hotels can also handle most mailing needs.

The Summerlin Hospital is located at 657 Town Center Drive (702/233-7000, www .summerlinhospital.org) and there is a UMC Quick Care facility for walk-in treatment of minor emergencies at 9320 W. Sahara Avenue (702/383-3850).

Getting There and Around

The best driving route to the area depends on the time of day and traffic. Unless it's afternoon rush hour, when everyone is trying to get home, the fastest route is probably I-95 West from Downtown Las Vegas to the Summerlin Parkway. This leads into the heart of the area, with the Rampart Boulevard off-ramp being the best choice for reaching the JW Marriott, Suncoast, and restaurants like Hannah's and Rosemary's. Continue on to the I-215 Las Vegas Beltway and take it south to Charleston to get to Red Rock Resort.

From the south side of town, take the I-215 Las Vegas Beltway, which wraps around the southern suburbs and then heads north past Red Rock Resort to meet up with the Summerlin Parkway.

Alternately, Charleston Boulevard and Sahara Avenue are major thoroughfares that run from The Strip all the way to West Las Vegas.

The Suncoast Casino offers a free shuttle to their property from The Strip and other sister properties, but without a car, the only way to explore other areas is to take cabs or use the bus system, neither of which are very good options. Rent a car or stay on The Strip.

Red Rock Canyon   Map 7

Most of the sights in the region, from The Strip to Lake Mead to Hoover Dam, were created by humans. This one was created by nature over hundreds of millions of years' worth of water and wind, shaping a vast 197,000-acre wonderland of deep arroyos, sandstone peaks, and desert landscapes, most with the trademark red hue of the oxidized minerals the ground contains.

The conservancy area is one of the best choices for nature and recreation lovers visiting Las Vegas. It's a mere 20 miles west of The Strip and offers a plethora of outdoor activities in a setting that will make you forget all about how much money you lost at the craps table the night before. Go and be healed.

SIGHTS
BONNIE SPRINGS/OLD NEVADA
One Gunfighter Ln., Blue Diamond, 702/875-4191, www.bonniesprings.com
HOURS: Daily 10 A.M.–6 P.M. (hours vary seasonally)
COST: $20 per vehicle (up to 6 people)
Just a few miles past the Red Rock Canyon Visitors Center is this charming Old West theme park of sorts. Done up as a replica of an 1880s mining town, Old Nevada and the Bonnie Springs Ranch offer a bunch of activities mainly geared toward families with children.

Start by wandering through the Wild West street scene, with its faithful re-creations of period buildings (the saloon, the blacksmith, etc.), horse-drawn carriages, and the like. A couple of small museums (the site has a history back to the 1850s as an actual prospector stopover and working ranch) and a bunch of shops with souvenirs and era-appropriate jewelry and clothing fill in the gaps along the street.

A petting zoo and miniature train ride will amuse the smaller children while a wax museum might just be creepy enough to amuse the slightly older ones. They have a series of "melodramas" throughout the day, staging everything from gunfights in the streets to a public hanging (don't worry, it's done with enough stuntman silliness to reassure all but the most sensitive of little tykes).

Stables, a small restaurant, and a motel are detailed later in this section.

SPRING MOUNTAIN RANCH STATE PARK
P.O. Box 124, Blue Diamond, 702/875-4141, http://parks.nv.gov/smr.htm
HOURS: Daily 8 A.M.–dusk, daily 10 A.M.–4 P.M. (Visitors Center)
COST: $5 entry fee per vehicle (allows access to all public areas of the park)
Also conveniently located just a few miles past the Red Rock Canyon scenic drive off Highway 159, the park was once a working ranch on 520 acres of spring-fed meadows and forest lands owned by a succession of famous names, including Howard Hughes.

The human history of the area actually dates back to the 1830s, when "Westward Ho" types stopped at the natural springs and established campsites. Over the years that followed, the land was owned by a series of folks who used it for a variety of purposes, including as a cattle ranch, a boys' camp, and a vacation home for the wealthy, until it was deeded to the state after Howard Hughes's death.

The grounds have a number of buildings to explore (including the spectacular 1940s-era main ranch house), picnic areas, living history programs with reenactments of historic events, and summer theater programs.

13-MILE SCENIC DRIVE

Highway 159 at Red Rock Canyon, 702/363-1921, www.nv.blm.gov/redrockcanyon

HOURS: Daily 6 A.M.-dusk, hours vary seasonally

COST: $5-per-vehicle access fee

The easiest way to see Red Rock Canyon is from the comfort of an air-conditioned automobile on this 13-mile loop through the park. Visitors must stop at the Red Rock Canyon Visitors Center to pay the $5-per-vehicle access fee, but this also provides the opportunity to pick up many of the helpful maps and informative brochures about the area.

The road is a 13-mile, one-way loop that twists and turns through a colorful landscape. Stop the car at any of the handy scenic turnoffs for some excellent photo opportunities. If you're lucky, you might just catch a snapshot of one of the wild burros that roam the area, descendents of the animals left behind by prospectors who traveled through the area back in the 1800s.

RESTAURANTS
BONNIE SPRINGS RANCH
RESTAURANT ❺

One Gunfighter Ln., Blue Diamond, 702/875-4191, www.bonniesprings.com

HOURS: Daily 10 A.M.-6 P.M. (hours vary seasonally)

If you've decided to spend some time at Bonnie Springs Ranch, you might want to consider having a bite to eat at the restaurant located on the facility. It's basic diner food with some hearty

breakfasts (steak and eggs, hotcakes, a chili, bean, and cheese omelet for the daring), sandwiches and burgers for lunch, and pork ribs, steaks, and a couple of seafood options for dinner. There's nothing here that could provoke fits of gastronomic delight, but it's all perfectly fine and substantial enough to get you through the day. Note that since it's inside the ranch, guests must pay the $20 vehicle access fee to get there—don't do it unless you were planning on visiting anyway.

RECREATION
Hiking

Red Rock Canyon has miles of well-marked trails for most levels of hiking ability (although all of them require at least a moderate level of physical activity, so those with health issues may want to wait in the shade somewhere). The most popular trail is the Lost Creek path, less than a mile long and winding through the arroyos past a waterfall, but there are much longer and more strenuous routes available. Stop at the **Red Rock Canyon Visitors Center** (Highway 159 at the Red Rock Canyon Park entrance, 702/363-1921, 8:30 A.M.–4:30 P.M. daily) to a pick up a map of all of the options. Even the adventurous should get one, because while most of these trails are well traveled and signposts are common, it's easy to get lost by wandering too far off the beaten track.

Rock Climbing

The thrust faults that created much of the topography of Red Rock Canyon conveniently provided a number of opportunities for rock climbing up the sheer faces of the sandstone cliffs. Challenge levels vary depending on the point of ascent, but there's enough here for even the most serious of climbers. Maps of some of the more popular destinations within the park are available at the **Red Rock Canyon Visitors Center** (Highway 159 at the Red Rock Canyon Park entrance, 702/363-1921, 8:30 A.M.–4:30 P.M. daily).

Cycling

The same trails that provide good hiking opportunities are also terrific for mountain biking. If you're not in the best shape, you probably wouldn't be considering such tomfoolery anyway, but it's worth noting that this is not for the faint of heart. For the willing and able, it offers a great workout in a beautiful environment. A map of trails is available at the Red Rock Canyon Visitors Center (Highway 159 at the Red Rock Canyon Park entrance, 702/363-1921, 8:30 A.M.–4:30 P.M. daily). A number of companies rent bikes, but the best is probably the **Las Vegas Cyclery** (8221 W. Charleston Ave., #101, 702/838-6966, www.lasvegascyclery.com, Mon.–Fri. 10 A.M.–6 P.M., Sat. 9 A.M.–6 P.M., Sun. 8 A.M.–4 P.M.), which offers a full range of on-road and off-road bikes for every level of ability. Rentals start around $30 a day or $100 a week and go up from there for the fancier bikes. They also offer a variety of bike tours of Red Rock Canyon.

Horseback Riding

If you're feeling a need to say "Get along, little doggie" without people laughing at you, the Red Rock Canyon area offers a number of horseback-riding facilities and tours designed to put guests in a cowboy (or cowgirl) spirit.

The best of the bunch is the **Red Rock Riding Stables** at Bonnie Springs Ranch (One Gunfighter Ln., Blue Diamond, 702/875-4191, www.bonniesprings.com, 10 A.M.–6 P.M. daily), which offers guided tours through the canyons and across the desert plains. You can almost hear the chuck wagon calling, can't you? Prices start at $40 per hour per person and they offer a variety of different programs at different times of the year, so call to see what's available.

Rocky Trails, Inc. (1930 Village Center Cir., #3–155, Las Vegas, 888/892-5380, www.lasvegashorsebackriding.com) offers more immersing horseback-riding experiences. One is a sunset trail ride (about an hour and a half) and barbecue, complete with Western music entertainment, a full meal and beverages, a campfire, and transportation to and from your hotel. The other is a four-hour morning ride

that doesn't have all the add-ons, but provides more time on the horse and more time to appreciate the natural beauty of the surroundings. Prices and schedules vary seasonally, so call for details.

PRACTICALITIES
Information

The best source for information is at the **Red Rock Canyon Visitors Center** (Highway 159 at the Red Rock Canyon Park entrance, 702/363-1921, 8:30 A.M.–4:30 P.M. daily), located at the entrance to the 13-mile scenic drive. Alternatively, contact the **Bureau of Land Management Las Vegas Field Office** (4701 N. Torrey Pines Dr., Las Vegas, NV 89130, 702/515-5000, www.nv.blm.gov/redrockcanyon) for information, but under most circumstances, they'll just refer you to the visitors center.

Fees

There is currently a $5-per-vehicle access fee to the Red Rock Canyon National Conservation Area. There are no additional fees for using any of the trails, but there is a $10 fee for overnight camping, which is only allowed in designated areas. No hunting or fishing is allowed.

Getting There

Unless going with a tour, visitors must drive themselves to Red Rock Canyon or the area ranches. The easiest way to get there is to take The Strip north to Charleston Boulevard (just past the Stratosphere) and take that street west for about 11 miles or so. After passing Desert Foothills Drive, Charleston becomes Highway 159 and curves to the left toward Red Rock Canyon. The entrance to the scenic drive and the visitors center is another five miles or so ahead on the right.

Bonnie Springs Ranch is located up Highway 159 about six miles past the Red Rock scenic drive (look for the Old Nevada signs). Spring Mountain Ranch is a few miles past that. Both are on the right.

BACKGROUND

The Setting

The city of Las Vegas is situated roughly at the center of a basin known as the Las Vegas Valley, an adjunct of the Great Basin area of the southwestern United States. Surrounded by mountains (the tallest being Mt. Charleston to the west at nearly 12,000 feet) and nothing but miles of desert in every direction, Las Vegas is considered to be the most geographically isolated major city in the United States.

GEOGRAPHY

The region was sculpted by a combination of forces, mostly tectonic in nature. Although there is some hearty and healthy disagree-ment among scientists, the most commonly accepted theory is that a series of faults in the earth's crust created the Sierra Nevada mountain range on the west of the Great Basin and the Wasatch Mountains on the east some 3–5 million years ago.

The land in between was not affected by the Ice Age glaciers—they never reached this far south. Instead, the natural drainage from the mountain ranges flowed through the basin, carving canyons in some spots and leaving untouched desert plains in others. Unlike the rivers to the west of the Sierra Nevada that flow to the Pacific Ocean and those to the east of the Wa-

LAS VEGAS NEWS BUREAU/LVCVA

satch range that flow into the Mississippi River, the waterways in the Great Basin are self-contained and do not empty into any ocean.

The Las Vegas Valley itself straddles the two major regions of the Great Basin with the colder desert highland plains to the north and the warmer Mojave Desert region to the south. Because it is technically a wash that drains to the Colorado River, the valley itself is not considered a part of the Great Basin, but this is really more of an academic argument than anything else.

The high alkaline content of the soil around the Las Vegas Valley seems to indicate that the region was once under a great salty sea or lake, but it was not associated with Lake Bonneville, the ancestor to the Great Salt Lake in Utah. As a result, early attempts by Mormon settlers in the 1800s to plant crops failed.

Although much of the Las Vegas Valley is barren desert sand, scrub brush, and rocky outcroppings, the center of the valley, near modern-day Downtown Las Vegas, was once filled with verdant meadows fed by natural artesian springs. The fresh water sources were a natural lure to the people who inhabited this land, from the ancient Native American Patayan and Paiute tribes to the modern settlers who first "discovered" the region in the early 1800s.

The city's elevation is roughly 2,178 feet, depending on where it's measured. The southern end of the valley is the low point, sloping gently up as it goes north and west toward Mt. Charleston.

CLIMATE

Most people think of Las Vegas as being hot all the time. Supernova hot. And during the summer months, they'd be right. After all, that's what you get when you go and put a big city in the middle of a desert.

According to the National Weather Service, the average daytime high in July is 104°F. And that's an average, mind you. That means that for every day in July that it's "only" 98°F, there's an equivalent day when it's 110°F. The record high of 117°F was originally set way back in 1942, but that record was tied on July 19, 2005, lest

you think hot days are a thing of the past. Another record was set for the highest nighttime low temperature when it only got down to 95°F in the wee hours of that morning.

It's probably worth noting that things like official record temperatures are measured in or near the Downtown area. Temperatures on The Strip and on the outskirts of town are often a couple of degrees higher. The former is due to all the concrete and metal of the giant resorts, the latter due to the general lack of natural shade to stop the relentless sun.

The flip side to all of this, however, is that at an elevation of more than 2,000 feet, it also gets chilly in Vegas and sometimes downright cold. The average nighttime temperature in December is 36°F and that's without the windchill factor. The record low was on January 13, 1963, when it got all the way down to 8°F. In January 2007, as we celebrated my parents' 50th wedding anniversary in Las Vegas, the temperature never got above 25°F during the day—and it snowed! I blamed them for getting married in January, but the point is bring a coat if you're coming to town during the winter.

Throw out all the extremes and you have a fairly moderate climate here. Annually, the average high is 80°F and the average low is 56°F. The months most likely to see such temperatures are April and October.

Getting back to that whole desert thing, it isn't surprising that Las Vegas doesn't get a lot of rainfall, averaging about 4.5 inches a year. For comparison purposes, in sunny Southern California, Los Angeles averages three times that amount.

The wettest months are January, February, and March, with just over a half inch falling as a norm. June is the driest, at less than one-tenth of an inch on average.

Surprisingly, late July and August are the second set of wet months, pulling in around a half inch apiece. This is due to the annual monsoon season that blows in warm, wet air from the Gulf of California or Gulf of Mexico. The superheating of the air by the brutal summer sun causes convective thunderstorms (created by all that moist air rising rapidly as it

HOW TO BEAT THE HEAT

The time of year when most people take their vacations is unfortunately one of the worst times to visit Las Vegas: summer. Temperatures hover at or well above 100°F from late May through early September, with 110°F or even 120°F days not uncommon in July and August. And I don't care what anyone says about it being a "dry heat" – 120°F is roughly the same temperature at which meat begins to cook, so rationalize it any way you want, but it's still really, really hot.

Luckily, there are several good ways to avoid getting baked. The first, and most obvious, is to not go outside. And no, that doesn't mean you can never leave your hotel. The bulk of worthwhile activities are indoors anyway, so let's look at this from a real-world perspective. Get up in a nice, air-conditioned room, have breakfast in one of the nice, air-conditioned restaurants, spend a while losing little Johnny's tuition in the nice, air-conditioned casino, and do a little shopping with whatever is left over in the nice, air-conditioned adjoining mall or shopping gallery. Then, go out to the covered parking garage where you can jump in the car and blast the nice air-conditioning until the next destination to eat lunch, do some more gambling, visit a museum, or what have you. The total time outside can be measured in minutes and I guarantee you'll be grateful for it.

Those without a car at their disposal will have to use the taxis or public transportation systems to get around – and that will involve a little bit more "outside time." The numerous indoor walkways that connect major hotels are perfect for these situations. For example, it's possible to get from Mandalay Bay to Luxor to Excalibur without ever setting foot outside.

Effective planning is also key to staying cool. Focus daytime activities on things that can be done inside and/or in one localized area. For instance, plan one day to see everything on the southern end of The Strip and you can make the quick jaunts from hotel to hotel and attraction to attraction without risking major sunburn. Try to schedule outdoor activities for the cooler nighttime hours.

Lastly, bring plenty of sunscreen and water with you wherever you go. Blocking out the sun's rays with a simple lotion and keeping yourself hydrated between stints at the slot machines will go a long way toward making your vacation memorable for good reasons rather than bad ones.

"Remember that time we went to Vegas and I got sunstroke?"

---

heats). These thunderstorms are usually short-lived but can be spectacular in nature, both in terms of the brilliant lightning shows and the violent downbursts of rain they create.

Las Vegas wasn't built with an eye toward storm runoff, and although massive flood control efforts have been underway for years to create washes and diversion channels, heavy and hard rains here in Vegas usually result in flooding. Most of it is of the minor surface-street variety, with a stranded motorist here and there. But occasionally, it gets more dramatic than that. Heavy rains in 1999 and 2003 caused severe property damage throughout the area, and an infamous 1969 storm sent cars floating through hotel parking lots like bathtub toys.

Another climatological concern is the wind that blows down from the Great Basin and then picks up speed as it zooms down the mountains that ring the Las Vegas Valley. When weather conditions are right, a steady wind of 20 miles per hour or more is not uncommon, and heavy gusts have been recorded as high as 93 miles per hour. A particularly violent windstorm in 1994 knocked down a portion of the 365-foot-tall sign in front of the Las Vegas Hilton. It has since been redone on a slightly smaller scale.

FLORA AND FAUNA
Plants and Flowers
Look closer at the desert landscape, past the seemingly endless stretches of little more than

native cactus and other succulents

dirt and rock, and you'll find a surprising number of indigenous wild plants, flowers, and trees thriving in the hot sun.

Cacti and other succulents are the staple crop around here, although few of them are the tall saguaro type that one usually associates with the breed. Instead, smaller barrel or beavertail cacti are more common, the former a basketball-sized plant with brown or reddish prickly thorns and colorful blooms in season, the latter a more traditional cactus green with a series of flat palms resembling their namesake animal's tail. The beavertail blooms with brilliant purple flowers, a splash of yellow seedlings at their center.

Cholla is a totally different kind of cactus, one that might not even be recognized as such since they are all spiny thorns and very little body. The thorns themselves are covered in a papery sheath, often in different colors, depending on their regional location within the desert.

Wildflowers are also common, often scattered in bunches around the scrub brush patches. Brittlebush is omnipresent, turning the brownish crags of the scrub into festive yellow patchworks with their small blooms. Slightly larger but similar in appearance is the desert marigold, which to the untrained eye can look a lot like a patch of dandelions.

Every now and then, more colorful desert flora appears, fascinating in both presentation and the sheer fact that something so seemingly delicate can survive in such harsh climate. The Apache plumes evoke another dandelion comparison, only this time with their fuzzy pink blooms amid white petals. They are actually an evergreen shrub, a member of the rose family, and can grow as high as six feet.

Even more delicate in appearance are the aptly named ghost flowers, with their translucent white crowns tucked in the green bushes that grow primarily in washes or slopes near the bases of the local mountains. They are in the same family as the snapdragon.

One of the most beautiful flowers in the area is the desert five-spot, so named for the five deep purple or crimson blotches inside pink or light purple cup-like globes. When the light hits them in the right way, they appear to glow, lending them the "lantern flower" nickname.

In the actual city, there are all types of non-native species, brought in by the truckload to dress up the multibillion-dollar casinos that dot the landscape. Water is a big issue around here, though, so the concept of Xeriscaping has taken root for developments both big and small.

From the Greek word *xeros* (dry), Xeriscaping goes beyond simple desert landscaping, heavily dependent on succulents and rock gardens. Instead, when done properly, it aims to create a virtual oasis with verdant green grasses, blooming wildflowers, and evergreen trees and shrubs from different regions that can thrive with very little water. The University of Nevada Las Vegas has a large Xeriscape facility, filled with red yucca evergreens and fragrant desert birds-of-paradise, among other plant life, all designed to turn the brittle desert surroundings into a lush garden without using the increasingly depleted water resources of the area.

Animals

Most of the wildlife in the area is of the two-legged variety, often found prowling trendy nightclubs looking for someone to buy them drinks. While fascinating to study, they can rarely survive outside of their tightly controlled environments featuring soft lighting and comfortable furnishings.

Instead, let's talk about the real wildlife that has called this southern Nevada desert home for much longer than humans have.

Reptiles are the most prevalent, with iguanas, tortoises, lizards, and plenty of snakes roaming the brush and barren plains surrounding the city. Although mostly harmless, this group does include the occasional rattler, so hikers and other naturists should be careful to tread lightly when out exploring.

Field mice, gophers, and prairie dogs make their homes burrowing in the softer areas of the landscape, meaning they're less common in the rocky slopes near the mountains. Prairie dogs are common; they look like overgrown hamsters and are known for their high-pitched barking (hence the name), used as an alarm to warn of approaching predators.

Mule deer and wild burros can be found in scattered areas further from the population centers, although Red Rock Canyon, located about five miles from the westernmost housing developments, is rife with the burros. These are descendents of the animals left behind by prospectors in the 1800s and they, along with the wild horses of the region, are protected by a 1971 law that mandates their survival through a program of management and control. If you're so inclined, you can even "adopt" one through the Bureau of Land Management, and while you can't take it home with you, you can feel like you're helping maintain the species.

Coyotes and gray foxes are found in the higher elevations surrounding the Las Vegas Valley, although during times of drought or other ecological imbalances, they may wander down into civilization for a drink or a snack. Likewise with the rarer bobcats and mountain lions, which are much more easily spotted at one of the local casino animal exhibits than out in the wild.

ENVIRONMENTAL ISSUES
Drought

When early American settlers first came to this area, they set up their camps near the artesian springs that bubbled near what is now Downtown Las Vegas. Overuse and poor city-development planning put too much of a strain on the system and the springs dried up around 1962. As a result, the region relies on the nearby Colorado River for most of its day-to-day water resources.

As with much of the western United States, Nevada has spent the better part of the last decade in various stages of drought. Lake Mead, the manufactured reservoir behind Hoover Dam, has receded so much in the last few years that the relics of small towns that were flooded during its creation have resurfaced, foundations of buildings and streets appearing as the water slips away.

This has brought about a stringent series of drought-relief efforts, mainly centered on development around the Las Vegas area. The acres of new tract homes and commercial centers are heavily regulated in terms of water usage, landscaping requirements, and conservation techniques. While the occasional green lawn dots the landscape here and there, most newer developments rely on desert flowers and plants or Xeriscaping to turn the rocky terrain into places where people want to live.

Of course, the question arises: How do those giant hotels on The Strip get away with their enormous waterfalls and lakes out front, not to mention their 4,000-odd rooms of people leaving the showers on for too long inside? Most of them are not tied into the city water system, instead preferring to dig their own wells to provide water to the properties. In the long run, this is probably only helping to destabilize the water table (those springs dried up for a reason) and could put more pressure on the Colorado River to supply the region's needs, but for the short term, it seems to be making everyone happy.

Yucca Mountain

Roughly 90 miles northwest of Las Vegas is a visually innocuous bit of real estate known as Yucca Mountain. It's not a mountain, really, at least not in the traditional sense of the word. It's more of a tall hill, rising 1,200 feet along a ridge of flat-topped peaks looming over the desert. It's not at all scenic or even very interesting from a geological standpoint and most people wouldn't give it a second glance.

It's odd then that this boring little mountain is at the center of one of the biggest environmental and political battles in the nation's history.

Nearly 1,000 feet below the surface of Yucca Mountain is where the federal government wants to store the nuclear waste produced by the nation's power and defense plants. The project has been in development for years and took on a new urgency after the September 11th terrorist attacks as safety experts posited that the unstable material would be better off in one protected place instead of in the various facilities, which are required to store and watch over the stuff on their own.

The voices on both sides of this debate are loud and emphatic. Local lawmakers and the majority of residents in the area (according to polling data) don't want the Yucca Mountain facility in their big backyard. Environmentalists claim proper study of the geological forces at work in the area has not been done and warn of dire consequences to the area's groundwater or even possible volcanic activity under the mountain. Everyone admits the latter is historically rare, but since the nuclear waste is expected to be lethally radioactive for at least the next 10,000 years or so, they say it's at least worth considering.

Getting the waste to the repository also poses problems, according to those on the con side of the argument, with trucks or trains carrying the highly dangerous nuclear material near, or in some cases through, major population centers. While final shipping routes have not been determined, early reports put much of the waste on carriers up I-15 or the Union Pacific train tracks through Las Vegas, both of which sit mere feet from The Strip.

The people in favor of the repository say that years of careful research, development, and money have gone into the program and that environmental and safety studies are exhaustive in their scope and preparedness. Virtually every major government agency that could be involved in the Yucca Mountain facility has signed off on it.

But it's the safety argument they keep coming back to, suggesting that the waste maintained in facilities around the country is much more dangerous to nearby population centers through natural or human-created disasters. In some cases, they say, the waste is guarded by little more than a chain-link fence and a too-small security force, leaving such facilities vulnerable to terrorist attacks.

Until early 2005, the Yucca Mountain project seemed to be a done deal, with Congress and President George W. Bush giving their endorsements. Since then, a series of investigations into alleged falsifications of important geological studies and continued court challenges from Nevada lawmakers leave the project in limbo, but as of this writing it looks as if it will happen someday.

History

EARLY HISTORY (TO 1829)

It is believed that the first inhabitants of the region took up residence as far back as 20,000 years ago. Known as the Anasazi, or Ancient Ones, these nomadic tribes left behind few clues for modern-day anthropologists and archaeologists to sift through. But crude artwork of animals of the era seems to support the theory that they roamed the region alongside the woolly mammoths and mastodons that were once indigenous to the area.

Somewhere around 1,000 B.C., the Pueblo Indians moved north out of Mexico and settled in the southern Nevada vicinity. Ruins of the Pueblo Grande de Nevada, an ancient town site known as The Lost City, is still visible in the Moapa Valley area just northeast of Las Vegas. Their descendents are the Paiute, who are still living in the Las Vegas Valley.

A series of expeditions by Spanish explorers in the late 1700s tried to establish trade routes through the area, linking the American colonies with the Spanish territories along the west coast of North America, but hostile terrain (and perhaps hostile Native Americans) kept that from happening for another 50 years or so.

In 1829, a Spanish merchant named Antonio Armijo led another attempt to create a trade route between New Mexico and California. One of his scouts, Rafael Rivera, was separated from the party and wandered lost through region until he stumbled upon a wide valley with thick meadows and natural springs at its center. After making his way back to the main group, he led them to the area and it became a stopping point known as The Meadows, or as it is said in Spanish, *Las Vegas,* on the famous Old Spanish Trail.

THE PIONEER DAYS (1829-1905)

As the trade route became more established, more expeditions came through the area, most notably one led by Captain John C. Fremont, a U.S. military officer, in 1844. Not only was he

the historic Flamingo Las Vegas

COURTESY HARRAH'S ENTERTAINMENT

the first to lend the name "the Great Basin" to the Nevada region, but he also led the charge to map the Old Spanish Trail. It is believed he was the first person to ever put the term Las Vegas on a map and it's only fitting that the first main street in the area was named in his honor.

The United States took control of the territory in 1848, putting the entire Utah Territory, which encompassed most of modern Utah, Idaho, and Nevada, under the control of Brigham Young, leader of the Mormon Church.

The natural artesian springs in the Las Vegas Valley provided a rest stop for travelers heading west, but the region didn't begin to take shape as a formal enclave until 1855, when William Bringhurst, a Mormon missionary under directive from the church to settle the Utah Territory, led a group of 30 men from Salt Lake City to the springs and set up camp. They built a fort and erected homes inside its adobe walls while attempting to farm the land outside.

But the area proved to be too difficult to manage, with the alkaline soil unable to sustain enough crops to keep the settlers fed. This, in combination with financial difficulties in the Mormon Church, resulted in the outpost being abandoned around 1857.

After the Mormons left, ranchers began moving into the area, with one of them, Octavius Decatur Gass, taking over the fort and setting up a series of grain and fruit fields surrounding it. Emboldened by formal Nevada statehood in 1864, cattle and horse ranches sprung up and the Las Vegas Valley began to take shape as more than just a way station on the road to something bigger and better.

One of those ranchers, Helen Stewart, sold the biggest parcel of land, including much of the area's water rights, to the San Pedro, Los Angeles, and Salt Lake Railroads, which would eventually become Union Pacific. The railroads were looking for a place with water for their steam locomotives to stop on the way from Utah to California. The purchase of 1,864 acres of land in the Las Vegas Valley was completed in 1902 for $55,000 (a huge sum then, of course, but it wouldn't get you a one-bedroom condo in the same neighborhood 100 years later).

As construction of the railroad moved north from California, workers came with it, populating the land owned by the railroad in temporary buildings and tents. As people flowed into the area, the owner of the railroad, Senator William Clark (as in Clark County) sensed an opportunity and decided to see if the people wanted something a little more permanent.

In May 1905, Clark held a land auction, allowing settlers to have their own part of the new community. Although formal incorporation didn't occur until March 1911, the 1905 land auction is widely considered to be the date when Las Vegas was born.

THE EARLY DAYS (1905-1941)

The railroad pushed the development of Las Vegas in the early years, with a Spanish missionary–style depot at the head of Fremont Street (where the Plaza Hotel now stands), businesses, an ice plant, and homes popping up all around what is now modern-day Downtown Las Vegas.

The first hotel opened in 1906 at the corner of Fremont and Main Streets, right across from the train depot. Known then as the Hotel Nevada, it charged a princely $1 a night for the privilege of staying in the small, 10- by 10-foot rooms with electric lighting, but no air-conditioning, of course.

On the ground floor of the hotel was the first formal casino. The region was filled with rough-and-tumble railroad workers, creating a real Wild West type of scene with drinking, shooting, gambling, and womanizing all popular pastimes. The center of this activity was at Block 16, along North 1st Street between Ogden and Stewart Avenues (a block north of today's Fremont Street Experience). It was the only area where liquor could be legally sold and this was where locals could find prostitution and most of the gaming, with roulette and poker tables being the major mainstays.

The Hotel Nevada put the concept of gambling on the road toward legitimacy, taking it out of the "dens of iniquity" on the streets and putting it in a nice hotel. (That hotel and casino still stand, by the way, known today as The Golden Gate, home of the world-famous 99-cent shrimp cocktail. And yes, they have air-conditioning now.)

The legitimacy of gambling came to a screeching, grinding halt when it was outlawed in 1909. The formal casinos folded up shop, but that didn't stop Las Vegas from being a gaming Mecca. In fact, legend has it that gambling became even more prevalent during the time it was outlawed than it had been when it was legal, with "underground" casinos operating with abandon in the largely lawless region. So when gambling was legalized again in 1931, all they did was put the signs back up.

In the interceding years, Las Vegas took a downturn. The railroad, which for more than three decades had been the biggest employer and single most influential factor in the development of the town, picked up stakes and moved its base of operations to Caliente, Nevada. The layoffs, in combination with the start of the Great Depression, decimated the town's fortune, and its future was in doubt.

Bringing gambling back helped a little, but it wasn't until 1932, with the commencement of construction of the massive Boulder Dam project about 40 miles southeast of the city, that things started looking up for Las Vegas. Over the next five years, more than 21,000 workers poured into the region, and while many lived in the company town of Boulder City, most traveled into Las Vegas for their entertainment. Most of that was found along the burgeoning Fremont Street, as legal casinos started opening in greater and greater numbers.

By the time the dam opened in 1937, Las Vegas was well on its way to becoming the economic and political centerpiece of the region.

THE BUGSY SEIGEL ERA (1941-1950)

By 1941, Las Vegas was booming. World War II brought even more economic power to the region with the opening of Nellis Air Force Base just northeast of Downtown and a giant magnesium-producing plant to the southeast in what is now Henderson.

Vegas had also become a popular tourist destination, with ever-growing numbers of visitors making the drive from Los Angeles to partake in the Sin City ethos of Fremont Street, which had been christened as Glitter Gulch for its bright neon signs towering over the street.

To get there, those Los Angeles visitors had to travel up US Highway 91, a two-lane road carved through the barren desert that became 5th Street as it crossed the city limits at what is now Sahara Avenue. South of that demarcation line were a few lonely hole-in-the-wall casinos or bars here and there, but not much else.

A few years earlier, in 1938, a Los Angeles hotelier named Thomas Hull was making one of his regular sojourns to Las Vegas when his car broke down along Highway 91 just outside of the city limits. As he sat there waiting for assistance in the hot desert sun, he surveyed the desolate land nearby and wished for a cool pool to dive into. That dream stuck with him,

and when he returned to Los Angeles, he announced his intentions to build a full-scale resort hotel on that property. Although a casino would eventually be included in the plans, the primary focus of the hotel was to provide a rest stop for weary travelers coming in across the desert.

Hull's dream became reality in 1941 with the opening of El Rancho, a western-themed resort on the corner of what is now Sahara Avenue and Las Vegas Boulevard (across from today's Sahara Hotel and Casino). It had 63 cabin-like rooms, the city's first all-you-can-eat buffet, riding stables, a casino, a neon-topped windmill, and, of course, a big sparkling pool visible from Highway 91. The Strip had been born.

Imitators soon followed, moving the focus of Las Vegas outside of Las Vegas city limits. The similarly western-themed Hotel Last Frontier opened in 1942, around the same time that the Alamo Airport started bringing passenger air service to the city with a small field several miles south along Highway 91. It was renamed McCarran Field in 1948 and is today the sixth busiest airport in the country.

As these new resort hotels along The Strip began raking in the dough, they caught the attention of a Los Angeles mobster named Benjamin Siegel. Bugsy, as he was called (although never to his face), muscled his way into the development of a new hotel-casino being developed just south of the Frontier. Using less-than-gentlemanly tactics, Siegel took over the property and used mob money to fund its construction. It opened in December 1946 as the Flamingo, named by Siegel after his long-legged girlfriend, Virginia Hall.

The hotel was not nearly ready when it opened, with tarps covering ongoing construction as the tuxedo-clad guests began to arrive. It struggled financially, a situation that led to Bugsy being fired from his position at its helm. And when you're fired by the mob, it usually involves bullets. Siegel was gunned down in Los Angeles in 1947, coincidentally just before the fortunes of both the Flamingo and The Strip as a whole began to improve.

A series of major resort hotels opened over

Caesars Palace circa 1966

the next few years, including the Thunderbird in 1948 and The Desert Inn in 1950. Each attempted to outdo the last in terms of amenities and luxury, and the race for Strip dominance was on.

THE RAT PACK ERA (1950-1969)

The Las Vegas Strip had become cool: a place to party, relax, gamble, lie by the pool, drink, and carouse in equal measure. It was a getaway for the rich and famous, while the average Joe was relegated to the Downtown area if he was able to afford to visit at all (sound familiar?).

A big part of that "cool" factor came with the entertainers who often performed there. Frank Sinatra, Sammy Davis Jr., Dean Martin, and Joey Bishop were mainstays on the Vegas stages starting in the early 1950s and they became known as The Rat Pack, a moniker allegedly bestowed upon the group by actress Lauren Bacall when she saw them stumbling in from a night of debauchery.

These men, nearing the zenith of their individual careers, were friends and cohorts, often showing up at each other's performances in Las Vegas for impromptu shows and late-night jam sessions at local clubs. Their onstage antics became the stuff of legend and the showrooms in town were packed to the brim with people trying to get near the iconic bunch.

They played at historic hotels like the Sahara and The Sands, both opened in 1952, helping to fuel a building boom, the likes of which would not be seen for another 40 years. In the next decade, The Strip welcomed The Royal Nevada (1955, later absorbed into The Stardust), The Riviera (1955, the first high-rise on The Strip at nine stories, still in business today), The Dunes (1955, now home to Bellagio), The Hacienda (1956, torn down in the 1990s to make way for Mandalay Bay), the Tropicana (1957, the Tiffany's of The Strip, still in business today), and The Stardust (1958, torn down in 2007), each more lavish than the last.

Meanwhile, out in the desert, a different kind of boom was happening when the Nevada Test Site began above-ground testing of

THE MOULIN ROUGE (1955)

Sammy Davis, Jr. was just one of the many African-American entertainers who played in the big showrooms on the Las Vegas Strip. But despite his fame, wealth, and popularity, Sammy couldn't leave the showroom to play in the casino with his Rat Pack pals. During their heyday, Las Vegas casinos were not integrated and African Americans were not allowed except as staff (or, in Sammy's case, performers).

That changed in 1955 with the opening of the Moulin Rouge. Built just west of Downtown Las Vegas in a predominantly black neighborhood, it was the first racially integrated hotel-casino in the city. Its splashy opening in May of that year was attended by co-owner Joe Louis (the heavyweight boxing champ) and a raft of celebrities, including Dinah Washington and the Platters, who provided the opening-night entertainment. It even made the cover of *Time* magazine.

The hotel was modeled after the joints on The Strip, with 110 rooms surrounding a big pool and patio area, a restaurant, a casino, a showroom, and other amenities typical of the era. It was hailed as not only a showplace for its French design (stunning murals of cancan dancers and Paris scenery adorned the walls) but as an important step forward in race relations for the city.

It became an instant hit, especially when Frank Sinatra, Dean Martin, and the rest of the Rat Pack made it their late-night, after-show haunt, allowing them to continue partying with Sammy Davis, Jr.

The success was short-lived, though, and it closed four short months after it opened.

Some say the investors behind the project were not being smart with their money, while others suggest it was pressure brought to bear by the big Strip casinos who hated seeing their entertainers and guests leaving their properties to have fun. Whatever the reason, the property sank into bankruptcy and never officially reopened.

In March 1960, a group of African-American leaders met at the Moulin Rouge with community and state government types to sign a historic agreement ending segregation at the Las Vegas casinos. Despite its business failure, the hotel had created a long-term social success.

The building passed through a series of owners, each promising to revitalize and reopen the hotel and casino, but it never happened. Most recently, the hotel rooms were used as low-income housing while the main building, where the casino and showroom once were, sat empty, its colorful murals fading slowly over time.

In May 2003, a fire broke out in the abandoned main building and destroyed this important piece of Las Vegas history. All that is left today is the front wall and the fanciful Moulin Rouge sign above it.

A consortium of African-American entrepreneurs has been trying to resurrect the property with ambitious plans to re-create the hotel and casino with a $200-million investment, including a cultural center and civil rights museum. As of this writing, there is no formal plan or timetable set for bringing back the Moulin Rouge.

nuclear weapons. Located a mere 60 miles from Las Vegas, the giant mushroom clouds could be seen from The Strip and Downtown—yes, even the atomic age could be turned into a tourist attraction.

There seemed to be a turning point in 1960, as the boom turned to a bust. Many of the hotels (The Royal Nevada, The Riviera, The Dunes) suffered severe financial difficulties shortly after their openings. Bankruptcies and closures followed, and what once seemed like an unstoppable force stumbled. It was just a coincidence that in 1960 the Strip's first major hotel, El Rancho, burned to the ground in a massive accidental fire, but it seemed to signal the dawn of a new era.

The Rat Pack remained a major draw, but The Strip faltered and only two major properties opened—Caesars Palace and The Aladdin, both in 1966. With the railroad long gone and much of the military money dried up, gaming and tourism had become the region's primary economic force, but those alone couldn't drive the significant development the city had seen for decades prior. As a result, Las Vegas of the 1960s didn't have quite as powerful an allure to the money men—those who could put up a new hotel and draw in a new crowd. It was time for a comeback.

THE ELVIS ERA (1969-1976)

Elvis Presley's once-hot career had faded much in the way that the once-hot Las Vegas had. Both were in need of a serious infusion of excitement, so it was almost ordained that Elvis should stage his big comeback specials at the International Hotel (now the Las Vegas Hilton) in 1969.

Those hugely successful shows kick-started Elvis's career, but they had both a positive and negative effect on Las Vegas. On one hand, the city was seen as being relevant again, at least in the eyes of the entertainment world. But it also began a period when performers who were past their peak came to town to try to rescue their flagging careers. Playing Vegas became almost a joke—a symbol that you were a has-been.

During this time period, development of major new properties almost stopped. The Landmark and International Hotels opened off The Strip in 1969, but with the exception of Circus Circus adding a hotel tower in 1972 (it was just a big-top casino until then), there was only one significant property debuting in the early 1970s. But what a property it was.

The original MGM Grand (now Bally's) opened in 1973 with Dean Martin hosting the gala premiere. At the time, it was the biggest, most expensive hotel in the world with more than 2,100 rooms and a football field–size casino. It was spectacular when the city needed spectacular, but it didn't touch off a new wave of development as many expected it would.

Part of the reason was due to a lack of funding for new projects. The early 1970s economy certainly didn't help, but the bigger reasons involved the U.S. government and Howard Hughes.

Many of the early hotels in Las Vegas were built with mob money and organized crime basically ran the city well into the 1970s. But in the late 1960s, the government itself got organized and went on a serious campaign to move the mob out of Vegas. Part of that was accomplished by a relatively minor rule change governing who could hold gaming licenses, which effectively forced the casinos to clean up their act. The government also quietly encouraged Howard Hughes to get into the gaming industry.

The billionaire businessman had been enamored of the city for decades, buying up land around the Las Vegas Valley and planning at one time to move his entire aviation business to a big tract of desert on the outskirts of town. In 1966, Hughes had rented the top two floors of the Desert Inn and basically moved himself and his business operations into the building. When the owners of the hotel grew weary of his extended stay, which stretched into months and threw a crimp in their servicing of high rollers, they asked him to leave. Instead, Hughes bought the place.

From there, he went on a spree, prodded by government types who rightly figured if American hero Hughes owned the casinos, the mob couldn't. He bought The Sands, The Frontier, The Castaways, and The Silver Slipper, and later tried to buy The Stardust. His dealings put a new face of respectability on the city in the business world and legitimate investors (like Kirk Kerkorian) started coming to play. Unfortunately, the money to build lavish new resorts wasn't as accessible to most businesspeople as it was to the mob.

And while corporate America began to have a newfound sense of respect for Las Vegas, the rest of the country didn't.

THE DAN TANNA ERA (1976-1985)

By the late 1970s, Las Vegas's image was completely tarnished. Instead of a glamorous Strip of luxurious resort hotels, it was a tacky Strip of neon—a resting place on the road to obscurity for entertainers who couldn't find work anywhere else.

THE MGM GRAND FIRE (1980)

November 21, 1980. Ronald Reagan had just been elected president, the hostages were still in Iran, and J. R. had been shot.

But in Las Vegas, the "real world" seemed a million miles away. Then, as now, Vegas was a place where the harsh realities of everyday life were held at bay by bright neon lights, slot machines, and showgirls.

All of that changed that November morning at around 7 A.M. when what should have been an inconsequential electrical fire at the MGM Grand turned into an inferno that killed and injured hundreds of people and caused millions of dollars' worth of damage. And it all started in a pie case.

Buried in a wall in a small deli off the main casino, copper pipes supplying coolant to the case rubbed against an aluminum conduit containing wires that had supplied electricity for more than six years. Eventually, the weaker aluminum wore through, exposing the wires – a spark was inevitable.

It's unknown exactly when the spark happened. The leading theory is that it may have occurred when the pie case compressor turned back on after a 15-minute defrosting cycle that happened every night after the deli was closed, around midnight. The sudden start-up vibration could have been just enough to bump the copper pipes into the exposed wire.

Regardless, there was a spark, and in the dark recesses of the wall, a fire began to burn. It smoldered for hours, sending heat up through the wall into the crawl space that ran from above the deli, above the casino, all the way to the front door of the hotel, more than 400 feet away. As the ambient heat rose, the ignition point of the materials that made up the ceiling fell.

Then, at shortly after 7 A.M., a maintenance worker opened the door of the deli. Air rushed into the room, feeding the smoldering beginnings. The wall, already tinder-dry and superheated, burst into flames, sending more heat and thick smoke up into the crawl space. Within minutes, the entire room was ablaze.

With no fire walls to impede it in the crawl space, the fire rushed through the ceiling out into the casino. There was a moment when the thick black smoke hung above the restaurant landing as the fire gained strength and the heat intensified. And then it pounced.

The casino ceiling burned first, but flames stretched to the floor. An enormous wall of fire rushed through the room, gobbling up carpeting and furnishings, plastics and fabrics, and anything and anyone in its path at an astounding rate – 20 feet per second. That's approximately 14 miles per hour, faster than many people can run.

Then came *Vega$*.

The sexy-suave allure of private eye Dan Tanna (as played by actor Robert Urich) was undeniable as he zipped around town in his red '57 Thunderbird, mixing it up with beautiful showgirls and low-life hoodlums in one fell swoop, all with the backdrop of what was obviously the most glamorous, most decadent, most id-inspiring city in the world. The TV show captured the era perfectly—slightly debauched, beyond tacky with zippy modern glass chandeliers, riotous disco-era carpeting, and smoky mirrors covering every available surface.

Sadly, it didn't do much more than shine a spotlight on how far the city had fallen in stature, and as the show passed into syndication heaven, Las Vegas continued its slide toward obscurity.

A few smaller hotels debuted along The Strip. The Barbary Coast (now Bill's) opened its roughly 150 rooms in 1979. A few months later, the low-cost Flamingo Capri, which had been used for overflow guests who couldn't find rooms at next-door Flamingo, was rebranded as the Imperial Palace. Several other existing hotels added more rooms and features, but for the most part, development all but stopped. It would take a visionary to get things back on track again.

The heat was incredible – 3,200°F. Enough to melt metal. It is estimated that as many as 14 people may have died in the first 90 seconds of the fire.

By the time the flames reached the front door of the casino, glass and metal were no match and no impediment. A fireball blew out the front of the door and swept through the porte cochere. A lone car, waiting to be parked, was incinerated in an instant. The heat of the fire reduced other cars in the adjacent parking lot to scorched wrecks, sitting on melted pools of rubber.

At this point, less than 10 minutes had passed since the worker first noticed the flames. In that short amount of time, the fire had destroyed the bulk of the casino and had killed more than a dozen people.

But that was only the beginning.

The fire and smoke quickly spread into the hotel guest tower, which was at 99 percent capacity – nearly 5,000 people were estimated to be in the building at the time, most sleeping soundly in their rooms. The smoke or maybe the screaming woke them.

Guests rushed for the fire exits, but design elements that were intended to keep the structure safe in the event of an earthquake turned the stairwells into chimneys as thick, poisonous smoke roiled up from the casino level and burst out the top of the hotel towers. Those on the lower floors managed to make it down or were rescued by fire engine ladders that could only reach so high. People on the upper floors went to the roof, where an unprecedented chain of helicopters, both official rescue choppers and private aircraft flown by volunteers, lined up to take people to safety.

It was the middle floors that proved most deadly. The bulk of the victims were found on the 20th and 23rd floors, far out of reach of the flames but overcome by the unstoppable smoke.

When it was all over a few hours later, 87 people were dead and almost 700 were injured. The disaster ranks as the second worst hotel fire in U.S. history.

The large loss of life, and the resultant media coverage the fire received, spurred government officials into action. The sprinkler systems that are found in most hotels and high-rises are a direct result of the MGM Grand fire.

The MGM reopened in July 1981 with a state-of-the-art fire safety system and a dapper Cary Grant greeting guests. By touting their new system, the MGM Grand was able to return quickly to its glory days, which remained until the hotel was sold in 1985 and renamed Bally's.

THE CORPORATE ERA (1985-PRESENT)

It might be going too far to suggest that Steve Wynn saved Las Vegas, but it's not hyperbole at all to say that modern-day Las Vegas wouldn't exist without him.

Wynn got his start through a bluff of sorts. In 1971, he used his own savings and borrowed money to buy up some land that Howard Hughes wanted. Wynn offered to trade the land for a tiny sliver of essentially useless property, a small parking lot next to Caesars Palace along Flamingo Road that the big hotel leased from Hughes.

When Wynn gained control of the land, he almost immediately made grand pronouncements about a major new hotel-casino he intended to build on it, acreage issues be darned: It would be the narrowest casino in the world. Whether or not he would've actually done it is an academic discussion best left to biographers and historians, but what is certain is that the owners of Caesars Palace flipped out over the possibility of their hotel being in the shadow of Wynn's project and offered to buy the land from him for double what he had invested to get it.

He used his money to buy stock in the aging Golden Nugget hotel downtown, eventually gaining enough of it to take over. Under his management, the hotel expanded and became a big moneymaker, generating enough wealth for the company and for Wynn that he was able to build a sister hotel in Atlantic City with no less than Frank Sinatra as its pitchman.

In 1986, Wynn became Caesars' neighbor once again when he purchased the land just to the north of that hotel, home at the time to the rundown Castaways resort. The bulldozers came in the following year and work was begun on a property that would revolutionize Las Vegas: The Mirage.

By that time, Vegas had become worn, with even the once-grand Dunes and Sands mere shadows of themselves. Yes, they were successful and, yes, they brought in tourists, but mostly a leisure crowd clientele, not the wealthy vacationers who had driven the early success of the city. No one who "was anyone" went to Vegas in the '80s. It had become a punch line.

So Wynn's plan was audacious. He envisioned the biggest, most expensive hotel ever built, with more than 3,000 luxurious rooms, a casino that dwarfed those at other hotels, world-class restaurants, and spectacle-size entertainment. It would all cost an estimated $630 million, a sum that was unheard of at that time for almost any building, let alone a Vegas casino.

Financed in large part through junk bonds, it was a huge gamble—especially since no one knew if the city could support that much room inventory priced miles above other hotels in the area. Until that time, rooms, shows, and restaurants were considered loss leaders, often priced below cost just to get people in the casinos. Wynn's theory was that if you offer the public something unique, they'll come to see it, and if you offer them something great, they'll pay for it. And they did.

The Mirage was an instant success, generating headlines around the world for its luxury and over-the-top features, such as an indoor rainforest. It was jaw-dropping—unlike anything the city, or the planet for that matter, had ever seen, and it literally stopped traffic. When it debuted, people would stop their cars in the middle of the street to gawk at the faux volcano erupting in front of the hotel every 15 minutes.

Overnight, Vegas was cool again and the people came in droves, dropping their money in casinos as if they didn't know they ever had it. Corporate America took note and came running to get a share of the action.

For the next decade, a wave of new casino development reshaped The Strip in a way that hadn't been seen since the 1950s. Billions of dollars flowed toward Las Vegas Boulevard, transforming it parcel by parcel into a wonderland of grand hotels, each more lavish, more expensive, or simply more eye-catching than the last. The company that owned Circus Circus built Excalibur's wacky castle and brought another 4,000 rooms in 1990. Right next door, they threw up a giant pyramid and opened the Luxor in 1993, and six years later built their grandest exercise, a gleaming gold tower called Mandalay Bay. Across the street, billionaire Kirk Kerkorian started work on his billion-dollar baby, the MGM Grand—the biggest hotel in the world (again) with more than 5,000 rooms. It opened in 1993 and helped fund the development of the wild New York-New York, which opened in 1997. Wynn parlayed his Mirage winnings into Treasure Island (1993), a pirate-themed resort with another 3,000 rooms. Later, he doubled down on Bellagio (1998), a 3,000-room resort that surpassed even the luxury benchmarks he himself had set. Replicas of famous locales were popular, so along came Monte Carlo in 1996, and The Venetian and Paris Las Vegas in 1999. The Strip was reaching for the stars, embodied perhaps by the tallest observation tower west of the Mississippi: the Stratosphere (1996).

The massive development of that four-mile stretch of road filtered out into the community as a whole. In the 1990s, Las Vegas became the fastest-growing city in the country, averaging more than 5,000 new residents every month. Eager vacationers flocked to the city, making it the number-one tourist destination in the world.

There were downsides, of course. To make room for the new grand resorts, formerly famous faces were shown the door. Tearing down a building became a spectator sport with broadly staged implosions of The Sands, The Dunes, The Hacienda, The Stardust, The Frontier, and the original Aladdin (which was replaced by a new Aladdin, which later became Planet Hollywood).

And while the resorts became grander, so did their prices. The days when a hotel would offer a nice room, a meal, and a show for next-to-no money just to get people into the casino are long gone, with rates reaching higher and higher every year. Today, the Las Vegas casinos bring in more money from those "sideline" ventures than they do from gaming.

But progress demands change, and despite a few stumbles along the road, the success of the town in the last 20 years has been astounding and richly rewarding for the people who believed in Vegas all along. For proof, witness the 2005 return of the man who defied all expectations in 1989 with The Mirage, spend-ing a reported $2.7 billion to build a palatial resort with his name on the front of it: Wynn Las Vegas.

Today, Las Vegas is poised to move forward into a new era of development, buoyed in no small measure by the record-breaking gaming revenue (more than $1 billion a month) the state generates. Nearly a dozen major new resorts are under construction or in the planning phases (see the *Future Vegas* sidebar in the *Hotels* chapter), each aiming to be larger and more lavish than the one before it. Unlike the early days, when casino developers would trump each other by having a few more hotel rooms or a slightly bigger casino, these days they are adding entire floors—entire wings, in fact—to make sure their casino is the biggest and the best. It's a spectacle done on a scale that no one could've imagined. In other words, it's Las Vegas.

Government

The story of the Las Vegas area government is the tale of two 800-pound gorillas who get along with each other most of the time, but occasionally devolve into fits of banana throwing. On one side of the cage, you have the Las Vegas mayor, city council, and planning commission, who rule everything inside of city limits. On the other side, you have the Clark County commissioners, who handle everything else.

The reason this is important, and sometimes contentious, is because The Strip is located outside of Las Vegas city limits—it is actually a part of Paradise Township, an unincorporated district under county supervision. That means the part of town that gets all the attention, all of the headlines, and the bulk of the money isn't really a part of the town at all.

In the past, Clark County government often overshadowed Las Vegas city government much in the way that the area's politicians are just as powerful (if not more so) than the state's governor, senators, and legislature. Politics is about money, after all, and since that four-mile stretch of road in Clark County generated the lion's share of the state's revenue (tax and otherwise), they were pretty much left alone to do whatever they wanted.

That started to change in 1999 when the city's residents elected a former mob attorney as their mayor. Oscar Goodman had built his career representing some of the most infamous alleged mafia figures in Las Vegas, including Meyer Lanksy, Frank Rosenthal, and Anthony "Tony the Ant" Spilotro, who was played by Joe Pesci in the semi-factual movie *Casino* (Goodman himself had a cameo in the film).

The colorful Goodman turned the Las Vegas political landscape on its ear, seeming to go out of his way to challenge tradition and try everything he could to steal some of Clark County's thunder. The mayor has built a huge fan base (and tremendous political capital) through his notoriously blunt manner, no-nonsense approach to governing, and good-natured humor about the city and himself. He jokes about settling differences with baseball bats or taking care of problems with shovels and flashlights in the desert at night; once called a high-ranking government official "a piece of garbage" (and repeated it gleefully when asked); dressed up as a member of the Village People and sang "Y.M.C.A." on a street corner when he lost a bet over the Super Bowl; and told a group of fourth graders that if stranded on a desert island, the one thing he would want with him is a bottle of gin. The last item caused a firestorm of media criticism, to which the mayor simply said, "If they didn't want the truth, they shouldn't have asked."

Most politicians get punished for such behavior. Goodman was reelected in 2003 with 86 percent of the vote and his 2007 victory was only slightly smaller at 84 percent.

Economy

HISTORY

The Las Vegas economy has certainly seen its share of ups and downs over the years. The railroad brought jobs and money in the early days, but when the railroad company left in the 1920s, things took a serious downturn. The construction of Hoover Dam and World War II brought in government dollars, but that money also dried up eventually. The mafia came in with their almost limitless funding, but then the Feds had to go and get all picky about things like laws. Finally, corporations came to town and turned The Strip into one of the biggest moneymaking pieces of real estate in the world.

It's worth noting that while The Strip soared, the once-popular Downtown area suffered. Despite attempts to lure the crowds back to Glitter Gulch with a high-tech light and sound show, the area declined and hasn't been able to find a solid footing since.

By 2000, it seemed as if nothing could stop Las Vegas's growth, but then the terrorist attacks of 2001 happened. A broad economic decline was led by the dramatic downturn in the travel industry, and in 2002, visitor volume and tourist revenue actually declined for the first time in more than a decade. Casino corporations downsized, cut back on their big expansion plans, and, in one dramatic case, went bankrupt. The sparkling new Aladdin was already straining under the weight of its massive debt, and a combination of fewer tourists overall and the unfortunate timing of a Middle Eastern theme conspired to create the state's largest bankruptcy filing in history: approximately $700 million.

But while the U.S. economy continued to falter, Las Vegas made a shockingly quick rebound. By 2003, the numbers were on the rise and casino development picked up again. Today, the city and the corporations that run it are making record profits, and most economic analysts believe it would take another catastrophic event like September 11th to slow things down.

TOURISM

There are other businesses in town, but most of them wouldn't be in Vegas if it weren't for the effects of tourism. Las Vegas is the number-one tourist destination in the world, swelling its population of 1.8 million people to more than 40 million over the course of a year. More people visit Las Vegas annually than the number of people who go to Disneyland, Disney World, and every other theme park in the country combined.

On holiday weekends, virtually every one of the city's 140,000 (or so) hotel rooms are full, bringing in nearly half a million visitors. Think about that for a second. During really busy weekends, one out of every four people in the city doesn't actually live there. Imagine adding 25 percent more people to Manhattan for a weekend and you start to get the scope of things.

And all those people bring money with them. According to figures from the Las Vegas Convention and Visitors Authority, tourism in 2004 generated an estimated $39.4 billion worth of economic impact, nearly two-thirds of every dollar spent in the state. That's higher than the gross national product of many countries and was up nearly $4 billion over the 2003 figures.

Gaming revenue is figured into that, of course, but almost two-thirds of the tourism-related dollars are generated by things like hotel rooms, food, entertainment, shopping, travel-related expenses, taxi fares, strip club cover charges...well, you get the point.

And those numbers don't take into account the indirect impact of tourism. Yes, it's clear that people come to Las Vegas and spend a lot of money, but those dollars help pay the salaries of hundreds of thousands of Las Vegas's residents, who then turn around and spend their money on things that aren't counted in the tourism-impact numbers, like food and gas and strip club cover charges. (We're talking about the economy—I just wanted to see if you were still paying attention.)

Taxes are another big factor here. With hotel, sales, and gaming taxes, the casinos fund virtually every statewide program, from roads to airport expansion to schools. There is no state income tax in Nevada, and non-casino business taxes are lower than the national average.

GAMING

In 2006, Las Vegas generated $8.2 billion in gaming revenue, and that number is expected to be significantly larger when the 2007 reports are complete. In fact, in March 2005, the state as a whole generated $1 billion in gaming revenue—the first time that had happened in a single month—and the casinos on The Strip alone contributed more than half of that.

Keep in mind this is real revenue. In March 2005, players actually wagered more than $15 billion. So the next time you lose $100 in a slot machine, console yourself by remembering that players actually won back nearly $14 billion in that particular month. It might not make you feel any better, but it could make for interesting dinner conversation (as long as someone else picks up the check).

While studies show that most Las Vegas visitors do not list gambling as their primary reason for coming to the city, most of them wind up dropping at least a few bucks inside the casinos. The average gambling budget for a Las Vegas visitor is more than $650 per person, according to the Las Vegas Convention and Visitors Authority.

OTHER INDUSTRY AND COMMERCE

The non-gaming, non-tourism side of Las Vegas has been booming as much as the rest of the city over the last decade and a half. Lured by lower taxes (companies do not pay corporate income, franchise, or inventory taxes, among others) and relatively low real estate prices, a number of high-profile corporations have moved their businesses from less profitable climes and set up shop in Sin City.

Nevada is the fastest-growing state, according to the United States Census, and according to the Las Vegas Chamber of Commerce, two acres of land are developed for residential or commercial use on average every hour, 24 hours a day, seven days a week. Things are happening so fast that the phone companies put out two phone books every year just to try to keep up with the changes.

It's no big surprise then that construction is the second largest industry in Las Vegas behind gaming. Roughly one-third of the 100 highest-grossing Las Vegas companies are construction-related, and only a fraction of those hammers and nails are being used on casino development. Houses and condominiums can't be built fast enough to shelter all of the new people wanting to move here, with residential construction alone generating more than $2 billion annually in the city.

The only thing hampering these numbers from being bigger is that so much is going on that the various projects can't find enough labor and resources to keep them going. The $7.4 billion CityCenter is running crews 24 hours a day to meet its 2009 opening date, and the thousands of new homes being built use up a lot of manpower and construction supplies.

This has driven up costs, which has resulted in more than a few high-profile projects falling by the wayside.

Harking back to the days when Las Vegas was a pit stop for travelers heading somewhere else, the city has also become a major hub for air travel and consumer product distribution. Virtually every airline in existence flies here, and with a modern network of rail and roads, companies have flocked to the region to set up distribution centers to serve the entire American Southwest.

But those are just the tip of the iceberg. The low costs of doing business in the area have drawn a wide variety of companies, from manufacturing to high-tech, financial, and governmental. And the low cost of living continues to draw workers to fill those jobs.

People and Culture

The roughly 1.8 million residents of the Las Vegas area are a diverse lot, drawn from all over the country and all over the world. According to the Las Vegas Perspective, an annual demographic report on the region, the population is 56 percent Caucasian, 23.1 percent Hispanic or Latino, 8.6 percent African American, and 6.6 percent Asian or Pacific Islander. Although they used to rule the land, Native Americans make up less than 1 percent of the Las Vegas population.

It's a relatively new crowd of people as well. Nearly one-third of residents have lived in the area for five years or less, outnumbering by a couple of percentage points the number of people who have lived there more than 20 years. This, in combination with the heavy tourist influx, has resulted in a somewhat transitory attitude among the people. Neighborhoods are younger and therefore less firmly established, so a real sense of community is harder to find, both on a citywide basis and on a block-to-block one.

The unemployment rate is consistently lower than the national average, the education level is on par, and the bulk of the residents fall into the 25–54 age range. The median household income in Las Vegas is around $44,000, only slightly higher than the U.S. average, but due to the lowered tax structure (no state income tax), there is more disposable income among area residents. Now, if they could just stay away from those casinos.

Although less than one-eighth of the city's population (approximately 200,000 people) is employed by the gambling industry, casinos inform virtually every aspect of the culture—often in surprising ways.

According to the Las Vegas Perspective, more than half of the residents rarely or never go to a casino to gamble, although they regularly partake in the dining, shopping, and entertainment options. Most locals only go to The Strip for truly special occasions or when they have out-of-town visitors.

Regardless, gambling pervades virtually every corner of the city. Most convenience stores, grocery stores, bars, and more than a few restaurants have some form of gambling available, even if it's only a couple of video poker machines tucked in a corner somewhere. Beyond the giant casinos on The Strip are dozens of smaller ones, many no bigger than the local McDonald's. About the only places guaranteed to be free from the pinging of a slot machine are the schools and churches (although many of the latter have bingo, so they're not even safe).

Sex is also a big seller here, perhaps even more so than in other major metropolitan areas. Taxis are covered with placards advertising topless shows or strip clubs, and giant mobile billboards hawking "escort services" trundle down the major streets through and near the tourist centers. After a failed attempt in the early 1990s to make Las Vegas more family-friendly for visitors, everyone seems to be working hard to put the sin back in Sin City.

On the flipside of all this, there is culture in the form of art, museums, symphonies, a major university, and plenty of well-funded schools. There are also more churches per capita in Las Vegas than in any other city in America.

Get married to someone you just met and get divorced just as quickly. Buy alcohol 24 hours a day. Gamble a few bucks while you're pumping gas. Pay a few more bucks for a lap dance. Then go to church the next day and be absolved of your sins.

It's true, Vegas is about vice. But the effect of all this vice on the local culture is up for debate. Some say it has a deleterious impact, continually reinforcing the concept that fortunes can be made by the pull of a handle or the roll of the dice and that the ideal woman can most likely be found wrapped around a stripper pole. Others suggest that it's all part of the show—pure entertainment, no worse than what can be found on the average night of television. It's interesting to note that most of the locals

fall in the latter category, while it's primarily outsiders who complain about how dangerous the whole place is.

In practice, the residents of the city both embrace and repel the prurient aspects that make the place tick. Go a few blocks from The Strip and it looks almost like any major metropolitan area in the American Southwest–Phoenix, perhaps—with mile after mile of strip malls and residential communities behind gates or cinder-block walls, perhaps trying to seal themselves off from the negative influences that bring some of the highest suicide rates, the highest alcoholism rates, and the highest automobile accident rates in the nation.

But ask any of those residents behind the gated walls and most will tell you they'd never live anywhere else. They'd say the opportunities for jobs, education, affordable housing, low taxes, and financial stability far outweigh the downsides, which are merely the price you pay for living in a big city.

ESSENTIALS

Getting There

As of this writing, there are only two ways to get to Las Vegas: via something with wings or via something with wheels. Well, three, I suppose, but it's an awfully long walk from just about anywhere, so the something-with-legs option really isn't a good one.

BY AIR

If you choose to fly, you'll arrive at McCarran International, one of the most well-organized, modern airports in the country, owing in part to the massive amounts of money the state spends trying to make sure everyone can get in and out with relative ease. Having said that, it's impor-tant to note McCarran is a very busy airport, so the lines can be long at baggage claim, check-in, and especially security. Allow yourself plenty of time both coming and going—at least an hour on your return home and two if it's the end of a weekend or holiday period.

Most major domestic carriers fly into Mc-Carran and there are several smaller airlines that service the area as well, so your choice of flights is usually broad. Southwest and JetBlue seem to offer the most reasonable fares no mat-ter where you're flying from, but take the time to do the research via phone calls or the Inter-net for the best deal.

AIRLINE CONTACT INFORMATION

The following airlines currently service McCarran International Airport:

- **AeroMexico,** 800/237-6639, www.aeromexico.com

- **Air Canada,** 800/776-3000, www.aircanada.ca

- **AirTran,** 800/247-8726, www.airtran.com

- **Alaska Airlines,** 800/426-0333, www.alaskaair.com

- **Allegiant Air,** 877/202-6444, www.allegiant-air.com

- **Aloha Air,** 800/367-5250, www.alohaairlines.com

- **American/American Eagle,** 800/433-7300, www.aa.com

- **American Trans Air,** 800/435-9282, www.ata.com

- **America West,** 800/235-9292, www.americawest.com

- **Continental,** 800/525-0280, www.continental.com

- **Delta/Skywest,** 800/221-1212, www.delta.com

- **Frontier Airlines,** 800/432-1359, www.flyfrontier.com

- **Harmony Airways,** 866/248-6789, www.hmyairways.com

- **Hawaiian Airlines,** 800/367-5320, www.hawaiianair.com

- **Japan Airlines,** 800/525-3663, www.jal.co.jp/en

- **JetBlue,** 800/538-2583, www.jetblue.com

- **Korean Air,** 800/438-5000, www.koreanair.com

- **Mexicana Airlines,** 800/531-7921, www.mexicana.com

- **Midwest Express Airlines,** 800/452-2022, www.midwestairlines.com

- **Northwest,** 800/225-2525, www.nwa.com

- **Philippine Airlines,** 800/435-9725, www.philippineairlines.com

- **Song,** 800/359-7664, www.flysong.com

- **Southwest,** 800/435-9792, www.iflyswa.com

- **Spirit Airlines,** 800/772-7117, www.spiritair.com

- **Ted Airlines,** 800/225-5833, www.flyted.com

- **United,** 800/241-6522, www.united.com

- **US Airways,** 800/428-4322, www.usairways.com

- **Virgin Atlantic Airways,** 800/862-8621, www.virgin-atlantic.com

For the latest information on airlines and scheduled flights into McCarran, visit their website at www.mccarran.com or call 702/261-5211.

There are two terminals at McCarran (although a third should be up and running before 2010). Terminal 1 has four concourses, labeled A, B, C, and D, mostly serving domestic flights. The A and B gates are connected to the main terminal (where baggage claim and check-in are located) via walkways; the C gates are connected via a walkway and a tram; and the D gates are connected only by a tram that shuttles under the runway to a satellite facility. Terminal 2 is primarily for international flights, although some domestic carriers do fly in and out.

Baggage claim for all Terminal 1 concourses is centrally located near the main exit where

DRIVING DISTANCES

Distances are measured by the most common available route.

CITY	DISTANCE
Chicago	1,808 miles
Dallas	1,215 miles
Denver	747 miles
Los Angeles	270 miles
Miami	2,828 miles
New Orleans	1,834 miles
New York City	2,560 miles
Orlando	2,571 miles
Phoenix	287 miles
Salt Lake City	419 miles
San Francisco	570 miles
Seattle	1,257 miles
St. Louis	1,594 miles
Washington, D.C.	2,447 miles

desks so you can get your room key right there without having to go to the hotel first. However, due to security restrictions enacted after September 11th, you can no longer check your bags and have them delivered to your room.

There are plenty of restaurants and stores inside all concourses, although they are typically airport overpriced. McCarran also has a 24-hour fitness center, an art gallery and aviation museum, a kids' play area (in concourse D only), foreign currency exchange, banking and postal services, and let's see, what else? Oh yeah, gambling. That's right. You can step off your airplane and be plugging bills into one of the hundreds of slot or video poker machines in minutes.

Can you actually win anything? Usually not. The machines here tend to pay out less often than the ones at the major casinos, but occasionally players can get lucky. I once put a $20 bill in a video poker machine and walked onto my flight a little while later $500 richer.

Also worth noting, unlike most airports in the country, McCarran International does have smoking areas inside the terminals.

BY TRAIN

There is currently no passenger rail service to Las Vegas. The Amtrak line shut down in the late 1990s, and while they have talked for years about starting it back up again with high-speed trains from Los Angeles, it has just been talk so far. I anticipate we'll be well into the second decade of the century before anything gets going, if it ever does. In the meantime, **Amtrak** (800/872-7245, www.amtrak.com) does offer a bus service from Los Angeles, so you can take a train to the City of Angels and then go Greyhound to Sin City.

you have to go for taxis and shuttle buses (or Aunt Ida's Buick, if she's picking you up).

Near the baggage claim area, several of the major Strip resorts have convenient check-in

Getting Around

McCarran is very close to The Strip, less than a mile as the crow flies from hotels like the MGM Grand and Mandalay Bay. Getting to those places requires a taxi, a shuttle bus, or a rental car. I highly recommend the last option, especially if you're planning on seeing anything more than The Strip. Rentals save money in the long run and allow more options in the "see and do" category of your vacation planning.

BY CAR OR BUS

If you choose to drive to Las Vegas, you'll solve a major problem once you get there, which is how to get around town. Keep in mind that parking is plentiful and free at every major hotel, casino, restaurant, show, and attraction, so you don't need to worry about that as a line item in your budget. Even valet parking is free at the big hotels with a buck or two tip for the attendants. Just keep in mind that dropping off and retrieving your car can take some time, so be sure to allow yourself a few extra minutes when you're thinking of getting from where you are to where you're going.

Las Vegas is located in the southern tip of Nevada and is most easily accessible by I-15, which runs right through the heart of the city, a few hundred feet from the big casinos on The Strip. I-15 is the major route to Los Angeles to the south and intersects with Interstates 40 and 10, and is the major route to Salt Lake City to the north and connects with Interstates 70, 80, and 90.

Greyhound (800/231-2222, www.greyhound.com) offers regularly scheduled service to Las Vegas from all points on the United States map. **The Las Vegas Bus Terminal** (200 S. Main St., 702/384-9561) is located in Downtown, two blocks south of Fremont Street adjoining The Plaza Hotel, and is open 24 hours a day.

RENTING A CAR

In 2007, McCarran International opened a multimillion-dollar consolidated rental car facility off airport property, and the method by which you rent a car is drastically different. The counters inside the terminal are gone, and now instead of individual company buses, there is one bus for all of the car companies. Well, there are lots of buses, but they are all marked "McCarran Rent-A-Car Center" instead of branded with the corporate logos. Buses leave the main terminals roughly every five minutes, so waiting won't be a problem.

Hop on the bus and it'll take you off of airport property to the new facility on Gilespie

CAR RENTALS

The following car rental agencies service McCarran International Airport:

- **Advantage,** 800/777-5500, www.arac.com

- **Alamo,** 877/227-8367, www.alamo.com

- **Avis,** 800/230-4898, www.avis.com

- **Budget,** 800/527-0700, www.budgetvegas.com

- **Dollar,** 800/800-3665, www.dollar.com

- **Enterprise,** 800/736-8227, www.enterprise.com

- **Hertz,** 800/654-3131, www.hertz.com

- **National,** 800/227-7368, www.nationalcar.com

- **Payless,** 800/729-5377, www.paylesscarrental.com

- **Savmor,** 800/634-6779, www.savmorrac.com

- **Thrifty,** 800/847-4389, www.thrifty.com

MAJOR ROUTES AND SHORTCUTS

Las Vegas Boulevard (otherwise known as The Strip) and Main Street are ground zero for east and west addresses, while Fremont Street in Downtown is the borderline between north and south addresses. So if you're going someplace that is, for instance, at the corner of Sahara Avenue West and Decatur Boulevard South, you know you're going to want to be west of The Strip and south of Downtown.

Everyone wants to drive The Strip at least once, but when you've gotten that out of your system it's best to avoid using it as a way of going north or south. The traffic on The Strip, especially on busy weekend nights, approaches gridlock and what should be a pleasant four-mile cruise turns into an hour-long nightmare of brake lights and bus fumes.

Likewise, getting across The Strip from east to west (or vice versa) can be just as challenging.

The following is a list of major routes and short cuts that can help navigate drivers around the worst of the traffic.

NORTH/SOUTH ROUTES

Frank Sinatra Drive runs behind the hotels on the west side of The Strip from Industrial Road at the north to Russell Road at the south. It provides easy back-door access to hotels like Mandalay Bay, Luxor, Monte Carlo, and Caesars Palace.

Industrial Road continues north from Frank Sinatra Drive into the Downtown area and will help guests sneak in the back way at hotels like Treasure Island and Circus Circus.

Dean Martin Drive is the new moniker for what used to be Industrial Road south of Twain Avenue. Confused? Yes, me too. But basically the road crosses under I-215 at Twain, heading north as Industrial on the east side of the freeway and south as Dean Martin Drive on the west side of the freeway. Whatever you want to call it, it usually has a lot less traffic than The Strip.

Koval Avenue runs just behind the hotels on the east side of The Strip from the airport up to Sands Avenue, allowing back entry to hotels like The Venetian, Harrah's, Imperial Palace, and the MGM Grand, among others. As Koval heads south, it curves to the west and joins Reno and Hacienda Avenues, which lead straight into Luxor and Mandalay Bay, respectively.

Paradise Road, home to the Las Vegas Convention Center, the Hard Rock, and the Las Vegas Hilton, among other interesting sights, is the next major north-south thoroughfare to the east of The Strip. Although busy, it is usually less heavily congested than The Strip.

EAST/WEST ROUTES

Tropicana Avenue is the major cross street for the South Strip area with access to New York-New York, MGM Grand, and I-15.

Harmon Avenue crosses The Strip near Planet Hollywood and goes east to the Hard Rock and beyond and west across the freeway (no access) to the west side of town.

Flamingo Road is the main cross street for the Center Strip area with entrances to Bally's, Barbary Coast, Bellagio, and Caesars Palace, plus on- and off-ramps to I-15.

Twain/Sands/Spring Mountain is a confusingly named road that crosses The Strip between Wynn Las Vegas and The Venetian. Everything east of Paradise Road is Twain Avenue, between Paradise and The Strip is Sands Avenue, and everything west of The Strip is Spring Mountain with access to I-15.

The Desert Inn Arterial is a convenient way to get across The Strip without actually having to deal with cross traffic. Heading west from Paradise Road (near the Convention Center), it becomes a mini-freeway of sorts, crossing underneath The Strip, then up a bridge over I-15. There is limited or no access to the streets it crosses, so only use this if you want to get from the east side to the west side quickly.

Sahara Avenue is the main cross street for the North Strip area and provides access to the Sahara Hotel and side streets that lead to the Stratosphere.

© RICK GARMAN/VERN GARMAN

McCarran Rent-A-Car Center

Street, near the intersection of Warm Springs and Las Vegas Boulevard South, which, for the familiar, is where the Las Vegas Outlet Mall is located. The new facility has counters for Avis, Advantage, Budget, Enterprise, Hertz, Dollar, Alamo, National, Payless, Savmor, and Thrifty car rental agencies and most of the vehicles are housed in multistory parking garages, thereby making the prospect of hopping in that Ford Taurus a little less intimidating than it was when it was sitting in the middle of a hot parking lot in July.

Rental Car Insurance

To insure or not to insure? That is the question. Here are the potential answers:

Every car rental agency in every state in the United States is required to provide liability insurance with every rental. So we're only talking about damage to the actual rental car itself, not damage inflicted on anyone else.

Now that we have that established, your first call should be to your own insurance company. You should ask if you are covered for col-

lision, if you are covered for "loss," and if there are any limitations on any of that coverage.

Collision coverage means that your insurance company will pay for the damage to the rental car if you run it into one of those big bronze lions outside of the MGM Grand. Loss means that your insurance company will pay not only for the damage, but also for the loss of revenue the rental company will incur by not being able to rent the car while it's being repaired.

You should keep in mind that no matter what answers you get, you will still be responsible for paying your normal deductible and will face whatever higher premiums may result from your insurance company having to pay for the car you backed into the lake in front of Bellagio.

Your second call should be to your credit card companies. Many credit cards will offer insurance on cars if you use their card to rent it. However, the restrictions they impose usually mean this isn't a good deal. Most credit card coverage is for a limited time or amount, is only good at certain rental car agencies or for certain types of vehicles, and usually includes a high deductible and no loss coverage. So read the fine print on these policies or you may have to pony up a lot of dough to repair the car if you get attacked by a rabid band of showgirls and Elvis impersonators.

Your final call should be to the rental car company itself to find out if they charge for downtime while a car is being repaired, if they offer a Collision Damage Waiver and/or a Loss Damage Waiver, and how much it costs. Just as above, a collision waiver covers damage to the car and is usually with no deductible, but does not cover loss of income to the rental car agency. A loss waiver covers everything and means that if you accidentally park too close to the volcano at The Mirage, you can just go back to the rental car company and say "Oops" and walk away. Well, there may be forms involved, but you get the drift.

For the record, I always take the Loss Damage Waiver when I rent a car. I think it's worth the extra $10 a day to not have to worry about it.

TAXIS AND SHUTTLES

Taxis are omnipresent in Las Vegas, and with the exception of trips in the far-flung residential areas, do not require a call ahead. Lines of them wait outside all the hotels, ready to take passengers wherever they need to go.

As of this writing, the cab fares in Las Vegas are among the most expensive of any major city. It costs $3.20 just to get in the taxi and an additional $2 per mile thereafter. In addition, if the taxi is moving less than eight miles per hour, there's an additional $0.20 added for every 33 seconds of wait time. There is also a $1.20 surcharge for fares originating at McCarran International Airport. Fares are good for up to five people in the cab.

A taxi from the airport to the South Strip runs about $10 including tip, Center Strip $10–15, North Strip $12–18, and Downtown around $20.

An alternative for airport-to-hotel transportation is to use one of the common shuttle buses that regularly patrol McCarran and most major resorts. Fares average around $5 per person to

and from Strip hotels, and $6 per person to and from Downtown hotels. As with taxis, they almost never require a call ahead—in fact, they'll be lined up and waiting at the shuttle bus stand at the airport. For return trips to the airport, there may be a longer wait (calling ahead won't get immediate service, but may speed things up a little). The major shuttle companies are Bell Trans (702/739-7990), C. L. S. (702/740-4050), Grayline (702/739-5700), Las Vegas Limousine (702/736-1419), ODS (702/876-2222), and Showtime Shuttles (702/261-6101).

The only major downside to using an airport shuttle is that it serves a number of people, who may not be going to your destination, meaning the ride may include several stops.

LAS VEGAS MONORAIL

The privately funded $650-million monorail was hailed as being one of the most technologically advanced transportation systems in the world—a gleaming wonder that would zip people from the south end of The Strip to the north and back again in about 15 minutes for only a few bucks.

And then it opened.

Well, first, it opened months later than originally planned due to issues that cropped up during testing, and then, once it did start running, things started going wrong. Pieces of the train literally fell off—a guidance wheel here, a driveshaft there—they crashed to the ground underneath and luckily avoided hitting anything other than concrete. Only a few weeks after it opened, the system was shut down and remained so for nearly four months in late 2004. Engineers from the company that built it were called in to do a top-to-bottom overhaul and finally got it running again around New Year's 2005.

Since then, the Las Vegas Monorail has been performing well, at least mechanically. Financially is another story as the system continues to lose money at an alarming rate, raising doubts about its long-term viability.

The 4.4-mile system has six air-conditioned trains, each capable of holding up to 200 passengers. There are seven stations servicing

the Las Vegas Monorail

MGM Grand, Paris and Bally's, the Flamingo Las Vegas, Harrah's and the Imperial Palace, the Convention Center, the Las Vegas Hilton, and The Sahara. In addition, many Strip hotels (such as Wynn Las Vegas) are offering free shuttles to and from monorail stations. There is a proposed expansion of the system to be completed by 2011, but with the existing route's financial difficulties, many doubt that it will actually be constructed.

Rides cost $5 one way, whether you're going to the next station or the all the way to the last one. Multiple-ride or day passes are also available at a discount, with the best deal being a one-day pass with unlimited rides for $8. Children five and under ride free, but must be small enough to be carried through the fare gates by an adult passenger who has paid full fare.

Tickets may be purchased at any monorail station with the handy automated machines just outside the gates. Insert the appropriate bills, pick the type of fare you want, and away you go. Tickets may also be purchased in advance on the Las Vegas Monorail website at www.lvmonorail.com.

The system runs from 7 A.M.–2 A.M. daily.

OTHER PEOPLE MOVERS

The Las Vegas Monorail is not the only convenient way to get around on The Strip without walking outside in the hot sun. There are three other monorail/tram systems and several indoor walkways between casinos to aid in your exploration.

There is a monorail that connects Excalibur, Luxor, and Mandalay Bay from 6 A.M.–2 A.M. daily. It is free of charge. It's worth noting that southbound trains originating at Excalibur do not stop at Luxor. Only northbound trains originating at Mandalay Bay make that stop.

A tram ferries passengers from the valet parking area of The Mirage to near the parking garage of Treasure Island. It's open from early in the morning until late at night and is free of charge.

There are indoor walkways that connect Mandalay Bay with Luxor, Luxor with Excalibur, and Paris with Bally's.

BUSES AND TROLLEYS

Up until recently I insisted that people only take the city buses if they had absolutely no other choice. **The Citizen's Area Transit** buses are clean and modern and, if you're riding them in the residential portions of town, they are terrific, usually on schedule, and very convenient. But if you're planning to ride them anywhere near The Strip or other major tourist areas, forget it. They're notoriously late and overcrowded, often running so far behind schedule and with so many people on board that they don't even bother to stop for new passengers.

The good news is that in 2005 they introduced a new service called **The Deuce,** double-decker buses that troll The Strip and have replaced the aging and inadequate fleet that came before it. These clean and modern conveyances are everywhere and are quite a bargain to boot, with $5 getting you an all-day pass. Of course, there are still major downsides. Just because the buses are nicer and there are more of them doesn't mean they aren't still crowded, and they still have to sit in the gridlocked traffic of The Strip, so getting places requires patience.

Fares must be paid in exact change or with tokens or passes that can be purchased online at www.rtcsouthernnevda.com. You can also do it by mail, but you'll have to go online to choose the exact token or pass package you want and then send a money order (no out-of-state checks) to an accompanying address.

For up-to-date route and schedule information, visit the Citizen's Area Transit website at www.rtcsouthernnevda.com or call 800/228-3911.

The Las Vegas Trolley, a replica of a classic trolley, runs up and down The Strip, from the Las Vegas Hilton on Paradise Road around to the Sahara on The Strip, and down The Strip to the Hacienda and back. There is also a Downtown route and another that goes to the Meadows Mall.

The trolley is scheduled to stop at each of the major hotels about every 20 minutes, 9:30 A.M.–1:30 A.M. daily. Like The Deuce, an all-day pass is $5 and exact change is required when boarding the trolley.

Conduct and Customs

Despite the "What happens in Vegas stays in Vegas" marketing campaign, the normal codes of conduct (and laws surrounding them) are pretty much the same here as they are in any city in the United States. Yes, you can drink 24 hours a day, but you can still get arrested for public intoxication. Yes, you can gamble all you want, but don't be a sore loser when the house takes all your money. Yes, you can look at beautiful, naked people dancing for your pleasure, but you can't touch them.

The moral of the story is have fun, but don't be a jerk about it. Las Vegas is a city that celebrates the id in all of us, but where you draw the line should be no different than where you draw it when you go out to have a good time in your own hometown.

Smoking

For years, Las Vegas was a smoker's paradise with virtually every place but the airport, showrooms, and parts of restaurants off-limits. But in 2007, a new law went into effect that dramatically changed the landscape. Today, smoking is only allowed in gaming areas of major casinos, in bars or nightclubs that do not serve food, and in designated hotel rooms. Everywhere else is now off-limits, including all restaurants, shopping facilities, and even the lobbies and non-gaming public areas of the major hotels.

Gambling Etiquette

The "rules" for gambling go beyond the specifics of how to play, and vary not only from

TIPPING GUIDELINES

Here's a general guideline on who to tip, how much, and when, but keep in mind that these are just generalities and you can tip more, less, or nothing at all if you are so inclined.

Bartenders: A minimum of $1 for a mixed drink and $0.50 for opening a bottle of beer or water is common.

Buffet Waitstaff: Although the food is do-it-yourself, most buffets have servers bringing guests drinks. If that's the case, be sure to leave a couple of bucks on the table as a tip when you leave.

Casino Cocktail Waitstaff: $1 per drink is not too much to ask, considering you're getting it for free.

Dealers: There is no formula for this, but tipping the dealer on big wins (blackjack, etc.) is common and, if they were especially good to you, tip them a few bucks again at shift changes or when you leave the table.

Housekeeping: Leave a couple of bucks each night of your stay for the people who clean your room, with a few bucks more if there's a big mess. Be sure to mark it as a tip, otherwise they won't know it isn't just cash lying around.

Restaurant Waitstaff: As with anywhere else, 15 percent is customary – more for especially good service. Worth noting: If you are lucky enough to be getting your meal comped,

remember that it doesn't include gratuity to the waitstaff. Tip based on what you would have paid for the meal.

Showroom Maître d': There are very few of these left as most shows have preassigned seating, but if you run across one, consider 10 percent of the ticket price, per ticket, to get a better seat.

Skycaps and Bellmen/women: Anyone who picks up your bag for you should get $1-2 per bag (more for heavier luggage), so, yes, if two different people handle your luggage at the hotel (which is becoming customary), two different people should get tips.

Slot Attendants: If you're in an old-school casino where they still have to fill the machine with coins when it runs out, give the people carting those heavy bags around a buck or two. If you've won a big jackpot requiring a hand pay (usually anything more than $1,200), it's common to give each of the people who assist a small cut (at least $5 apiece).

Taxi Drivers: 10-15 percent of the fare.

Valet Parking Attendants: $1 to the person who gives you the ticket upon arrival and $1-2 for the person who brings the car back. More on hot days would be nice, especially if they've turned on the air-conditioning for you when they bring the car back.

---

game to game but within variations of each game. For instance, at a blackjack table where the cards are dealt from a shoe (a plastic container holding multiple decks), you're not allowed to touch the cards, but at single- or double-deck tables, you are. Check the *Gaming* chapter for more information on specific games and general casino guidelines, but if you're still unsure, don't be afraid to ask. The dealers want you to join the game and will be happy to tell you anything you need to know.

Legalized Prostitution

Despite what you may have heard, prostitution is not legal in Las Vegas. The state of Nevada

does allow the world's oldest profession, but only in counties with populations of less than 200,000 and only in very strictly supervised brothels. That leaves Clark County, home to Las Vegas's roughly 1.8 million people, out of the running, and it criminalizes the kind of prostitution that happens on street corners and in yellow-pages ads for "escorts."

The closest legal brothels to Las Vegas are in and around Pahrump, Nevada, about 60 miles to the west. This is where the once-infamous Chicken Ranch and several other establishments devoted to the trade are located. In days gone by, these generally consisted of a collection of barely inhabitable trailers, but now the brothels have moved into a more modern era, with clean, comfortable facilities that mimic homes, motels, or even glorified mini-malls.

I am not including any specific information on the locations or amenities of specific brothels, not for prudish reasons but simply because I'm not sure how I'd go about reviewing such facilities to be able to say which ones are worth visiting and which ones should be avoided. However, a quick Google or Yahoo search on "Nevada brothels" will bring up a plethora of informative (and usually adult-oriented) sites that can provide a good overview.

By the way, there are no legally run brothels with male prostitutes. Doesn't seem fair, does it?

Tips for Travelers

FOREIGN TRAVELERS

To enter the United States, foreign visitors must have a valid passport that expires at least six months after the end of their visit, a round-trip airplane or cruise ship ticket, and a nonimmigrant visa from the United States government.

The last item is waived if you are from one of the 27 countries currently accepted under the Visa Waiver Program. These countries are Andorra, Australia, Austria, Belgium, Brunei, Denmark, Finland, France, Germany, Iceland, Ireland, Italy, Japan, Liechtenstein, Luxembourg, Monaco, the Netherlands, New Zealand, Norway, Portugal, San Marino, Singapore, Slovenia, Spain, Sweden, Switzerland, and the United Kingdom. As of 2005, visitors from these countries *must* have machine-readable or biometric passports to qualify for the Visa Waiver Program. If you don't have one, get one or you'll have to get a visa also.

In addition, visitors from Canada, Mexico, Bermuda, and certain other South and Central American countries do not need a visa, but as of 2007 must show a valid passport.

To apply for a visa, first go to the special website set up to assist in the effort at www.unitedstatesvisas.gov. Immigration and border security laws are changing regularly in the United States, so it's best to double-check that nothing important has changed since this book was written. The website will help you determine which class of visa you should apply for (student, tourist, business, etc.) and provide links to download the appropriate forms you must fill out. Next, contact the United States Embassy or Consulate in your country to set up an appointment (a full list of them is available on the website) and bring in all your completed paperwork, support documentation, and appropriate fees.

Getting a visa used to be a relatively easy thing, but these days the process is more complex and takes longer. Additional interviews or documentation may be requested, especially if you happen to be unlucky enough to have a name that matches, or comes close to matching, one in a big database of people who raise red flags when they try to come to the United States. Give yourself at least a month to accomplish the process, two if you've got it. It's possible to get a visa on the same day you apply for it, but why not plan ahead just in case and have one less thing to worry about before your trip?

It's also worth noting that citizens from Cuba, Iran, Libya, North Korea, Sudan, and Syria will be put through more hoops, including additional forms and in-person interviews before a visa is granted. While other Middle Eastern nations are not on the above list, visitors from the region should expect additional scrutiny when trying to obtain the proper clearances to visit.

There are additional restrictions for persons with certain health issues, such as HIV or conditions that require intravenous injections or treatment with narcotic drugs.

For more information on passports, immigration, and the latest up-to-date travel restrictions, visit the U.S. State Department website at www.travel.state.gov or call 202/663-1225.

Once in the United States, there is a small arrival fee (less than $20) and then the customs screening. For information on what can and can't be brought into the country and what must be declared, visit the U.S. Customs and Border Protection Agency website at www.customs.gov or check with the United States Embassy or Consulate in your home country.

After all the paperwork has been checked, the cigarettes declared, and the baggage inspected, please accept a hearty "Welcome to America." You are free to travel to any of the states in the union (including Nevada) without having to provide any documentation at the borders between them (the most you'll see is a sign letting you know you've just entered the Hawkeye State or the Buckeye State or whichever state you happen to be visiting). It is important, however, that you keep your passport and visa with you at all times and be ready to offer it to any law enforcement officer who asks for it.

The driver's license from your country of origin is good here, but if it's not written in English, it may not be a bad idea to get an International Driver's License (check with the motor vehicle and driver licensing bureau in your country). This may help if you get pulled over at 4 A.M. by a state trooper who has seen one too many Vin Diesel movies.

DISABLED ACCESS

Las Vegas is one of the most accessible cities in America for people with disabilities, owing partly to their stringent adherence to laws but probably more to the fact that they don't want to put any impediments between their slot machines and your wallet.

Every hotel has ADA-compliant rooms and, in many cases, hotels go the extra mile to accommodate persons with vision or hearing loss with both safety and comfort equipment modified for such use. Most of the things to be seen and done in hotels or casinos are on one level, with ramps, elevators, and other accessibility devices available when they aren't.

There are some downsides. The distances between locations are often epic, even when

having to go from the valet parking to the showroom, for instance, let alone from hotel to hotel; so if walking is a problem, consider renting a wheelchair or electric scooter. These can often be arranged through the major hotels or resorts or by calling **Mesa Medical Equipment** (5225 S. Valley View Blvd., 702/367-0737). They offer reasonable rates on a full range of medical equipment and provide hotel delivery and pickup for the equipment.

For additional information on local services for persons with disabilities, contact **The Southern Nevada Center for Independent Living** (6039 Eldora St., Suite F, Las Vegas, NV 89146, 702/889-4216, www.sncil.org). They can help in finding suitable accommodations and with arranging personal care attendants, transportation, and much more.

SENIORS

I've said it before and I'll say it again: Vegas wants your money. Age is not a deterrent in gaining access to places. The problem is, it isn't as much of a benefit in Las Vegas as it is in other cities, at least not financially. Many of the smaller chain hotels will offer discounts for senior citizens or AARP members, but none of the major Strip or Downtown resorts do. Likewise, very few of the major restaurants and almost none of the big shows offer any kind of senior discount.

The biggest category for discounted admission for seniors is in the attractions and recreation area. Museums, movie theaters, bowling alleys, amusements, and other entertainment draws often do knock at least a couple of bucks off their ticket price for folks above 60 or 65 (note that the low age mark varies from place to place).

The city of Las Vegas does have an active Senior Citizens Program (dance instruction, exercise programs, recreation and entertainment outings, arts and crafts, etc.), but it's geared mostly toward locals. That doesn't mean visitors can't join in, it just means that the locations for most of their events or activities are far away from the major tourist centers. For more information, visit the city website at

WALKING DOWN THE AISLE

The fact that this discussion of how and where to get married in Las Vegas appears near the bars section of this book is in no way meant to be a commentary on people who get drunk and wind up betrothed to a total stranger in the morning. Okay, maybe it is, but hey, if Britney did it, why not you?

All a person needs to get married here is a willing participant and a marriage license from the **Clark County Marriage Bureau** (Clark County Courthouse, 200 S. 3rd St., Downtown, 702/455-4415, www.co.clark.nv.us/clerk/marriage_information.htm). A license from a person's home state is no good here.

The Marriage Bureau is open 8 a.m.–midnight daily, so if you see the person of your dreams standing at a slot machine at 10:30 in the morning on a weekend, you're in luck. Appointments are not accepted, so be warned that you may have a substantial wait, especially on busy weekends or holiday periods. Budget a couple of hours for this process.

Licenses cost $55 and must be paid in cash only – no checks or credit cards are accepted. All it takes is a partner (both must be present and accounted); some sort of proof of age, like a birth certificate, driver's license, or passport

(you must be 18 or, with parental consent, 16); and a social security number. There's no blood test and there is no waiting period, so again, that future spouse at the slot machine can be yours almost immediately.

Those who are divorced needn't bring any paperwork to prove it, but they do need to know the month, year, city, and state in which it was final.

Most wedding chapels will help arrange all of this and some will even provide transportation to and from the courthouse.

As far as where to get married, well, that's a totally different animal. There are hundreds of chapels in the city, ranging from elegant to "What's your name again?" Couples have their pick of serious (gowns, flowers, limos) to silly (come on, you know you want to get married by an Elvis impersonator!). They can exchange vows in a traditional church-like setting, on top of the Eiffel Tower, or even in a helicopter. The choices are almost limitless.

For a more traditional experience, I highly recommend using one of the chapels at the major hotels. It costs a little extra money, but the service, the settings, and the wedding bells and whistles are of a much higher caliber than at

www.lavegasnevada.gov or call 702/229-6297 8 a.m.–5 p.m. Monday–Friday.

If you are over 50 and aren't already a member of **AARP** (601 E St. NW, Washington, D.C. 20049, 888/687-2277, www.aarp.org), you may want to consider joining. It may not get you a lot of discounts or benefits in Las Vegas, but AARP does offer a wide range of programs and services that can provide assistance in other areas.

GAY AND LESBIAN TRAVELERS
Accommodations

There is only one hotel that caters exclusively to the gay community: **Blue Moon Resort** (2651 Westwood Dr., 866/798-9194, www.bluemoonlasvegas.com) is tucked away

on a side street next to the freeway just off Sahara Avenue. They took what was a boring box of a pedestrian three-story motel and turned it into a lovely (at least on the inside) collection of upscale rooms with comfortable furnishings and plenty of amenities. There's an onsite café, a sauna, and lushly landscaped pool area (complete with a Playboy Mansion–style grotto) that is clothing-optional and offers day passes for residents and visitors. Although certainly frisky at times, this is not a glorified bathhouse and is more comparable to the nicer Palm Springs resorts.

Safety

Gay and lesbian visitors should exercise the same amount of care for their personal safety in Las Vegas that they would in any other major

the independent chapels. Almost every hotel has some form of a chapel, but the best can be found at **Bellagio** (3600 Las Vegas Blvd. S., 888/987-3344, www.bellagio.com), **Caesars Palace** (3570 Las Vegas Blvd. S., 877/279-3334, www.caesarspalace.com), **Mandalay Bay** (3950 Las Vegas Blvd. S., 877/632-7701, www.mandalaybay.com), **Paris Las Vegas** (3655 Las Vegas Blvd. S., 877/650-5021, www.parislv.com), **The Venetian** (3355 Las Vegas Blvd. S., 866/548-1807, www.venetianweddings.com), and **Wynn Las Vegas** (3131 Las Vegas Blvd. S., 888/320-7115, www.wynnlasvegas.com). Each offers spectacular chapels, opportunities to get married in locations around the properties (poolside at Caesars, by the fountains at Bellagio), a full range of wedding services, and the most professional staffs.

On the other hand, those looking for either a less expensive wedding or something a little less traditional (you're thinking about that Elvis impersonator, aren't you?) can try one of the following:

Cupid's Wedding Chapel (827 Las Vegas Blvd. S., 800/543-2933, www.cupidswedding.com), while not very fancy, is very friendly and the staff treats every couple like members of their own family.

Little Church of the West (4617 Las Vegas Blvd. S., 800/821-2452, www.littlechurchlv.com) lives up to its "little" name, but the traditional church architecture (instead of a strip mall) and exceptionally caring staff has made this a local favorite, plus the building dating back to 1942 is on the National Register of Historic Places.

A Special Memory Chapel (800 S. 4th St., 800/962-7798, www.aspecialmemory.com) is done up as a New England-style church with two chapels, a drive-up window, and a staff of people who know how to take the edge off the stressful day.

The **Viva Las Vegas Wedding Chapel** (1205 Las Vegas Blvd. S., 800/574-4450, www.vivalasvegasweddings.com) is the place for a wacky theme wedding. Outer space? Western? James Bond? Graveyard? Egyptian? They've got it all covered, and if they don't have a pre-existing package, they'll make one to suit about any taste.

The **Wee Kirk o' the Heather** (231 Las Vegas Blvd. S., 800/843-5266, www.weekirk.com) is the oldest continually operating wedding chapel in the city, hitching folks in the same spot since 1940. For a sense of history, this is the place.

---

city. Ultimately, the casinos and hotels don't care who you're dating or sharing a bed with, they just want your money, but the "anything goes" ethos of the city only extends as far as the attitudes of the people standing next to you at the craps table. Since Vegas draws a widely diverse crowd, it's likely that holding hands with your significant other in public is going to bother someone in the vicinity (especially in these increasingly conservative times in America). Whether or not that stops you from doing it is a matter of personal choice that should balance "I don't care what they think" pride with "People are capable of anything" discretion.

Resources

Before your trip, visit **www.gaylasvegas.com,** a professional and very complete online resource

for entertainment, community services, special events, and much more. While not as slick (and with more pop-up ads), **www.gayvegas.com** offers a more personal touch to the information they put on their website.

Once in town, stop at any of the clubs to pick up a copy of one of the local gay lifestyle magazines: *QVegas* or *Out Las Vegas*. Both have online editions and are run by the same company, **Stonewall Publishing** (2408 Pardee Pl., Las Vegas, NV 89104, 702/650-0636, www.qvegas.com or www.outlasvegas.com).

Get Booked (4640 Paradise Rd., 702/737-7780, www.getbooked.com) is a small but complete community bookstore and resource adjacent to many of the gay bars near The Strip. This is a good place to find information about what's happening around town.

The Las Vegas GLBT Center (953 E. Sahara Ave., Suite B-31, Las Vegas, NV 89104, 702/733-9800, www.thecenterlv.com) offers a host of services and helpful information for gay, lesbian, bisexual, and transgender locals and visitors alike.

TRAVELING WITH CHILDREN

Back in the early 1990s, Las Vegas tried a marketing experiment designed to make the city more family-friendly. This was the period when the MGM Grand theme park, the Disney-fied Excalibur and Luxor, and a variety of kid-centric attractions opened. It failed miserably and now most of that stuff is gone. Even Excalibur has gotten rid of their dragon show out front and put in male strippers inside.

Adult entertainment is the focus now, with sexually charged shows and nightclubs, advertisements for strip clubs and escort services, and even folks handing out leaflets on the street for all manner of sins-of-the-flesh–style entertainment everywhere you look. There's a Hooters Hotel just off The Strip, a Playboy boutique inside The Forum Shops mall, and a bunch of other decidedly family-unfriendly attractions at every turn, so bring your kids to Las Vegas at your own risk.

More bad news: Children are not allowed in the casinos, and many of the nicer hotels place restrictions on entry for children anywhere in the building; many major hotels do not offer any kind of discount for children staying with parents and charge an additional $20–30 per person above double occupancy; and there is a strictly enforced curfew on The Strip that says children under the age of 18 cannot be out after 9 P.M. without a parent or guardian. Add in the fact that there are fewer and fewer things for kids to do around the major tourist centers and it all adds up to suggest that for a good family vacation, perhaps Disney World would be a better option than Las Vegas.

If you are insistent about bringing the tykes with you on your Sin City adventure, the only good Strip option for accommodations is Circus Circus. They have a full indoor theme park and lots of other activities for children, although it's worth noting that most of them are geared toward younger kids. Teenagers will most likely be bored here, but teenagers are bored just about everywhere, so what the heck.

A better alternative is to get away from The Strip. Lake Las Vegas has a lot of recreation and entertainment options that are more kid-appropriate and many of the locals' casinos (Boulder Station, Sunset Station, or Orleans, for example) have things like movie theaters, bowling alleys, "playcare" centers, and large video game arcades designed to keep the young ones busy while the adults are off gambling. (Check the *Recreation* chapter for more information on family-friendly activities.)

For additional information on how to do Vegas with your family, check out the website **www.lasvegaskids.net.** They have plenty of recommendations for hotels, shows, attractions, and more. The **Las Vegas Convention and Visitors Authority** (877/VISIT-LV, www.visitlasvegas.com) can also provide helpful advice.

TRAVELING WITH PETS

Fido and Fluffy are not really welcome in Las Vegas, so it's best to leave them at home with a sitter. If that's not feasible, your hotel accommodation choices will be severely limited.

Policies change often, but as of this writing there are only three major hotels in the city that allow pets: **The Four Seasons** (3950 Las Vegas Blvd. S., 877/632-7800, www.mandalaybay.com), **The Westin Casuarina** (160 E. Flamingo Rd., 866/837-4215, www.westin.com), and **Green Valley Ranch** (2300 Paseo Verde Pkwy., Henderson, 702/617-7777, www.greenvalleyranchresort.com). Each has restrictions on the size of the pet, though. (Great Danes? Probably not.) There are several other smaller, non-casino hotels that accept pets, and you can get the most up-to-date list from the **Las Vegas Convention and Visitors Authority** (877/VISIT-LV, www.visitlasvegas.com).

Pets are not allowed inside any of the casinos, restaurants, showrooms, or attractions in Las Vegas, so even if you can find a hotel that will accept them, they will have to sit there alone while you go out and play.

The two closest animal hospitals to The Strip are the **Paradise Pet Hospital** (1060 E. Flamingo Rd., 702/734-1711) and the **Sahara Animal Hospital** (4301 W. Sahara Ave., 702/876-2338).

For more information or advice on how to care for your pet in Las Vegas, contact the **Las Vegas Valley Humane Society** (2250 E. Tropicana Ave., 702/434-2009, www .lvhumane.org).

Health and Safety

MEDICAL FACILITIES

There are two major hospitals with full emergency care centers located near The Strip. The closest is **Sunrise Hospital** (3186 S. Maryland Pkwy., 702/731-8057, www.sunrisehospital.com) near the corner of E. Desert Inn Road. Only about a mile further away is **Desert Springs Hospital** (2075 E. Flamingo Rd., 702/733-8800, www.desertspringshospital.net) between Maryland Parkway and Eastern Avenue.

If the emergency is not hospital-worthy but still requires a doctor's visit, try the **Harmon Medical Center** (150 E. Harmon Ave., 702/796-1116, www.harmonmedicalcenter.com), an urgent-care facility just a block east of The Strip, open 24 hours.

Pharmacies

For filling a prescription, there is a 24-hour **Walgreen's** (3765 Las Vegas Blvd. S., 702/739-9645, www.walgreens.com) on The Strip next to the MGM Grand. There's another one across from The Stardust, but this **Walgreen's** (3025 Las Vegas Blvd. S., 702/836-0820, www.walgreens.com, pharmacy open 9 A.M.–7 P.M. Mon.–Sat., 10 A.M.–6 P.M. Sun.) is not open 24 hours.

In Downtown, try the **White Cross Drug Store** (1700 Las Vegas Blvd. S., 702/382-1733, open 24 hours) or the **Walgreen's** (495 Fremont St., 702/385-1284, www.walgreens.com, pharmacy open 9 A.M.–7 P.M. Mon.–Fri., 9 A.M.–6 P.M. Sat., 10 A.M.–6 P.M. Sun.) near the Fremont Street Experience.

LAWS

The most important laws to be aware of in Las Vegas surround gambling and drinking.

A person must be 21 to enter a casino, much less gamble in one. People under the age of 21 are allowed inside to use the walkways through the casinos to the restaurants or showrooms, but are not allowed to approach any of the slot machines or gaming tables. Those who look young should carry identification because they do card people playing the games.

A person must also be 21 to drink in Las Vegas, and alcohol is served 24 hours a day, 7 days a week. It is legal to have open containers on the streets provided you are on one of two very specific streets: The Strip or Fremont Street in Downtown Las Vegas. If you're wandering the casinos in those tourist areas you are allowed to take your beers or those giant Eiffel Tower–shaped margarita containers. Wander off those streets and you're breaking the law.

In addition, Nevada has some of the toughest drunk driving laws in the country. If alcohol is a part of the night's entertainment plan, take a cab.

As mentioned earlier, prostitution is illegal in Clark County, including Las Vegas. While escort services are common, anything beyond a nice conversation with these women or men could result in jail time.

GENERAL SAFETY TIPS
The Educated Visitor

There's a particular brand of person who preys on tourists, so it is extremely important to be educated in making travel plans. Know where you're going, check operating hours, study maps for alternate routes, and get as much information as possible so you can look like you know what you're doing (even if that's not the case). Visit websites, read travel guides, and do your homework! Not only will you have a more fulfilling vacation, you'll have a confidence that may keep you out of trouble.

Stick to Well-Traveled Areas

I actively encourage visitors to get off The Strip to explore other parts of town, but like any major city, Las Vegas has some bad neighborhoods, so it's important to stick to the well-traveled thoroughfares and highly trafficked areas whenever possible, especially late at night. A general rule of thumb is to go where the taxis go. Cab drivers tend to stick to the areas where tourists want to travel. Of particular concern are the neighborhoods just east and west of Downtown Las Vegas and just north of The Strip. There are no major hotels or tourist attractions in these areas, so there's no good reason to go there anyway.

Crowds

It's hard to go anywhere in Vegas without being in a big crowd, a potentially dangerous situation if something bad were to happen. Be aware of your surroundings wherever you go, whether it's an outdoor attraction, a packed casino, a big showroom, or even a crowded buffet. Take a moment to identify the nearest exits or quickest routes to safety so you can get out quickly if you need to.

Watch the Wallet

No, I'm not talking about blowing money in the casino—that's a totally different problem. I'm referring to the fact that pickpockets love Las Vegas, especially in areas where people are distracted by things like volcanoes, dancing fountains, and bright neon lights. Carry cash and cards in a front pocket if possible or get a wallet with a security chain or other theft deterrents. If carrying a purse (which I discourage whenever possible), be sure to wear it in a protective fashion (strung across your body as opposed to slung loosely over your arm) and try not to let the flashing lights make you forget that there may be someone around who wants to take it.

Pedestrian Safety

True, Vegas is great at putting up distracting things (like the aforementioned volcanoes, fountains, and neon lights), but there seems to be a problem in this town with people not looking both ways before they cross the street. The local papers seem to have a story every other week about someone wandering into a busy roadway without looking, often with tragic results. I know pedestrians in other cities don't always pay attention to things like "Walk" and "Don't Walk" signs, but they should here, just in case the guy in the big SUV barreling ahead is distracted by the volcanoes, fountains, and neon lights as well.

Don't Overdo It

Yes, Vegas is a city built on the concept of having fun, but it should be done as responsibly as humanly possible. There's something unique about this town that makes people, often fueled by excesses of alcohol or other mind-altering substances, want to drop all of their inhibitions. I'm not passing any kind of judgment here—God knows I've had a couple of cocktails in my life—but there are ways to do it without being stupid or ending up in dangerous situations. Don't let a wild Vegas dream vacation turn into a nightmare by making the wrong decisions.

HOTEL SAFETY

Today, the hotels in Las Vegas are among the safest in the world, with some of the most advanced fire safety systems in existence. But that doesn't mean the dangers can be ignored, especially in the behemoth 4,000-room resorts, which present unique challenges unlike other hotels. All of the fire safety systems are mechanical and/or controlled by computers and, although many will say they are infallible, that kind of thinking has led to disaster in the past. Can you say *Titanic*?

Following are some guidelines that specifically address hotel safety in the event of a fire:

Pack Smart

Safety preparedness should begin with packing, and the list of essentials should include a small flashlight. Although the hotels are equipped with emergency lighting, it may fail or be obscured by smoke, so a flashlight could be instrumental in finding the exits.

Counting Things Other Than Cards

After arriving in the hotel room, take the time to identify where the emergency stairwells are located. Count the number of doorways from your room to the stairwell and walk the route to familiarize yourself with any hallway twists or other obstacles. During a fire, the halls may be filled with blinding smoke, but you'll be able to feel your way along the path, counting off doorways by touch until reaching the one that leads to safety.

You Are Here

Take a moment to identify where your room is situated in the overall scheme of the hotel tower and how it can be distinguished from the thousands of other rooms in that tower. While knowing the room number can be helpful, knowing its placement can help direct rescuers to a room in the event of an emergency. For instance: Is the room in the north or south end of the tower; does it face the Strip or the freeway; how many rooms are between it and the elevator or stairwell?

Fire Safety

As with car alarms, many people have gotten blasé about fire alarms in public places. Don't be. If you're in your room and the fire alarm sounds, grab the room key and head for the door. It may be tempting to collect other belongings, but that temptation can cost you your life. During the MGM Grand fire in 1980, several people were found in an elevator bay with their suitcases. Despite the billowing smoke, they had taken the time to pack—a decision that proved fatal.

It's also important to take immediate action. Don't wait for someone to give instructions on what to do because, in many cases, by the time those instructions come (if they come at all) it could be too late.

Be sure to feel the door and knob first to check for heat. If it's warm, don't open it. There

may be fire on the other side. If it is cool to the touch, open the door carefully and head immediately to the emergency stairwells. Do not use the elevator as these systems may fail during a fire, leaving you trapped or worse. At the MGM Grand in 1980, the heat from the fire was so intense that it melted elevator cables, sending them crashing to the ground floor with people onboard.

If the halls are filled with smoke, try crawling to the nearest exit as the freshest air will be near the floor. But if the smoke is too dense even at floor level, turn around and return to the room.

Stairwells are supposed to be constructed to keep smoke and fire out, but in many situations, especially when there is damage to the structure, stairwells act as chimneys funneling smoke to the top of the building. If the stairwell is too dense with smoke, return to the room.

If trapped in the room by smoke or flames, there is a quick decision to make between calling for help or sealing the room. Which you do first totally depends on the situation.

If smoke is coming into the room, try to seal up the bottom of the doorway with wet towels before making the phone call. (In the time it takes to see if the phone is working and relate the situation to someone, the smoke could overwhelm you.) Check the air-conditioning vents as well. If smoke is coming in through them, stuff more wet towels into the openings.

Filling the bathtub (if the room has one) with water may also be helpful.

Once this is accomplished, check the phone and, if it is still in operation, give anyone who answers the room number, location in the hotel tower, and a brief rundown of the situation, including injuries, if there are any.

If the smoke has not begun filtering in the room, make the call first and then start placing the wet towels around the doors and vents.

Although most modern hotel rooms in Vegas do not have windows that open, many have vents at the top or bottom of the sills that open to let in a little fresh air. It may be tempting, but do not break the windows. Fire needs oxygen to survive and it will seek the best available source, thereby drawing the flames and smoke toward the room.

In addition, most fire departments are not equipped with ladders that can reach much past the seventh floor of a high-rise, so if help is going to come, it's going to come through the door and not the window.

It sounds a lot easier than it actually is, but the most important thing to do in an emergency situation is stay calm. Panicking will lead to bad decisions, and bad decisions will lead to disaster.

Information and Services

HOTEL AMENITIES
So you're sitting there facing a suitcase that won't close and wondering what you did wrong. Never fear—there are some things you may have put in your bag that you don't actually need to bring with you because the hotel provides them.

All major hotels in town offer telephones; air-conditioning; a television (or two or three) with in-room, pay-per-view movies (some with built-in Internet browsers and games); a telephone; an alarm clock; an iron and ironing board; and a hair dryer. Many rooms come with a safe, but if they don't have one, the hotel will offer the use of safety deposit boxes at the front desk (usually at no charge). All have maid service and towels.

Most hotel rooms have standard amenities like shampoo, soap, and hand lotion gratis in the rooms, but I recommend that these things be packed anyway. The quality of the in-room amenities varies wildly, and if the item in question is of poor quality, a replacement from the hotel sundry shop can cost a small fortune. Bottles of basic shampoo for $8 are not uncommon.

Although an iron and ironing board usually come standard, if they don't, they can be requested from housekeeping at no charge at most hotels in the city.

Sunscreen is not provided and is a must, even during the winter. While it may be cool during the day in January, the sun is still unrelenting on most days and people can get burned if they stay out in it for too long. Hats and sunglasses are also highly recommended.

If you're traveling on business or just can't bear the thought of being away from your email for more than a day, most rooms have data ports on the phone that you can hook your laptop up to. Many offer high-speed Internet connections and/or Internet service that can be browsed through the television set, both for a fee. Some hotels have even gone wireless, allowing guests to wander around the pool while looking for the latest baseball scores. (Not that you'd actually do something like that, would you?)

As noted above, every room has a phone, but the charges to use it are often exorbitant. A cell phone with free or low-cost roaming charges can save a few bucks.

In terms of services the hotels offer, all have room service (most 24 hours); laundry and dry-cleaning services; some form of a business center for checking email or sending faxes; and a bell desk. Use of these services costs extra, of course.

Most hotels offer some form of concierge service, a tour desk, a show desk, and a rental car counter (or the ability to get a rental car for guests).

Speaking of cars, all hotels offer free parking (self or valet), although some of the Downtown hotels require that tickets be validated inside the casino.

MONEY
Here's a shock: Getting access to your money in Las Vegas is not difficult. Every casino in town has multiple ATMs, check-cashing services, travelers check services, and credit card

cash-advance systems, and some even have foreign currency exchange. The question is whether it's a good idea to use them.

Most of the above charge a hefty fee, with ATMs charging as much as $3.50 (in addition to whatever your bank charges) to use them, and cash-advance systems charging 2–5 percent of the amount being withdrawn. It's better to make your money arrangements before getting to town, not only because it saves money, but it also helps with budget control when you get near that slot machine you're absolutely convinced will pay off soon.

My recommendation is to bring only the cash that you intend to gamble with and pay for everything else on a credit card. ATM cards should stay at home.

POSTAL SERVICES

Most of the major resorts can assist with whatever mailing or shipping needs their guests have; otherwise, the closest major post office is at 3100 Industrial Road (702/792-4503, www.usps.com). There is also a FedEx/Kinko's

(395 Hughes Center Dr., 702/951-2400, www.fedex.com) near Paradise and Flamingo.

MAPS AND TOURIST INFORMATION

Maps are plentiful in Las Vegas. All car rental agencies and most of the major hotels offer basic ones for free. For something more detailed, every gift shop, gas station, and convenience store in town has some form of a Las Vegas map, but for the tourist areas, the free basic ones should suffice.

There are lots of tourist information places along The Strip, many of them using the word "official" in their names—but they aren't. These are just fronts for getting people to buy the show or tour packages they are trying to sell. Avoid them.

Instead, head to the **Las Vegas Convention and Visitors Authority (LVCVA)** (3150 Paradise Rd., 877/VISIT-LV, www.visitlasvegas.com). They are located at the Convention Center and are open 8 A.M.–5 P.M. daily to assist with brochures, maps, directions, and more.

RESOURCES

Glossary

Action The amount of money wagered by a player.

All In To wager all of your money on one hand.

Ante The first bet of a new hand. Used mainly in poker and variations of the game.

Bankroll The amount of money players have with them to gamble.

Beltway I-215, which encircles Las Vegas.

Bet The amount of money wagered.

Betting Limits The minimum and maximum wagers allowed per bet.

Black At a gaming table, the $100 chips.

Boxman The person in charge of the craps table.

Burn Card A card placed in the discard rack without being entered into play. Usually the first card of a new shuffle.

Bust To go over 21 in blackjack.

Cage/Cashier's Cage The main place in a casino where players can exchange money for chips or change or cash in winnings.

Card Counting A system, usually used in blackjack, by which players keep track of how many high and low cards are remaining in a deck. While not expressly illegal, if a casino suspects you of doing it, they will ask you to leave.

Cardsharp Technically, one who habitually cheats at cards. However, the more common usage refers to a person who is an expert at card games.

Carousel A group of slot machines. This used to refer only to groups that were arranged in a circle or square with room for a change attendant in the middle, but is now common usage

for any grouping of slot machines.

Cash Out Removing winnings or credit balances from a slot or video poker machine.

Chip The round plastic tokens used at gaming tables.

Color Up/Out To exchange lower value chips for higher value chips. For instance, 20 $5 chips (usually red) can be colored up to a single $100 chip (usually black).

Comp Free (or discounted) meals, rooms, or other offers. Short for complimentary.

Croupier The person who runs the roulette wheel. Also sometimes used to describe a baccarat dealer.

Cut To divide a deck of cards into two sections. Used in shuffling.

Cut Card A plastic card used to cut the deck.

Dealer The person who deals cards at various casino games.

Deuce A card with a value of 2.

DI Nickname for Desert Inn Road or Desert Inn Arterial roadway.

Dime Bet At a gaming table, a $1,000 wager.

Discard Rack A plastic or metal container on the table where used cards are placed after each hand.

Dollar Bet At a gaming table, a $100 wager.

Drop Box The metal container where dealers deposit cash, markers, and chips.

Edge The statistical amount of advantage the casino has in a game.

Even Money 1:1 payouts (a $5 bet wins you $5).

Face Cards The king, queen, or jack of each suit.

First Base The seat at a gaming table that receives the first cards of a hand. Most tables go from the dealer's left to right, so first base is the seat on the far right side of the table as you're looking at it.

Flat Top A slot machine with a fixed top payout, as opposed to a progressive or changing amount.

Front Money Cash deposited with a casino in advance of play.

George A player who tips well.

Glitter Gulch Fremont Street in Downtown Las Vegas.

Green At a gaming table, the $25 chips.

Hand Each deal of a card game.

High-Roller A player who wagers a lot of money.

Hit To take another card. Usually used in blackjack.

Hole Card The dealer's face-down card.

Hopper On older slot machines, the internal tray that holds the coins.

IP Nickname for the Imperial Palace hotel and casino.

Jackpot A big win on a slot or video poker machine. Derived from poker games that required a pair of jacks or better to be eligible to win the pot.

Locals' Casino Any casino located in a mostly residential area away from The Strip or Downtown.

Loose Term to describe a slot machine that is paying well or often.

Marker A check that can be written at gaming tables by players with established credit at the casino.

Nevada The state in which Las Vegas is located is pronounced Neh-va-duh (with a hard "a" like "cat"), not Neh-vah-duh. It makes the locals cranky when you say it wrong.

Nickels At a gaming table, the $5 chips.

Odds The statistical chances of winning.

Pay/Payout/Payoff The amount paid upon winning. Usually written as 3:1 or 3 to 1 (for example), the first number is the payout expressed as a multiplier of the second number, which is the wager. So, for example, if a wager pays 3:1 and you bet $5, you will win 3 times the bet, or $15.

Pay Cycle On a slot or video poker machine, the number of plays required to go through all

winning and non-winning combinations.

Payline On a slot machine, the line on which the symbols on the reels must line up for a win.

Payout/Payoff Percentage The percent of each dollar a slot or video poker machine returns to the players.

Pit The area between gaming tables where the casino employees stand.

Pit Boss The casino employee in charge of a group of table games.

Pot The amount of money in play, usually used in poker.

Player You, every time you put a coin in a slot or a wager on a table.

Players' Club A system that tracks play and offers rewards to players.

Porte Cochere The covered driveway area at the entrance to a hotel or casino where vehicles arrive.

Progressive A slot or video poker machine with a top jackpot that grows with each coin played until it is won.

Push When the dealer and the player have hands with the same total. No one wins or loses.

Quarters At a gaming table, the $25 chips.

Random Number Generator A computer chip inside a slot or video poker machine that determines wins or losses.

Red At a gaming table, the $5 chips.

Reel The wheels inside a slot machine on which the symbols are printed.

Shill An employee of the casino hired to play at empty gaming tables in the hopes of luring other players into the action.

Shoe A plastic device containing multiple decks of cards from which they are dealt.

Shuffle To mix the cards.

Silver At a gaming table, the $1 casino tokens.

Spaghetti Bowl The interchange of Interstates 15, 93, and 95 near Downtown Las Vegas.

Sports Book The bets taken on a fixed odds event, usually sports.

Stake The amount of money bet each hand.

Stand To not take any more cards.

Stick The wooden or plastic device used to collect bets and dice at a craps table.

Stickman At a craps table, the dealer who calls the numbers rolled and controls the stick.

The Strat Nickname for the Stratosphere hotel and casino.

The Strip Roughly, the 2000–4000 blocks of Las Vegas Boulevard South where the major casinos are located.

Surrender To give up half the wager before the hand is complete.

TI Nickname for Treasure Island hotel and casino.

Ticket On modern slot and video poker machines, the paper slip that prints out with the monetary balance of the cash out.

Tight Term to describe a slot machine that is not paying well or often.

Toke Slang for tip or gratuity.

Token Coin-like objects used in higher-limit slot machines ($1 and above).

Upcard The dealer's exposed card.

Whale A high roller; big spender.

Suggested Reading

ART AND ARCHITECTURE

Venturi, Robert; Steven Izenour; and Denise Scott Brown. *Learning from Las Vegas, Revised Edition: The Forgotten Symbolism of Architectural Form.* Cambridge: M.I.T. Press, 1977. While a bit dry and certainly academic in nature, this treatise on the form and function of the architectural side of early Las Vegas is fascinating.

BIOGRAPHIES

Castleman, Deke. *Whale Hunt in the Desert: The Secret Las Vegas of Superhost Steve Cyr.* Las Vegas: Huntington Press, 2004. Steve Cyr has been described as the best casino host in town, catering to the rich, and often wacky, demands of high rollers. A great behind-the-scenes look at the world of big-money gambling.

Otfinoski, Steve. *Bugsy Siegel: And the Postwar Boom (Notorious Americans and Their Times).* Woodbridge, CT: Blackbirch Press, 2000. Although this book covers Bugsy's life before Las Vegas, it also does a good job of examining his impact on The Strip and vice versa.

Smith, John L. *No Limit: The Rise and Fall of Bob Stupak and Las Vegas' Stratosphere Tower.* Las Vegas: Huntington Press, 1997. Bob Stupak has variously been described as a genius and a madman. Read all about his wild exploits in this well-researched book.

Smith, John L. *Of Rats and Men: Oscar Goodman's Life from Mob Mouthpiece to Mayor of Las Vegas.* Las Vegas: Huntington Press, 2003. The most colorful mayor in America has had a remarkable progression from mafia lawyer to running Sin City.

DINING AND ENTERTAINMENT

Clarke, Norm. *Vegas Confidential: Norm Clarke! Sin City's Ace Insider 1,000 Naked Truths.* Las Vegas: Stephens Press, 2003. *Las Vegas Review Journal* gossip columnist Clarke has had his finger on the pulse of the city's hot-or-not scene for years, encapsulated in this handy guide.

Knapp Rinella, Heidi. *Personal Favorites: The Chefs of Las Vegas.* Las Vegas: Stephens Press, 2005. Rinella is the head food critic of the *Las Vegas Review Journal* and her book highlights some of her favorite chefs, restaurants, and recipes. A must for foodies!

Weatherford, Mike. *Cult Vegas: The Weirdest! The Wildest! The Swingin'est Town on Earth.* Las Vegas: Huntington Press, 2001. Those *LVRJ* columnists have been busy. Weatherford is the paper's entertainment specialist and his behind-the-scenes tales are both informative and hilarious.

ESSAYS AND FICTION

Connelly, Michael. *Murder in Vegas: New Tales of Gambling and Desperation.* New York: Forge Books, 2005. A collection of crime-centric short stories using Vegas as a backdrop from the award-winning author of *The Narrows* and other well-known writers.

O'Brien, John. *Leaving Las Vegas.* New York: Grove Press, 1995. Certainly not the most uplifting read, but this tale of the seedy side of Las Vegas is just as good as, if not better than, the award-winning movie of the same name.

Tronnes, Mike, ed. *Literary Las Vegas: The Best Writing About America's Most Fabulous City.* New York: Henry Holt & Co., 1995. Another collection of stories set in and around Las Vegas from legendary authors like Noel Coward, Hunter S. Thompson, and Joan Didion, among others.

GAMBLING INSTRUCTION

Brisman, Andrew. *Mensa Guide to Casino Gambling: Winning Ways.* New York: Sterling, 2004. You don't have to be a genius to learn from this well-researched and informative guide to all things gaming, which goes beyond basic instruction into theories of winning and strategic playing.

Harroch, Richard D., et al. *Gambling for Dummies.* New York: For Dummies, 2001. If Mensa is too intimidating for you, try this guidebook aimed at the gambling layperson.

Nestor, Basil. *The Unofficial Guide to Casino Gambling.* New York: Wiley, 1998. Striking a good balance between the two aforementioned books, the *Unofficial Guide* helps with the basics but also directs readers toward winning strategies.

Shackleford, Mike. *Gambling 102.* Las Vegas, Huntington Press, 2005. This one is definitely for people who already know how to play and want to know how to win.

LAS VEGAS HISTORY

Basten, Fred E. and Charles Phoenix. *Fabulous Las Vegas in the '50s: Glitz, Glamour & Games.* Santa Monica, CA: Angel City Press, 1999. A colorful book of photographs from the most glamorous era of Las Vegas.

Chung, Kim Su. *Las Vegas Then & Now.* San Diego: Thunder Bay Press, 2003. Compare old Las Vegas to the modern-day city with a series of before-and-after–style photographs.

Denton, Sally and Roger Morris. *The Money and the Power: The Making of Las Vegas and Its Hold on America.* New York: Vintage, 2002. You may never look at Las Vegas the same way again after reading this well-researched book about the shadier side of the city.

Hopkins, A. D. and K. J. Evans. *The First 100: Portraits of the Men and Women Who Shaped Las Vegas.* Las Vegas: Huntington Press, 1999. Biographical portraits of the 100 most influential people in Las Vegas history from the editors of the *Las Vegas Review Journal.*

Knapp Rinella, Heidi. *The Stardust of Yesterday: Reflections on a Las Vegas Legend.* Las Vegas: Stephens Press, 2006. The Stardust opened in 1958 and was torn down in 2007. In those nearly 50 years, stories, photos, and history were made, and this coffee-table book has a lot of each between its covers.

Land, Barbara and Myrick Land. *A Short History of Las Vegas.* Las Vegas: University of Nevada Press, 2004. "Short" is not exactly the word I'd use to describe this nearly 300-page compendium of the city from the early days all the way up to its recent 100th anniversary.

Moehring, Eugene P. and Michael S. Green. *Las Vegas: A Centennial History.* Las Vegas: University of Nevada Press, 2005. Written by a professor of history at the University of Las Vegas, this tome focuses less on the events and more on the reasons they happened and their lasting impact.

PEOPLE AND CULTURE

McManus, James. *Positively Fifth Street.* New York: Picador, 2004. McManus was sent by *Vanity Fair* to cover the World Series of Poker and wound up writing this amazing book—part memoir, part true crime—about his participation in the competition and the murder of casino owner Ted Binion.

Rothman, Hal. *Neon Metropolis: How Las Vegas Started the Twenty-First Century.* London: Routledge, 2003. Another professor at UNLV, Rothman examines the ever-shifting face of Las Vegas and the people behind it.

Simich, Jerry L. and Thomas C. Wright, eds. *The Peoples of Las Vegas: One City, Many Faces.* Las Vegas: University of Nevada Press, 2005. More than a dozen scholars contributed to this collection of essays about the various ethnic cultures of Las Vegas.

TRUE STORIES

Mezrich, Ben. *Bringing Down the House: The Inside Story of Six M.I.T. Students Who Took Vegas for Millions.* New York: Free Press, 2003. What these brainy college kids got away with is almost jaw-dropping. Read the book before the movie starring Kevin Spacey comes out.

O'Brien, Matthew. *Beneath the Neon.* Las Vegas: Huntington Press, 2007. The managing editor of the local alternative paper went into the storm drains for a look at what goes on under Las Vegas and came out with a fascinating snapshot of a side of the city few ever see.

Internet Resources

CITY GOVERNMENT AND BUSINESS

www.lasvegasnevada.gov
www.lvchamber.com

ENTERTAINMENT LISTINGS

www.ilovevegas.com
www.reviewjournal.com/neon/

HISTORY

www.lvstriphistory.com

MARRIAGE AND WEDDINGS

www.co.clark.nv.us/clerk/marriage_information.htm
www.lvweddingchapels.com
www.vegasweddings4u.com

MEDIA AND COMMUNICATIONS

www.fox5vegas.com
www.klas-tv.com
www.ktnv.com
www.kvbc.com
www.lasvegassun.com
www.lasvegasweekly.com
www.reviewjournal.com

RESERVATIONS

www.lasvegas.com
www.vegas.com

REVIEWS AND OPINION

www.cheapovegas.com
www.vegas4visitors.com

TOURISM INFORMATION

www.travelnevada.com
www.visitlasvegas.com

Index

nuclear waste repositories: 255
Nurture: 159

O

O: 15, 25, 112
Ocean's 11 (film): 20, 141
Ocean's 13 (film): 20
off season: 13-14
Old Las Vegas Mormon Fort State Historic
    Park: 20, 228
Old Nevada: 247
old-school gambling: 56
Orleans: accommodations 189; casinos 18, 75;
    entertainment 122; general discussion 11;
    recreational activities 166; restaurants 100
Orleans Arena: 122
Orleans Bowling Center: 166
Orleans Showroom: 122
outlet malls: 144, 155

P

packing tips: 286-287
Pai Gow poker: 60
Palace Station: 189
Palms, The: accommodations 190; casinos 75-
    76; entertainment 122; general discussion
    11; itinerary tips 21, 24; nightlife 125, 126, 127,
    128; restaurants 101, 103
Paradise Road at Naples Drive: 134
Paris Las Vegas: accommodations 182-183;
    casinos 19, 70-71; entertainment 112-113;
    general discussion 10; itinerary tips 15;
    nightlife 132-133; restaurants 91-92;
    sightseeing tips 30, 39, 42-44
Paris Las Vegas Eiffel Tower Experience: 30,
    39, 43-44
party scene: *see* Nightlife Index
passports: 280
Pearl, The: 122
pedestrian safety: 286
Penn & Teller: 15, 115
penny slot machines: 18
performing arts: 241
pet care: 145
pets, traveling with: 284-285
Phantom: The Las Vegas Spectacular: 112
pharmacies: 285
pickpockets: 286
planetariums: 226-227
Planet Hollywood: accommodations 183;
    casinos 56, 71; entertainment 113, 120;
    nightclubs 21; restaurants 87, 91, 93-94;
    shopping 25, 152; sightseeing tips 39

Planet Hollywood Theatre for the Performing
    Arts: 120
planning tips: 12-14
plants: 252-254
players' clubs: 64-65
Plaza Hotel: 106
poker games: 59-61
Polaris: 133
pool clubs: 23, 124, 160-161
population: 268
postal services: 289
Presley, Elvis: 261
The Price is Right Live: 117
The Producers: 112-113
production shows: 109-113
prostitution: 268, 279-280

QR

Qua Baths & Spa: 16, 26, 162
rainfall: 251-252
Rampart Casino: casinos 236; entertainment
    240; restaurants 237-238, 239
Rat Pack: 259-261
reading suggestions: 292-294
recreational activities: 157-169; best of Las
    Vegas 158; Boulder Highway 217-218; family
    fun activities 167-169; general discussion
    157; Henderson 206-207; high-roller
    itinerary tips 24; Lake Las Vegas 213; Las
    Vegas vicinity 196, 219-222; North Las
    Vegas 233-234; pools 160-161; Red Rock
    Canyon National Conservation Area 248-
    249; sightseeing tips 50-51; spas 158-159,
    162; sports 163-166; West Las Vegas 242-
    244, 246; *see also specific place*
Red Rock Canyon National Conservation Area:
    225, 247-249
Red Rock Lanes: 243
Red Rock Resort: accommodations 224, 245;
    casinos 17, 18, 236-237; entertainment
    241-242; general discussion 12; itinerary tips
    26; nightlife 240; restaurants 238, 239-240;
    spas 243
Reflection Bay Golf Club: 163, 196, 213
Rehab: 124
rental cars: 273, 275-276
resources: 290-294
restaurants: 79-106; alternative choices 27;
    bargain restaurants 82; best of Las Vegas
    80; Boulder Highway 216; Center Strip
    86-94, 96; Downtown Las Vegas 104-106;
    general discussion 79-81; Henderson
    202-205; Just Off the Strip 96, 99-103;

Restaurants Index

Nightlife Index

Shops Index

Hotels Index

MOON LAS VEGAS

Avalon Travel
a member of the Perseus Books Group
1700 Fourth Street
Berkeley, CA 94710, USA
www.moon.com

Editor and Series Manager: Erin Raber
Copy Editor: Melissa Brandzel
Graphics and Production Coordinator:
  Tabitha Lahr
Cover Designer: Tabitha Lahr
Map Editor: Albert Angulo
Cartographers: Kat Bennett, Suzanne Service
Indexer: Judy Hunt

ISBN-10: 1-59880-062-0
ISBN-13: 978-1-59880-062-3
ISSN: 1556-7702

Printing History
1st Edition – 2006
2nd Edition – March 2008
5 4 3 2 1

Front cover photo: Neon signs of Fremont Street © 2005 Kelly Mooney/Digital Railroad
Title page photo: Courtesy of Las Vegas News Bureau/LVCVA
Color interior photos: Page 2 Courtesy Harrah's Entertainment; Page 3 Courtesy of Las Vegas News Bureau/LVCVA; Page 4 Courtesy Wynn Las Vegas/Jon and Jeannine Henebry; Page 5 © Robert Lahr; Page 6 Courtesy MGM Mirage; Page 7 MGM Grand's *Crazy Horse Paris, Courtesy of MGM Mirage;* Page 7 Caesar's Palace, Courtesy Harrah's Entertainment; Page 7 The Steak House at Circus Circus, Courtesy of MGM Mirage; Page 10 South Strip/ exterior of the Excalibur, Courtsey of MGM Mirage; Page 10 Center Strip/ the Bellagio exterior, Courtsey of MGM Mirage; Page 11 North Strip/ Chaos Ride at Circus Circus, Courtsey of MGM Mirage, Page 11 Just Off the Strip/ the pool at The Flamingo, Courtesy Harrah's Entertainment; Page 11 Downtown/ Vegas Vicky watches over The Fremont Street Experience, Courtesy of Las Vegas News Bureau/LVCVA; Page 12 East and South of Las Vegas/ Green Valley Ranch, Courtesy Station Casinos; Page 12 North and West Las Vegas/ Santa Fe Station, Courtesy Station Casinos

Printed in USA by RR Donnelley

KEEPING CURRENT

If you have a favorite gem you'd like to see included in the next edition, or see anything that needs updating, clarification, or correction, please drop us a line. Send your comments via email to feedback@moon.com, or use the address above.

MAP SYMBOLS

⬌ Expressway	🄲 Highlight	✗ Airfield	⚲ Golf Course
⬌ Primary Road	○ City/Town	✈ Airport	🄿 Parking Area
⬌ Secondary Road	◉ State Capital	▲ Mountain	⬟ Archaeological Site
⌁ Unpaved Road	⊛ National Capital	✛ Unique Natural Feature	⬤ Church
------ Trail	★ Point of Interest		⛽ Gas Station
········· Ferry	• Accommodation	≋ Waterfall	◌ Glacier
─┼─┼─ Railroad	▼ Restaurant/Bar	▲ Park	Mangrove
▒ Pedestrian Walkway	■ Other Location	⊟ Trailhead	Reef
⊞ Stairs	Λ Campground	⛷ Skiing Area	Swamp

CONVERSION TABLES

$°C = (°F - 32) / 1.8$
$°F = (°C \times 1.8) + 32$
1 inch = 2.54 centimeters (cm)
1 foot = 0.304 meters (m)
1 yard = 0.914 meters
1 mile = 1.6093 kilometers (km)
1 km = 0.6214 miles
1 fathom = 1.8288 m
1 chain = 20.1168 m
1 furlong = 201.168 m
1 acre = 0.4047 hectares
1 sq km = 100 hectares
1 sq mile = 2.59 square km
1 ounce = 28.35 grams
1 pound = 0.4536 kilograms
1 short ton = 0.90718 metric ton
1 short ton = 2,000 pounds
1 long ton = 1.016 metric tons
1 long ton = 2,240 pounds
1 metric ton = 1,000 kilograms
1 quart = 0.94635 liters
1 US gallon = 3.7854 liters
1 Imperial gallon = 4.5459 liters
1 nautical mile = 1.852 km

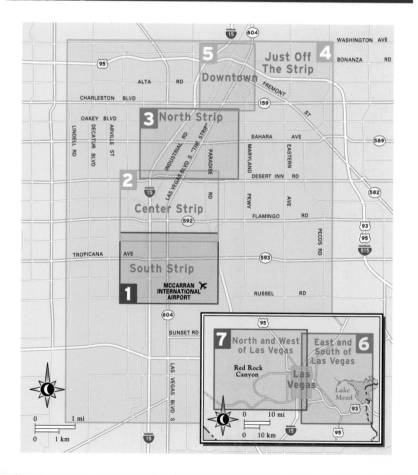

W HARMON AVE

W NAPLES DR

W TOMPKINS AVE

W TROPICANA AVE

W RENO AVE

W ALI BABA LN

W HACIENDA AVE

W DIABLO DR

W DEWEY DR

W RUSSELL RD

S POLARIS AVE

PROCYON ST

VALLEY VIEW BLVD

PROCYON ST

POLARIS AVE

DEAN MARTIN DR

FRANK SINATRA DR

RUE DE MONTE CARLO

MANDALAY BAY

E RUSSELL

CITYCEN

FUTURE SIT

MONTE CARL

NEW Y
NEW

EXCALIBUR

LUXOR
LAS VEGAS

MANDALAY BAY

MONTE CARLO

GAMING
MONTE CARLO

RESTAURANTS
MONTE CARLO PUB &
BREWERY

ENTERTAINMENT
LANCE BURTON

HOTELS
MONTE CARLO

NEW YORK-NEW YORK

SIGHTS
NEW YORK-NEW YORK
NEW YORK-NEW YORK
TRIBUTE TO HEROES

GAMING
NEW YORK-NEW YORK

RESTAURANTS
ESPN ZONE
JODI MARONI'S SAUSAGE KINGDOM
NINE FINE IRISHMEN

ENTERTAINMENT
BAR AT TIMES SQUARE
COYOTE UGLY
ZUMANITY BY CIRQUE DU SOLEIL

RECREATION
MANHATTAN EXPRESS ROLLER
COASTER

HOTELS
NEW YORK-NEW YORK

EXCALIBUR

SIGHTS
EXCALIBUR

GAMING
EXCALIBUR

ENTERTAINMENT
LOUIE ANDERSON
THUNDER FROM DOWN
UNDER
TOURNAMENT OF KINGS

HOTELS
EXCALIBUR

LUXOR LAS VEGAS

SIGHTS
LUXOR LAS VEGAS

GAMING
LUXOR LAS VEGAS

ENTERTAINMENT
LUXOR IMAX THEATER

RECREATION
LUXOR IMAX RIDEFILM
NURTURE

HOTELS
LUXOR LAS VEGAS

SEE
"MAP 4 JUST OFF
THE STRIP"

MANDALAY BAY

SIGHTS
MANDALAY BAY
MANDALAY BAY SHARK REEF

GAMING
MANDALAY BAY

RESTAURANTS
AUREOLE
BORDER GRILL
CHARLIE PALMER STEAK
THE CHOCOLATE SWAN
FLEUR DE LYS
HOUSE OF BLUES LAS VEGAS
MANDALAY BAY BAYSIDE
BUFFET
RED SQUARE

ENTERTAINMENT
CORAL REEF LOUNGE
HOUSE OF BLUES
HOUSE OF BLUES: LATE NIGHT
IVAN KANE'S FORTY DEUCE
MAMMA MIA!

ENTERTAINMENT continued
MANDALAY BAY EVENTS
CENTER
MIX
RUMJUNGLE

SHOPPING
THE CHOCOLATE SWAN
55 DEGREES
LUSH PUPPY
MANDALAY PLACE
THE READING ROOM

RECREATION
THE BATHHOUSE SPA
AT THEHOTEL

HOTELS
FOUR SEASONS
MANDALAY BAY
THEHOTEL

WEDDINGS
MANDALAY BAY

SEE
"MAP 2 CENTER STRIP"

HARLEY
-VIDSON
CAFÉ

S KOVAL LN

E HARMON AVE

LAS VEGAS MONORAIL

SHOWCASE MALL
ENTERTAINMENT
UNITED ARTISTS SHOWCASE 8
SHOPPING
M&M WORLD
SHOWCASE MALL
RECREATION
GAMEWORKS

EMPIRE
LLROOM

E TOMPKINS

MGM GRAND
CONFERENCE
CENTER

S DECKOW LN

MGM GRAND

MGM GRAND
SIGHTS
MGM GRAND
MGM GRAND LION HABITAT
GAMING
◖ MGM GRAND
RESTAURANTS
EMERIL'S NEW ORLEANS FISH
HOUSE
◖ L'ATELIER DE JOEL
ROBUCHON
RAINFOREST CAFÉ
WOLFGANG PUCK BAR & GRILL
ENTERTAINMENT
CRAZY HORSE PARIS
◖ KÀ BY CIRQUE DU SOLEIL
MGM GRAND GARDEN ARENA
MGM GRAND HOLLYWOOD
THEATRE
STUDIO 54
TABÙ
HOTELS
MGM GRAND

E TROPICANA AVE

SEE
"MAP 4 JUST OFF
THE STRIP"

TROPICANA

P

E RENO AVE

S HAVEN ST

TROPICANA
GAMING
TROPICANA
ENTERTAINMENT
FOLIES BERGERE
HOTELS
TROPICANA

E HACIENDA AVE

DANVILLE LN
BETHEL LN
S HAVEN
GILES ST

MCCARRAN

INTERNATIONAL

AIRPORT

E DIABLO DR

ST

★ LITTLE CHURCH
OF THE WEST

0   250 yds
0   250 m

E DEWEY DR

SEE
"MAP 4 JUST OFF
THE STRIP"

AI GOLF CLUB

SEE
"MAP 3 NORTH STRIP"

W SPRING MOUNTAIN RD

FASHION SHOW D

SPRING

POLARIS AVE

HIGHLAND DR

TWAIN AVE

15

THE MIRAGE

SIGHTS
C THE MIRAGE
MIRAGE SECRET GARDEN
& DOLPHIN HABITAT

GAMING
THE MIRAGE

RESTAURANTS
CRAVINGS BUFFET AT THE
MIRAGE
ONDA
STACK

ENTERTAINMENT
DANNY GANS
DANNY GANS THEATRE
JET
LOVE BY CIRQUE DU SOLEIL
REVOLUTION LOUNGE

HOTELS
THE MIRAGE

SEE
"MAP 4 JUST OFF
THE STRIP"

THE
MIRAGE

VIKING RD

S VALLEY VIEW

W FLAMINGO RD

W NEVSO DR

BLVD

DEAN MARTIN DR

THE FORUM
SHOPS

CAESARS
PALACE

CAESARS PALACE

SIGHTS
C CAESARS PALACE

GAMING
CAESARS PALACE

RESTAURANTS
BOA
BOBBY FLAY'S MESA GRILL
JOE'S SEAFOOD, PRIME STEAK,
& STONE CRAB

ENTERTAINMENT
BETTE MIDLER IN CONCERT
THE COLOSSEUM AT
CAESARS PALACE
ELTON JOHN IN
THE RED PIANO
C PURE
PUSSYCAT DOLLS LOUNGE

SHOPPING
AGENT PROVOCATEUR
EXOTIC CARS AT
CAESARS PALACE
FAO SCHWARZ
THE FORUM SHOPS AT
CAESARS PALACE
HARRY WINSTON
KIEHL'S COSMETICS
NANETTE LEPORE
PLAYBOY
TRUEFITT & HILL

RECREATION
QUA BATHS & SPA

HOTELS
C CAESARS PALACE

P

P

BELLAGIO

BELLAGIO

SIGHTS
BELLAGIO
BELLAGIO CONSERVATORY AND
BOTANICAL GARDENS
C BELLAGIO FOUNTAIN SHOWS

GAMING
C BELLAGIO

RESTAURANTS
THE BUFFET AT BELLAGIO
FIX
OLIVES
PICASSO

ENTERTAINMENT
BELLAGIO GALLERY OF
FINE ARTS
CARAMEL
FONTANA LOUNGE
O BY CIRQUE DU SOLEIL
PETROSSIAN BAR

SHOPPING
TIFFANY & CO.
VIA BELLAGIO

RECREATION
SPA BELLAGIO

HOTELS
BELLAGIO

FRANK SINATRA DR

COSMOPOLI
FUTURE SITE

| 0 | 250 yds |
| 0 | 250 m |

HARMON A

CITYCENTE
FUTURE SITE (3

W HARMON AVE

15

SEE
"MAP 1 SOUTH STRIP"

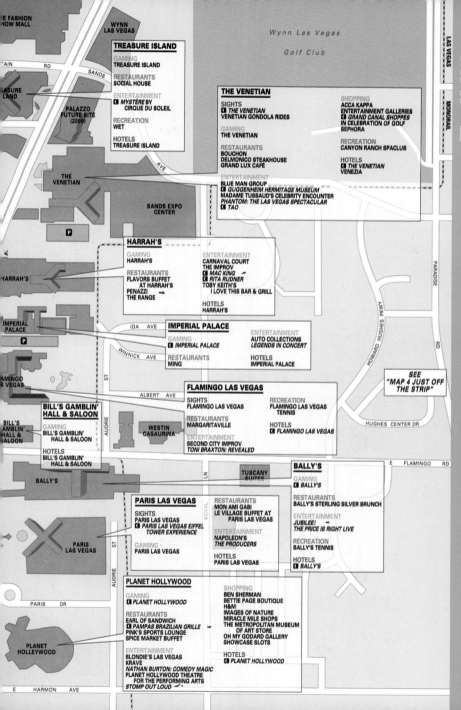

E FASHION
HOW MALL

WYNN
LAS VEGAS

Wynn Las Vegas
Golf Club

TREASURE ISLAND
GAMING
TREASURE ISLAND

RESTAURANTS
SOCIAL HOUSE

ENTERTAINMENT
MYSTÈRE BY
CIRQUE DU SOLEIL

RECREATION
WET

HOTELS
TREASURE ISLAND

THE VENETIAN
SIGHTS
THE VENETIAN
VENETIAN GONDOLA RIDES

GAMING
THE VENETIAN

RESTAURANTS
BOUCHON
DELMONICO STEAKHOUSE
GRAND LUX CAFÉ

ENTERTAINMENT
BLUE MAN GROUP
GUGGENHEIM HERMITAGE MUSEUM
MADAME TUSSAUD'S CELEBRITY ENCOUNTER
PHANTOM: THE LAS VEGAS SPECTACULAR
TAO

SHOPPING
ACCA KAPPA
ENTERTAINMENT GALLERIES
GRAND CANAL SHOPPES
IN CELEBRATION OF GOLF
SEPHORA

RECREATION
CANYON RANCH SPACLUB

HOTELS
THE VENETIAN
VENEZIA

PALAZZO
FUTURE SITE
(2009)

THE
VENETIAN

SANDS EXPO
CENTER

HARRAH'S
GAMING
HARRAH'S

RESTAURANTS
FLAVORS BUFFET
AT HARRAH'S
PENAZZI
THE RANGE

ENTERTAINMENT
CARNAVAL COURT
THE IMPROV
MAC KING
RITA RUDNER
TOBY KEITH'S
I LOVE THIS BAR & GRILL

HOTELS
HARRAH'S

IMPERIAL PALACE
GAMING
IMPERIAL PALACE

RESTAURANTS
MING

ENTERTAINMENT
AUTO COLLECTIONS
LEGENDS IN CONCERT

HOTELS
IMPERIAL PALACE

IDA AVE

WINNICK AVE

SEE
"MAP 4 JUST OFF
THE STRIP"

HUGHES CENTER DR

FLAMINGO LAS VEGAS
SIGHTS
FLAMINGO LAS VEGAS

RESTAURANTS
MARGARITAVILLE

ENTERTAINMENT
SECOND CITY IMPROV
TONI BRAXTON: REVEALED

RECREATION
FLAMINGO LAS VEGAS
TENNIS

HOTELS
FLAMINGO LAS VEGAS

ALBERT AVE

BILL'S GAMBLIN' HALL & SALOON
GAMING
BILL'S GAMBLIN'
HALL & SALOON

HOTELS
BILL'S GAMBLIN'
HALL & SALOON

WESTIN
CASAURINA

BALLY'S

TUSCANY
SUITES

BALLY'S
GAMING
BALLY'S

RESTAURANTS
BALLY'S STERLING SILVER BRUNCH

ENTERTAINMENT
JUBILEE!
THE PRICE IS RIGHT LIVE

RECREATION
BALLY'S TENNIS

HOTELS
BALLY'S

E FLAMINGO RD

PARIS LAS VEGAS
SIGHTS
PARIS LAS VEGAS
PARIS LAS VEGAS EIFFEL
TOWER EXPERIENCE

GAMING
PARIS LAS VEGAS

RESTAURANTS
MON AMI GABI
LE VILLAGE BUFFET AT
PARIS LAS VEGAS

ENTERTAINMENT
NAPOLEON'S
THE PRODUCERS

HOTELS
PARIS LAS VEGAS

PARIS
LAS VEGAS

PARIS DR

PLANET HOLLYWOOD
GAMING
PLANET HOLLYWOOD

RESTAURANTS
EARL OF SANDWICH
PAMPAS BRAZILIAN GRILLE
PINK'S SPORTS LOUNGE
SPICE MARKET BUFFET

ENTERTAINMENT
BLONDIE'S LAS VEGAS
KRAVE
NATHAN BURTON: COMEDY MAGIC
PLANET HOLLYWOOD THEATRE
FOR THE PERFORMING ARTS
STOMP OUT LOUD

SHOPPING
BEN SHERMAN
BETTIE PAGE BOUTIQUE
H&M
IMAGES OF NATURE
MIRACLE MILE SHOPS
THE METROPOLITAN MUSEUM
OF ART STORE
OH MY GODARD GALLERY
SHOWCASE SLOTS

HOTELS
PLANET HOLLYWOOD

PLANET
HOLLYWOOD

E HARMON AVE

HARRAH'S

IMPERIAL
PALACE

AMINGO
S VEGAS

BILL'S
AMBLIN'
HALL &
ALOON

RD
SANDS

AIN
RD

ASURE
LAND

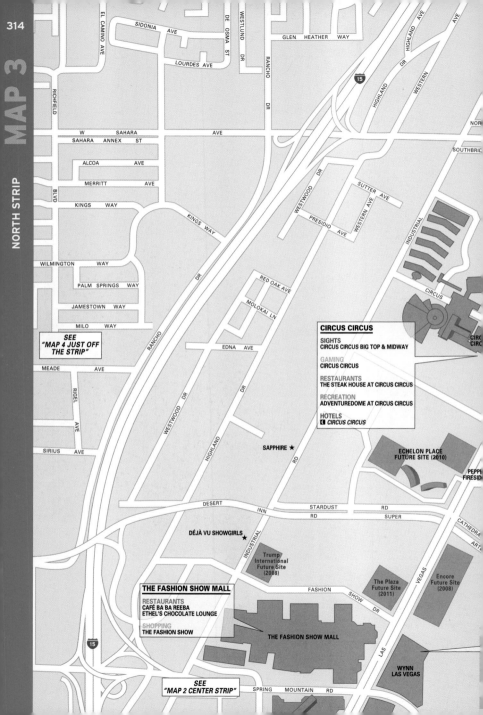

EL CAMINO AVE

SIDONIA AVE

DE OSMA ST

WESTLUND DR

GLEN HEATHER WAY

HIGHLAND AVE

AVE

RICHFIELD

LOURDES AVE

RANCHO DR

15

HIGHLAND DR

WESTERN

AVE

NOR

W SAHARA AVE
SAHARA ANNEX ST

BLVD

ALCOA AVE

MERRITT AVE

KINGS WAY

KINGS WAY

WESTWOOD DR

PRESIDIO AVE

SUTTER AVE

WESTERN AVE

SOUTHBRID

INDUSTRIAL

WILMINGTON WAY

PALM SPRINGS WAY

JAMESTOWN WAY

MILO WAY

**SEE
"MAP 4 JUST OFF
THE STRIP"**

MEADE AVE

RIGEL AVE

SIRIUS AVE

RANCHO DR

WESTWOOD DR

RED OAK AVE

MOLOKAI LN

EDNA AVE

HIGHLAND DR

DR

CIRCUS

CIRC
CIRC

CIRCUS CIRCUS

SIGHTS
CIRCUS CIRCUS BIG TOP & MIDWAY

GAMING
CIRCUS CIRCUS

RESTAURANTS
THE STEAK HOUSE AT CIRCUS CIRCUS

RECREATION
ADVENTUREDOME AT CIRCUS CIRCUS

HOTELS
◖ CIRCUS CIRCUS

SAPPHIRE ★

**ECHELON PLACE
FUTURE SITE (2010)**

PEPP
FIRESID

RD

DESERT INN RD

STARDUST RD

SUPER

CATHEDRA

ART

DÉJÀ VU SHOWGIRLS ★

INDUSTRIAL

Trump
International
Future Site
(2008)

The Plaza
Future Site
(2011)

VEGAS

Encore
Future Site
(2008)

THE FASHION SHOW MALL

RESTAURANTS
CAFÉ BA BA REEBA
ETHEL'S CHOCOLATE LOUNGE

SHOPPING
THE FASHION SHOW

FASHION SHOW DR

THE FASHION SHOW MALL

LAS

WYNN
LAS VEGAS

15

**SEE
"MAP 2 CENTER STRIP"**

SPRING MOUNTAIN RD

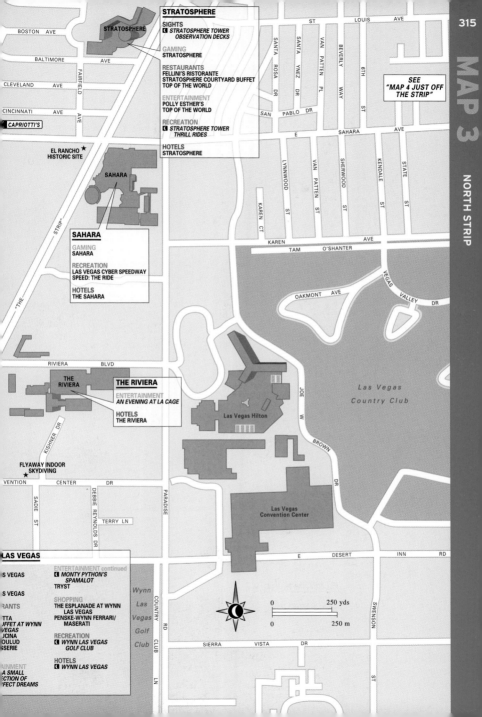

COMMERCIAL CENTER MALL
RESTAURANTS
LOTUS OF SIAM
ENTERTAINMENT
BADLANDS SALOON

ANTIQUE SQUARE

LAS VEGAS HILTON
GAMING
LAS VEGAS HILTON
ENTERTAINMENT
MANILOW: MUSIC AND PASSION
RECREATION
STAR TREK: THE EXPERIENCE/BORG INVASION
HOTELS
LAS VEGAS HILTON

LAS VEGAS NATIONAL

ZIA RECORDS

THE TILLERMAN

BOULEVARD MALL

JASON'S DELI

MEDITERRANEAN CAFÉ
MARKET
HOOKAH LOUNGE

THE BUFFALO ANTIQUES
EXCHANGE MALL

ATOMIC TESTING MUSEUM

CAFÉ HEIDELBERG

SHALIMAR

LAWRY'S THE PRIME RIB

PF CHANG'S

TUSCANY SUITES

WESTIN CASAURINA

RED ROOSTER ANTIQUES
NOT JUST ANTIQUES MART
LITTLE DARLINGS

CHEETAH'S

TREASURES

ENTERTAINMENT
CHIPPENDALES
PENN & TELLER
VOODOO LOUNGE
SHOPPING
MASQUERADE VILLAGE
HOTELS
RIO ALL SUITE HOTEL & CASINO

RIO ALL SUITE HOTEL & CASINO
SIGHTS
RIO'S MASQUERADE VILLAGE SHOW IN THE SKY
GAMING
RIO ALL SUITE HOTEL & CASINO
RESTAURANTS
GAYLORD INDIA
RIO CARNIVAL WORLD BUFFET

PALACE STATION

GOLD COAST
GAMING
GOLD COAST
RESTAURANTS
GOLD COAST PORTS O' CALL BUFFET
RECREATION
GOLD COAST BOWLING CENTER

SPRINGS PRESERVE

M&M SOUL FOOD

PLAY IT AGAIN SAM
SAND DOLLAR BLUES LOUNGE

BRITISH FOODS, INC.

THE PALMS
GAMING
THE PALMS
RESTAURANTS
ALIZÉ
N9NE
ENTERTAINMENT
GHOSTBAR
MOON
THE PEARL
THE PLAYBOY CLUB
RAIN
HOTELS

MOJAVE RD
FREMONT ST
SAHARA AVE
KAREN AVE
MOJAVE DR
VEGAS VALLEY DR
DESERT INN RD
TWAIN AVE
EASTERN AVE
PARADISE RD
FLAMINGO RD
VIKING RD
ROCHELLE AVE
CHARLESTON BLVD
S MARYLAND PKWY
OAKEY BLVD
ST LOUIS AVE
LAS VEGAS BLVD S • THE STRIP
INDUSTRIAL RD
KOVAL
S
M L KING BLVD
SHADOW LN
RANCHO DR
CAMPBELL DR
VALLEY VIEW BLVD
SAHARA AVE
ARVILLE ST
DECATUR BLVD
LINDELL RD
W SPRING MOUNTAIN RD
W FLAMINGO RD
HINSON ST
OAKEY
TWAIN AVE
MEADOWS LN
ALTA DR
CASINO CENTER BLVD
GRAND CENTRAL PKWY
GRAGSON AVE
STEWART AVE
ORAN
BRIDGER AVE
13TH ST
4TH ST
N
E
W
DESERT INN RD
PENNWOOD AVE
95
15
515 93 95

RESTAURANTS
C CARLUCCIO'S TIVOLI GARDENS

ENTERTAINMENT
G LIBERACE MUSEUM
GOOD TIMES

HARD ROCK HOTEL

SIGHTS
HARD ROCK HOTEL

GAMING
C HARD ROCK HOTEL

RESTAURANTS
HARD ROCK CAFÉ
NOBU

ENTERTAINMENT
BODY ENGLISH
THE JOINT

HOTELS
HARD ROCK HOTEL

UNIVERSITY OF
NEVADA LAS VEGAS

ENTERTAINMENT
THOMAS & MACK CENTER

RECREATION
UNIVERSITY OF NEVADA LAS VEGAS

HOOTER'S CASINO HOTEL

RESTAURANTS
DAN MARINO'S

ENTERTAINMENT
PETE & SHORTY'S BOOK & BAR

HOTELS
HOOTER'S CASINO HOTEL

ORLEANS

GAMING
ORLEANS

RESTAURANTS
ORLEANS FRENCH MARKET BUFFET

ENTERTAINMENT
CENTURY ORLEANS 18
ORLEANS ARENA
ORLEANS SHOWROOM

RECREATION
LAS VEGAS WRANGLERS HOCKEY
ORLEANS BOWLING CENTER

HOTELS
ORLEANS

SILVERTON

SHOPPING
BASS PRO SHOPS

HOTELS
SILVERTON

LAS VEGAS
OUTLET CENTER

LORRAINE'S
BOOTLEGGER
LOUNGE

WELCOME TO FABULOUS
LAS VEGAS SIGN

ANCHOR PUB

DOUBLE DOWN SALOON

PT'S GOLD

MCCARRAN
INTERNATIONAL
AIRPORT

Sunset
County Park

0.5 mi

0.5 km

0

215

15

95

N

S   PECOS   RD

PATRICK

MCLEOD   DR

S   EASTERN   AVE

AVE

HACIENDA

RUSSELL   RD

E

E

E

TROPICANA   AVE

PARADISE   RD

PARADISE   RD

SUNSET   RD

E

WELL   RD

BERMUDA   RD

ROBINDALE   RD

WINDMILL   LN

GILLESPIE   ST

E

E

LAS   VEGAS   BLVD   S

HIDDEN   RD

DIAMOND   RD

BLUE

SPRINGS

VALLEY   VIEW   BLVD

SUNSET

WARM   RD

W

SINATRA   DR

MARTIN   DR

RD

N   ST

TROPICANA   AVE

RENO   AVE

HACIENDA   AVE

LINDELL   RD

RUSSELL   RD

W

W

W

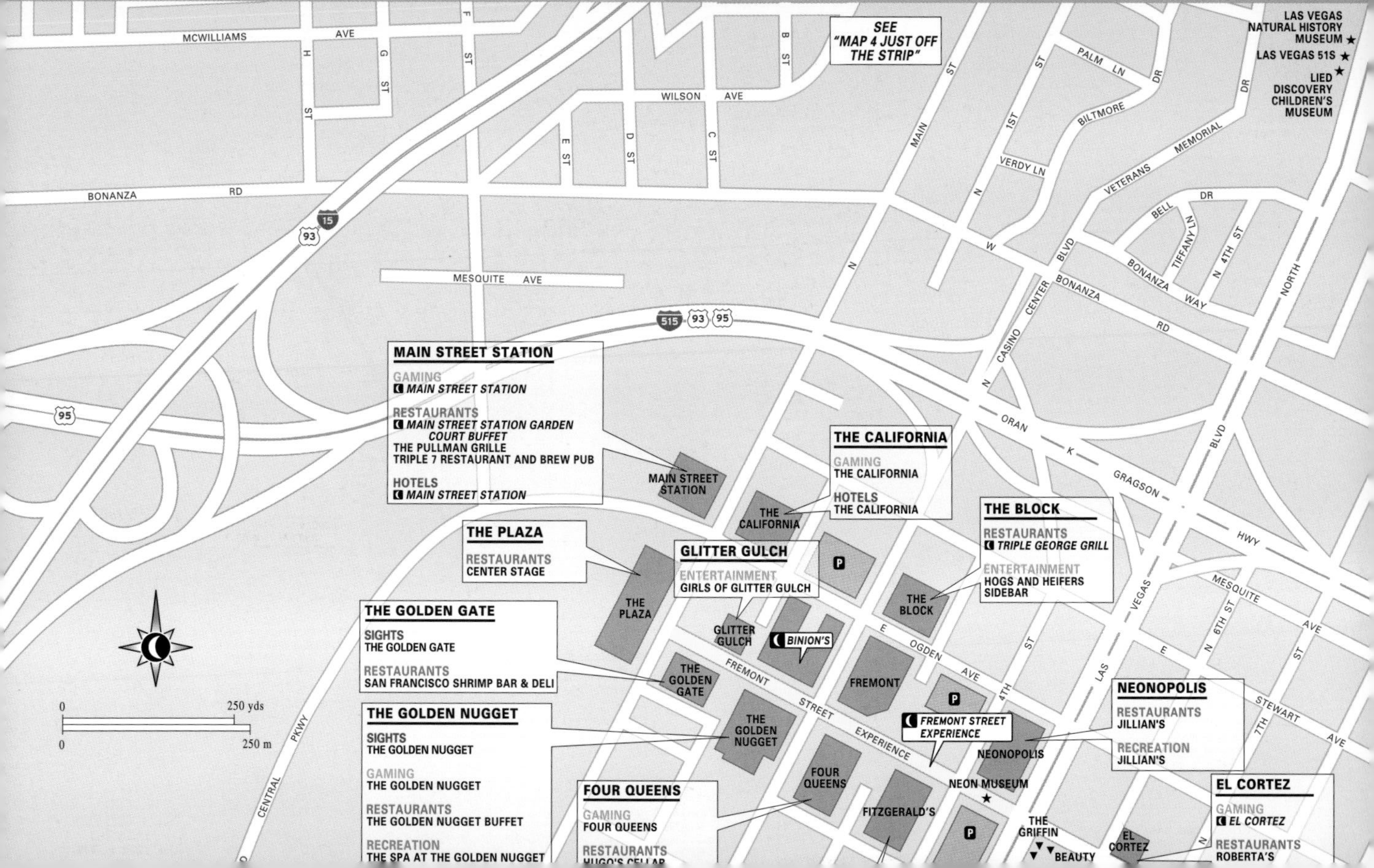

MAP 5   DOWNTOWN   318

LAS VEGAS NATURAL HISTORY MUSEUM ★
LAS VEGAS 515 ★
LIED DISCOVERY CHILDREN'S MUSEUM ★

SEE "MAP 4 JUST OFF THE STRIP"

EL CORTEZ
GAMING
◀ EL CORTEZ
RESTAURANTS
ROBERTA'S

NEONOPOLIS
RESTAURANTS
JILLIAN'S
RECREATION
JILLIAN'S

THE GRIFFIN ▼
BEAUTY ▼

NEON MUSEUM ★

THE BLOCK
RESTAURANTS
◀ TRIPLE GEORGE GRILL
ENTERTAINMENT
HOGS AND HEIFERS
SIDEBAR

◀ FREMONT STREET EXPERIENCE

NEONOPOLIS

THE BLOCK

FITZGERALD'S

THE CALIFORNIA
GAMING
THE CALIFORNIA
HOTELS
THE CALIFORNIA

THE CALIFORNIA

FREMONT

FOUR QUEENS

GLITTER GULCH
ENTERTAINMENT
GIRLS OF GLITTER GULCH

◀ BINION'S

GLITTER GULCH

THE GOLDEN GATE

THE GOLDEN NUGGET

FOUR QUEENS
GAMING
FOUR QUEENS
RESTAURANTS
HUGO'S CELLAR

THE PLAZA

MAIN STREET STATION
GAMING
◀ MAIN STREET STATION
RESTAURANTS
◀ MAIN STREET STATION GARDEN COURT BUFFET
THE PULLMAN GRILLE
TRIPLE 7 RESTAURANT AND BREW PUB
HOTELS
◀ MAIN STREET STATION

MAIN STREET STATION

THE PLAZA
RESTAURANTS
CENTER STAGE

THE GOLDEN GATE
SIGHTS
THE GOLDEN GATE
RESTAURANTS
SAN FRANCISCO SHRIMP BAR & DELI

THE GOLDEN NUGGET
SIGHTS
THE GOLDEN NUGGET
GAMING
THE GOLDEN NUGGET
RESTAURANTS
THE GOLDEN NUGGET BUFFET
RECREATION
THE SPA AT THE GOLDEN NUGGET

250 yds
250 m

0
0

SEE "MAP 4 JUST OFF THE STRIP"

Huntridge
Circle Park

GAMBLERS' BOOK SHOP ■

ANDRE'S ►

MARYLAND PKWY

11TH

10TH

CLARK AVE

9TH

BONNEVILLE AVE

GARCES AVE

LEWIS AVE

8TH ST

7TH ST

6TH

SOUTH

BLVD

LAS VEGAS

BLVD

4TH ST

3RD

CENTER AVE

CASINO

BONNEVILLE

GARCES

CLARK

1ST

MAIN

CARSON AVE

BRIDGER AVE

CHARLESTON BLVD

YUCCA AVE

FRANCIS AVE

PARK PASEO

PARK PASEO

GASS AVE

HOOVER AVE

COOLIDGE AVE

GASS AVE

DONA MARIA ► TAMALES

D'LOE HOUSE OF STYLE
THEN AND NOW ■

CHARLESTON BLVD

CASINO CENTER BLVD

3RD ST

MAIN ST

ART BAR ►

COMMERCE ST

EL SOMBRERO CAFÉ ■

GAMBLERS GENERAL STORE

THE ATTIC ■

BOULDER AVE

COMMERCE ST

"MAP 4 JUST OFF THE STRIP"

BONNEVILLE AVE

LAS VEGAS PREMIUM OUTLETS ★

HOTELS FITZGERALD'S

CRAIG RD

NORTH LAS VEGAS

15

604

Sunrise Mtn
3,364ft

BUS 95

CHEYENNE AVE

NORTH LAS VEGAS AIRPORT

JONES BLVD

CAREY AVE

LAS VEGAS BLVD N

LAMB BLVD

LAKE MEAD BLVD

HOLLYWOOD BLVD

Frenchman Mtn
4,052ft

95

CHARLESTON BLVD

FREMONT ST

"THE STRIP"

BOULDER STATION

GAMING
BOULDER STATION

ENTERTAINMENT
BOULDER STATION

HOTELS
BOULDER STATION

ARIZONA CHARLIE'S

GAMING
ARIZONA CHARLIE'S

RESTAURANTS
THE WILD WEST BUFFET

ENTERTAINMENT
ARIZONA CHARLIE'S

HOTELS
ARIZONA CHARLIE'S

SAHARA AVE

LAS VEGAS BLVD S

EASTERN AVE

NELLIS BLVD

DESERT INN RD

LAS VEGAS

FLAMINGO RD

SAM'S TOWN

GAMING
SAM'S TOWN

RESTAURANTS
SAM'S TOWN
FIRELIGHT BUFFET

ENTERTAINMENT
SAM'S TOWN

RECREATION
SAM'S TOWN
BOWLING CENTER

HOTELS
SAM'S TOWN

TROPICANA AVE

RAINBOW BLVD

BOULDER HWY

SAM BOYD STADIUM

ETHEL M CHOCOLATE FACTORY

GALLERIA AT SUNSET

582

HENDERSON BIRD VIEWING PRESERVE

W SUNSET RD

SUNSET STATION

GAMING
SUNSET STATION

RESTAURANTS
THE SONOMA CELLAR STEAKHOUSE

ENTERTAINMENT
SUNSET STATION

RECREATION
STRIKE ZONE BOWLING CENTER

HOTELS
SUNSET STATION

CAPRIOTTI'S

FIESTA HENDERSON

GAMING
FIESTA HENDERSON

RESTAURANTS
FIESTA HENDERSON
FESTIVAL BUFFET

HOTELS
FIESTA HENDERSON

WARM SPRINGS RD

MEMPHIS CHAMPIONSHIP BARBECUE

BLUE DIAMOND RD

160

WIGWAM PKWY

THE CUPCAKERY

PEBBLE RD

215

SWEET WATER PRIME SEAFOOD

THE DISTRICT RETAIL CENTER

RESTAURANTS
LUCILLE'S SMOKEHOUSE BAR-B-QUE
PF CHANG'S CHINA BISTRO

SHOPPING
THE DISTICT

BLACK MOUN GOLF AN COUNTRY C

HORIZO DR

515

95

SILVERADO RANCH BLVD

SOUTH POINT

146

BONEFISH GRILL

GREEN VALLEY RANCH

GAMING
GREEN VALLEY RANCH

RESTAURANTS
FATBURGER
FEAST AROUND THE WORLD BUFFET
HANK'S

ENTERTAINMENT
GREEN VALLEY RANCH
WHISKEY BAR/WHISKEY BEACH

RECREATION
WHISKEY BEACH AND
GREEN VALLEY RANCH SPA

HOTELS
GREEN VALLEY RANCH

ST ROSE PKWY

EASTERN AVE

15

RIO SECCO

HENDERSON-SKY HARBOR AIRPORT

REVERE AT ANTHEM

Black Mtn
5,092ft

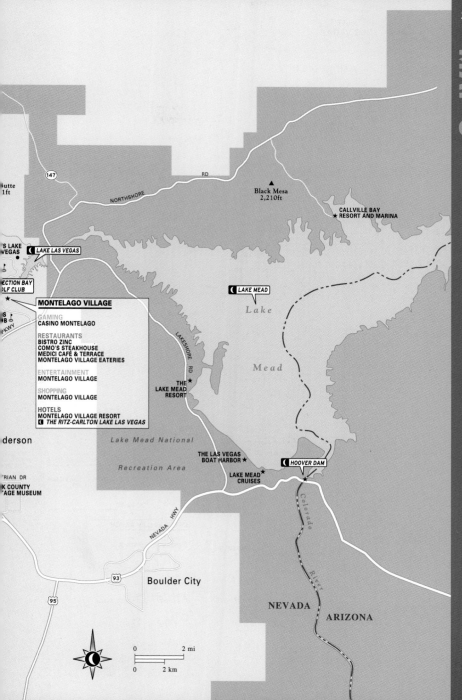

147

RD

NORTHSHORE

Butte
1ft

▲ Black Mesa
2,210ft

★ CALLVILLE BAY
RESORT AND MARINA

'S LAKE
VEGAS

☾ *LAKE LAS VEGAS*

ECTION BAY
OLF CLUB

☾ *LAKE MEAD*

S
B
PKWY

Lake

MONTELAGO VILLAGE

GAMING
CASINO MONTELAGO

RESTAURANTS
BISTRO ZINC
COMO'S STEAKHOUSE
MEDICI CAFÉ & TERRACE
MONTELAGO VILLAGE EATERIES

ENTERTAINMENT
MONTELAGO VILLAGE

SHOPPING
MONTELAGO VILLAGE

HOTELS
MONTELAGO VILLAGE RESORT
☾ *THE RITZ-CARLTON LAKE LAS VEGAS*

Mead

LAKESHORE
RD

★
THE
LAKE MEAD
RESORT

derson

Lake Mead National

Recreation Area

THE LAS VEGAS ★
BOAT HARBOR

☾ *HOOVER DAM*

RIAN DR

K COUNTY
AGE MUSEUM

LAKE MEAD ★
CRUISES

Colorado

NEVADA   HWY

93

95

Boulder City

River

NEVADA

ARIZONA

0   2 mi

0   2 km

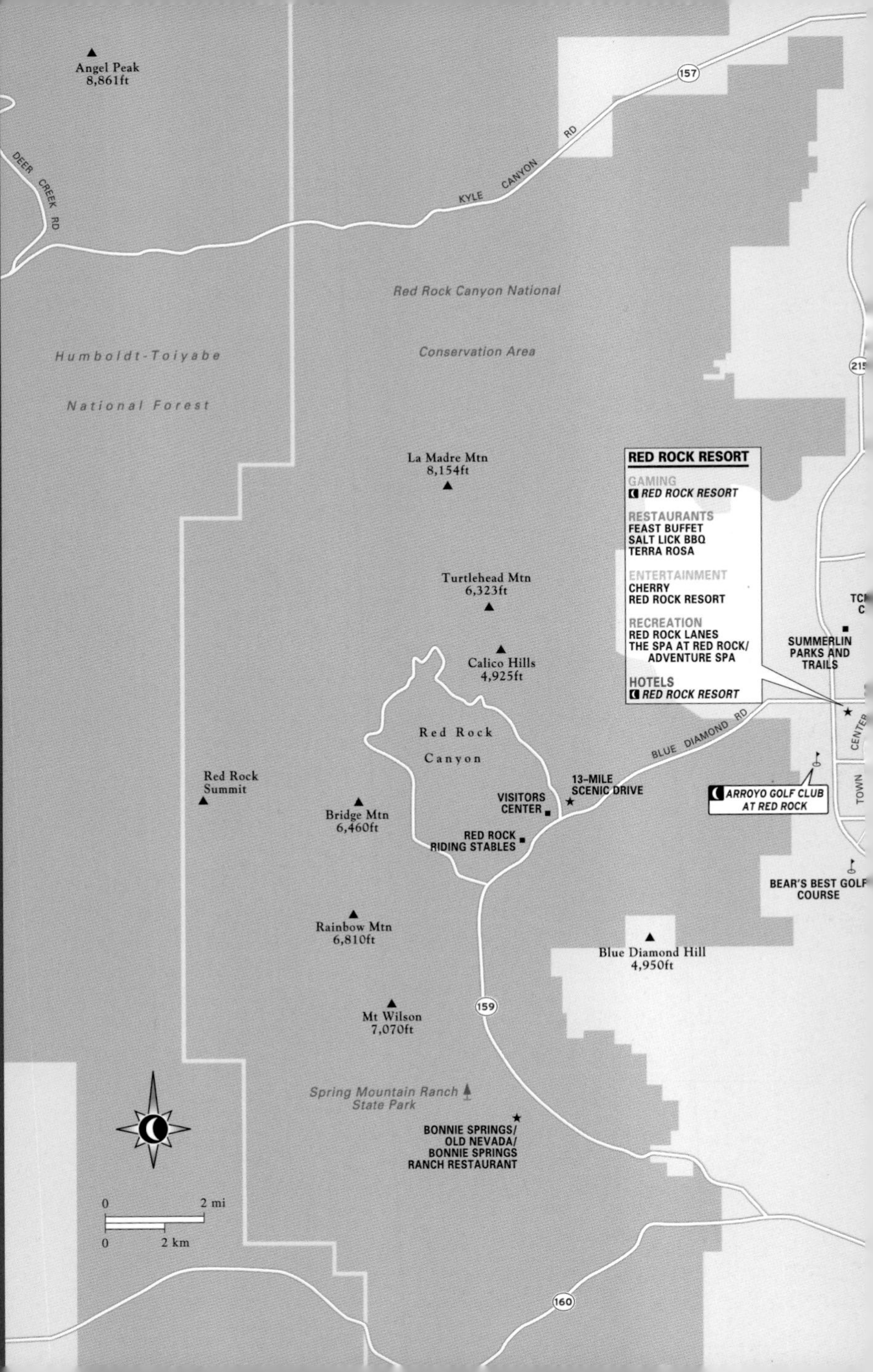

Angel Peak
8,861ft

DEER CREEK RD

KYLE CANYON RD

157

Red Rock Canyon National

Conservation Area

Humboldt-Toiyabe

National Forest

215

La Madre Mtn
8,154ft

Turtlehead Mtn
6,323ft

Calico Hills
4,925ft

Red Rock

Canyon

Red Rock
Summit

Bridge Mtn
6,460ft

VISITORS
CENTER

RED ROCK
RIDING STABLES

13-MILE
SCENIC DRIVE

BLUE DIAMOND RD

TOWN CENTER

TCH
C

SUMMERLIN
PARKS AND
TRAILS

ARROYO GOLF CLUB
AT RED ROCK

BEAR'S BEST GOLF
COURSE

RED ROCK RESORT		
GAMING		
RED ROCK RESORT		
RESTAURANTS		
FEAST BUFFET		
SALT LICK BBQ		
TERRA ROSA		
ENTERTAINMENT		
CHERRY		
RED ROCK RESORT		
RECREATION		
RED ROCK LANES		
THE SPA AT RED ROCK/		
ADVENTURE SPA		
HOTELS		
RED ROCK RESORT		

Rainbow Mtn
6,810ft

Blue Diamond Hill
4,950ft

Mt Wilson
7,070ft

159

Spring Mountain Ranch
State Park

BONNIE SPRINGS/
OLD NEVADA/
BONNIE SPRINGS
RANCH RESTAURANT

0   2 mi

0   2 km

160

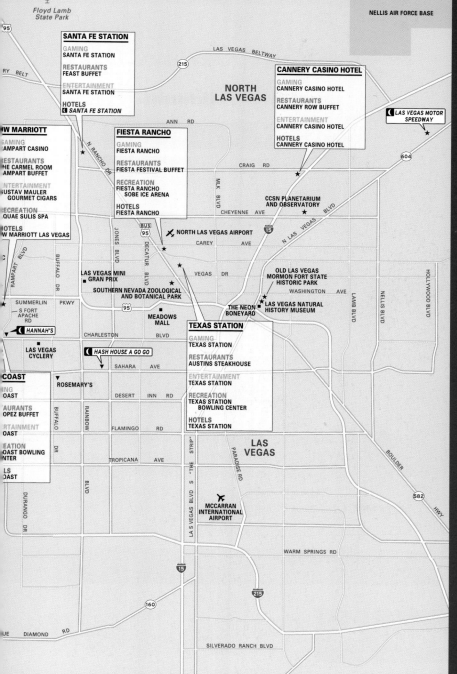

Floyd Lamb
State Park

95

RY BELT

NELLIS AIR FORCE BASE

LAS VEGAS BELTWAY

215

NORTH
LAS VEGAS

SANTA FE STATION
GAMING
SANTA FE STATION

RESTAURANTS
FEAST BUFFET

ENTERTAINMENT
SANTA FE STATION

HOTELS
SANTA FE STATION

CANNERY CASINO HOTEL
GAMING
CANNERY CASINO HOTEL

RESTAURANTS
CANNERY ROW BUFFET

ENTERTAINMENT
CANNERY CASINO HOTEL

HOTELS
CANNERY CASINO HOTEL

LAS VEGAS MOTOR
SPEEDWAY

W MARRIOTT
GAMING
AMPART CASINO

RESTAURANTS
HE CARMEL ROOM
AMPART BUFFET

ENTERTAINMENT
USTAV MAULER
GOURMET CIGARS

RECREATION
QUAE SULIS SPA

HOTELS
W MARRIOTT LAS VEGAS

FIESTA RANCHO
GAMING
FIESTA RANCHO

RESTAURANTS
FIESTA FESTIVAL BUFFET

RECREATION
FIESTA RANCHO
SOBE ICE ARENA

HOTELS
FIESTA RANCHO

ANN   RD

N RANCHO DR

CRAIG   RD

604

MLK BLVD

CHEYENNE   AVE

CCSN PLANETARIUM
AND OBSERVATORY

N LAS VEGAS BLVD

HOLLYWOOD BLVD

BUS
95

NORTH LAS VEGAS AIRPORT

CAREY   AVE

15

JONES BLVD

DECATUR BLVD

VEGAS   DR

OLD LAS VEGAS
MORMON FORT STATE
HISTORIC PARK

WASHINGTON   AVE

LAMB BLVD

NELLIS BLVD

RAMPART BLVD

BUFFALO DR

LAS VEGAS MINI
GRAN PRIX

SOUTHERN NEVADA ZOOLOGICAL
AND BOTANICAL PARK

THE NEON
BONEYARD

LAS VEGAS NATURAL
HISTORY MUSEUM

SUMMERLIN   PKWY

S FORT
APACHE
RD

HANNAH'S

95

MEADOWS
MALL

TEXAS STATION
GAMING
TEXAS STATION

RESTAURANTS
AUSTINS STEAKHOUSE

ENTERTAINMENT
TEXAS STATION

RECREATION
TEXAS STATION
BOWLING CENTER

HOTELS
TEXAS STATION

CHARLESTON   BLVD

LAS VEGAS
CYCLERY

HASH HOUSE A GO GO

SAHARA   AVE

COAST
ING
OAST

RESTAURANTS
OPEZ BUFFET

ERTAINMENT
OAST

EATION
OAST BOWLING
NTER

LS
OAST

ROSEMARY'S

DESERT   INN   RD

FLAMINGO   RD

DURANGO DR

BUFFALO DR

RAINBOW BLVD

LAS VEGAS BLVD S "THE STRIP"

PARADISE RD

LAS
VEGAS

BOULDER HWY

582

TROPICANA   AVE

15

MCCARRAN
INTERNATIONAL
AIRPORT

WARM SPRINGS RD

215

160

DIAMOND   RD

SILVERADO RANCH BLVD

www.moon.com

For helpful advice on planning a trip, visit www.moon.com for the **TRAVEL PLANNER** and get access to useful travel strategies and valuable information about great places to visit. When you travel with Moon, expect an experience that is uncommon and truly unique.

HANDBOOKS | METRO | OUTDOORS | LIVING ABROA